A. Mosso

Life of Man on the High Alps

A. Mosso
Life of Man on the High Alps
ISBN/EAN: 9783743407459
Manufactured in Europe, USA, Canada, Australia, Japa
Cover: Foto ©ninafisch / pixelio.de

Manufactured and distributed by brebook publishing software (www.brebook.com)

A. Mosso

Life of Man on the High Alps

LIFE OF MAN
ON THE HIGH ALPS

By ANGELO MOSSO

TRANSLATED FROM THE SECOND
EDITION OF THE ITALIAN BY E.
LOUGH KIESOW ❖   ❖   ❖   ❖

LONDON: T. FISHER UNWIN
PATERNOSTER SQUARE   MDCCCXCVIII

To

HER MAJESTY

QUEEN MARGARET OF ITALY

WHOSE LOVE FOR OUR MOUNTAINS

AND ZEAL FOR THE ADVANCEMENT OF SCIENCE

HAVE BEEN MY BEST ENCOURAGEMENT IN MY LABOURS

THIS BOOK IS HUMBLY DEDICATED

PREFACE

I MADE preparations for this expedition immediately after the construction of the Regina Margherita Hut (on the summit of Monte Rosa at a height of 4,560 metres above sea-level). The better to study certain problems of Alpine physiology a sojourn of a few weeks on the summit seemed to me necessary, and as it was not possible to carry out a series of exact researches on man with the sole assistance of the guides and porters, I asked the Minister of War for permission to take with me ten soldiers of the Alpine regiment under the command of an army-surgeon.

On the intimation of the acquiescence of the Ministry I went to Ivrea where the Alpine regiment was stationed. My errand being made known, a number of soldiers immediately offered to join the expedition to the glaciers of Monte Rosa. I shall often have occasion to mention by name those who accompanied me; I take, however, this early opportunity of remarking that their behaviour and discipline were worthy of all praise, and of giving expression to my feelings of admiration for the sterling qualities of these humble comrades of mine, to whom likewise my heartiest thanks are due.

The first month, from the 19th of June to the 11th of July, 1894, was devoted to preliminary researches with the object of ascertaining the physiological conditions of the soldiers. As it was necessary to know what was their power of resistance to fatigue at ordinary elevations, I let them march with arms and baggage from Ivrea to Turin, a distance of 60 kilometres. I had purposely chosen some soldiers who were very strong and others of average strength: these I divided into two squads. I started with one squad and made the ascent at a slow rate of progress, about 1,000 metres per week. The other division climbed up to the summit of Monte Rosa rapidly, employing only three days, the rest being by that time installed in the Regina Margherita Hut, awaiting their arrival. This arrangement was made with the intent of discovering the effect of slow and rapid changes of altitude on the organism.

Some physiologists have studied man in the Alps under conditions so unfavourable that they did not succeed in separating the effects of fatigue and cold from those of diminished barometric pressure. The liability to error under disadvantageous circumstances being known to me, I took every precaution to ensure all necessary comforts as well as satisfactory victualling.

To the Minister of Public Instruction, Sig. Guido Baccelli, who kindly contributed 1,350 lire towards the expenses of the expedition, I offer sincerest thanks.

One single misfortune cast a gloom over us during our sojourn on the Alps: the illness of the soldier Ramella, who was seized with an inflammation of the lungs while we were in the Regina Margherita Hut. The rather serious nature of the attack interrupted our investigations and obliged us to start homewards sooner than had been our intention, ten days having been spent on the summit of Monte Rosa.

My brother, Ugolino Mosso, Professor of Pharmacology at the University of Genoa, Dr. Vittorio Abelli, army-surgeon, and Sig. Beno Bizzozero, medical student, accompanied me on this expedition. The last-named, I sorrowfully record, died a year later in the flower of his age, to the deep regret of all who knew him. Sig. B. Bizzozero's artistic talent made me select him to be the photographer of our expedition. From his beautiful collection of photographs I have taken a few views which, reproduced as illustrations in the following work, give an idea of the surroundings amidst which our investigations were carried on. I am no less indebted to Sig. Vittorio Sella for several admirable photographs.

I have long cherished the project of writing an easily understood book, founded on the observation of human life under a special group of conditions, so as to show within this narrower field what is the modern tendency of physiology as well as the methods now followed in studying the wondrous mechanism of our body. I have been prompted not by the passion for mountaineering, nor even the wish to preserve some record of happy hours spent in the Alps, but by the hope of thereby making a humble contribution to human physiology.

CONTENTS

CHAPTER I.
MUSCULAR FORCE STUDIED AT GREAT HEIGHTS 1

CHAPTER II.
AN ASCENT OF MONTE ROSA IN WINTER (1885) . . . 17

CHAPTER III.
RESPIRATION ON THE MOUNTAINS 31

CHAPTER IV.
THE CIRCULATION OF THE BLOOD IN RAREFIED AIR . . 51

CHAPTER V.
FATIGUE OF THE HEART 67

CHAPTER VI.
ACCIDENTS CAUSED BY EXCESSIVE FATIGUE AND NERVOUS EXHAUSTION . 81

CHAPTER VII.
ASCENTS—OUR CAMPS—GNIFETTI AND REGINA MARGHERITA HUTS . 101

CHAPTER VIII.
ALIMENTATION AND FASTING 117

CHAPTER IX.
THE TEMPERATURE OF THE BODY—CLASSIFICATION OF MOUNTAIN-CLIMBERS 129

CHAPTER X.
INDIVIDUAL DIFFERENCES 137

CHAPTER XI.
TRAINING—VITAL CAPACITY—MOUNTAINEERING . . . 147

CONTENTS

CHAPTER XII.
MOUNTAIN-SICKNESS 160

CHAPTER XIII.
AN EXPEDITION UP MONT BLANC IN 1891 . . 173

CHAPTER XIV.
OBSERVATIONS ON MOUNTAIN-SICKNESS . . 180

CHAPTER XV.
CHEMICAL ACTIVITY OF THE RESPIRATION ON THE ALPS . 191

CHAPTER XVI.
ANALYSIS OF ASPHYXIA AND OF MOUNTAIN-SICKNESS . 200

CHAPTER XVII.
INFLUENCE OF MOUNTAIN AIR ON THE NERVOUS SYSTEM—HEADACHE—THE WIND 224

CHAPTER XVIII.
CIRCULATION OF THE BLOOD IN THE HUMAN BRAIN . 237

CHAPTER XIX.
SLEEPINESS DURING ASCENTS—EXPERIMENTS ON MONKEYS AND MARMOTS 252

CHAPTER XX.
THE ACTION OF LIGHT—PERSPIRATION—COLD . 265

CHAPTER XXI.
CHANGES IN THE BLOOD ON THE ALPS . . 277

CHAPTER XXII.
EXPLANATION OF MOUNTAIN-SICKNESS—ACAPNIA . 287

CHAPTER XXIII.
THE NEW OBSERVATORY AND ALPINE STATION ON MONTE ROSA . 308

APPENDICES.

FIRST—AN ATTACK OF INFLAMMATION OF THE LUNGS ON THE SUMMIT OF MONTE ROSA 319

SECOND—METEOROLOGICAL OBSERVATIONS . . 324

TABLES . . 331

LIST OF ILLUSTRATIONS

INDRA CAMP	*Frontispiece*
	PAGE
VALLEY OF GRESSONEY	1
ERGOGRAPH	2
THE SOLDIER SARTEUR PERFORMING DUMB-BELL EXERCISE ON THE BALCONY OF THE REGINA MARGHERITA HUT	5
HOTEL AT THE COL D'OLEN	17
VIEW OF MONTE ROSA FROM THE GRESSONEY SIDE	19
SKETCH BY ZUMSTEIN SHOWING HIS ROUTE AND THE PEAKS OF MONTE ROSA	21
MERCURIAL MANOMETER FOR THE REGISTRATION OF THE FORCE OF THE RESPIRATORY MOVEMENTS	24
VIEW OF THE VINCENT PYRAMID FROM OUR CAMP NEAR LINTY HUT	25
SNOW-SHOE USED ON WINTER ASCENT OF MONTE ROSA	30
INDRA CAMP	31
APPARATUS WITH LEVER FOR THE TRACING OF THE RESPIRATORY MOVEMENTS	32
GAS-METER, VALVES, AND GUTTA-PERCHA MASK FOR THE MEASUREMENT OF THE AMOUNT OF AIR INSPIRED	39
VALLEY OF ALAGNA	51
HYDRO-SPHYGMOGRAPH	53
SPHYGMOMANOMETER FOR THE MEASUREMENT OF THE PRESSURE OF THE BLOOD IN MAN	57
VALLEY OF MACUGNAGA	67

LIST OF ILLUSTRATIONS

	PAGE
Form and Position of the Heart Determined with the Bianchi Phonendoscope	69
Myosphygmograph for the Study of the Circulation of the Blood	71
Changes in the Form and Position of the Heart after Ascents	75
Shepherds' Cottages on Monte Rosa	81
Panoramic View of Monte Rosa from Rimpfischhorn on the North Side	85
Gressoney St. Jean	101
Camp near Linty Hut	109
Parrot Peak	111
The Two Gnifetti Huts	113
The Little Gnifetti Hut which served as a Laboratory	115
View of Regina Margherita Hut from Col Gnifetti	117
Regina Margherita Hut on Gnifetti Peak	119
Plan of Regina Margherita Hut	129
Carrying-frame on Sella Model	130
Sella Hut	137
Mattia Zurbriggen	139
Field-bed Set Up and another Packed ready for Transport	147
Greeting the Arrival of a Mountaineering Party at Regina Margherita Hut	160
Arrival of an Expedition at Regina Margherita Hut	173
Linty Hut	180
View of the Lys Glacier and of the Continuation of the Hoheslicht Rock on which Gnifetti Hut Stands	183
A Corner of the Alpine Laboratory	191
Experiment Performed by Professor U. Mosso in order to Measure the Quantity of Carbonic Acid Eliminated in Half an Hour by Beno Bizzozero	195
Hoar-frost on the Regina Margherita Hut after the Storm of August 13, 1894	200
View from the Regina Margherita Hut	219

LIST OF ILLUSTRATIONS

THE DESCENT OF THE PARTY FROM MONTE ROSA. THE LAST PART OF THE GARSTELET GLACIER	224
PANORAMIC VIEW TAKEN FROM REGINA MARGHERITA HUT	237
PNEUMATIC CHAMBER AND ARRANGEMENTS FOR THE EXPERIMENTAL STUDY OF THE BRAIN-PULSE IN RAREFIED AIR	239
REGISTRATION OF THE CEREBRAL PULSE DURING THE RESPIRATION OF ARTIFICIAL AIR	248
PANORAMIC VIEW TAKEN FROM REGINA MARGHERITA HUT	252
DE SAUSSURE'S CAMP AT THE COL DU GÉANT	265
ROMAN BALANCE MADE USE OF ON THE MONTE ROSA EXPEDITION	269
ALP-HUT LAVEZ IN THE VALLEY OF GRESSONEY	277
GRESSONEY LA TRINITÀ	287
INSCRIPTION BURNT INTO A TABLET OF WOOD BY H.M. THE QUEEN OF ITALY IN REGINA MARGHERITA HUT	307
THE NEW REGINA MARGHERITA OBSERVATORY TO BE CONSTRUCTED IN 1898 ON THE SUMMIT OF MONTE ROSA	308
PLAN OF THE NEW REGINA MARGHERITA OBSERVATORY	309
H.M. QUEEN MARGARET OF ITALY ABOUT TO MAKE THE ASCENT OF GNIFETTI PEAK, AUGUST 18, 1893	313
GROUP OF SOME OF THE MEMBERS OF THE EXPEDITION	319
ORSIA ABOVE GRESSONEY LA TRINITÀ	324

Valley of Gressoney.

CHAPTER I

MUSCULAR FORCE STUDIED AT GREAT HEIGHTS

I.

I SHALL always remember the account Joseph Maquignaz gave me of the construction of the first hut on the Matterhorn. We were sitting together in the Théodule Hut, near the fire, awaiting the cessation of a furious storm.

No work had ever before been continued for a whole week together at such a height on the Alps, Maquignaz told me. The hut, situated at an altitude of 4,114 metres, was constructed, I believe, in 1867. All the guides of Val Tournanche went up in relays and took about three weeks to finish it. Maquignaz and his companions found work much more fatiguing at this height; while hewing the blocks of stone they had to stop to take breath every time a few blows had been struck, a necessity unknown to them in the plain even after a much greater exertion.

During the time they were at this altitude, exposed to wind and snow, and sleeping on the rock at night, their appetite failed. Once, when Maquignaz wished to force himself to finish part of the wall in haste, he was seized with oppression on the chest and with such a difficulty in breathing that he almost fainted.

Maquignaz was a modest man. During the whole of the day that we spent together, he would not even have told me, if I had not asked him, that he had performed the same ascent on which he was accompanying me, when conducting the Queen of Italy up the Breithorn. He seemed to be ignorant of the fact that he was one of the greatest authorities in the Alpine world. Only once he said jokingly that the Matterhorn was the university for mountain climbers. I told him with a smile that as professor in this university he far surpassed me in mine.

Maquignaz was laconic, but answered willingly, nevertheless, the questions I kept putting to him for the pleasure of hearing his replies so full of good sense. "I did not pay the least heed," he said, "to the bodily disturbances caused by living at great altitudes, because I knew that the rarefied air does not hurt one, and a good rest puts all right again. The breathing alters,"

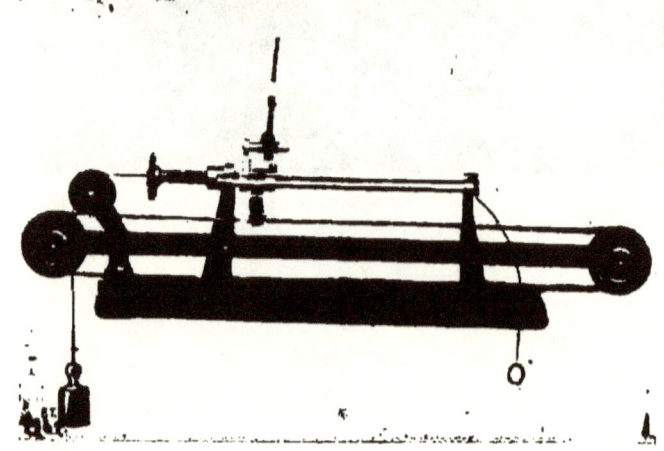

FIG. 1.—Ergograph.

he went on, "and a pipe will not keep alight in the same way. One needs the patience of a Job to prevent it from going out and to strike the matches. In fact we nearly all left off smoking. The ropes which we placed on the Matterhorn and the ladders we made are still as good as new even after so many years," he told me further, "whereas in the valley they would have rotted long since. I had forgotten a wallet on the Matterhorn in which there was some bread and cheese, and last year I found it again and ate up the contents, which were not at all musty."

In Sir W. M. Conway's last journey in the Himalayas, when a height of above 6,000 metres had been reached, the rate of progress had to be slackened so that the ascent continued at from 250 to 300 metres per day.[1] Conway's guide, Mattia Zurbriggen, told me that, at the last, he could not strike more than five or six blows with the ice-axe without stopping, when cutting steps

---

[1] W. Martin Conway, *Climbing and Exploration on the Karakoram Himalayas*. London, 1894.

in the ice; about a minute being necessary for him to regain his breath. "It was not strength which was lacking," he said, "but breath."

If one could believe everything the guides say, as one is inclined to do when they soberly enunciate their opinions, looking at one the while in their good-natured way, I might consider my subject as already exhausted and turn to something else. But before admitting that it is not the strength of the muscles but the breath which fails us when we work at great heights, I must chronicle the experiments which I performed in connection with this question. We shall see that the facts of the case are very complicated.

In order to register the mechanical work of the muscles, I constructed an apparatus [1] to which I have given the name of ergograph. Fig. 1 shows the registering part of the ergograph in its newest form. On a platform of iron two forked upright supports sustain two cylindrical steel bars which constitute the guides of the metal runner with the stylet which traces the muscular contractions of the middle finger on a smoked cylinder not shown in the figure. The clockwork which turns the cylinder, and which was used

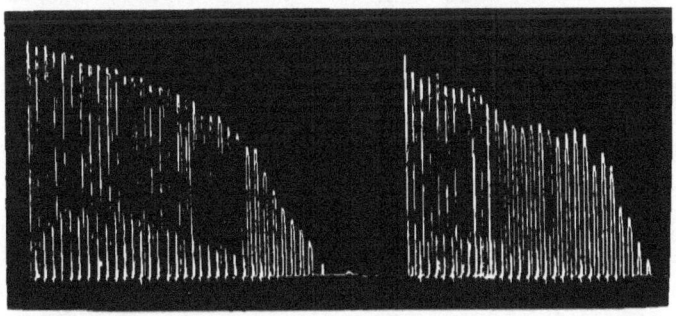

FIG. 2—Curves written with ergograph by Prof. Ugolino Mosso. A. Normal fatigue-curve in Turin.—B. Curve written on Monte Rosa at a height of 4,560 metres.

for these and all the other graphic experiments, is given in Fig. 9. A little cord passes through the aperture in the axis of the screw seen at the top of the apparatus, then runs over a pulley and descends, drawn downwards by the weight. The contractions of the middle finger are executed rhythmically, following the movements of a pendulum or of a metronome. In all the experiments made on Monte Rosa the rhythm was marked by a metronome which struck the seconds. Every two seconds a contraction was performed.

The part of the ergograph represented in Fig. 1 is constructed in such a manner that it not only writes the height of every contraction of the muscles, but also measures it in millimetres, and gives the sum of all the contractions executed within a given time. A tape-measure is seen in Fig. 1 running over two pulleys below the cylindrical bars. At every contraction of the middle finger a pair of nippers draws the tape on to a length corresponding to the height to which the weight is lifted. When the runner returns to its place, the nippers glide over the tape without moving it,

[1] A. Mosso, *La Fatica*, 1891, p. 180. *Die Ermüdung*, Leipzig, 1892, S. 86.

grasping it again at the next contraction. The number of centimetres to which the weight has been raised and the weight itself being known, the work accomplished may be determined in kilogrammetres.

In Fig. 2 the first curve to the left (A) was traced in Turin, the other (B) in the Regina Margherita Hut, by my brother, in the manner above described, a weight of four kilograms being raised with the middle finger of the right hand. The first vertical line to the left in this as in all other tracings forms the beginning of the curve. Immediately after every contraction the finger relaxes, returning to the position of repose. As the flexor muscles tire, the contractions become regularly lower, until at last fatigue renders the flexors incapable of raising the weight.

The lines are white on a black ground, because the paper which envelops the cylinder is smoked, and a very fine quill fixed at the extremity of the lever traces a white line by removing the soot in its passage.

My brother was one of the best possible subjects for this investigation, as he had worked with the ergograph for many years. From long experience we knew the profile of his normal curve, which is seen in Fig. 2 (A), as written in Turin before starting for Monte Rosa. In this experiment thirty-three successively decreasing contractions were performed, the work accomplished being equal to 3·48 kilogrammetres, a weight of four kilograms being lifted to a height of 0·870 metres, which is the sum of the contraction-heights in curve A.

The second curve, shown in Fig. 2 (B), was written several days after my brother's arrival at the Regina Margherita Hut, when he was acclimatised, for during the first few days he was not quite well. The quantity of mechanical work accomplished in curve B is a little less than in the preceding one. The weight of four kilograms was raised to a height of 0·707, the work accomplished in thirty contractions amounting only to 2·828 kilogrammetres. Excepting towards the end, where there is a slight rise, the curve preserves the type of the preceding figure registered in the plain.[1]

Similar experiments were made on myself, Beno Bizzozero, and on all the soldiers of the expedition. I did not find that the barometrical depression corresponding to the altitude of 4,560 metres had produced in any one a very considerable diminution of force. I refer, of course, to the curves registered after the fatigue produced by the ascent had disappeared.

Besides the slight decrease in the work accomplished, one circumstance becomes evident when we compare the series of curves obtained in Turin with those written on Monte Rosa; that is, a certain irregularity in these last.

We may therefore say that on Monte Rosa, at a height of 4,560 metres, the force of the muscles is slightly diminished and the characteristic and individual fatigue-type shown by the ergograph somewhat altered. Respecting the work accomplished, the difference between these curves in some persons was so small that the variations are, possibly, only the usual diurnal fluctuations. The greater irregularity in the curves is a sign that at a great height the motor-centres of the nervous system perform their functions less perfectly than in the plain.

---

[1] U. Mosso, *Action physiologique de la cocaïne.* Archives italiennes de Biologie, tome xiv. p. 9. *Action des principes actifs de la noix de kola sur la contraction musculaire.* Ibidem, tome xix. p. 241. *Influence du sucre sur le travail des muscles.* Ibidem, tome xxi. p. 293.

II.

Some will say that the fatigue of the hand, of a single finger, indeed, as studied by means of the ergograph, is too slight to admit of the above deduction. To meet this objection I had experiments performed before leaving Turin in which a greater number of muscles were exercised at once, in order to be able to establish a comparison in cases where a higher degree of fatigue is concerned.

In Fig. 3 we see one of these experiments, which used to be performed, when the weather was fine, on the balcony of the Regina Margherita Hut. The soldier Sarteur holds in his hands two dumb-bells, each weighing five kilograms. A metronome beats the seconds, and he raises the dumb-bells above his head every four seconds.

Let us suppose that the illustration shows the starting position; after one second the arms are bent and the dumb-bells lowered to the level of the thorax. In the next second the arms are stretched and the dumb-bells fall till parallel with the knees. After the lapse of another second the arms are again bent and the bells carried to the height of the thorax, and then at the last beat, the arms are extended upwards, holding the dumb-bells above the head, thus returning to the position indicated in the figure. In this position one second passes, then the dumb-bells descend to the thorax, and so on until the strength gives out. One of us always stood behind the persons exercising, in order to count how many times the dumb-bells were raised by each, the results then being noted. The number of times accomplished before strength fails varies certainly from one day to another, and the extreme limit is never exactly reached, but in spite of all sources of error there is a certain uniformity in the results.

We repeated these exercises at every encampment during our ascent of Monte Rosa, and to my surprise I found that at an altitude of 4,560 metres much more work was accomplished than in Turin.

FIG. 3—The soldier Sarteur performing dumb-bell exercise on the balcony of the Regina Margherita Hut (alt., 4,560 metres).

There are two causes of this augmentation. Even a slight acquaintance with gymnastic exercises suffices to render the first intelligible. This is the increasing resistance which a continued repetition of the same work enables us to oppose to fatigue. The second source of error might have been avoided, had I foreseen it, but it was too late when it forced itself upon my notice. So long as my soldiers remained in Turin they did not pay due heed to this method of determining their strength, owing to their excitement at being in a large town. Similarly during the week which we spent at the Indra Camp (alt., 2,515 metres) pastime was not lacking. We set up a target and had rifle-competitions, or else we hunted marmots. But when we were up amongst the glaciers, and still more so when shut up in the Regina Margherita Hut, the dumb-bell exercise became a favourite diversion, each trying to outdo the other in the number of lifts. In order to eliminate this spirit of rivalry I at last adopted the expedient of letting each perform his exercises alone on the balcony or in the end-room of the hut which served us as a laboratory and in which we had isolated the soldier Ramella, unfortunately suffering from an attack of inflammation of the lungs.

Before starting for Monte Rosa I reflected that it was not sufficient to measure the strength in the plain and on the heights, but that the modification in the breathing and action of the heart during the performance of the same work must also be studied. To this end I counted pulse and breathing in all before the commencement of the dumb-bell exercise and while they were well rested. When the exercise terminated owing to fatigue I again counted breathing and pulse. The amount of work accomplished by the men of the expedition thus trained did not, as already mentioned, diminish—it increased. I found, however, in all, that the heart and breathing-apparatus hastened their movements during the accomplishment of the same work in rarefied air.

III.

Many Alpinists believe that rarefied air produces an augmentation of strength. This is an illusion due to the fact that during an ascent a much greater amount of work is usually accomplished than we are accustomed to in the plain, and thus, because a true comparison is wanting, we imagine ourselves stronger. When an altitude of 4,000 metres is reached the diminution of resistance to work is evident in almost all. Before ascending Chimborazo Whymper made experiments in connection with this subject.[1]

The road which Whymper chose was perfectly level. He measured off half a mile in the neighbourhood of Quito and experimented on himself, counting the minutes which he took to cover one mile six times in succession. Comparing the time taken to go over the same distance in London with the time in Quito (about 3,100 metres higher), Whymper found that he walked more slowly at a great altitude. Striking the average of the time-lengths taken to cover a mile, the result was eleven minutes and four seconds for London and eleven minutes fifty-eight seconds for Quito. Whymper concludes "As regards myself, it appeared to me to be *conclusive* that a marked effect was produced, and an effect of a kind which I had never suspected at corresponding altitudes (pressures) in the Alps, where there was no possibility of applying a similar test."

We shall see from the following experiments that the action of the heart

---

[1] Ed. Whymper, *Travels Amongst the Great Andes of the Equator*. London, 1892, p. 300.

and the breathing alter more than in the plain, when the same muscular exercise is accomplished in the Alps. The data which I have collected allow of a more exact analysis of the phenomena observable in pulse and breathing in consequence of muscular exertion.

Chamois was one of the soldiers of the second squad, which came up rapidly from Ivrea to the summit of Monte Rosa. In Turin, after lifting dumb-bells weighing five kilograms each 121 times at four-second intervals, his pulse rose from 62 to 68 beats per minute. His breathing fell from 20 to 18 movements in the minute, but the inspirations after the exertion were deeper. Having reached the summit of Monte Rosa (alt., 4,560 metres), Chamois complained the first day of headache and stomach-ache, and remarked more than once that he could not breathe well. He did not, however, lose his appetite. As his radial pulse was too weak I was obliged to count that of the carotid artery.

On the 14th of August he raised the dumb-bells (five kilograms each in weight) 119 times; the pulse increasing from 94 to 120 beats per minute. The number of breaths rose from 22 to 27.[1]

After six minutes' rest the breathing had returned to its former rate, whereas the pulse was still accelerated, even after the lapse of twenty minutes.

In the greater number of cases I found that the acceleration of the breathing lasts somewhat longer; sometimes both cardiac and respiratory functions gradually became normal again together. Not wishing to inflict too many instances on the reader I restrict myself to one only of this kind.

The soldier Oberhoffer came up directly from Ivrea to the Regina Margherita Hut without first acclimatising himself. He, too, did not feel well the first day; his radial pulse was so weak and thready that in this case also I had to count the pulse of the carotid artery.

In Turin, after raising the dumb-bells (of the same weight) at four-second intervals 124 times, his pulse increased from 70 to 86 beats, the number of breaths diminished from 23 to 22 in the minute. On Monte Rosa, on the contrary, the pulse-frequency rose from 86 to 118, and the number of breaths

[1] Breathing and pulse in this observation and the following were counted during only 30″, so that I might better be able to follow their variations and take note of them. Every line of the following table corresponds to two minutes.

Chamois (soldier), August 14th (Regina Margherita Hut).

	Pulse in 30″.				Breathing in 30″.
4.29 p.m.	47	...	...	...	11
	48	...	...	...	11
	46	...	...	...	12
4.31 p.m.	The dumb-bells are raised 119 times.				
4.39 p.m.	64				14
	58				13
	53				14
	53				11
	52				11
	52				10
	50				11
	52				10
	52				11

from 24 to 28. This was after raising the five-kilogram dumb-bells 130 times.[1]

After twenty-two minutes' rest the heart-beats and breaths became normal together.

IV.

Cardiac and respiratory activity is more liable to alteration on the Alps after the accomplishment of the same amount of work as in the plain, but the rarefaction of the air does not exercise an immediate influence on the force and resistance of the muscles, because even at the height of 4,560 metres many persons preserve the same energy of which they have given proof at the foot of the Alps. Perhaps the products of fatigue affect the organism more intensely at a diminished barometrical pressure. Our pulses were rather more rapid in the Regina Margherita Hut when we stood. This agrees with and is explained by the fact that on Monte Rosa pulse and breathing presented for the same amount of work a more intense subsequent modification than they presented in the plain.

On account of the theories to be subsequently developed, I here communicate an instance showing that the rate of breathing was not always modified by fatiguing muscular work, even on the summit of Monte Rosa. Other data will be found in the tables at the end of the book.

To illustrate this fact I have selected an experiment made in the Regina Margherita Hut on one of the most robust men of our party: the soldier Marta, who acted as cook. He had told me several times that he had never felt so well as when acting cook on the summit of Monte Rosa, and, indeed, he worked on contentedly without ever taking a rest.

On the 14th of August I told him to exercise with the two five-kilogram dumb-bells.[2]

---

[1] Oberhoffer (soldier), August 14th, 1894 (Regina Margherita Hut).

	Pulse in 30".				Breathing in 30".
11.20 a.m.	43	...	...	...	12
	41	...	...	...	12

The dumb-bells are raised 130 times.

11.34 a.m.	59	...	...	...	14
	52	...	...	...	15
	48	...	...	...	13
	47	...	...	...	13
	44	...	...	...	15
	45	...	...	...	14
	45	...	...	...	13
	45	...	...	...	14
	44	...	...	...	13
	42	...	...	...	12

[2] Marta (soldier) (Regina Margherita Hut).

	Pulse in 30".				Breathing in 30".
10.15 a.m.	46	...	...	...	11 } Normal
	46	...	...	...	12 }

After 185 lifts of the dumb-bells.

10.28 a.m.	67	...	...	...	12
	55	...	...	...	10
	55	...	...	...	12
	59	...	...	...	12
	58	...	...	...	10
	57	...	...	...	10
	55	...	...	...	10

The frequency of the breathing was not augmented, indeed, there was a slight diminution; the depth of the respiratory movements was, however, much greater. This is an important result, because we have here an amount of mechanical work so considerable that few men would be able to accomplish it. Only the rhythm of the heart was modified, twenty minutes' rest being necessary before it again became normal.

Any one who takes two dumb-bells, each weighing five kilograms, into his hands and tries to raise them above his head at four-second intervals in the manner indicated, will be convinced that the strength of these soldiers was not diminished, surpassing as it did the average man's strength.

Oscar Eckenstein[1] made certain observations at an altitude of 3,350 metres, and did not find that his strength was diminished.

Fatigue, like emotion, produces a more serious alteration in the activity of the heart than in the respiratory functions.

This law, which I had already discovered in studying the modifications which the organism undergoes during psychic processes, is confirmed by the observations made during ascents. It is thus probable that the sudden alteration in the activity of heart and breathing-apparatus does not depend solely on the contraction of the muscles. The relations between brain, heart and lungs, present very complex phenomena. The supposition that during muscular exertion poisonous substances are generated is true; it is, however, also true that palpitation and oppression may be caused without preceding muscular work.

V.

The increase in our rate of breathing and cardiac pulsations when we perform any considerable muscular work suggests the comparing of our bodies to the gas-motors now used in many industries, which regulate their action automatically. In these machines, whenever a stronger movement is to be accomplished, we immediately notice that the action of the piston is more rapid and the belching more frequent.

The simile is not perfect because our machine is much more complicated. The oxygen inspired and carbonic acid produced do not represent all the energy called into play by the muscles. When the work is finished the respiration still continues more intense, and the palpitation of the heart lasts for some time, because the nervous system modifies the metabolic processes of the organism in a manner not proportional to the mechanical work accomplished.

In my book *La Fatica*,[2] I have already shown that poisonous substances are produced by working muscles. Having injected the blood of a fatigued dog into a sleeping dog, I noticed the laboured breathing and the palpitation of the heart reappear in the latter.

The increased rapidity of the pulse which often lasts for a very long time after the cessation of the exertion, is due most probably to the poisons which fatigue produces in the body.

Till very recently many thought that the breathing increased in rapidity, when we go upstairs, for instance, because the blood must eliminate a greater quantity of carbonic acid. The recent researches of Zuntz, Geppert,

---

[1] O. Eckenstein, *The Karakorams and Kashmir*, 1896, p. 152.
[2] A. Mosso, *La Fatica*, p. 145. *Die Ermüdung*, S. 119.

Filehne, and Kionka[1] have shown that the blood in the arteries is richer in oxygen during work than repose, and that it contains a lesser quantity of carbonic acid.[2]

The soldier Solferino performed dumb-bell exercise on the 2nd of August while we were encamped near Linty Hut (alt., 3,047 metres).

	Pulse in 30"					Breathing in 30"
5 p.m.	39	...	...	...	...	10
	40	...	...	...	...	10

The 5-kilogram dumb-bells are raised 104 times.

5.10 p.m.	55	...	...		...	14
	53	...	...		...	11
	45	...	...		...	11
	44	...	...		...	10
	43	...	...		...	10
	44	...	...		...	10

After four minutes the breathing had returned to its former rate; the cardiac movements only became normal after twenty minutes.

The day afterwards I sent this same soldier to Gressoney for the mail and to buy provisions. How he passed the night I never learnt, but probably enjoying himself in a tavern, because he returned very tired towards midday the next day, and gave me the impression that he had drunk more than usual over night.

The next day, August 5th, at 9.40 a.m., I told him to exercise with the dumb-bells shortly after he was out of bed. The results were as follows:—

	Pulse in 30"					Breathing in 30"
	29	...	...	...	...	9
	28	...	...	...	...	9
	28	...	...	...	...	9

The dumb-bells are raised only 67 times.

9.51 p.m.	55	...	...	...	...	16
	53	...	...	...	...	15
	40	...	...	...	...	14
	39	...	...	...	...	13
	35	...	...	...	...	10
	38	...	...	...	...	10
	38	...	...	...	...	9
	38	...	...	...	...	9
	38	...	...	...	...	9
	37	...	...	...	...	9
10.30 a.m.	39	...	...	...	...	9
10.45 ,,	37	...	...	...	...	9
11.0 ,,	35	...	...	...	...	9
11.30 ,,	30	...	...	...	...	9
11.50 ,,	28	...	...	...	...	9

We see from this experiment how a dietetic irregularity weakens us physically. Although considerably less work was performed, the dumb-bells being raised 34 times less, Solferino experienced a much greater degree of fatigue. The number of respirations rose to 32, this increased frequency continuing twelve minutes longer than normally, whereas in the preceding experiment the greater

---

[1] Pflüger's *Archiv für Physiologie*, vol. xlii. p. 189; vol. lxiii. p. 234.

[2] Johansson has studied the influence which the activity of the muscles exercises on the breathing and on the heart. He restricted his investigations to rabbits.—*Skandinavisches Archiv für Physiologie*, 1893, vol. v. p. 21.

frequency of respiration had only lasted for six minutes. But the most serious effects were those on the heart, this organ requiring two hours to recover its normal conditions, although the subject remained seated in the meantime.

Perhaps Solferino, being weaker, had become more sensitive to fatigue-poisons; or else in consequence of the depression of the organism their elimination required a longer time.

Professor Oertel, in a very well-known book [1] containing his studies on the beneficial influence which movement and moderate ascents exercise on diseases of the heart and lungs, shows that after the fatigue of an ascent the heart has already returned to its normal state while the blood-vessels are still dilated. Even twenty-four hours after a toilsome ascent he noticed that the tension of the arteries was less when registering the pulse with the sphygmograph. I did not measure the pressure in Solferino, but I believe it was little diminished, because the pulse rate was normal and less than what it had been on August 2nd.

The action of nervous system which is involved in the performance of an exertion produces, independent of the chemical work of the muscles, a sudden change in the breathing and in the action of the heart. As a normal emotion takes away our breath and gives us palpitation of the heart, so the nervous system, when it issues a series of orders to the muscles, is subjected to a species of unconscious emotion which would modify the breathing even though the muscles did not contract. I have seen an affectionate and sensitive dog take such fright at hearing the whiz of a rocket at a great distance that he immediately began to breathe as though he had been running hard. Half an hour later he was still panting, his heart beat fast and his breathing was laboured.

All this serves to show how close is the connection between the brain and the respiratory and cardiac functions, a connection of which emotions have made us all aware.

In the following chapters I shall show more clearly how the influence of a little irregularity of diet predisposes to mountain-sickness. The instance of the soldier Solferino is typical of a whole class of serious complications. These arise partly from poisonous products of intrinsic origin, partly from the action of each part of the organism on the others; often the phenomena become so inextricable that we do not succeed in distinguishing which is the cause and which the effect.

VI.

In works on mountain climbing one often reads of travellers fainting. Alexander von Humboldt's experience of this kind in South America [2] is well known.

"Once, on the volcano of Pichincha," he writes, "I was seized, though without any bleeding, with such violent pains in the stomach, accompanied by dizziness, that I was found lying unconscious on the ground immediately after parting from my companions. The altitude was inconsiderable, being only 13,800 feet (4,206 metres)."

In the study of fatigue at different heights I did not restrict myself to

[1] I. Oertel, *Handbuch der allgemeinen Therapie der Kreislaufs-Störungen.* Leipzig, 1891, p. 195.
[2] *Notice sur deux tentatives d'ascension du Chimborazo par Alexandre de Humboldt.* Annales de Chimie et de Physique, tome lxviii. 1838, p. 401.

counting the rate of breathing, but also registered it, because the respiratory depth may change, although the rate of movement remain the same. The necessity of brevity prevents my introducing the numerous curves registered so as to facilitate the analysis of these phenomena; one, however, it will be well to give, as it shows the effect of a fainting-fit produced by fatigue on the Alps.

On August 16, 1894, at 4.50 p m., in the Regina Margherita Hut, I registered the thoracic respiration of Corporal Camozzi with Marey's double pneumograph. The day before he had arrived from Linty Hut in good condition, without any load, and in fine weather. The normal respiratory curve is shown in the bit of tracing at the bottom and to the right of Fig. 4. The line 1 represents normal breathing of one minute's duration, twenty breaths being drawn in that time.

When I had removed the pneumograph from the thorax, Corporal Camozzi took the two 5-kilogram dumb-bells and raised them 150 times. At Indra Camp, where the last experiment had been made, the maximum number of lifts had been 108. The exceptional figure 150 shows how great was his strength at this height. As soon as the exercise was finished I applied the pneumograph again and registered the breathing.

Line 2 in Fig. 4 shows the respiratory curve taken immediately after the exertion. The rate is 29 to the minute. The pulse beats 128 times in the minute and immediately afterwards towards the end of the line it rises to 136 times per minute. In line 3, six minutes after the cessation of the dumb-bell exercise, I felt the radial pulse become so feeble that I could scarcely count it. I placed my finger on the throat in order to touch the carotid artery and counted sixty pulsations in thirty seconds. At this point Camozzi told me that he would like to sit down, as everything was growing dark around him. I looked at the curve and noticed at once that for more than a minute the breathing had been profoundly altered. At A I told Camozzi to sit down (till then he had been standing); immediately afterwards he fainted.

The curve, as we see, is interrupted. I sprinkled his face with water and he recovered immediately. As soon as he told me that it was over I began again to register the breathing. As may be seen from line 4 of Fig. 4 the respiration is much stronger than before, after the cessation of the muscular work, and almost twice as high as the last fragment which represents the normal breathing before exertion. The pulse, on the contrary, has slackened, beating only 104 times per minute.

The last part of the curve having been taken, I did not wish to continue the registration and told Camozzi to lie down on a mattress in the other room. He did so, drank a cup of coffee, and after ten minutes wanted to rise, assuring me that he was perfectly well.

Seldom, perhaps never, have physicians had an opportunity of following with equal precision the beginning and development of a fainting-fit. The observation that the respiratory and cardiac functions were contemporaneously modified is important. Six minutes passed after the cessation of the muscular exercise before the weakness manifested itself in the functions of the heart and breathing apparatus. The modification which the breathing underwent is interesting, slackening somewhat at the beginning of the fainting-fit, with a slight halt at the beginning of the expiration. The movements of the thorax became very superficial, gaining strength again after the fit was over.

The excitability of the nerve centres was diminished when the fainting-fit

took place. There was a species of paresis of the respiratory centre and cardiac nerves. The reason of this central effect I cannot tell, but this observation suffices to convince any one that it is not the insufficiency of breath which prevents our working on the Alps and that it is not oxygen which is wanting during work. During six minutes after the cessation of work everything seemed to be proceeding normally. The first morbid phenomenon was a diminution in the depth and rate of the breathing.

The blood continued to become venous during the swoon. This incipient asphyxia did not aggravate the conditions, which proves that this was not the cause of the sudden diminution of excitability in the nerve centres. As soon as the nervous force was re-established the respiratory centre sought to compensate for the preceding diminution of breathing. This explains why the respiration is nowhere stronger than at the beginning of line 4A of the curve.

Here, too, we observed that the maximum rate of the cardiac pulsation is not reached during exertion nor immediately after its cessation, but after a few minutes of repose. In the above instance the pulse rose from 128 to 136. We shall return to this point later. In the meantime we have come to the conclusion that when muscular exercise ceases, the physical condition is not improved but rendered worse. Perhaps the unconscious emotion of the nervous system during muscular exertion is an excitement which acts on the cardiac and respiratory centres. Perhaps when the exertion ceases, these centres, sinking into repose, are paralysed by fatigue-poisons.

Seeing that the same work produces on Monte Rosa a more serious and more lasting modification of the organism, we are inclined to think that we understand what mountain-sickness is. Indeed both mountain-climbers and physiologists have thought that fatigue was a sufficient explanation of this disturbance. In climbing mountains we consume a greater quantity of oxygen, they say, the respiration no longer suffices to compensate the losses which the organism incurs through muscular work, and, therefore, mountain-sickness ensues.

This is the theory which bears the name of Dufour, after whom also one of the peaks of Monte Rosa has been christened.

The experiment which gives the most satisfactory support to this theory would seem to be that of Regnard.[1]

Regnard placed under a large pneumatic bell, a wheel which rotated horizontally like a squirrel-wheel, and to which by means of an electric current he could impart a rotatory movement of the desired velocity. Within this wheel he placed a guinea-pig, and regulated the movement so that the animal walked 400 metres in the hour. He put another guinea-pig within the bell outside of the wheel in order to facilitate a comparison. The pressure being reduced till it corresponded to an altitude of 300 metres, there was little difference observable between the two animals, but from this degree of rarefaction onwards, the guinea-pig within the wheel began to fall frequently forwards and allow itself to be dragged on by the wheel, as though exhausted, whereas the other guinea-pig was quiet.

At a pressure corresponding to the height of 4,600 metres, the guinea-pig within the wheel fell on its back, no longer moved its legs, letting itself be dragged on as before. The machine was stopped and the animal taken out; its state was such that one would have thought it dead had it not been for the laboured breathing. The other was quite well.

[1] Paul Regnard, *La cure d'altitude*, 1897, p. 119.

This experiment of Regnard seems simple and reliable, but it is not really so. The fact that the one animal was in repose renders the comparison invalid.

The guinea-pig is an animal that offers very little resistance to work; it runs badly, and even in air not rarefied, if it is kept in movement, soon presents serious phenomena of exhaustion, unaccustomed as it is to running. Indeed, we see that in Regnard's apparatus, the guinea-pigs run only 400 metres per hour. The manner in which I have seen chamois run at an altitude of 3,500 metres, and the exertions undergone by some of the soldiers of my expeditions, who carried 30 and 40 kilograms up to the top of Monte Rosa by a steep and difficult road over the glacier of Gnifetti Peak without any ill effects, convinced me that the experiments on guinea-pigs are not the most suitable for the study of mountain-sickness. We shall presently see that this malady may be caused without fatigue.

VII.

Alexander von Humboldt [1] measured in the Andes the height at which he saw a condor fly, and found it to be 21,834 feet. The brothers Schlagintweit [2] relate that in Asia they saw eagles and vultures at a height of 23,000 feet and that for six days, while at an altitude of 6,000 metres on the Ibigamin, they were followed by Tibetan ravens that ate the remnants of their food at the various encampments.

Similar if more modest observations may be made also on our Alps, nor are they less worthy of wonder.

Alpine crows (*Graculus alpinus*) often left Alagna and flew in flocks up as high as the Regina Margherita Hut during our sojourn there. Once with the telescope I saw a number fly across the Vigne Glacier in a great spiral line. We shut ourselves into the hut, and I stood watching them through a crack, when they alighted near the door to eat the kitchen-remnants. They were only a few paces distant from me, and I could observe them well; their breathing was quiet, which surprised me considering that they had mounted so quickly, rising for about 2,000 metres without a halt.

Zumstein relates that he was surrounded by a number of these crows on his first ascent of Monte Rosa. I have often seen them circling round the highest and most desolate of the Monte Rosa peaks where, save for a few insects carried up by the wind, every sign of life is lacking. I have seen them also in winter, consequently it cannot be that they or the vulture and condor mount to these heights in search of food. I cannot say why they repair thither, but they certainly do not suffer any inconvenience, and this journeying through such rarefied air cannot cost them any great exertion.

The recent studies of the ablest experimenters tend to show that the oxygen absorbed in respiration increases in direct proportion to the work accomplished. We shall see later that there are other still more convincing facts which will oblige us to attribute less importance to the oxygen that we inspire as an immediate cause of the energy developed by the muscles.

Birds living in the most elevated regions of the atmosphere must perform such energetic muscular work in order to sustain themselves in the rarefied

---

[1] Alexander von Humboldt, *Ansichten der Natur*, Zweiter Band, Erläuterungen 2, S. 4.
[2] Hermann, Adolphe, and Robert Schlagintweit, *Results of a Scientific Mission to India and High Asia*. Leipzig, London, 1862, vol. ii.

air, as perhaps animals in the plains never do. Nothwithstanding this, it seems as if amongst all living beings, they had the least need of oxygen in breathing.

Often when looking at the birds circling round Monte Rosa, I used to think that perhaps the study of fatigue in these animals would open up new scientific vistas, for it is inexplicable that they should be the warmest of all animals and yet those which breathe the least frequently. The condor draws only six breaths in the minute (four times less than we draw), and flies with velocity at heights where man has never yet set his foot. Were he to do so, he would arrive, as Humboldt says, "in an alarming asthenic condition."[1]

[1] *Der Mensch befindet sich in solchen Höhen in einem beängstigenden asthenischen Zustande. Op. cit.*, p. 37.

Hôtel at the Col d'Olen (alt., 2,865 metres).

CHAPTER II

AN ASCENT OF MONTE ROSA IN WINTER (1885)

I.

MY studies having necessitated the experience of a great degree of fatigue, and especially of that fatigue of the eyes which only the perpetual dazzling white of the Alpine snows can cause, this winter ascent of Monte Rosa was undertaken, nor was it, I trust, utterly useless from a physiological point of view.

Let me first speak of the surroundings amid which my investigations were conducted, and devote a few words also to those mountain-climbers who first began scientific researches in those regions.

The Italians had already conquered the difficulties of Monte Rosa, and accurately mapped all its peaks before it was known on the north side where this mountain was situated.

G. Studer, in his story of the Alps, wrote " that till 1830 Swiss topographers and panorama-drawers confounded Monte Rosa with the Mischabelhörner."[1] Now, any one who, from the Zermatt side or from the Regina Margherita Hut (as seen in Chapter XVI.) contemplates the distance which separates the summit of the Mischabelhörner from the Monte Rosa group, can with difficulty believe so recent this almost prehistoric epoch of mountaineering, when the queen of the Alps was still unknown or confounded with the lower mountains stretching away to the north.

[1] G. Studer, *Ueber Eis und Schnee*, Bern, 1869, ii., Abth. S. 4.

In 1788 Count Morozzo, president of the Academy of Sciences of Turin,[1] attempted the first ascent of Monte Rosa. Unfortunately he made the attempt from the Macugnaga side, and only reached the height of 3,700 metres.

This path, the first tried, and the one from which the best view of Monte Rosa in all its grandeur is obtained was the last to be followed up, in 1872, after a century of attempts. The name of Count Morozzo recalls the most glorious epoch of Italian physiology. Towards the end of the last century, earlier than in any other country, an exact study of respiration had been begun in Italy. Spallanzani and Fontana were the greatest physiologists of that time. Besides these two, Cigna, whom I shall mention later, and Count Morozzo must be named. The memoir of this latter with the title: *Expériences eudiométriques sur l'air pur vicié par la respiration animale,* is a work which merits rescue from oblivion, because the researches contained in it are little different from those which are carried on in our own day. The fundamental idea in Paul Bert's book on Barometrical Pressure, that is, the analysis of the air in which an animal dies from asphyxia, with the object of learning the changes which the composition of the air has undergone, is one of Count Morozzo's ideas, and one which he was the first to verify by means of eudiometrical analysis.

The five ascents of Monte Rosa, by Joseph Zumstein, are perhaps from an Alpinist's point of view more important than the ascent of Mont Blanc, by Saussure, for Jacques Balmat had already twice ascended Mont Blanc, when he, with other seventeen guides, accompanied Saussure.[2]

The Academy of Sciences of Turin published in 1820 Zumstein's narrative in which is described the first expedition with Vincent, to the pyramid which now bears the name of the latter.[3] The accounts of the four subsequent expeditions were published in German in the monograph of Monte Rosa, written by von Welden, who was staying at that time[4] in Gressoney, whence he made many ascents with Zumstein. It was he who gave the name of Ludwig's Höhe to one of the Monte Rosa peaks.

In the Archives of the Academy of Sciences of Turin I found the autographic account which Zumstein, as corresponding member, presented to the society on March 1, 1824. At that time Monte Rosa was known only from the Macugnaga side, it being thought by all that below the peaks of its north side there was a deep valley. It was Zumstein who discovered the table-land of ice which lies like an immense amphitheatre in the middle of the crown formed by the Monte Rosa peaks. Amongst the papers of Zumstein I found also a fine painting in distemper of the highest peaks of Monte Rosa. It is reproduced in Fig. 5, and represents the southern side of the mountain, as seen from the hills in the valley of Gressoney.

There was also another of Zumstein's drawings in the Archives of the Academy of Sciences, which I give in Fig. 6. It is a valuable sketch, because it was executed by Zumstein when he had, for the first time, reached the great ice-plains situated amid the peaks of Monte Rosa, and helps to

---

[1] Morozzo, *Sur la mesure des principaux points des Etats du Roi*, M. ix. 1.
[2] Saussure, *Relation abrégée d'un voyage à la cime du Mont Blanc*, 1787.
[3] J. Zumstein et M. Vincent, *Voyage sur le Mont Rose et première excursion de son sommet méridional.* Memorie della R. Accademia delle Scienze di Torino, tome xxv., 1820, p. 230.
[4] Ludwig, Freiherr v. Welden, *Der Monte Rosa,* Wien, 1824. An abridgment of this book was printed in the "Bibliothèque universelle de Genève," vol. xxvii. p. 221, and vol. xxviii. p. 63, in 1824 and 1825.

FIG. 5.—View of Monte Rosa from the Gressoney side. Painting in distemper presented by Zumstein in 1824 to the Academy of Sciences of Turin. In length this production is shorter by 10 centimetres than the original; its breadth being correspondingly reduced.

elucidate the structure of the mountain. At the foot of Gnifetti Peak, which Zumstein ascended, is marked the spot where the distinguished traveller spent a night in a glacier-crevasse.

In the last chapter I have inserted the reproduction of a photograph, which was taken while her Majesty the Queen of Italy, after reaching the foot of Zumstein Peak, was about to begin the ascent of Gnifetti Peak. All the peaks marked in Zumstein's sketch simply with letters were then untrodden. In the foot-note [1] the reader will find the corresponding names afterwards given to them. The dotted line in the sketch indicates the path followed by Zumstein in his first ascent from Gressoney.

I shall, I hope, find time to publish a biographical sketch of Zumstein with the help of the new documents which I have collected; here I restrict myself to transcribing a fragment of the manuscript in which he relates his ascent of the peak which bears his name, and on which the cross of iron which he erected may still be seen. Zumstein slept at a height of 4,217 metres in a glacier-crevasse, no other, until Tyndall in 1859,[2] having passed the night so high up on the Alps.

"I saw with satisfaction from the spot where I stood that the peak which we had proposed as the end of our journey could be very easily climbed. The great sea of ice and snow showed no crevasses; it was smooth and of dazzling whiteness.

"In the midst of my observations my friends and a few porters arrived, the latter laying down their loads and going back to meet the others. After a few minutes' rest M. Molinatti, who had just arrived, hastened to set up his theodolite beside my instruments, but in vain, for no sooner was all ready than the clouds closed in around and above us, and the distant summits were hidden from our sight.

"Night was coming on, and our porters had still not returned. A great part of our effects was also in the rear, even the tent and the wood of which we had such need. It was six o'clock in the evening and no one came. The thermometer was at —7°. A change of 15° of temperature in so short a time had a bad effect on me. My people were benumbed, while an irresistible sleepiness began to creep over me. My companions saw me grow suddenly pale; I felt my strength and courage fail. Old Joseph Beck, an experienced hunter, began, however, to shake me, to make me move about so as to warm my blood, and to lend me every sort of assistance.

"The cold was increasing more and more, and likewise our dismay. It is easy to imagine what horror took possession of us. We were at a height of 13,000 feet above the level of the sea, with 10° of cold which continued to increase, without shelter, without fire, our feet on the ice, in the open air, exposed to all the rigour and dangers of the approaching night.

"We at last resolved to confront the greatest perils by retracing our steps

---

[1]
					Altitude.	
A.	Vincent Pyramid	...	...	...	4,215	metres.
B.	Balmenhorn	...	...	...	4,231	,,
C.	Schwarzhorn	...	...	...	4,334	,,
D.	Ludwig's Höhe	...	...	...	4,346	,,
E.	Parrot Peak	...	...	...	4,463	,,
G.	Gnifetti Peak	...	...	...	4,560	,,
H.	Dufour Peak	...	...	...	4,635	,,
I.	Lyskamm	...	...	...	4,529	,,

[2] J. Tyndall, *Hours of Exercise in the Alps*, London, 1871, p. 54.

in spite of the darkness of the night, for there was no moon, when at last the longed-for porters arrived with their loads. . . . We reached the edge of the fissure by a wall of snow with an inclination of about 65 degrees. The old hunter, Joseph Beck, was the most daring, and the first who ventured to descend to the bottom of the pit by a series of forty steps which he cut himself with his axe in the snow and ice. Having assured us that the bottom was formed of snow heaped up by the wind and very compact, we all went down, one after the other, into this species of tomb. We were all chilled with cold, I, almost benumbed, and unable to aid the others in setting up the tent which was raised by the intrepid Joseph Maurice Zumstein, while our robust Marty was laying and lighting a good fire, of which we stood much in need.

"Although little inclined to eat, we all partook of a savoury soup, and then huddled together in the tent. There were eleven of us lying on the ground, all on the right side and close together for fear of freezing during the night, and so we fell asleep in the arms of fate.

"In the course of the night I was attacked by strong palpitation; I felt

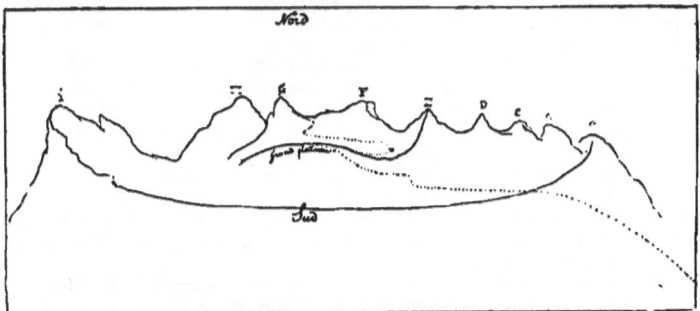

FIG. 6.—A sketch by Zumstein showing his route and the peaks of Monte Rosa.

as though I should choke, but having wriggled out from among the others I stood up, recovered my breath and was soon able to lie down quietly again and sleep till dawn.

"We were at a height of 2,188 toises above the level of the sea (about the height of the Jungfrau in the Haut Bernois) and 193 toises, or 1,158 feet, higher than the spot where M. de Saussure passed the night on Mont Blanc. . . . At half-past seven in the morning we were all ready. At the distance of about half a league we passed near the eastern peaks, over a great plain of snow undulating like the waves of the sea and a little sloping towards Valais, and a league further, still rising at an angle of about 30°, we arrived at the foot of the pyramidal summit which we began to climb. M. Molinatti, inconvenienced by the too great rarity of the air, was forced to stop from time to time.

"The last arête of snow which we had to surmount rose at an angle of 65 degrees. We attacked it, led by the bold hunter Castet, who, armed with his axe, cut steps in the snow and ice in which we could place our feet. As we advanced along this dreadful crest which dominated in part the Macugnaga valley, the snow disappeared almost entirely and we had only smooth, solid ice under our feet. If a foot had slipped we should have been lost, falling vertically downwards a depth of 8,000 feet, but luckily none of us suffered from dizziness in that decisive moment.

"As soon as young Vincent had reached the summit he turned towards us, crying: 'Long live the king, long live science!' We heartily repeated the cry, and, grasping the flag which we had planted in the ice, we all swore fidelity to our king and to our country."

II.

In his book, *The Pioneers of the Alps*,[1] Cunningham says: "None of those who have visited the Alps during the winter months can show such a splendid record of achievements as the Signori Sella." My winter ascent of Monte Rosa with Alessandro Sella took place at that time.

Seldom does such a quantity of snow fall as in the winter of 1885. Pietro Guglielmina, whom Alessandro Sella and I had requested to act as guide, wrote to us from Alagna that the snow was above man's height. We left Alagna in the morning of February 13th, wearing our snow-shoes. After three hours' toilsome march we came across a little chapel. The sun had melted the snow from the eaves, and we sat down on the slates of the roof to rest. Midway towards the Col d'Olen we tried a few times to find out the depth of snow, but even though we thrust the whole of the arm as well as the alpenstock into the snow, we did not strike the ground, not even on the slopes, where the depth was certainly least. The snow had filled up valleys and torrent-beds, making all one level plain. From time to time we stopped to take breath and shake our shoes free from the encumbering snow. But we kept sinking in more and more, and only with difficulty could we extricate our feet. We toiled on, stumbling, falling, crawling on our knees, entangling ourselves in our snow-shoes, and sinking sometimes as far as the waist into the snow.

At last we arrived below the Col d'Olen; our breathing was laboured, and our hearts beat so fast that it was an annoyance to me to hear mine pulsating. I counted as many as a hundred and ten beats in the minute. Although we were only at a height of 2,800 metres, the expedition halted at every thirty paces. We were all exhausted, and my purpose of experiencing a great fatigue was fully accomplished.

At Alagna at 7 a.m. before rising my pulse beat at the rate of 59 to 60 in the minute. Breathing, 14 per minute. Rectal temperature, 36·6°.

We arrived at the Olen inn at 4.10 p.m. Pulse 114–112. After a rest of fifteen minutes the temperature was 38·1°. Breathing, 16. We see here, too, that the breathing becomes regular much sooner than the heart. The temperature presented this circumstance worthy of note, that after the first two hours' march it had reached (at 10.45 a.m.) its maximum of 38·2°, while the pulse beat at the rate of 122 times in the minute. Afterwards there was a slight diminution of both temperature and pulse-rate, although the last part of the ascent was more fatiguing.

At 8 p.m. the pulse beat 80 times in the minute. Rectal temperature, 36·9°.

During the night I slept little and was feverish, with a temperature of 38·5°. In the morning at 7 o'clock the temperature had fallen to 38·1°. Pulse, 84. Breathing, 19.

[1] C. D. Cunningham, *The Pioneers of the Alps*, London, 1888, p. 40.

This is the fever of fatigue which attacks us when, after leading a sedentary life for some time we perform prolonged and tiring muscular work. That the temperature of the body rises in consequence of movement is a fact known to all, and we shall see in Chapter IX. that the internal temperature may reach 39·5° owing to the fatigue caused by a short ascent. I should like here to show the characteristic course of the fever of fatigue. When the movement ceases the temperature of the body sinks, and soon falls below the normal. If the exertion has been great I have noticed that in the majority of persons the body becomes somewhat colder, although this is not the case in all. If we then remain quietly in bed (as in my case) an attack of fever without shivering seizes us after an hour or two, and the temperature rises to about two degrees above the normal.

The study of fever is one of the most obscure points in medicine and we can say little positively about its mechanism and the actual nature of the processes giving rise to it. Judging by analogy we may compare the fever of fatigue to the fever which is caused by contusions, fractures, and wounds, studied by Billroth,[1] and later by Volkmann. The infection of a wound by germs which multiply rapidly and spread through the organism is sufficient to generate this fever. In subcutaneous fractures and contusions, when the skin remains uninjured, an attack of fever occurs after a few hours. I make this comparison in order that it may be understood how a serious blow in modifying the life of the cells in one part of the body, generates noxious substances which give rise to fever. In extraordinary exertions, with the excess of life in the muscles and nervous system is closely connected a proportionate excess of (so to speak) local death in the used-up tissues. Fatigue which consumes the chemical provisions of energy of the organism, acts in the manner of a fracture or contusion, immediately altering the vitality of the tissues in a great number of cells which change and die. The products of these cells passing into the blood act on the nervous system and cause fever.

The diminution of the temperature, when the ascent is accomplished, and its subsequent increase beyond the normal, is therefore a complex phenomenon, and to it I shall return when treating of the fatigue of the heart and of the nervous depression which follows great muscular exertion. One might think that the fatigue-fever was a beneficial reaction of nature, which seeks through the greater chemical activity of the organism to free it from the noxious substances which infest and foul the body in consequence of fatigue. The time which elapses between the moment of the cessation of work, and that in which the fever breaks out (in my case about six hours), may be thought a period necessary to the muscles and tissues to eliminate completely the noxious products which they contain. We may suppose that the blood and lymph take several hours after the beginning of repose to complete fully the cleansing of the muscles, and to absorb all the detritus and irritating substances which generate fever—or else that the nerve-cells which preside over the movements of the blood-vessels, and moderate the chemical processes of the organism, are so constructed that they do not immediately react when these impurities appear in the blood, but must be irritated for a certain time by the blood, corrupt with the products of fatigue, before their reaction becomes manifest in fever. These are hypotheses and, unfortunately, pathologists have up till now nothing better to offer respecting the subject.

[1] Th. Billroth, *Die allgemeine chirurgische Pathologie und Therapie.* Berlin, 1869, p. 91.

At 10.30 the next day I took a cup of coffee with milk and rose, completely restored, at midday for lunch. Appetite was, however, lacking.

3.15 p.m. Rectal temperature, 36·8°. Pulse, 67. Breathing, 16.

We left the Olen inn on Sunday, February 15th, at 1 p.m., the temperature of the air then being —5°.

12 p.m. Pulse, 68. Breathing, 16. Temperature, 37°.

We arrived at Gnifetti Hut at 6.30 a.m., staying here for half an hour while the sun rose. At 10 a.m. we were already on the Vincent Pyramid. Pulse, 180. Temperature, 39·1°. I was very tired. In my note-book I wrote : " Respiration rather panting, does not correspond to pulse. Temperature of the air, —10°; of the snow, —15°."

After the return to the Vincent Pyramid at 3.40 p.m. my temperature was 38·1°. Pulse, 80. At midnight the temperature was 37·1°.

I slept at night and had no fever. On Monday morning before rising and immediately on waking my temperature was 36·9°. Pulse, 60. Breathing, 16.

These figures suffice to show the course of the fever of fatigue.

From Alagna to the Olen inn is a distance of 1,674 metres (from 1,191 to 2,865 metres). My temperature rose rapidly during the first two hours of the march and reached 38·2°. At 8 p.m., after four hours' rest, it had become normal again. During the night an attack of fever occurred which lasted till about 11 the next morning. The ascent of the Vincent Pyramid demanded little less exertion, because though it is only of 1,350 metres (from 2,865 to 4,215 metres) the march by night, not without danger over the glaciers, certainly increased one's fatigue. Notwithstanding, the night after the ascent I slept soundly without fever.

FIG. 7.—Mercurial manometer for the registration of the force of the respiratory movements.

At 8.40 a.m. we left the Col d'Olen in a snow-storm, and descended towards Alagna.

The observation that the fever broke out in the night of the first twenty-four hours, after six hours' rest, and did not appear the next day when I ascended the Vincent Pyramid, and was fatigued to nearly the same degree, shows how intricate are the phenomena of fatigue. Probably my organism had already accustomed itself to exertion during the two days of exercise at the beginning of the expedition.

View of the Vincent Pyramid (alt., 4,215 metres) from our camp near Linty Hut (alt., 3,047 metres). On the horizon at the left-hand side is the rock on which Gnifetti Hut was built.

III.

"In a book on fatigue shortly to be published, I shall explain the physiological researches and experiments which were the principal object of this winter ascent." These were the concluding lines of an account which I wrote of this ascent of 1885.[1] The investigations into nervous fatigue took up so much space in the book on fatigue, that none was left in which to speak of ascents.

And now I see with surprise that those researches of mine are not yet antiquated. Twelve years have passed, and no physiologist has thought of continuing the study which I then began. The long neglect is regrettable, but still, the incomplete experiments of that time have given the impulse to the writing of this book, of which they form, as it were, the first nucleus.

I had taken with me a mercurial manometer with which to measure the action of the rarefied air, and of fatigue on the force of the thorax. This apparatus is shown in Fig. 7. In order to avoid a possible error arising from inspiration through the mouth, I always placed a cork stopper in one of the nostrils, which was in this way hermetically closed. Through this stopper, which may be seen at the end of the tube in the figure, passes a glass pipe, which communicates by means of an india-rubber tube with the manometer. The latter is a U-formed tube of glass half-filled with mercury. The stopper being fixed into the nose, the other nostril is closed with the finger, and the experimenter can then read to what height the mercury rises during a profound inspiration, on the scale divided into millimetres.

This is an easy experiment which any one may perform on himself, if care be taken to place the manometer so that the scale may be read. In Turin I obtained a negative pressure of from 88 to 92 mm. of mercury. In the evening, when I arrived at the Col d'Olen, I repeated the experiment, and found that the thoracic force was much diminished, the values marked being the following:—

70 mm. 60—60—64—68—64—60.

The day after, the force of inspiration returned to 80 mm., and the maximum reached amounted to 84 mm. of mercury.

When we left for the Vincent Pyramid I took charge of the manometer myself, thinking thus to assure its safe carriage, the guide Gilardi having to carry several instruments for optical research, as well as the provisions. Near the summit the wind had hollowed out the snow into great slippery steps. Here I stumbled, and the manometer was broken. I was very much exhausted when I reached the top, and wrote in my note-book, "I feel a difficulty in breathing, due probably to fatigue of the thorax."

Having returned to Turin I studied the fatigue of the muscles which affect the inspiratory movement, and found that they tire in the same manner as the other muscles. I introduce a curve here in order to give an idea of thoracic fatigue, the effects of which are here analysed for the first time.

Fig. 8 shows the curve obtained on the servant of the laboratory, Giorgio Mondo. The stopper having been placed into the right nostril, he executed a deep inspiration, then, as he closed the left nostril, the mercury rose in the leg of the manometer subjected to the aspiration and sank, of course, in the other. The floating stylet, in sinking, marked the first line to the left. After the inspiration a natural expiration followed, because the left nostril was

[1] A. Mosso, *Un' ascensione d'inverno al Monte Rosa*. Milano, Fratelli Treves, 1885.

immediately opened. Four seconds later an assistant made a sign with the hand for the subject to execute another inspiration, which is shown in the second line, and so on regularly in four-second intervals. In order to economise space that part of the oscillations registered above the line of repose is not shown in the figure. I need not remind the reader that quick-silver, being a very heavy liquid, oscillates, in accordance with the law of inertia, in the manometer tube, when its level is raised in one part, as in this experiment. We see the half of these subsequent oscillations at the top of the curve at the base of each line by which the force of the inspiratory movement is represented.

The lines gradually decrease in height, which proves that the respiratory muscles are likewise subject to fatigue.

To the many alterations which fatigue causes in our organism we must add one more—the diminution of the inspiratory force of the chest.

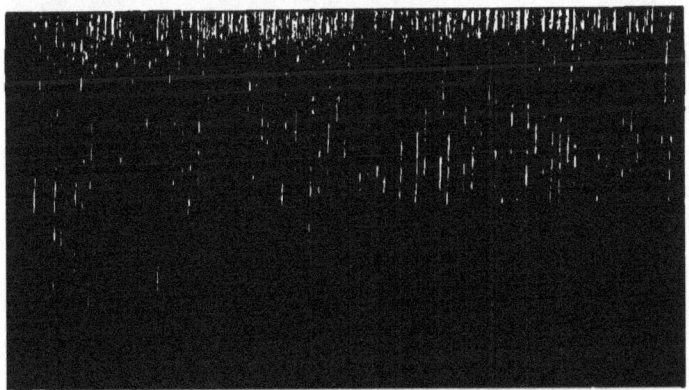

FIG. 8.—Giorgio Mondo. Curve registered by a manometer in communication with the nose in order to show the fatigue of the thorax after a series of deep respirations.

The curve, which is reproduced in its original size, gives us the measure of the inspiratory force which would amount in this case to 114 mm. of mercury. This is a useful datum which will be of use to us later in studying the action of the wind on the breathing.

The so-called oppression on the chest complained of by mountain-climbers suffering from mountain-sickness is perhaps the result of excessive fatigue of the muscles of the thorax, together with the sensation of anxiety which laboured breathing gives rise to.

IV.

The influence of fatigue on the acuteness of vision and the perception of colours are two important points in physiological optics which have not yet received that ample study which they demand. At the back of the eye there is a membrane on which luminous objects produce photographs. A red substance, discovered by Boll while professor in Rome, gives a purple colour to the back of the eye; this substance is destroyed by light, and continually reproduced by darkness.

I had taken with me a pair of very dark spectacles, which rested the eyes while the body was undergoing fatigue. I intended in this way to ascertain the influence of general fatigue on the eye, and then further to fatigue the eye with the dazzling white of the snow and glaciers in order to find out what degree of alteration there is in our perception of colours when a very intense light destroys the visual purple with unusual rapidity.

It is known that the sense of colours presents remarkable individual differences, and that there are persons who confound red with green, yellow with blue. I had taken with me a tablet of coloured wools arranged according to Holmgren's method,[1] in order to study the modification of the perception of colours from the effects of muscular and ocular fatigue.

Another method which I adopted consisted in measuring at what distance the gradations of colour could be distinguished in a series in which a given tint progressively diminishes in intensity, passing through a definite number of shades. For this purpose also I made use of the Holmgren wools, in which a colour, green, for instance, is given in seven gradations.

I perceived, however, when I had arrived at the Col d'Olen, that this method, which had seemed to me sufficiently exact for the study of ocular fatigue in the plain, was not of equal efficacy in the mountains, because on the heights the light is much more vivid, so that even at the Col d'Olen I could see, at a distance of two metres, all the shades of colour more distinctly than in the plain, and when I was on the summit of the Vincent Pyramid the light was so intense that, in spite of the glare, I could distinguish the colours still better.

I believe that our eye gains in strength after a few days spent in the Alps. Doubtless the eye undergoes a course of training. An artist who leaves his studio in winter and goes to the mountains to make studies, will see the details of nature less accurately than a week later, when his eye has adapted itself to the clear light. Great masses strongly lit up, which at first seemed uniform, will afterwards develop details and reliefs which at first were not perceived. The gradation of tints will become more distinct, and his eye will be able to analyse shadows and colours much better. When I made the final observations at the Col d'Olen, I had already been living for three days in the midst of snow strongly illuminated by the sun. To the greater intensity of light which enabled me to distinguish better the shades of the coloured wools, must, I think, be added the greater strength which my eye had acquired during three days' training.

In spite of this difficulty, which I was at a loss how to overcome, I yet learnt some important facts from these observations. Even when the visual purple is quite destroyed, as probably happens when our eye is dazzled by the continuous glare of the glaciers, we are still able to distinguish the colours. Secondly, we can distinguish red and violet, which are the extreme spectral colours, well, even when the eye is very tired.

According to a modern theory, we have in the retina, at the back of the eye, three substances, each of which gives rise to two fundamental sensations. The fact that I could see equally well both yellow and blue, for instance, when the eye was very tired, seems to me to militate against this theory.

As soon as I noticed that the light was too vivid, and that the possibility of a comparison with the experiments made in Turin was excluded, I deter-

[1] D. A. Daae, *Die Farbenblindheit und deren Erkennung.*

mined, nevertheless, to continue the study in another manner, by writing down the ocular impressions awakened by the landscape, with its constant variation of colour so characteristic of the Alpine world. More especially did I fix my attention on the rising and setting of the sun. This was the origin of that description of impressions of nature which forms the greater part of the little work *Un' ascensione d'inverno al Monte Rosa*. Some may have thought it a literary effort; on the contrary it was a physiological study of my eyes, with the object of determining the state of colour-perception during fatigue.

My idea was that when the eye was excessively fatigued by the dazzling snow, its luminous sensibility must diminish, a deficiency in its perception of green light be noticeable, and that, in other respects also, it must resemble the eyes of the aged. Many works have already been written on the alteration of colour-perception in aged artists, but as yet no one has studied with sufficient exactness the influence of fatigue of the retina on colour-perception and the influence which excessive bodily fatigue exercises on the eye.

Artists are certainly in much more favourable conditions than we physiologists for making a thorough study of these phenomena, because their long exercise enables them to judge better of the shades of colours and of their luminous intensity. Painters are much better acquainted than we are with atmospheric perspective, the tone of colours and their saturation. The study of shadows, of which non-artists are almost wholly ignorant, is to the artist an ample preparation for similar studies in the Alps, where he is able to analyse with accuracy the contrast of colours and of lights. Because this is a new study, and because its pursuit does not demand a physiological training, intelligence and some artistic feeling being the principal requisites, I have been tempted to dwell on the subject in the hope that it may inspire some worker who will contribute new observations towards its elucidation.

The alteration of sight in Titian during his last years is a fact known to many. Some think that a change of this kind arises from a growing opacity of the refracting media of the eye, from an alteration of the transparency of the cornea and crystalline lens, but this is not the only cause.

Let us consider Rembrandt, for instance. No painter ever exacted from his eyes more minute, continuous, and fatiguing work. His engravings alone fill us with admiration, and give us an idea of the continual effort made, and of the difficulties overcome, before he attained perfection. His wonderful ability to discern amid the darkest shadows, the minutest details of objects, his art of graduating the effect which the modification of a light more or less vivid, more or less oblique, produces in the appearance of forms, his powerful use of the chiaro-oscuro, all this was the result of long-continued exertion to which no artist before him had ever subjected himself. His eyes were so fatigued that he had to rest from his work from the age of fifty-six to that of fifty-eight years. And when, after this long pause, he returned to his work, his eye already gave signs of premature old age. His style was changed.

In fatigue the force of attention diminishes, and we become incapable of complicated mental work. We notice this in Rembrandt's pictures after 1664; these representing work which no longer demanded long preparation. It seems as though his life, so fertile in inspirations, his long experience, had been interrupted; his pictures have become simple in composition. They contain as a rule two or three large figures, as though the eye rebelled at minute work; his sketches are large and incomplete, like the representation of vaguer, more indefinite ideas. Michel wrote of Rembrandt: "In the course of time his harmonies have become less complicated, his effects less subtile. The number of colours which he employs becomes more and more limited, but he uses by preference the richest and most ardent; no more purples, but vermilion reds, with which are mingled vivid yellows and tawny tints."[1]

The experiments which I made on Monte Rosa when the eye was forcibly dazzled by the very vivid light reflected from the snow and glaciers, led me to conclude that even in the extreme degrees of dazzlement colours may still be distinguished; that they are, however, all more intense, more saturated. Light yellow melts into white. Pale and dark rose-colour seem dirty and blackish. The shadows are less soft and graduated, and seem darker to the tired eye. Green tends to melt into blue. Red seemed to me the colour which the eye best perceives even when excessively fatigued.

[1] Emile Michel, *Rembrandt, sa vie, son œuvre et son temps*. Paris, 1893, p. 486.

Indra Camp (alt., 2,515 metres).

CHAPTER III

RESPIRATION ON THE MOUNTAINS

I.

BREATHING is that function of the organism which is most noticeably altered during ascents. It is generally believed that on the mountains respiration is more rapid and more profound. Saussure, after his first ascent of Mont Blanc, said: "As the air at that height weighs little more than half its usual weight it was necessary to make up for the lack of density by a greater frequency of inspirations." And this was repeated by all down to Paul Bert who is a great authority in this branch of investigation. This statement I have been unable to confirm by my studies of man on the Alps.

I would fain invite the reader's immediate attention to this fundamental diversity of statements. We have here to do with facts, and when I have shown that the breathing on the Alps does not increase either in depth or in frequency, that both may even diminish, one step forward will thus be taken towards the consideration of the physiology of man on the Alps from a new point of view. The above-mentioned error originated in the long duration of the disturbing influence of an ascent, the observations being made on persons who were not in a state of complete repose.

In order to exclude this complicating factor, I counted the rate of breathing in my soldiers and in other persons who accompanied me on the ascent of Monte Rosa every day for two months in succession, always at the same hour; in the morning before rising and in the evening before dinner. As the rate of our respiration is apt to alter when we know it is being observed, we adopted the method of counting first the pulse, and then, still holding the fingers on the wrist as though continuing to feel the pulse, we determined the rate of respiration unknown to the person under examination. The afternoon observations were taken between three and five o'clock, the soldiers lying down for about ten minutes in a horizontal position before the breathing was counted; the morning observations were made at six o'clock while the soldiers were still in bed.

In the tables of the sixteenth chapter are indicated the observations made on five persons first in Turin, then during the ascent of Monte Rosa and the return. In the morning Dr. Abelli and I rose in turn to count the rate of pulse and breathing and to take the temperature, the soldiers, as just mentioned, being still in bed. Only those observations made while the subjects

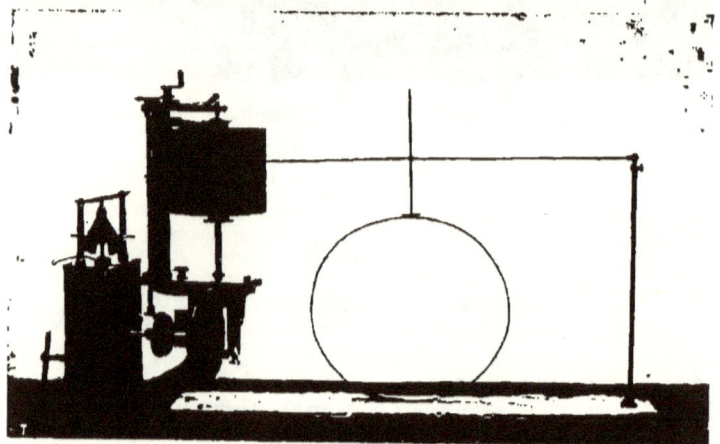

Fig. 9.—Apparatus with lever for the tracing of the respiratory movements. The circle beneath the lever represents theoretically the section of the thorax.

were in a state of complete repose are noted in the tables. The frequent interruptions in these tables with regard to the time are explained by the circumstance that for the service of the expedition certain of the soldiers had to rise before us, or were detained at a distance from us. Other observations made on Dr. Abelli, my brother, Bizzozero, and myself, I omit, as their results are in accordance with those in the tables referred to. The results lead us to conclude that on the summit of Monte Rosa the respiratory rate is not altered when one is well rested, several of us even breathing at a diminished rate.

Corporal Camozzi had, in the Regina Margherita Hut (alt., 4,560 metres), a minimum breathing rate of nine respirations per minute; in Turin (276 metres above the sea level) his breathing had never been so slow. The soldier, Sarteur, likewise showed a diminution of the rate of breathing, which on the summit of Monte Rosa fell as low as eight respirations in the minute. The respiratory rate remained unaltered in Corporal Jachini and in the soldiers Marta and Cento, being in the Regina Margherita Hut the same as in Turin.

A diminution of the rate of breathing was observable also in all the soldiers who ascended rapidly from Ivrea to the Regina Margherita Hut. (See Tables VII. and VIII. at the end of the book.)

I do not wish to interrupt the relation of facts by introducing here the statistical lists from which these conclusions are drawn. The comparison of respiration, pulse action, and temperature on high mountains will be facilitated by a reference to the appended tables

II.

The fact that on high mountains the rate of breathing remains the same, or is, in certain persons, diminished, awakens some surprise. We imme-

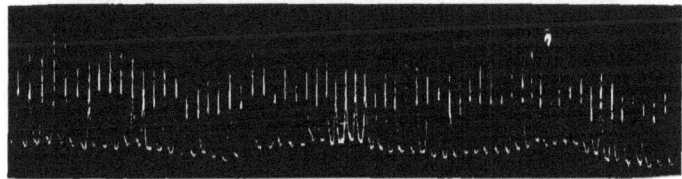

FIG. 10.—Corporal Camozzi. Abdominal respiratory curve traced in Turin with the lever.

diately reflect, however, that if the inspirations are more profound the rarefaction of the air will be compensated for.

The results which I obtained from the registration of the respiratory movements may in part reply to this supposition. In order to measure with precision the amplitude of these movements, I took with me up Monte Rosa

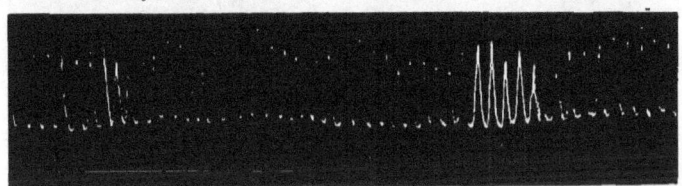

FIG. 11.—Corporal Camozzi. Abdominal respiratory curve written with the same lever in the Regina Margherita Hut (alt., 4,560 metres).

the apparatus shown in Fig. 9. A slender metal bar, turning on a pivot, rises and falls as it traces the respiratory movements on a rotating cylinder.

Let us suppose that a man is lying at full length on a table, and that the circle shown in the figure represents theoretically the section of the abdomen of this person. The metal bar is lowered so that the disc at the lower end of the perpendicular rod rests on the abdomen. The respiratory movements will raise the metal bar, the excursions of which will be traced on the smoked cylinder.

Fig. 10 shows a curve taken in this manner on Corporal Camozzi. Every lift is twice the actual height, as the abdomen exercises its pressure on the middle of the horizontal bar. At every inspiration the apparatus traces an ascending line, at every expiration a descending line on the smoked paper fastened round the vertically rotating cylinder. In Fig. 9 may be seen the construction of the clockwork which effects the rotation of the cylinder on which the lever writes the respiratory movements.

On July 5th, in Turin, at 6 p.m., I took the above tracing, Corporal Camozzi performing twenty respirations in the minute, and the rhythm of the breathing remaining regular.

In the Regina Margherita Hut (alt., 4,560 metres) on August 5th at 5 p.m., I obtained the respiratory curve shown in Fig. 11, the same apparatus

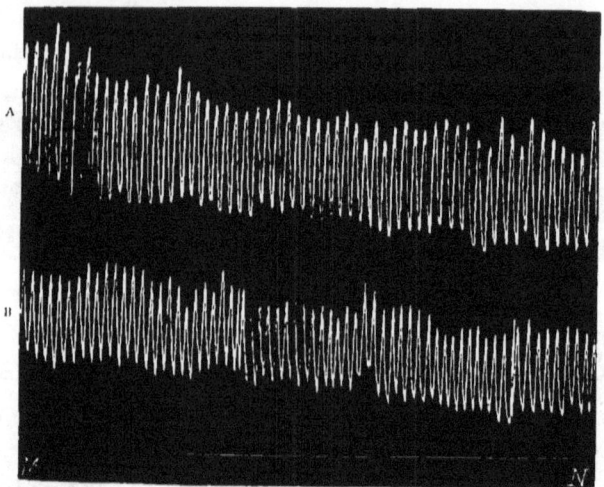

FIG. 12.—Marta (soldier). Abdominal respiration written with the lever.
A. Taken in Turin. B. In the Regina Margherita Hut.

having been made use of, and the position of the disc being as before. The respiratory rate was only sixteen to the minute, and the inspirations were not so deep.

The breathing shows periods of greater and lesser activity, so that the line is undulating, not all the expirations being equally forcible. In Fig. 11 we see five or six undulations in the upper profile of the tracing which are lacking in Fig. 10.

Here it appears evident that the amplitude and the rate of breathing are both less on Monte Rosa than in Turin.

In other persons I found that the number of respirations remained the same on the mountains and in the plain, but the amplitude was diminished in these cases also. On the soldier Marta, for instance, the upper curve in Fig. 12 was obtained on July 11th in Turin at 3 p.m., the rate of breathing being twenty-one to the minute. On Monte Rosa at a height of 4,560 metres, on August 12th, he had the same respiratory rate, but the abdominal excursions were less marked, as may be seen in the tracing.

These researches are valuable, inasmuch as I have never observed in persons awake so weak a respiration as in these two men on Monte Rosa. To give a convincing proof of this fact I measured the quantity of air which each of my companions inspired in the plain and on the mountain.

III.

In Fig. 12 the curves are slightly inclined, a circumstance not observable in Figs. 10 and 11. This calls for some explanation.

The vertebral column in man presents two very visible curves, one between the shoulders rounded exteriorly (forming when of undue size that deformity known as a humpback), the other rounded interiorly in the lumbar region. These curves change between morning and evening. When we rise in the morning the back is less rounded, and the belly, too, is less prominent. In the evening the posterior profile of our body forms an S more squat in appearance, and it is owing to this that our stature is less than in the morning. The more tired we are, the shorter do we become, because the trunk is less erect, and its exterior and interior curves are exaggerated. I

FIG. 13.—The line A B shows the flattening of the lumbar curve, after an ascent.

have found, according to measurements taken, that after an ascent mountain-climbers have lost on an average two or three centimetres of their stature since the morning. In persons who had carried knapsacks on their shoulders, and in some porters of our expedition who underwent extraordinary exertions, I even found a decrease of four centimetres.

It is, I think, unnecessary to give the figures resulting from all the different observations which I made. Any one who wishes to convince himself of the rapidity with which the stature diminishes need not perform an ascent; if he take a dumb-bell weighing ten kilograms in each hand, and go up and down the stairs of a house several times in succession, he will find that his stature has diminished by about a centimetre. After laborious exercise of an hour, or an hour and a half, the stature may be decreased by two centimetres.

Rest, taken by lying down or otherwise, slowly restores the former stature. The curves of back and loins open, and the trunk lengthens.

The same apparatus described in Fig. 9, slightly modified, serves to trace the change of the lumbar curve.

All know that when we lie down we can without difficulty pass the hand under the loins. During repose this arch sinks gradually lower. The change which takes place in fifteen minutes when one is tired may be seen in Fig. 13. The beginning of the line A B was written a few minutes after the arrival of the subject at Gnifetti Hut at 9 a.m., after walking from the encampment near Linty Hut. The inclination of the curve A B is similar to that of the curves in Fig. 12. As the lumbar curve gradually becomes flatter, the body causes the sinking of the lever with which it is in contact. The metal rod terminating in the stylet which traces the line A B on the smoked cylinder is held in a raised position by a thin elastic ring. The movement of extension in the lumbar region gradually slackens, so that its representative line A B runs towards the last almost parallel with the line M N. In this case the tracing is three times the magnitude of the actual change of the lumbar curve.

This inclination is lacking in Figs. 10 and 11 because the person on whom I took those curves was not so tired, and had, moreover, been lying on the table for a greater length of time.

It is perhaps in consequence of this straightening of the vertebral column that persons who have been in bed for many days seem taller to us when they get up again. This exaggeration of the dorsal curve which is produced in all during the exertion of an ascent certainly does not facilitate respiration. We may convince ourselves of this fact by drawing a deep breath, and we shall immediately notice that the vetebral column straightens. It is well to load one's self as little as possible, and not to carry a knapsack on the shoulders, but rather an ordinary bag, which may be fastened round the waist when breathing becomes difficult.

IV.

In 1869 Lortet wrote the respiratory movements on Mont Blanc.[1] He was the first physiologist who carried a registering instrument to that altitude, but the apparatus used was so imperfect [2] that it is impossible to compare the curves which he obtained with those published in this book. He found that the quantity of air inspired and expired was less on the summit of Mont Blanc than at the Grands-Mulets, and less here than at Lyons. He observed that the duration of the inspiration, compared to that of the expiration, was much less on the summit of Mont Blanc than at the above-mentioned stations. In Lortet's tracings there is, besides the action of the rarefied air, also the influence of fatigue.

The experiments on the form of respiration I made by means of Marey's double pneumograph. I do not stop to describe it in detail, as a description may be found in all treatises of physiology. I shall merely mention that as the thorax dilates, the air becomes rarefied within two capsules closed by an elastic membrane, to which is attached the band which fastens the pneumograph round the thorax. By means of the elastic tube this rarefaction of the air is transmitted to the tympanum with lever, so that at every inspiration the lever falls, rising at every expiration. This instrument of Marey is very convenient as it registers the movements at a distance, and with it the observations may be continued or interrupted without the subject's knowledge. In the Gnifetti and Regina Margherita Huts I made a hole in the wall which separated one room from the other; the elastic tube of the pneumograph could thus be extended from the bed of the sleeping or resting subject through the hole into the next room, where it put in movement the

---

[1] Lortet, *Physiologie du mal des montagnes. Deux ascensions au Mont Blanc.* Revue des cours scientifiques, 1870, p. 119.
[2] *Anapnographe de Bergeon et Kastus.*

registering tympanum; in this manner I was enabled to work without difficulty during the night.

Fig. 14 shows the respiratory curve of the soldier Sarteur, taken in the Regina Margherita Hut on August 11, 1894, at 4 p.m. Sarteur was one of the strongest youths of our party. Early in the morning he had left Gnifetti Hut with Solferino and a guide, all three with twenty kilograms of provisions on their shoulders. When the curve was taken he had been resting for about four hours in the hut. Rate of breathing, 11. Pulse, 74. Temperature, 37·1°.

In Fig. 15 is shown the respiratory curve of the soldier Solferino, written three hours and forty-five minutes after his arrival at the Regina Margherita Hut with twenty kilograms of wood for fuel on his back. Rate of breathing, 21. Pulse, 76. Temperature, 36·9°. The temperature of the room was 11·5°.

These two persons of the same age, of about the same height, living on the same food, and who had walked the same distance, show a remarkable difference in the rate of breathing.

The most important phenomenon is the respiratory pause noticeable in

FIG. 14.—Sarteur (soldier). Thoracic respiration, written with the Marey pneumograph (Regina Margherita Hut).

both tracings. At the end of an expiration the thorax remains still, and the stylet writes an almost horizontal line in which three or four (occasionally even six) cardiac pulsations are visible, which produce an undulating line. This form may be considered typical of the respiration at great heights.

Many physiologists deny that there is a pause between expiration and inspiration. According to these the thorax is never motionless—as soon as the inspiration is finished the expiration begins, and *vice versâ*. If we consider these tracings we shall notice that in both there are, undeniably, long intervals between each expiration and the inspiration following.

This respiratory arrest is of importance to us because it shows that at that height there is in the air a sufficient quantity of oxygen to permit of so slow a respiration of the organism that the movements are in a manner detached one from the other, there being a longer interval between them than is generally observable in the plain.

This is another proof of the statement I have made, namely, that we breathe less at great heights.

At 6 p.m. Sarteur was still in bed dozing. I went to call him to dinner, but before waking him I counted his rate of breathing. I counted eight breaths in the minute several times in succession. This is the lowest rate that I have ever observed in man; it is less than half the rate given in physiological treatises as the average for his age. When I called him he told me that he was not sleeping. He ate with appetite, and was quite well.

As to the respiratory form, we see in Sarteur (Fig. 14) that the inspiration lasts longer than the expiration. In Solferino (Fig. 15) we have the contrary phenomenon. I shall not detain the reader with a discussion of this difference, only remarking that the Sarteur type resembles the breathing during sleep, the Solferino type the waking respiration.

Two important facts result from these observations. The first is, that at great heights the respiratory organs tend to pause at the end of the expiration; the second, that the respiratory type may become, on the mountains, during the waking condition, similar to the type characteristic of sleep. The expiration lasts a shorter time than the inspiration, whereas in the plain, in the waking condition, the opposite phenomenon takes place.

FIG. 15.—Solferino (soldier).—Thoracic respiration written with the Marey pneumograph (Regina Margherita Hut).

V.

In order to measure the volume of air which we breathe on the Alps, I took with me two gas-meters similar to those used in houses for the measurement of the consumption of lighting gas. These meters, which are used in physiological research, are, however, much more sensitive and graduated with much greater accuracy than those which serve for gas lighting, marking as they do the hundredth part of a litre. I was, perhaps, the first to use a gas-meter as a means of studying the respiration in man. This circumstance, otherwise of no importance, I mention merely as a species of introduction to the following account of my first studies on this subject. In 1877, in Milan, I made certain researches on the physiological action of compressed air.[1] The air was compressed in an iron chamber by means of a steam-

---

[1] A. Mosso, *Sull' azione fisiologica dell' aria compressa.* R. Accademia delle scienze di Torino, vol. xii. Giugno, 1877.

engine. The apparatus was constructed for clinical use, and guaranteed to resist an internal pressure of only thirty or forty centimetres of mercury.

Wishing to experience the pressure of two atmospheres, I took the precaution of strengthening the window panes to prevent them from breaking. For several days I experimented together with the laboratory servant, Agostino Caudana. By means of taps which were in the iron chamber, we were able slowly to graduate the pressure until the mercurial manometer marked seventy-six centimetres above the atmospheric pressure. The pressure thus obtained would correspond to that at the bottom of a shaft 6,000 metres deep, for had we been able to descend towards the centre of the earth, we should have experienced the same pressure at that distance below sea-level.

FIG. 16.—Gas-meter, valves and gutta-percha mask for the measurement of the amount of air inspired.

For the collection of the air which enters and issues from the nose in breathing through the meter, I made use of a gutta-percha mask, modelled on the face, with a tube corresponding to the position of the nostrils. Although twenty years have passed since then, this gutta-percha mask still seems to me the best method for studying the breathing. I have tried various apparatus used by physiologists for the collection of the air, the nose being closed by nippers, but all occasioned such discomfort compared with the gutta-percha mask, that I abandoned them again.

On the expedition up Monte Rosa I took with me six of these gutta-percha masks. Of these one or more served for two or three persons in whom the conformation of the face was about the same. By means of putty softened with oil or vaseline, the mask is hermetically closed about the root of the nose, the cheeks, and under the chin.

The tube divides at a short distance from the mask into two branches communicating with two valves known as Müller's valves. These valves serve the purpose of impelling into the meter all the air breathed by the subject, which may thus be exactly measured. Other figures contained in subsequent chapters will show how the mask was applied to the face. For these experiments we lay down on the ground, the head being slightly raised by an india-rubber cushion.

From the experiments communicated at the end of this volume we see that the depth of the respiratory movements does not increase on Monte Rosa when the subjects are in a state of complete repose.

VI.

My first Alpine investigations into breathing were begun in 1882 at the Col du Théodule (alt., 3,333 metres), where I made use of a meter such as has just been described. Giorgio Mondo, laboratory servant, was my subject in these experiments. He was at that time a robust young man of twenty-six years of age. On September 1st we halted at Châtillon (alt., 1,566 metres) in the valley of Aosta, where I took some measurements of respired air in order to compare them with those taken in Turin. " On the day following at 9 a.m., we proceeded with two guides and two mules laden with the cases of instruments. As it was part of my programme to study the effects of a long march on the Alps without previous training, we walked on till evening with our mountain knapsacks on our shoulders, making a halt in Val Tournanche and another at the Matterhorn Hotel in order to eat. In the evening, towards 5 p.m., we arrived at the foot of the glacier of Val Tournanche. We were surprised by a very dense fog which rendered the crossing of the glacier rather arduous. At 8.30 p.m. we arrived at the Théodule Hut, so tired that it was not possible to perform any experiments. One hour after our arrival at the Col du Théodule, Mondo's temperature was 38·7° and mine 38·3°. This fatigue fever continued through the night, and we slept little and badly. We were both troubled by intestinal pains and were very thirsty.

" In the afternoon of the next day we performed the ascent of the Breithorn (alt., 4,148 metres) a great exertion for Mondo, who had never before been on a glacier. In the evening, when we returned to the Col du Théodule, Mondo was very much exhausted, and went to bed at 6 p.m. I was very tired, had lost my appetite and did not feel well. On the morning of September 3rd, Mondo's face was swollen and the eyelids so œdematous, that he could scarcely open his eyes. The erysipelas in the face and hyperæmia of the eyes increased so rapidly that in the afternoon we decided to leave the Col du Théodule, hoping to be able to return another time when we would take the precautions necessary to allow of a longer stay."

This quotation from the memoir which I published in 1884 on the *respiration of man on high mountains*,[1] serves as a critique of those first observations which form the basis of the more complete researches recently carried out on Monte Rosa. It is evident that at the Théodule my subject was tired and not in perfect physiological conditions.

A sufficient proof of this was the feverish temperature of his body on our arrival at the hut and on our descent from the Breithorn. It must be under-

---

[1] A. Mosso, Atti della R. Accademia medica di Torino. 1884.

stood therefore that the results given in the following table, apply to an individual not completely rested.

Places where the observations were made.	A Average number of inspirations per minute.	B Amount of litres of air breathed in half an hour.	C Litres of air breathed in half an hour reduced to the pressure of 1 m. and to the temperature 0°.
Turin, August 24th, 1882	11.6	191.88	129.48
,, ,, 25th	10.9	172.26	119.47
Châtillon	11.5	167.28	111.07
Col du Théodule, September 2nd	14.5	199.26	98.150
Col du Théodule, September 2nd	13.7	189.42	93.109
Descent from the Breithorn	18.0	239.78	118.110
Col du Théodule, September 3rd	14.2	199.26	98.150
Turin, September 6th ...	15.3	134.00	85.75
,, ,, 8th ...	11.2	171.02	119.26
,, ,, 8th ...	11.6	169.12	117.78

VII.

"At the height of 3,333 metres a much smaller quantity of air is breathed than in Turin and at Châtillon. This fact is interesting, showing, as it does, that there is in man a respiration *of luxury*,[1] as I have termed it. At the usual pressure of 740 millimetres, such as prevails in Turin, and still more so at the sea-level, we breathe a quantity of air which surpasses by far the needs of our body. In regions above the height of 3,000 metres, although the weight of the air which we breathe is much less, the organism shows itself scarcely susceptible to it, providing for compensation by a slight increase in the rate of the inspiratory movements."

This was the conclusion which I drew from my studies at the Théodule in 1882.

That a smaller weight of air is introduced into the lungs at a height of 3,333 metres appears evident from column c of the preceding table, and this was the case in spite of the persistent fatigue and the high temperature of the body. But that the increased respiratory rate was due to the rarefaction of the air I can no longer affirm, holding it rather to be an effect of fatigue which the subject had not recovered from.

The fact that we, in the plain, breathe in more air than is necessary, I have called the *respiration of luxury*[2] (*respirazione di lusso*). Certainly one is reluctant to look upon breathing as a luxury, but the expression recommended itself to me as an appropriate denomination for our superfluous respiration, by which I mean that the number and amplitude of the respiratory movements are not in strict proportion to the chemical needs of our body.

Loewy,[3] in his recent work on respiration and circulation during changes of pressure, and of the amount of oxygen in the air, says : "The limits of the

---

[1] *Respirazione di lusso.*

[2] A. Mosso, *La respiration périodique et la respiration superflue ou de luxe* Archives italiennes de Biologie, tome vii. p. 48. *Archiv für Anatomie und Physiologie*, 1886. Supplementband, S. 55.

[3] A. Loewy, *Untersuchungen über die Respiration und Circulation bei Aenderung des Druckes und des Sauerstoff-Gehaltes der Luft*, Berlin, 1895, s. 57.

rarefaction of the air within which we may speak of a respiration of luxury are represented by a pressure of about 300 mm. of mercury (from 760 mm. to 450 mm.)," which corresponds to a height of 4,000 metres.

Not only by ascents but in several other ways I have proved that the bellows-play of the lungs, which represents the mechanical part of breathing, and the chemical needs of the organism are in a certain measure independent of each other. This is necessary, because if man and animals were only to inhale the strict amount of air indispensable to them, the consequence would be, that every ascent, even the climbing of a hill, would call for an increase in either the number or the depth of their respirations.

As every natural phenomenon incites to the research of its cause and its object, we may say that the respiration of luxury promotes an economy of the functions, because it renders the regulating processes of our organism less complex. If it were otherwise, at every variation of the barometer, and these are often considerable, men and animals would be obliged to alter at once the rate and depth of the breathing in order to compensate for the change in the air.

VIII.

Tyndall relates that when he accomplished his first ascent of Mont Blanc, he was so exhausted that when he was near the summit he lay down on the snow and immediately fell asleep. He was in company of Mr. Hirst; Huxley, who was also of the party, had been obliged to stop at the Grands Mulets. Mr. Hirst roused the sleeper at once, saying: "You quite frighten me, I have listened for some minutes and have not heard you breathe once."[1]

This is the first hint which I have found in Alpine literature of the remarkable diminution of the breathing which I observed on Monte Rosa.

A further mention I found in a writing of Dr. Egli-Sinclair on mountain-sickness. It runs as follows: "On August 17th, the third day, that is (in M. Vallot's hut at a height of 4,400 metres), I still notice the duration of the lack of appetite and the rapidity of the respiration. Concerning the breathing, I distinctly observed that it had the Stokes character, that is, it seemed regular during a certain time, after which a few rapid and profound breaths were drawn, a total suspension of a few seconds then following."

The Riffelberg Hotel (alt., 2,560 metres) is the lowest station at which I noticed a change in my breathing.

I had travelled by rail from the Lake of Geneva to Zermatt, and ascended the Riffelalp on foot. I did not sleep as well at night as I usually do. Early in the morning I made an excursion to the Hut Bétemps, crossing the Görner glacier. Having returned to the inn I lay down towards 2.30 p.m. to rest. I could not fall asleep at once, and several times I noticed, on rousing myself, that my breathing was more forcible than usual, and that periods then followed during which it became so superficial that it seemed almost to have stopped altogether.

During repeated sojourns at the Olen Inn (alt., 2,865 metres), I noticed that the breathing became less regular and uniform. I need not here enumerate the persons in whom I observed this phenomenon of common enough occurrence at a height of from 2,500 to 3,000 metres.

At the beginning of August, while we were at Gnifetti Hut (alt., 3,620 metres), my brother and I noticed that our breathing had become periodic, not only during sleep but also when we were awake.

[1] Tyndall, *The Glaciers of the Alps*, 1860, p. 80.

FIG. 17.—Angelo Mosso. Thoracic respiration. First appearance of periodic respiration in waking condition (Gnifetti Hut, alt., 3,620 metres).

I communicate one of these observations (Fig. 17) made on myself. On August 8th we were alone in the little hut which served us as laboratory. I was sitting on a chair and leaning with my back against the closed door, while my brother registered my breathing on the cylinder, which was kept in continuous rotation. This was necessary in order that I might not know when the curve was being traced. For the sake of brevity I do not here introduce any of my respiratory curves taken in the plain, which are in general so regular that the bases of the respiratory movements form a horizontal line. Here, on the contrary, it is at once apparent that the thorax does not always return to the same position of equilibrium at the end of the expiration.[1] A species of waves are formed, an indication of the periods which we shall see very markedly in other persons.

On the day following I repeated this observation. For four days I had not moved from Gnifetti Hut, and was therefore in a state of complete repose. Fig. 18 shows at a still more evident periods, during which the respiratory activity is below the normal. If we look at the beginning of the curve, at the left hand, we see that the third respiration is a little less profound than the one preceding, while the fourth and fifth are still more superficial. At a the thorax tends to become motionless. There is a little pause as though breath were lacking; then comes a weak inspiration followed by another stronger one. In the upper part of the curve we can trace the rise of the next pause. At E there is a slight arrest at the end of the expiration which is repeated in the expirations following, until in F a brief interval appears. Then there is another period of greater respiratory activity. There is, therefore, in myself also, as in the soldiers Sarteur and Solferino, a tendency to respiratory pauses which was never observed in the plain.

During the sojourn at Gnifetti Hut I found in two other persons very evident respiratory periods. One of these was my brother. In Fig. 19 I give one of the curves taken on him during sleep. So that the noise of the clock-work which puts the cylinder in rotation might not disturb him, I had made, as already mentioned, a hole in the partition of wood which separates the kitchen from the other room. I was in the former room while my brother slept in the latter.

The respiratory movements are less ample than mine, as my brother had been sleeping for more than an hour when I took the tracing; he has, moreover, always a more superficial respiration. In the upper line one notices the tendency of the breathing to stop. Thrice in succession at the points marked A we see an abortive inspiratory movement. In the lower line, written immediately afterwards, a period marked B appears, in which five breaths are drawn which are more superficial than the others.

Four methods were open to nature by which to diminish the intensity of the respiratory movements. 1. To lessen the rate of the respirations. 2. To diminish their depth. 3. To detach one respiration from the other by a pause. 4. Merely to weaken a series of respirations by periods of minor activity. All four methods we have seen exemplified in the curves here introduced. Sometimes they all appear in the same person. We may therefore affirm that the respiration tends to diminish on the Alps and not to increase as has hitherto been thought.

---

[1] The line descends during the inspiration and ascends during the expiration following.

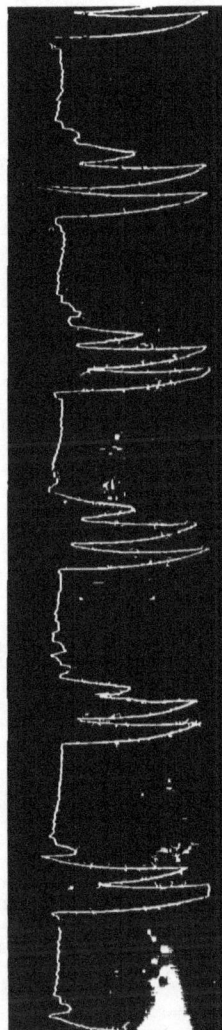

FIG. 19.—Ugolino Mosso. Thoracic respiration with periods, taken during sleep (Gnifetti Hut, alt., 3,620 metres).

FIG. 20.—Ugolino Mosso. Periodic respiration during sleep at the Regina Margherita Hut. The periods of arrest last twelve seconds.

IX.

At the Regina Margherita Hut the periods of respiratory arrest assumed an unexpected and almost morbid intensity.

Fig. 20 [1] shows the periodic respiration of my brother at the Regina Margherita Hut. The breathing sometimes continued for hours with this rhythm, three descending movements, of which the first is forcible and the other two or three weak, being followed by a pause which lasted regularly twelve seconds before the return of another series of three descending respirations. When the thorax is still and the line becomes horizontal, the pulsations of the heart, fourteen or sixteen in number, are clearly noticeable in the latter.

A physician would say, on seeing these tracings, that they were of a dying person. This interrupted respiration is, indeed, often observed shortly before death. Two English physicians, Cheyne and Stokes, first described this intermittent respiration, as a characteristic sign of several maladies. This form of breathing bears, therefore, the name of Cheyne-Stokes.

Respiration interrupted by long pauses is not a new form of breathing, but the exaggeration of a physiological phenomenon, for in every one the breathing tends to assume a periodic form when the excitability of the nerve-centres diminishes. We need only administer a dose of chloral or morphia to a person predisposed to periodic respiration, and this intermittent form immediately appears.

And yet we cannot say that sleep is more profound on Monte Rosa than in the plain; it seemed to me, indeed, lighter.

It is a proof of the incipient paralysis of the nerve-centres that during the respiratory pause the heart becomes insensible to the action of carbonic acid. If we observe the cardiac pulsations during the periods of repose of the thorax we see that the pulsations are all equal, whereas so long an arrest of the breathing ought somewhat to slacken the last beats.

The presence of a paralysis of the nerves of the heart will be shown more clearly in the sequel. As mountain-sickness is due in great part to weakness of the heart, I wished to show the reader whither these studies lead us.

A question much debated and not yet resolved is, whether the respiratory movements are produced by the accumulation of carbonic acid in the blood or by the diminution of oxygen. Rosenthal is the most strenuous upholder of this last hypothesis according to which the respiratory centre is automatically excited by the diminution of oxygen in the blood. In Chapter XXII. I shall show that the slackening of the breathing on the Alps is caused by the diminution of carbonic acid in the blood.

The observations made in the Regina Margherita Hut showed that the phenomena of respiration are very complex and that, to explain the unexpected fact that the respiratory movements are less rapid and less profound in rarefied air, at a height of 4,560 metres where there is a smaller ration of oxygen, we must admit a diminution in the excitability of the nerve-centres.

We have here to do with a very evident phenomenon which I observed in almost all, even in the most robust of those who were with me on Monte Rosa. Dr. Gurgo, whom I asked to make observations when he was accompanying a large party of students to the Regina Margherita Hut, told me that in the night, in nearly all, the respiration was periodic.

[1] All the curves in this chapter are reduced from twenty-eight to eighteen centimetres.

A   B   C

The nerve-centre which regulates the breathing does not apparently accustom itself easily to rarefied air. After twenty days spent on the slopes of Monte Rosa, at heights above 3,000 metres, the periodic respiration had not in the least decreased in any of us, continuing to be as pronounced as on our arrival.

In order to show that this phenomenon stands in no relation to mountain-sickness, I introduce a curve (Fig. 21) taken on the keeper of the hut, Francioli, a very robust man who had spent two or three months in summer, two years in succession, in the Regina Margherita Hut.

That these periods, now established as a phenomenon characteristic of the breathing on the Alps, should be due to deficient energy of the respiratory muscles, is out of the question. Many of us who had this periodic respiration were well in health and quite rested; the force of the inspiratory muscles was likewise normal as we shall see from the researches executed with the spirometer.

X.

The most important result of these observations is that in healthy men at a height of 4,560 metres there are generally pauses in the respiration. That the breathing should become periodic during sleep would not have surprised me, for I had shown as far back as 1884 that the fundamental type of our respiration consists of periods of greater and others of lesser activity. But I should never have supposed that the pauses would become more marked as the altitude was increased, and in proportion as the amount of oxygen in the atmosphere decreased.

The observation that at great heights the respiratory centre does not act so well, and that the nerves regulating the movements of the heart are less active enables us to recognise the nature of mountain-sickness. I think it well, therefore, to communicate other observations, which show that on Monte Rosa there is really a depression in the activity of that part of the nervous system which is of the most fundamental importance to life.

Fig. 22 shows a curve traced with Marey's pneumograph applied to the thorax of the soldier Chamois.

The upper curve A was written in Turin on July 10th. The middle toothed line marks the time in seconds. The line showing the periodic respiration was written at a height of 4,560 metres, the day after the subject's arrival from Ivrea, whence he had proceeded directly to the Regina Margherita Hut without stopping at the intermediate stations to acclimatise himself.

While the last curve C was being traced, Chamois half-closed his eyes from time to time, without, however, quite falling asleep.

We see here how greatly the intensity of our breathing may diminish on Monte Rosa. We must remember, however, in order to have a correct idea of our condition at that height, that there was a similar depression in the activity of the heart, for the pulse was weak and filiform. The cardiac centre and that which enervates the blood-vessels, being nearest to the respiratory centre, had likewise become less excitable.

XI.

Dogs suffer from mountain-sickness and exhibit the same symptoms as man. They are troubled with nausea, somnolence, vomiting, laboured breathing, muscular weakness, and inability to stand on their legs. For the sake of observation I took, therefore, a dog with me up Monte Rosa. I had at first had two with me, but the annoyance they caused us in our encampments and in the laboratory tent decided me to send one back to Gressoney.

These dogs were of the same litter and resembled each other perfectly in appearance, but they presented a marked difference in their resistance to the action of rarefied air.

I had often placed them together under a pneumatic bell, when one of them would sleep and show symptoms of mountain-sickness at a pressure much less diminished than that which affected the other. Of course, I took the most sensitive with me. Nerino, as he was called, was of the common foxhound kind, and though he had certainly never seen the mountains, having always lived in the laboratory where he was born, he showed, nevertheless, such adaptability to mountain life, that after my return I left him with an acquaintance in the valley of Gressoney.

As I meant him to go with me over the glaciers, I tried first, and with success, to gain his affection. At the first encampment at Alpe Indra (alt., 2,515 metres), however, he abandoned me on making the acquaintance of the soldier Marta, who was the cook of the party. While we were at Gnifetti Hut (alt., 3,620 metres), it happened that our cook had to go to the Linty Hut encampment for provisions. Foreseeing that the dog would want to follow Marta, we shut him into the little hut which served as a laboratory.

Two hours later we let him out. He sought all around, snuffed everywhere, began to whine, and then set off like an arrow. He rushed down the glacier, ran about hither and thither for a time, and then disappeared. Three hours afterwards he had rejoined Marta. Later we found his traces in the snow, and noticed that he had taken a different path to the usual one, had leapt over glacier-brooks and got safely over the most difficult parts. The next day he returned with Marta, happy and lively in spite of a few slight wounds on the legs.

In Nerino, too, the breathing was periodic in the Regina Margherita Hut, as may be seen in Fig. 23, this curve being taken on August 17th at 8.30 a.m. The dog breathed from 26 to 28 times per minute, the heart-beats numbering from 120 to 126 while he dozed.

This was the first time that I had observed periodic respiration in a dog during light slumber; during the deep sleep caused by narcotics it is often noticeable.

The dog, as we see at A and B in the figure, drew a very deep breath from time to time. This often occurs in animals and in man when the respiration becomes inadequate. These deep breaths, the periodic respiration, and a slight diminution of cheerfulness are the only phenomena by which we are made aware that dogs also are affected by the rarefied air at a height of 4,560 metres.

We cannot say, however, that these deep breaths were caused by lack of oxygen. When, in consequence of bad weather, we could not open the windows, the thermometer, in the room which served as kitchen, rose to 25° and even 27°. I then noticed that the dog lay curled up near the stove, his breathing accelerated, as is characteristic in dogs suffering from heat, the respiration in these being sometimes even ten times quicker than usual.

Richet [1] showed the profound difference between this form of breathing,

[1] Ch. Richet, *Une nouvelle fonction du bulbe rachidien. Régulation de la température par la respiration.* Travaux du Laboratoire, tome i. p. 430.

which he called polypnœa, and asphyxia. An animal cools through rapid breathing, but in order that this automatic process of the organism, which affects a more abundant evaporation of water in the lungs, may be established, the blood must, firstly, not contain an excess of carbonic acid; secondly, the amount of oxygen in the blood must be sufficient to obviate the necessity of the dog's breathing in order to renew the supply. Without these two conditions that accelerated respiratory rhythm, which all have noticed in dogs in summer when they are hot, cannot be originated. The observation of polypnœa in our dog in rarefied air at a height of 4,560 metres is a proof that there is at that height really no lack of oxygen.

Animals and man resist the action of rarefied air much more than is thought. It is well to convince ourselves that our notions as to the lack of oxygen are exaggerated, for then we shall more easily understand that there are other and no less important factors which give rise to mountain-sickness. For these experiments it is necessary that the animals, when placed under the pneumatic bell, should be neither excited nor frightened.

The greater the composure of the nervous system, the greater is the resistance to the action of rarefied air; the greater the agitation, the weaker the resistance. This is a law which, as we shall see, is of constant application in the physiology of man on the Alps.

A very quiet and sleepy dog can remain for fifteen and even thirty minutes in an atmosphere reduced to one-third without any alteration in the rate and depth of its breathing. A greater rarefaction of the air, as when the barometric height is only 220 millimetres, causes an augmentation of the respiratory activity also in a quiet dog, but not immediately. This delay renders probable the supposition that there is in the organism a store of oxygen which is consumed little by little. My investigations on this subject are incomplete, but I am almost convinced that there are substances in the organism besides the hæmoglobin of the blood from which a supply of oxygen may be obtained. This is at any rate the simplest hypothesis for the explanation of the resistance of dogs and men to great depressions; namely, that oxygen is drawn from the tissues when the amount contained in the atmosphere and in the blood is no longer sufficient. This period of resistance lasts from about six to eight minutes when the barometer indicates less than one-third of an atmosphere, that is, 220 millimetres; when the reserve-stores are consumed there is an augmentation in the rate of breathing which, after a longer or shorter lapse of time, is followed by an abatement due to the depression of the nerve-centres.

The great resistance of dogs to lack of oxygen was shown by Drs. Daddi and Treves[1] by a series of experiments, conducted in my institute, in which the animals themselves were made to deprive the atmosphere little by little of oxygen.

If the carbonic acid is not withdrawn, the rate of breathing increases rapidly; but if, while the animal is consuming the oxygen, the carbonic acid is drawn off, we notice that the respiration does not change, even though the animal is breathing an air which only contains one-third of oxygen. Here, then, we have one difference between slow asphyxia from carbonic acid and without carbonic acid. Mountain-sickness is an asphyxia without carbonic acid, as shall be more distinctly shown in subsequent chapters.

[1] L. Daddi e Z. Treves, *Osservazioni sulla asfissia lenta.* Memorie Accademia delle Scienze di Torino, 1897.

Valley of Alagna.   *V. Sella.*

CHAPTER IV

THE CIRCULATION OF THE BLOOD IN RAREFIED AIR

I.

AT the beginning of the last century a youth, the celebrated Haller of later days, returned to his native place, Berne, after completing his medical studies in Germany, and solicited a position as physician at the hospital. It was refused him, because he was too crude, he was told. He then tried for a position as professor of history in the gymnasium of Berne. This was refused him because he was a physician. In despair he began to write poetry, publishing in 1729 a short poem on the Alps. These verses, which now seem rather Arcadian to us, met then with general admiration, and exercised a decided influence on German literature.

In his great treatise on physiology,[1] which embraces all that was known of this science up till the middle of last century, Haller repeatedly speaks of the influence of rarefied air, and says: "Even though the air be reduced to half its weight, it may still be breathed without difficulty, as I experienced on the mountain *Jugo et Furca*, and as others have experienced in the Caucasus." The exact altitude reached by Haller is unknown to me, but it certainly

[1] Alb. Haller, *Elementa physiologiæ*, tome iii. p. 139.

cannot have amounted to 5,520 metres, which corresponds to half an atmosphere.

In another volume of his work,[1] in speaking of the pressure which the air exercises on our body, he says that it is equal to that pressure which we should feel, were we at a depth of ten metres under water. When the pressure diminishes in any part of the body, there is immediately a more copious flow of blood to that part which makes it swell and redden.

"Rarefied air does not dilate the lung equally," says Haller. "When the pressure is diminished on all the vessels of the body, these present less resistance to the heart and easily burst."[2]

These two notions that rarefied air does not sufficiently dilate the lungs and that the hemorrhage observed during mountain or balloon ascents is due to the diminished pressure at the surface of the body, held their ground till the present day.

The older scientists imagined the effects of diminished pressure to be similar to those manifested in the redness of any portion of the body which has been sucked with the lips. The conditions are, however, very different on the mountains, where the depression envelopes the whole body and penetrates to the interior through the lungs. In this case all the parts are equilibrated and there is a compensation of depression. When the barometric depression on one part of the body is not counterbalanced, a serious dilatation of the blood-vessels is immediately produced. We see this when the cupping-glass is made use of. Although the negative pressure which it exercises differs little from the diminished barometric pressure on the Alps, it yet causes a far-reaching disturbance in the circulation of the blood and lymph.

If mountain-climbers observe the colour of their skin during ascents they will, as a rule, notice that the blood-vessels on the mountains are paler than in the plain. This is a sufficient proof that the above theory is unreliable.

II.

Chauveau, in 1866, and Lortet, in 1869, took the first pulse-curves with the sphygmograph on the summit of Mont Blanc. Lortet says that these tracings resemble that of the pulse in typhus and other persistent fevers.

FIG. 24.—A. Mosso. Pulse-curve taken at Alagna.

Let us first consider the phenomenon and then seek the cause of this modification of the pulse. In the winter ascent of Monte Rosa in 1885 I had taken with me a Marey sphygmograph. As this instrument, of frequent use in medicine, is well-known, I shall not trouble the reader with a description of it. It is applied to the wrist where the pulse beats, every dilatation of the artery raising a very delicate lever which effects the tracing. A strip of paper which glides under the stylet receives the registration of the curve.

Fig. 24 shows the writer's pulse-curve at Alagna. At every beat of the heart the artery dilates and the stylet is raised. A wave of blood rolls into the arterial ramifications of the hand and fingers and the radial artery shows

[1] *Op. Cit.*, tome ii. p. 159.   [2] Idem, tome iii. p. 196.

THE CIRCULATION OF THE BLOOD IN RAREFIED AIR 53

oscillations due to its elasticity. On the summit of the Vincent Pyramid the writer's pulse-curve was again taken. (See Fig. 25.)

We see at once that the pulsations are closer together. At Alagna the pulse only beat sixty-two times in the minute, on the Vincent Pyramid it beat one hundred and fifteen times. The contraction of the heart was more forcible and the fatigue of the ascent had caused a slight palpitation.

The temperature of the air was $-10°$, but the blood-vessels were neverthe-

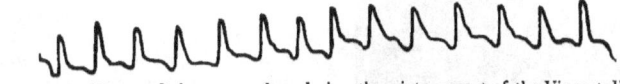

FIG. 25.—A. Mosso. Pulse-curve taken during the winter ascent of the Vincent Pyramid (alt., 4,215 metres).

less dilated, their contractibility being diminished by fatigue. This pulse form is similar to that which may be artificially produced by warming the arm. When the arteries become more yielding the pulse assumes this form characteristic of fever. The artery dilates and empties itself more rapidly. These changes are caused by the fatigue of the heart and the greater pliability of the arterial walls.

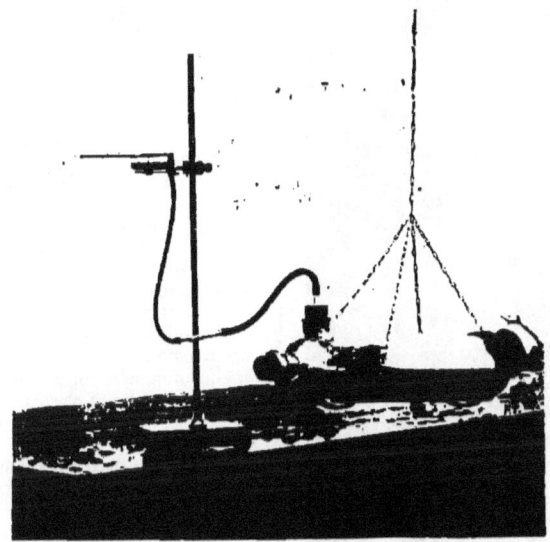

FIG. 26.—Hydro-sphygmograph.

III.

The observations made with the Marey sphygmograph did not give me complete satisfaction. In order to follow the circulatory changes for a greater length of time, I took with me two other instruments. In Fig. 25, which shows my own pulse-curve, we see that the pulsations rise gradually towards the end. This is a phenomenon of frequent occurrence in the tracings taken at great heights. I obtained a more complete picture of the movements taking place in the blood-vessels by making use of the hydro-sphygmograph by means of which the pulse, not merely of the artery but of the whole forearm is taken. The forearm of the subject is introduced into a glass cylinder, as is shown in Fig. 26, and closed in by means of an india-rubber cuff.[1] The apparatus is then suspended to the ceiling of the room, in order to secure freedom of movement, and the cylinder filled with tepid water as high as the basis of its anterior opening. At every contraction of the heart a wave of blood penetrates the forearm, producing an augmentation of volume which raises the level of the water at the basis of the opening. The air therein contained is lightly compressed and escapes by the caoutchouc tube, transmitting thus the movement to a lever which traces the pulsations.

Besides the pulse-beats, there are registered in Fig. 27 the movements of contraction and relaxation of the blood-vessels. When the arm loses colour owing to the contraction of the little arteries, the forearm decreases in volume and the pen moves downwards while still describing the pulsations. When there is a dilatation of the vessels the pen in mounting marks

Fig. 27.—Oberhoffer (soldier). Pulse-curve of forearm taken in Regina Margherita Hut (alt., 4,560 metres).

[1] A. Mosso, *Sulle variazioni locali del polso*. R. Accademia delle Scienze di Torino, xiii. 1877. *Die Diagnostik des Pulses*, Leipzig, 1879.

exactly the augmentation of volume in the forearm. The undulations of the curve in Fig. 27 are therefore the faithful image of the movements taking place in the blood-vessels. Let us now see under what conditions this diagram of the pulse was written.

The soldier Oberhoffer was a robust young man whose condition during fatigue and in repose was well known to me, as, during the preliminary studies performed in July in Turin, I had had him march with arms and baggage from Ivrea to Turin, a distance of sixty kilometres.

On August 10th he left Ivrea, and arrived at Gressoney St. Jean in the evening. The day afterwards he reached Gnifetti Hut, and on August 12th he arrived at the Regina Margherita Hut carrying baggage of the weight of twelve kilograms on his shoulders. He felt well during the march on the glaciers, and even his breathing was easy. We went to meet him at the base of Gnifetti Peak, and relieved him of his knapsack during the last part of the ascent, which is laborious. At 9.15 a.m. he reached the hut, the skin of his hands, cheeks and lips being livid. Pulse, 112. Breathing, 32. Rectal temperature, 38°.

After fifteen minutes' rest he became pale. Fearing he was about to faint I asked him how he was, to which he replied that he did not feel quite so well as before, that his strength was exhausted and his head aching violently. The radial pulse had become imperceptible. The pulse at the neck beat 108 times per minute. Breathing, 32. Temperature, 37·7°.

This indisposition lasted more than an hour, during which time he remained lying down, well covered. At 9.45 the pulse-rate was 100. Breathing, 29. Temperature, 37·6°. He said that he did not feel at all well. Then he fell asleep. When he awoke two hours later, the cyanosis (livid colour) had disappeared, but he had rings around the eyes, a sign that the circulation in the veins was still defective, and he had no appetite. Even in the evening, at 5.45, the pulse was still so weak that it could only be counted by placing the hand on the neck or on the heart. Pulse, 100. Breathing, 24. He was still troubled with headache, sat down to table, however, and ate with fair appetite.

In Oberhoffer (as has been already observed in other persons) the bodily conditions became worse on the cessation of great exertion. The other three soldiers who came up with him from Ivrea to the Regina Margherita Hut presented the same phenomena.

During the following day the livid, purplish colour of the skin persisted in all these soldiers who had come together from Ivrea. Oberhoffer's pulse was filiform. The respiration was rapid, the movements numbering from 26 to 28 in the minute. The temperature was slightly above the normal, 37·8°. We auscultated the heart and found its tones regular.

On August 13th, twenty-four hours after Oberhoffer's arrival at the Regina Margherita Hut, I registered his pulse with the hydro-sphygmograph; with the Marey sphygmograph it was impossible to obtain a tracing, the pulse being too weak and filiform. With the hydro-sphygmograph the curves were taken which are shown in Fig. 27. The cyanosis of face and hands showed that the circulation was weak and languid, the blood-vessels were, however, more unstable than I had ever observed in Turin. The vaso-motor centre manifested profound alterations similiar to those of the respiratory centre, for the respiratory movements were likewise irregular. The periods of greater and lesser activity of the breathing do not exactly correspond to the dilatation and contraction of the blood-vessels of the forearm.

The curve in Fig. 28 was taken in the Regina Margherita Hut. From it we see that at every respiratory movement the volume of the forearm alters. At the first inspiration (to the left of the figure) the pen sinks, whereas in the line below, which marks the volume and the pulse of the forearm, there is an augmentation.

The lower festooned line which marks the pulse of the forearm with the respiratory oscillations, forms an undulation which sinks in a manner similar to that of the curve in Fig. 27. There was, however, no corresponding change in the respiratory movements. The duration of the inspiration is somewhat shorter than of the expiration, but this relation between the two is the same as in the plain.

From these and numerous similar observations made on Monte Rosa I conclude with certainty that the diminished barometric pressure at a height

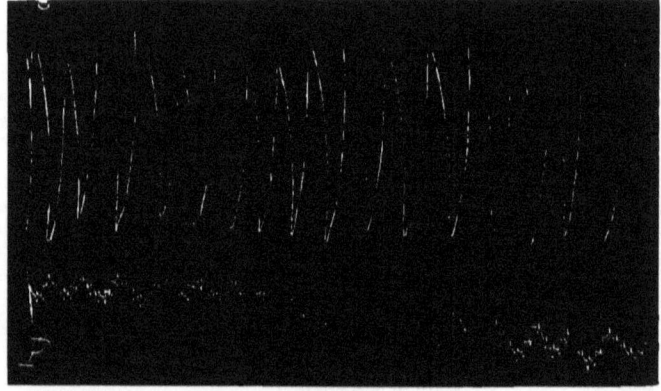

FIG. 28.—A. Mosso. Pulse-curve of forearm registered at the same time as the respiratory curve (Regina Margherita Hut, alt., 4,560 metres).

of 4,560 metres did not modify the physiological conditions of the blood-vessels either in my companions or in myself.

Those physiologists who maintained that the state of the blood-vessels is modified in rarefied air because the pressure of the atmosphere on the skin is diminished had attributed great importance to the more pronounced dicrotism of the pulse, to the undulation, that is, which appears in the curve of every pulsation and which is visible in a very marked form in the curves of Figs. 24 and 25 written with the Marey sphygmograph. In Oberhoffer's pulse-curve (Fig. 27) dicrotism is visible almost in every pulsation, but in other persons, Jachini, Marta, Sarteur, for instance, the pulse-curve was quite normal, in no way differing from that registered in Turin. This proves that the pulsatory oscillations of the walls of the blood-vessels do not undergo any alteration when the diminution of the atmospheric pressure on the surface of our body corresponds to a height of 4,000 metres. This difference of pressure causes no variation in the form of the pulse, but fatigue and the altered chemical conditions of the organism render the blood-vessels more unstable, the heart weaker and the circulation less active.

IV.

The movements of the blood-vessels which we have considered in the preceding section have made us acquainted with a local phenomenon of the circulation of the blood; in order to form an idea of the general pressure of

FIG. 29.—Sphygmomanometer for the measurement of the pressure of the blood in man.

the blood I made use of the sphygmomanometer. Fig. 29, which is the reproduction of a photograph taken during an experiment on Dr. Kiesow, shows the construction of this instrument.

The apparatus is filled with water and the middle and third fingers of both hands are introduced into the metal sheaths which are lined with india-rubber finger-stalls. The hands are then firmly fixed by means of two supports worked by screws, the arms being held close to the trunk. The fingers being thus shut into the metal tubes, a pressure is effected on the water contained in the cylinder by means of a little piston (to the right of the figure). This pressure is communicated to the surface of the fingers and thence to the mercurial manometer which indicates its height in millimetres. This apparatus, to which I have given the name of sphygmomanometer, registers at the same time pulse and pressure.[1]

Fig. 30 gives the writer's pulse-curve during the measurement of the blood-pressure which fluctuates between eight and ten centimetres of mercury.

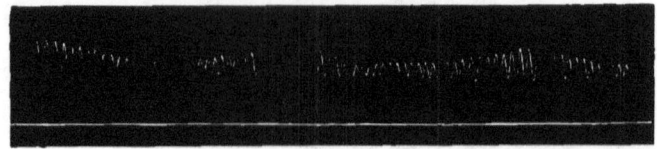

FIG. 30.—A. Mosso. Curve of blood-pressure (Regina Margherita Hut, alt., 4,560 metres).

In this case also the pressure of the blood remained the same at a height of 4,560 metres on Monte Rosa as in Turin. In this curve three undulations are observable similiar to those which till now had only been noticed in animals when a manometer was introduced into an opened artery. The fact

FIG. 31.—U. Mosso. A. Curve of blood-pressure. B. Respiratory curve taken at the same time (Regina Margherita Hut, alt., 4,560 metres).

that the pressure of the blood in the Regina Margherita Hut was normal confirms what has been already stated, namely that the diminished barometric pressure does not cause a dilatation of the blood-vessels at the height of 4,560 metres. We shall presently consider the modifications of circulation produced by fatigue and mountain-sickness.

[1] A. Mosso, *Sphygmomanomètre pour mesurer la pression du sang chez l'homme*. Archives italiennes de Biologie, xxiii. p. 177. F. Kiesow, *Versuche mit Mossos Sphygmomanometer über die durch psychische Erregungen hervorgerufenen Veränderungen des Blutdruckes beim Menschen*. Wundts Philos. Studien. Bd. xi. s. 41 ff.

The simultaneous registration of the pressure of the blood and the respiration acquainted me with the fact that on the Alps there is an intimate relation between these two phenomena, as may be seen from Fig. 31. When the breathing increases in intensity the pressure augments likewise, and decreases when the respiration diminishes in intensity. The synchronism of these two phenomena is evident. I do not think, however, that the one is the cause of the other; probably both are the effect of a simultaneous change in the centre of respiration and in that of the vasomotor nerves.

In my brother, in whom the respiratory periods are more marked, the undulations in the blood-pressure are also more pronounced. These observations seem important to me, because until now it was not known to physiologists that such a close relation existed between the pressure of the blood and the respiratory periods.

An equally new and fundamental fact is established by these curves: the periodic change in the rate of the cardiac pulsations. When the breathing is more forcible we see (Fig. 31) that the heart-beats become stronger and less frequent. When the breathing slackens or ceases, the pulsations of the

heart become weaker and more frequent. In myself (Fig. 30), as in my brother, the same periodic variations in the rate of the pulse, which I have never observed in the plain, were observable.

From the circumstance that I have noticed these periodic changes in the force and rate of the pulse in persons suffering from mountain-sickness, I conclude that the action of the heart is altered on the Alps, so that, even during complete repose and when one feels quite well, there are periods during which its activity diminishes, an incipient paralysis of the organ manifesting itself. After this diminution in the energy of the systole, there is a period during which the action of the heart seems more vigorous, the pulsations being stronger and less frequent.

I know of no other fact in the physiology of man more likely than this (which indicates the beginning of a functional alteration of the heart), to afford us an explanation of the mechanism which causes the outbreak of mountain-sickness.

In other respects, too, the simultaneous registration of the respiration and of the pressure of the blood was of service to me. Certain modes of breathing which seem irregular when examined singly, lose this character when considered together with the curve of the blood-pressure.

I give the instance of an English gentlemen, Mr. G. Thompson, who arrived, with a friend and a guide, in such good condition on Peak Gnifetti that he did not even wish to enter the hut. The weather was fine and the party seemed disposed to remain on the sunlit terrace enjoying the mountain panorama until they set off again. Having looked into the hut, however, they became interested in the work of our expedition, and willingly agreed to contribute their share to physiological research by offering themselves for examination.

In Fig. 32, as in the one preceding, the pressure-curve is registered above, the respiratory curve below. If we consider the latter we might be inclined to think that the irregularities due to deep and superficial inspirations were a casual occurrence, as similar irregularities are observable in nearly all persons, especially during fatigue. But if we examine the undulations of the upper curve, we note that whenever the respiration becomes more ample, a more vigorous beating of the heart is indicated in the pulse-curve taken with the sphygmomanometer and that *vice versâ* the pressure of the blood diminishes when the force of the breathing decreases. The rate of the cardiac pulsations is greater, therefore, in this case also, when the pulse is weak, and less when the pulse becomes stronger.

There is, therefore, an incipient alteration in the functions of the heart and breathing-apparatus even in persons who feel quite well. These symptoms, which escape the less attentive observation of travellers who have reached great heights and who seem to be in normal conditions, mark the beginning of mountain-sickness when it is so slight that it remains unnoticed.

V.

The number of pulsations increases considerably during an ascent. On this point all are agreed. It is, however, further believed that the pulse beats much more rapidly on the mountains even when one is in a state of profound repose. In the tables given in Chapter XVI. are entered the observations which I made every day on five soldiers belonging to the expedition. Specially important are the figures indicating the rate of the pulse in the morning before the subjects had risen. We see from them that there is a slight change, for in the Regina Margherita Hut the pulse never sank to the minimum observed in Turin. The differences are, however, much less considerable than physiologists, who have studied the question, maintain. Physicians at climatic stations have contributed most of the publications on the subject. The contradictions in the results they obtain prove that the conditions of the persons examined were not determined with sufficient exactness.

Jaccoud found at St. Moritz (alt., 1,856 metres) an augmentation of from 12 to 18 pulsations and about five respirations per minute. Armieux maintains a diminution of about four pulsations and an augmentation of two respirations per minute at Barège. Dr. Vacher even speaks of a *fièvre d'altitude* from the observation of an increase of about 10 heart-beats at Davos (alt., 1,558 metres). Veraguth, too, found, at St. Moritz, an augmentation of about eight pulsations in the first week, while afterwards the pulse neared its normal rate, without, however, quite recovering it. Mercier, Mermod, Weber found that the pulse augments at heights of about 1,800 metres (which Mercier calls *grandes altitudes*)[1].

These observations in the climatic stations, although very abundant, are not very reliable, for being made at relatively inconsiderable heights, the exciting influence of surroundings may have been confounded with the action of rarefied air. Vacher found, in fact, a diminution of the pulse-activity and out of ten cases Veraguth found two in which the pulse became slower after the arrival at St. Moritz.

Dr. Mermod says that the pulse increased by 2·21 pulsations per minute in going from Lausanne to St. Croix, a rise of 600 metres. Conway found, on the contrary, that at a height of 6,000 metres his pulse-rate was normal during repose. If at this height of 6,000 metres, ten times greater than that mentioned by Dr. Mermod, the rate of the pulse is unaltered, it must be acknowledged that it is somewhat difficult to draw general conclusions. Mermod's results are rendered doubtful when we remember that there are continual barometric variations which must be taken into account. At an ordinary pressure there are sometimes storms which rapidly establish a difference of pressure of 40 millimetres. If a similar variation (corresponding to a height of 600 metres) were to produce an augmentation in the rate of the pulse, it would have been noticed. The physicians who have studied the influence of barometric variations, as, for instance, Vierordt, maintain the contrary, expressing the opinion that there is a slackening in the pulsations of the heart when the atmospheric pressure diminishes in the plain.

VI.

Serviceable data on the augmentation in the rate of the pulse and breathing were collected by Dr. Francesco Gurgo in July, 1896, at the Regina Margherita Hut. Six members of the Italian Alpine Club accompanied eight students and one young lady up Monte Rosa, in one of the so-called scholastic excursions [2] which the Turin section often organises for the purpose of training young mountain-climbers. Dr. Gurgo was the physician of the party. His observations (see tables, p. 63), are the more

[1] Société de Biologie, 9 Juin, 1894, p. 481. [2] *Carovane scolastiche*.

noteworthy as the subjects were young people who were little trained and had never been at great heights.

They left Turin by train, went on foot from Pont St. Martin to Gressoney la Trinità, a walk of about ten hours. Here I had the pleasure of making the acquaintance of all the members of the expedition. After resting the night at Gressoney, they went on the next day at about 9 a.m.

After sleeping at Gnifetti Hut, they reached the summit of Monte Rosa on the 27th of July at 10.30 a.m., the weather not being very favourable. The observations on the breathing were almost all made during sleep, or while the subjects were lying down, resting. Those on the pulse were likewise made during a state of repose, so far as this was possible.

On the second day after their arrival at Regina Margherita Hut they tried to descend, but after two hours and a half of ineffectual effort they were obliged to return owing to the violent storm which was raging. This explains why pulse and breathing are more rapid in nearly all on the second day. On the third day the sun had reappeared and the party left at 12 a.m., although the weather was still threatening. The observations of the third day were therefore made in the morning, whereas those of the two days preceding were made towards evening. The incidents of the expedition were described by the leader of the expedition, Sig. Guido Rey.[1]

It is important to note that none of these persons suffered from mountain-sickness with serious symptoms, only two complained of nausea during the time spent in the Regina Margherita Hut. All had headache, which ceased or diminished when they went out into the open air. This was, however, not always possible on account of the storm.

In order to give an idea of the unfavourable hygienic conditions in the hut at this time, I must mention that in consequence of the bad weather two scholastic parties had taken refuge there and were obliged to stay together for three days. There were, therefore, forty-five persons in a space 9·20 metres long and three metres wide, so that, taking the furniture into account, each person had less than 0·613 square metre of space, and scarcely 1·29 cubic metres of air. By day the stove served as a ventilator, and from time to time the windows were opened in order to renew the air. But by night when, as a rule, the phenomena of mountain-sickness are more pronounced, the air was certainly worse. If we bear in mind the barometric depression produced by the tempest and the impoverishment of the air within, where so many persons were breathing, we are astonished that only two out of fifty suffered from slight symptoms of mountain-sickness.

During the storm, when there was no possibility of renewing provisions, the fear of their running short made itself felt on the second day, when the leaders of the two expeditions decided to diminish the rations. This uneasiness must certainly have had a very unfavourable influence on the nervous system of the two member of the two parties.

However difficult it may be to make statistical comparisons, these figures noted by Dr. Gurgo indicate, nevertheless, a minimum percentage of cases of mountain-sickness, much below the usual average on Mont Blanc and in Vallot Hut, situated about 200 metres lower, and also below the average of the cases which came under my notice in the Regina Margherita Hut. One certain fact is, that the diminution of oxygen caused by the presence of so many persons in a limited space did not aggravate their condition, and this is of importance to the theory of the origin of the indisposition.

[1] G. Rey, *Una escursione scolastica al Monte Rosa*. Torino, 1897.

THE CIRCULATION OF THE BLOOD IN RAREFIED AIR

OBSERVATIONS MADE BY DR. GURGO ON THE RATE OF THE PULSE AND OF THE BREATHING DURING A SOJOURN OF THREE DAYS AT THE REGINA MARGHERITA HUT (ALT., 4,560 METRES).

		Normal.		1st Day.		2nd Day.		3rd Day.		Observations made during the days spent in the hut.
		Pulse	Breathing	Pulse	Breathing	Pulse	Breathing	Pulse	Breathing	
1	Adele Bona	68	20	104	24	112	24	96	16	Pulse irregular and intermittent the first day.
2	Alcide Bona	76	14	100	20	110	22	100	16	Idem.
3	Livio Cibrario	61	23	110	20	116	24	94	16	Breathing irregular during first and second day, sometimes deep and sometimes very superficial.
4	Silvio Salza	61	23	92	20	80	18	68	16	During 1st day regular alternation of one deep and one superficial inspiration.
5	Carlo Toesca	66	17	96	20	104	22	88	16	During 1st day respiratory pause after every 7 or 8 breaths.
6	Giorgio Volla	66	16	104	22	102	22	86	18	Respiration with distinct periods of greater and lesser amplitude.
7	Adolfo Hess	68	18	110	24	98	22	96	18	Breathing and pulse always regular.
8	Giovanni Negri	68	19	108	24	108	22	92	18	
9	Pietro Goffi	73	14	98	18	90	16	76	14	
10	Basilio Bona	80	20	100	34	108	36	88	30	Slight indisposition before the ascent. During 1st and 2nd day typical Cheyne-Stokes breathing, in waking condition likewise.
11	Massimo Cappa	56	14	88	19	90	20	88	17	
12	G. B. Devalle	76	16	102	20	98	24	82	18	Suffered from nausea. During 1st and 2nd day every 5 or 6 respirations were followed by a fairly long pause.
13	Guido Rey	64	17	82	18	97	24	82	20	
14	Gustavo Turin	75	16	104	22	100	20	80	16	Periodic respiration during sleep.
15	Gustavo Nasi	75	14	110	20	104	20	88	16	

The observations on the normal rate of the pulse and breathing were made a few days later in Turin and in other neighbouring towns of the plain whither the members of the expedition had returned. I had begged them all to count pulse and breathing before rising in the morning, after their return to their homes, and here express my thanks for their punctual response to my request. In the table the rate of the pulse and respiration in Signorina Bona and the students, who were all of an age varying from eighteen to nineteen years, is first given, then follow observations on the members of the Alpine Club.[1]

[1] Basilio Bona, 50 years of age; Massimo Cappa, 42; G. B. Devalle, 22; Guido Rey, 36; Gustavo Turin, 33; Gustavo Nasi, 45.

I have already mentioned that the augmentation in the rate of pulse and breathing found in the climatic stations much surpasses that observed by me at great heights. Dr. Gurgo's statistical results on the third day that the fifteen persons whom he was observing had been in the Regina Margherita Hut confirm those which I obtained. These data correspond in fact to Veraguth's observations at St. Moritz, on persons immediately after their arrival, although the station of St. Moritz in situated 2,704 metres lower than the Regina Margherita Hut. We shall presently see that when the sojourn on the summit of Monte Rosa is prolonged, pulse and breathing approach still more nearly their ordinary rate.[1]

The average pulse-rate in the six members of the Alpine Club, on the third day in the hut, was 84, that of the students, 88; this difference arising probably from the greater age and strength and better training of the members of the Club. On the last day the pulse was regular in all, whereas during the first day it presented in many of them remarkable variations in strength, being sometimes filiform and imperceptible. These variations are not taken account of in the tables, only the greater variations observed in the rate being given.

Here, too, we notice, in Signorina Bona and in the students Cibrario, Salza, Toesca, that the breathing may become slower than the normal on the mountains, in spite of the rarefaction of the air. In Signori Hess and Turin the rate of breathing did not alter. On the second day four students showed an augmentation in the rate of pulse and breathing. This increase must be attributed to the less favourable condition of the organism resulting from the rarefaction of the air, as we know that the exertion undergone on this day was less than that on the first day when the entire ascent had been accomplished.

VII.

If there is the same augmentation in the rate of pulse and breathing during the first days at St. Moritz as on the summit of Monte Rosa, we must not therefore think that the causes are in both instances the same. Where inconsiderable heights are concerned it may be the exciting influence of the Alpine climate which makes itself felt; on Monte Rosa the causes lie deeper and are more complex. At St. Moritz and other climatic stations the augmentation is not a constant phenomenon, whereas in the Regina Margherita Hut I observed it invariably in all, and there a longer period of acclimatisation is necessary before the organism adapts itself to the new conditions due to the rarefied air. The two keepers of the hut had, although at a height of 4,560 metres, the same pulse-rate at the end of the season as in the plain before performing the ascent.

Haller's conception, that on the mountains there lacks a counter-pressure at the surface of the body and that the beating of the heart is accelerated owing to the dilatation of the blood-vessels, was made by many physiologists to serve as an explanation of the increased pulse-rate, but we have already seen that this hypothesis cannot stand before criticism and experiment.

Many imagined that the greater frequency of the cardiac pulsations was a means of compensation for the lack of oxygen, and that the blood must

---

[1] The results of the observations on the members of our expedition are given in five tables of Chapter XVI. and in other tables at the end of the book.

circulate more actively in the lungs because the air is poor in oxygen. At the Alpine stations and on mountains lower than 3,000 metres the acceleration in the activity of the heart is certainly not due to a deficiency of oxygen, for till now no one has proved that the blood is influenced by so slight a rarefaction of the air.

The tracings (Figs. 30 and 31) indicating the periodic modifications which the rate and strength of the pulse undergo, I have introduced in order to show that this augmentation is not due to a mechanical perfection of our organism, but is, on the contrary, the beginning of a morbid condition. In all probability it is the inhibitory nerves of the heart which, at great heights, become irregular in their action.

Since Paul Bert mountain-sickness has been considered by all as an asphyxia. The study of the pulse suffices, however, to show that it is quite a different process. In asphyxia, the rate of the pulse diminishes, and it augments, on the contrary, in rarefied air.

The better to establish these facts which prepare the way for a new theory of mountain-sickness, I communicate two experiments made in the pneumatic chamber, in order to exclude the effects of fatigue.

The mechanician of my institute, Luigi Corino, had, on July 17, 1895, at 3.10 p.m., a pulse-rate of 81 beats to the minute, after remaining seated and resting for ten minutes, the atmospheric pressure being 742 millimetres.

He then entered the pneumatic chamber and the air was rarefied. At 4 p.m., when the inner pressure was 412 mm., the pulse-rate was 94. The depression had therefore caused an augmentation of 14 pulsations, although the subject remained seated and motionless and was quite free from apprehension, as he was already accustomed to these experiments. The normal pressure being restored at 4.22 p.m., the pulse became slower than before, beating only 76 times in the minute.

The same day I made another experiment on myself. In repose my pulse beat 62 times in the minute. At 4.40 p.m. I entered the pneumatic chamber and the rarefaction of the air was begun. At 5.22 p.m. the barometer marked 422 mm. The pulse-rate was 68. After the return to the normal pressure the pulse fell to 58.

The slackening of pulse and breathing when one passes from rarefied air to a normal pressure shows that the nervous system rapidly accustoms itself to a diminution of the quantity of carbonic acid and oxygen in the blood. The fact that the rate of breathing and of the cardiac pulsations sinks below the normal on the cessation of the rarefaction of the air must be attributed, I believe, to the nervous system being affected by the normal condition of the blood, as if by an excess of carbonic acid and oxygen.

The opinion maintained by some that the quickened movements of the heart in rarefied air are a means of compensating automatically for the lack of oxygen by the promotion of a more active circulation, is combated by the fact that the mechanism is inadequate to its supposed end, the circulation remaining languid, notwithstanding the increased activity of the heart.

This fact becomes very apparent when the barometric depression is great, as in the following experiment on the servant of the institute, Giorgio Mondo. The external pressure was 740 mm. The subject's pulse, after he had sat still for half an hour, beat 59 times in the minute. When the pressure had been reduced to half an atmosphere, that is to 370 mm. (= 5,520 metres), the pulse beat 90 times per minute, while afterwards at the normal pressure it sank to 53 beats in the minute. The increase of one-third in the frequency of the pulse was accompanied by phenomena similar to those which appear in mountain-sickness. The pressure had been reduced to 370 mm. in about half an hour, when Mondo informed us that he did not feel as well as at first, his cheeks and lips were bluish and the skin had become rather pallid. The circulation of the blood was therefore less active, for, as shall be further explained at the end of Chapter XIV., this livid colour arises from the stagnation of the blood in the vessels of the skin, the heart lacking strength to promote the circulation as usual.

The action of the heart having been considered, a few words remain to be said on the course of the blood in the capillaries. Alexander von Humboldt's observation that on Mount Chimborazo, at a height of 5,700 metres, there was a bleeding of the gums in himself and in his companions and that the conjunctiva was blood-shot has been hitherto explained, together with all similar facts, by the old Haller hypothesis; namely, that the blood-vessels are, to use Saussure's words, "faiblement contrebandés par la pression."

This conjecture has not an experimental basis, and my readers are, I hope, convinced by the foregoing explanations that physical action alone is not capable of producing these disturbances. The cause of these bleedings must be sought in the weakness of the heart and in the languid peripheric circulation. The blood stagnates in the dilated blood-vessels and the skin assumes that characteristic livid hue which all have observed when on the summit of mountains.

Much importance has been attributed to these hemorrhages, as phenomena bearing out the old theories respecting the physiology of man on the Alps. My observations do not enable me to say that bleedings are very frequent. At present I only mention this fact, to which I shall return in the sequel. The hemorrhages often mentioned by travellers are never so abundant as they would be were they due to a physical cause. They arise, as Payot has said, from a passive congestion. The venous colour of the skin shows that the blood circulates badly, the walls of the vessels grow weak and burst easily; but this is a sufficiently rare phenomenon not ascribable to the exercising of a local, aspiring action on the blood by the diminished pressure, still less to the palpitation of the heart which, according to others, might burst the vessels through some too vigorous pulsation.

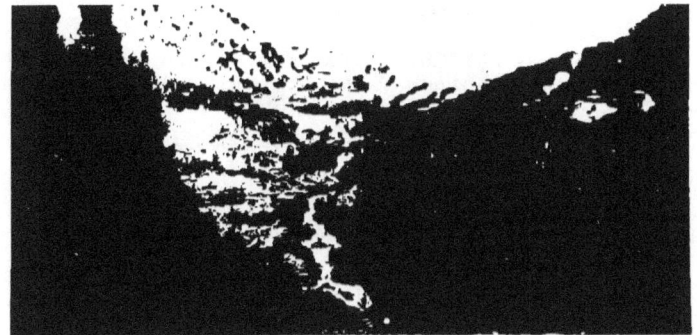

Valley of Macugnaga.   V. Sella.

CHAPTER V

FATIGUE OF THE HEART

I.

WHEN the heart performs excessive work it dilates and alters. Prolonged muscular action causes fatigue of the heart.
  In 1870 an English physician (Clifford Albutt) drew the attention of his colleagues to this phenomenon. Pathological facts and symptoms were collected and a definite acquaintance was made with the new disease which has been called cardiac overstrain, cardiac irritability, sub-paralysis of the heart, according to the various authors.
  I shall here relate Albutt's first observation on himself and then the investigations which I made on Monte Rosa in collaboration with Dr. Abelli, and in Turin with Dr. Z. Treves, and which prove that the first traces of this disease may appear in healthy men in consequence of an ascent.

In the summer of 1868 Albutt[1] began a series of excursions in the Alps without sufficient previous training. At first he felt perfectly well, but on climbing the Aeggischhorn at rather a more rapid pace than usual he was suddenly seized with a strange need of breathing never till then experienced, and which was accompanied by a disagreeable feeling of tension and throbbing in the epigastrium. He laid his hand on his heart and felt that the beating was diffused throughout the epigastrium, opened his shirt and ascertained by means of percussion that the right ventricle of the heart was much dilated. After a short rest in a horizontal position the symptoms partially subsided, but returned immediately when an attempt was made to climb higher. When at length Albutt had reached the height of the Aeggischhorn inn and had one or two miles to go on level ground, the indisposition disappeared at once. During the night spent at the inn, he was suddenly roused by a strong palpitation, the heart beat violently in the epigastrium and there was great difficulty in breathing, but the cardiac dulness did not pass beyond the sternum. He opened the window, drew a few deep breaths and recovered.

Of late years the attention of physicians has been turned to the poisons which certain diseases produce. Toxic inflammations and local affections of the heart are more especially due to infective processes. It is on this account that persons who have just recovered from typhoid fever, diphtheria, or even a simple influenza, must exercise the greatest caution in the performance of muscular effort. Clinical studies on this subject are now very numerous, the experiments of the physiologists having prepared the ground for them, as Prof. Stefani showed in a recently published work.[2]

In an article in the *British Medical Journal*,[3] by Roy and Adami, the former writes that he too had experienced overstrain of the heart from intense muscular exercise. During convalescence after typhoid fever he was called upon as physician to perform a rapid and fatiguing march over the Mer de Glace, as far as the Jardin, in order to attend a guide from Chamonix who had met with an accident and was seriously injured. The symptoms experienced coincided perfectly with those described by Albutt.

Roy and Adami showed experimentally that a very short time suffices to produce a dilation in the heart of the dog when the pressure of the blood is augmented beyond a certain limit.

II.

The form and volume of our heart may be ascertained with sufficient accuracy, externally, by means of percussion. This method of investigation resembles that by which the level of wine in a pipe is determined without the opening of the latter. By slightly knocking the pipe one is able to tell, from the difference of sound resulting, how high the liquid rises in it and what part of it is filled with air. In the same manner the percussion of the thorax enables us to determine the extent of the lungs. These resound to a knocking on the chest, because they are full of air. In that part, on the contrary, where the heart touches the thorax or lies very close to it the sound is duller, more obtuse.

An instrument, called a phonendoscope by its constructor, Dr. A. Bianchi,

[1] Clifford Albutt, St. George's Hospital Reports, vol. v., 1870, p. 29.
[2] A. Stefani, *Action de la pression artérielle sur les vaisseaux et sur le cœur*. Archives italiennes de Biologie, tome xxvi. p. 173.
[3] Roy and Adami, *Remarks on failures of the heart from overstrain*. British Medical Journal, Dec., 1888.

facilitates this investigation, the volume of the organs contained in the cavities of chest and abdomen being determined, by its aid, with much greater accuracy. The phonendoscope reinforces the sounds in such a manner that the percutient process is now no longer necessary, it suffices to draw a finger lightly over the skin to produce vibrations so distinct that the limits of any given organ in the cavity of thorax or abdomen may easily be ascertained.

Fig. 33 represents the form of the heart, traced by Dr. Z. Treves by means of the Bianchi phonendoscope.

FIG. 33.—Form and position of the heart determined with the Bianchi phonendoscope.

The upper oval, which touches with its apex the left mamma, indicates the periphery of the left ventricle; the oval below by which it is intersected marks the outline of the right ventricle. Higher up, on the breast-bone, we see the contour of the left auricle, the little circle below it indicating the right auricle. This drawing was verified several times by Dr. Treves on corpses. The figure traced by means of the phonendoscope corresponded exactly to the limits of the heart when the thorax was opened.

The examination of the heart, repeated at intervals of about three hours, showed that the volume of the heart changes during the day and is different in the evening from what it is

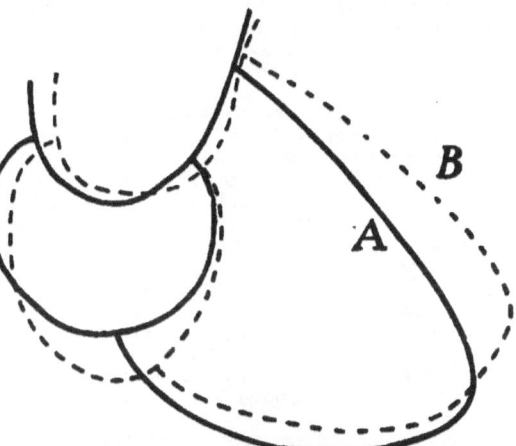

FIG. 34.—Augmented volume of the heart after exertion of an hour and a half.

in the morning. I restrict myself to the communication of an experiment which shows how the form of the heart may be altered by a brief exertion. The subject, a very robust person (see Fig. 33), was examined at 8.30 a.m. with the phonendoscope, the limits of the heart then being as indicated by line A in Fig. 34. At 10 a.m., after the tiring exercise of carrying, during an hour and a half, two dumb-bells, 10 kilograms each in weight, up and down the laboratory stairs, the form of the heart was as shown by the dotted line B. In order to render the figure less complex the ventricular septum has been omitted in both A and B. The augmented volume of the heart after exercise of an hour and a half is very evident in this experiment. The axis of the heart is displaced and there is an increase of volume in the upper part corresponding to the left ventricle.

III.

The facts contained in this chapter concerning overstrain of the heart are of more general interest than the simple study of mountaineering. All who perform great exertions in cycling, rowing, &c., are subject to the same disturbances.

The causes of the alteration of the heart during fatigue are two in number: the one is of mechanic or hydraulic origin and depends on the pressure of the blood, the other is chemical or toxic and is to be sought in the products of decomposition of the organism.

Many observations have been made on the circulation in contracting muscles. Authors of the greatest authority, such as Ludwig and Chauveau, have maintained that the blood circulates more freely in the contracting muscle. My experiments on man do not enable me to confirm this stated augmentation of the circulation. The problem is, however, not restricted to the determination of the course of the blood in the working muscle, the general pressure of the blood must be ascertained. We all know from the palpitation of the heart how profoundly the circulation of the blood is altered, even when only a small group of muscles is called into action.

Together with Dr. F. W. Tunnicliffe, of London, I studied this problem of the circulation of the blood in the contracting muscle by means of new experiments. The method we adopted consisted in the examination of the pulsations proper to the muscles. For this object we constructed an instrument, shown in Fig. 35, which, in some points, resembles another apparatus already known in physiology: Marey's cardiograph. It consists in the same capsule of wood which is applied by means of a bandage to the calf of the leg, or to the flexor muscles of the fingers, as in Fig. 35. Within the wooden capsule there is a tympanum with an elastic membrane, an inner spiral screw and an external knob of wood. By means of a metallic spring enclosed within the tube above the tympanum, the muscle may be compressed until its pulsations become visible. These are then traced by means of a tympanum with lever on a smoked cylinder. To this instrument we gave the name of myosphygmograph as it serves to register the pulse of the muscles.

When the myosphygmograph is applied to the surface of a muscle without a sufficient pressure, no pulsations are seen, but if a pressure equal to two or three centimetres of mercury is exercised a curve is obtained similar to the upper tracing of Fig. 36. These pulsations were obtained from the calf of the leg, that is, from the muscles *gastrocnemius* and *gemelli*. The observation already made with the sphygmomanometer, that the pulsations increase in height to a certain limit in proportion as the external pressure is augmented, is here verified. The little veins and lymphatic vessels give to the uncompressed muscle an almost fluid consistency, so that the pulsations of the little arteries are not seen, but when part of the muscle is compressed by means of the myosphygmograph the resistance is increased and the transmission of the pulsations of the little arteries through the skin to the registering tympanum effected. On this account the pulsations are stronger when the arm is raised as in Fig. 35.

The circulation of the blood in the contracting muscle has already been studied by Sadler[1] and Gaskell.[2] I shall not detain the reader with a criticism and comparison of the experiments of these investigators, as our object of learning the changes in the circulation of the blood in the working muscle is sufficiently attained by examining Fig. 36, which shows a myosphygmographic curve obtained on Dr. Tunnicliffe, the instrument being applied to the calf of the leg. The subject lay on a table with his leg raised, the foot resting on the shoulder of an assistant. The first part of the curve as far as the sign ∝ being written, a forcible contraction of the posterior muscles of the leg of one minute's duration was executed. In the tracing written during the contraction the pulse is not visible.

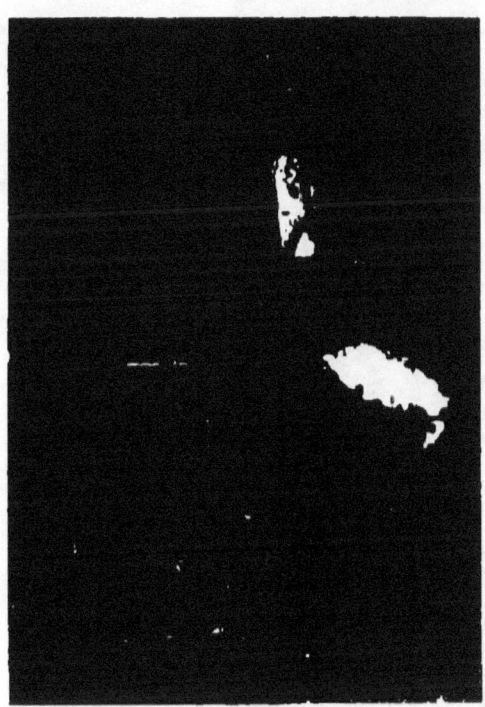

FIG. 35.—Myosphygmograph for the study of the circulation of the blood.

This is owing to the hardening of the muscle which, in contracting, swells and becomes shorter. According to this experiment, there is not that dilatation of the blood-vessels during muscular contraction which is now generally asserted. Rather are we inclined to maintain that the

[1] W. Sadler, *Ueber den Blutstrom in den ruhenden, verkürzten und ermüdeten Muskeln.* Ludwig's Arbeiten, 1869, p. 189.
[2] W. H. Gaskell, *Ueber die Aenderungen des Blutstroms in den Muskeln durch die Reizung ihrer Nerven.* Ludwig's Arbeiten, 1876, p. 45.

circulation in the muscles is less vigorous during their activity. This fact may be a partial cause of the augmented pressure of the blood observed when the muscles are at work.

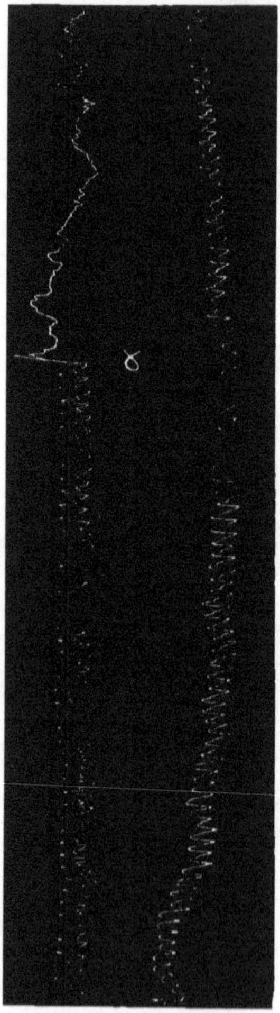

Fig. 36.—Dr. Tunnicliffe. Pulse-curve of the calf of the leg written with myosphygmograph. The first part of the upper line was traced during repose, the last during a contraction. The lower line was written after the cessation of a forcible contraction of the duration of one minute.

The lower curve of Fig. 36 was taken as soon as the contraction had ceased. We see that the profile of the pulsations is altered. The second dicrotic elevation has disappeared. The pulsations are nearer to each other, because the beating of the heart is accelerated. The point of the pulsations is blunted and only after fifteen or twenty of these have been registered do we see the dicrotism slowly re-establish itself, but even after one minute the form of the pulse is still different from what it was before the contraction. These changes in the form of the pulse prove that the blood-vessels of the muscles dilate after a forcible contraction, yielding more easily to the wave of blood which passes through them. This subsequent dilatation of the vessels is probably due to the arrest of circulation taking place in the muscle during its contraction.

Analogy would lead us to suppose, knowing as we do that working organs are more abundantly supplied with blood, that the blood-vessels of the muscles would dilate during contraction. It may be, however, that since the muscles have very brief periods of activity, their vessels do not dilate when they are contracted, their needs being sufficiently supplied by the subsequent dilatation of the vessels observed by means of the myosphygmograph. The friction automatically exercised by the muscle on its vessels in the act of contracting suffices alone, perhaps, in rapid and brief contractions, to render the circulation more active in its interior. However this may be, we have ascertained that the circulation becomes more vigorous in the muscle after the cessation of the contraction. This is certainly of benefit to the muscle, which is thus cleansed of the noxious substances and scoriæ which work has produced within its fibres.

IV.

With Dr. Tunnicliffe I further studied the changes produced in the pressure of the blood by walking. The first researches on this subject were conducted by Basch, Maximowitsch, Rieder, Oertel, and established the increase of the blood-pressure during work and ascents. Our studies of the pressure of the blood in walking man proved that there is an augmentation of two or three centimetres of mercury when the usual walking pace is kept.

Professor Oertel says that the pressure of the blood increases during ascents because there is a more abundant flow of venous blood to the heart and an equilibrium established between the arterial and venous pressure of the blood.[1]

We observed that there is a contraction of the blood-vessels at the surface of the body whenever we perform intense muscular work. This process, too, must increase the pressure of the blood during ascents.

Another important phenomenon, besides the two facts already studied, is the contraction of the blood-vessels in the organs of the abdominal cavity. In no other way can the elevated pressure of the blood be explained, when the skin is red and perspiration abundant as in ascents. Of necessity there must be less blood in the internal organs if the supply of blood in the muscles at work is greater and the blood-vessels of the skin are dilated. This explains why some persons when they run or walk much suffer from nausea and vomiting. The disturbances produced by fatigue in the digestive system due to an anæmia of the viscera consequent on the contraction of the muscles shall be considered with greater attention further on.

If the dilatation of the vessels at the surface of the body and in the muscles becomes too great and the heart too weak, the pressure of the blood diminishes. This fact was already observed by Oertel, who, on measuring the pressure of the blood during an ascent, found that it was greater half-way up the mountain and less when the summit was reached.

We have now seen what mechanisms come into play in order that the pressure of the blood may be regulated when the muscles are in action. The peculiar perfection of our organism consists in the co-operation of these mechanisms, the one making up for the deficiencies of the others, when work has diminished their activity.

As another illustration of the manner in which the blood circulates in the organism I communicate the following experiment performed in my institute by Dr. Colombo on the 28th of February, 1894. Dr. Colombo was then twenty-three years of age and weighed 66 kilograms. At 3.45 p.m. his blood-pressure, pulse, breathing and internal temperature were determined. Immediately afterwards, at 4.10 p.m., he went ten times in succession up and down the stairs of the laboratory, 64 in number, holding in each hand a dumb-bell weighing 5 kilograms. He then returned, panting and bathed in perspiration, to the room where we were awaiting him. Blood-pressure and temperature were immediately measured, the pulse and breathing counted. The following table contains the results of these observations which were continued for more than twenty minutes until the pressure of the blood and the rate of breathing were normal once more :—

NORMAL VALUES.

	Blood-pressure.	Pulse.	Breathing.	Temperature.
3.45 p.m.	80 mm.	65	20	37·0°

[1] Oertel, *Handbuch der Allgemeinen Therapie und Kreislaufstörungen*, 1891, p. 189.

AFTER EXERTION.

	Blood-pressure.	Pulse.	Breathing.	Temperature.
4.25 p.m.	105 mm.	108	37	37·1
4.30 ,,	100 ,,	98	20	37·0
4.35 ,,	98 ,,	79	18	,,
4.40 ,,	90 ,,	70	16	,,
4.45 ,,	80 ,,	70	17	,,

We see from this experiment that the brief exercise of going up and down the stairs caused an augmentation of 25 millimetres of mercury in the pressure of the blood, the normal pressure being recovered after the space of twenty minutes.

It is a wonderful perfection of our organism that the blood flows more abundantly to fatigued organs. The quantity of blood contained in our body amounting, however, to scarcely 5 litres, all the vessels contract when intense work of brain or muscles is called for. The canals in which the blood circulates become narrower, the velocity of the current is consequently increased in the organs which are at work or which have worked, the activity of these is augmented and the normal conditions are more rapidly re-established.

The data furnished by this last experiment serve to measure the surplus work performed by the heart during the exercise of going up and down stairs. The pressure of the blood measured in the little arteries of the fingers is certainly inferior to the pressure of blood in the heart, but up till the present time we possess no more exact instrument than the sphygmomanometer for the pursuance of these researches in man.

Let us therefore compute the surplus work of the heart; we shall thus see in what manner fatigue of this organ is produced. The left cavity of the heart resembles a muscular pouch and contains 180 cubic centimetres of blood. In a state of repose every pulsation of the heart forces normally 180 cubic centimetres up to a height of 80 millimetres of mercury; after the exercise up and down the stairs, the same volume of blood is forced up to a height of 105 millimetres.

Let us suppose that the weight of blood is equal to that of water. We find that before the experiment, in a state of repose, the heart performed work equal to 13·92 kilogrammetres (0·085 × 14 = 1·190. 1·190 × 0·180 = 0·2142 × 65 = 13·92).

After the exertion, the heart performs a double amount of work: 28·57 kilogrammetres (105 × 14 = 1·470. 1·470 × 0·180 = 0·2646 × 108 = 28·57).

Before this double amount of work can be performed it is probable that the heart, as it grows tired, does not empty itself completely. As yet we have no means of rectifying these calculations, but it is, at any rate, certain that the work accomplished by the heart is greatly increased. If the exercise is continued, not only does it cause fatigue of the heart but also a dilatation of this organ which gives rise to inadequate action although the valves and circulating apparatus are intact. To this state, which excessive work has rendered pathological, the name of overstrain of the heart has been given.

V.

Now that we have examined the physiological conditions which generate fatigue of the heart, let us return to our observations on Monte Rosa. The accompanying figure shows the form and position of the heart in Corporal Cento as determined by percussion of the thorax, first, under normal conditions, and then immediately after a walk over the glaciers. The black line

1 of Fig. 37 showing normal form and position was traced on August 7th, while we were in Gnifetti Hut. The precise point where the apex of the heart beat and the limits of the relative and absolute obtusity were first carefully traced with a blue pencil on the thorax, the drawing being afterwards copied by means of transparent paper. After every experiment the tracing on the thorax was rubbed out, with the exception of the little line (reproduced in the figures) indicating the upper rim of the second rib, so that the precise demarcation of the area of obtusity might not be influenced, in subsequent examinations, by preconceived ideas. This examination of the heart was conducted by Dr. Abelli, while the subject was in a sitting posture, the

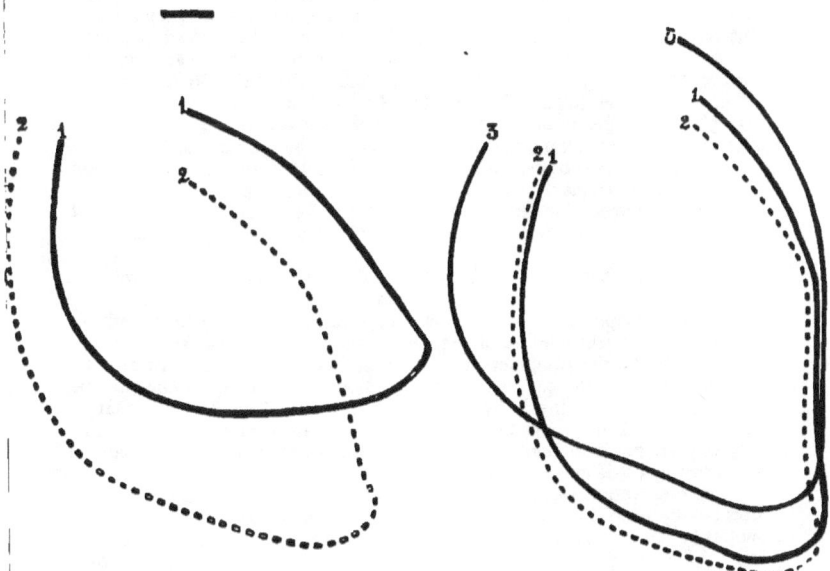

Fig. 37.—Corporal Cento. 1. Form and position of the heart before the ascent. 2. After the ascent.

Fig. 38.—Solferino (soldier). Position and form of the heart: 1. In repose. 2. After a short ascent. 3. On arriving at the Regina Margherita Hut.

thorax therefore being vertical. On the next day Corporal Cento left the encampment near Linty Hut, and mounted slowly to Gnifetti Hut, carrying a weight of fifteen kilograms on his shoulders. This is a short ascent with a walk over the glacier of the duration of about an hour and a half.

As soon as Cento arrived at Gnifetti Hut we determined again the position of the heart, the outline then being as is shown by line 2 of Fig. 37. A comparison of this outline with the one preceding shows that after this ascent the apex of the heart beat lower down, and that the whole organ was slightly displaced towards the right.

Dr. Abelli was of opinion that Corporal Cento, in spite of his robust appearance, must have a heart somewhat below the average size. The kicking of the apex of the heart against the thorax was felt at the upper rim of the fifth rib. One very fine calm day he performed the journey between Gnifetti and Regina Margherita Hut with difficulty, although he had a weight of only ten kilograms on his shoulders.

In stronger men the sinking of the heart in consequence of so inconsiderable an ascent is less marked as may be seen in Fig. 38, which shows the measurements taken by Dr. Abelli on the soldier Solferino. Line 1 marks the position of the heart in repose at Gnifetti Hut on August 8th, at 8 a.m., after a good night's rest. The upper rim of the second rib to the left side of the sternum is shown here as in Fig. 37 by the short black line at the top of the figure. The point of the heart was felt in the sixth intercostal space. After Solferino's return to Gnifetti Hut from the encampment near Linty Hut, having carried a weight of only four kilograms on his back, the dull cardiac sounds were heard rather lower down, and the point of the heart had also slightly sunk, as may be seen by the dotted line in Fig. 38. On August 18th he arrived at the Regina Margherita Hut without any load. Line 3, Fig. 38, shows the form of the heart after this ascent. The volume is augmented, the transverse diameter is greater and the apex is higher up.

The upward displacement of the heart inclined us to think that a distension of the gases of stomach and intestines due to the diminished barometric pressure had forced the diaphragm upwards. The observation in Turin of the same rising of the heart in consequence of fatigue showed the supposition to be incorrect.

It is an old hypothesis that mountain-sickness arises from an expansion of the gases of the abdominal cavity, and that these gases impede the breathing by raising the diaphragm. With a view to ascertaining whether this hypothesis was correct, I took a number of measurements and found that at an altitude of 2,000 metres, the circumference of the abdomen had not altered even by a millimetre. In the persons on whom I made these measurements the muscles of the abdominal walls were well-developed. I do not deny that in those individuals in whom the walls are less resistant a slight expansion may be produced, but it will certainly never be so pronounced as to force diaphragm and heart upwards and to impede the breathing.

The observation made on Corporal Cento is instructive in this respect, because between Linty and Gnifetti Hut the difference of level is of 600 metres (3,047 to 3,620 metres); and Fig. 37 shows plainly that the heart has sunk. This is due to the dilatation of the heart. This organ contains a greater quantity of blood, because its walls are more relaxed, and probably is not able to empty itself completely in its contractions, and on this account sinks lower.

At Regina Margherita Hut Dr. Abelli found that in Sarteur, on whom he made a series of exact measurements, the transverse diameter of the heart was likewise augmented, and that the apex of the heart rose after the ascent from Gnifetti Hut.

We shall presently see that fatigue of the heart is one of the most weighty factors in mountain-sickness.

VI.

I have already said that when we stop during ascents, our condition does not at once improve, and often grows worse. Let us now investigate more carefully what takes place in the heart after an ascent.

The soldier Chamois started on August 10, 1894, from Ivrea with others of the party. When they arrived at Pont St. Martin they continued the journey on foot, slept the night at Gressoney, and arrived at Gnifetti Hut at 5.30 p.m. on August 11th. Chamois slept little, probably owing to digestive disturbances. When he arrived at Gnifetti Hut he felt a pricking pain at the base of the lung, at the left side when breathing inwards. On the 12th at 5.30 a.m. he left with the others, quite restored and carrying on his back a load of 16 kilograms. When the party arrived below Gnifetti Peak, Chamois was suddenly seized with great tiredness in the legs. Those of the expedition who had come down to meet them at the foot of peak relieved him of his load. He arrived at the Regina Margherita Hut at 9.12 a.m., and complained of feeling very cold, but of nothing else. He lay down at once. His pulse was so feeble that I had to count it on the artery of the neck, as it was impossible to do so at the wrist.

	Pulse.	Breathing.	Temperature.
9.20 a.m.	109	27	$37\cdot8°$
9.30 ,,	106	22	$37\cdot2°$
9.45 ,,	106	21	$37\cdot2°$
11.10 ,,	116	21	$37\cdot1°$
5.30 p.m.	108	22	$36\cdot9°$

I observed a similar augmentation of the pulse in other persons, but not in all; it is due, I think, to fatigue of the heart.

The last climb up to Regina Margherita Hut is very fatiguing. Notwithstanding this, the frequency of the pulse in the many persons whom I examined never reached the 166 pulsations, which was the maximum found by Jaquet and Christ after work with the ergostat [1] of only fifteen or twenty minutes' duration. I attribute this difference to the greater fatigue of the cardiac muscle, which is produced by the tiring march over the glaciers of Monte Rosa. When Lortet ascended the last part of Mont Blanc he counted 160 pulsations. I never met with this maximum at the altitude of 4,560 metres. This shows how complicated these studies are. It is of little use to feel the pulse unless one takes carefully into account the conditions and numerous factors which modify the action of the heart and blood-vessels.

When Saussure performed the ascent of Mont Cenis in 1787 he counted the pulse in his two companions, first on the summit and afterwards at the Mont Cenis post-office. On the top he made his observations after two hours of repose; below, immediately after the arrival, and found that in one companion the pulse was less frequent on the summit than below, while in the other it was in both places the same. Zumstein, when on the Vincent Pyramid, counted 77 pulse-beats per minute in one of his companions, a hunter, who had been feeling unwell, while in himself the pulsations amounted to 101, in Vincent to 80, and in a guide to 104 per minute. According to Saussure, those who suffered from mountain-sickness on Mont Cenis had a more rapid pulse, whereas according to Zumstein's observations the pulse was in these cases slower.

I have dwelt on these early observations, as they indicate so plainly the difficulty of the subject. Even now, a century later, these individual differences are still but little explained.

[1] H. Christ, *Ueber den Einfluss der Muskelarbeit auf die Herzthätigkeit*. Leipzig, 1894, p. 16.

VII.

In the accounts of bicycle-races we often read of some competitor having fainted. Arthur Linton fainted during the race Bordeaux-Paris, but recovered and arrived the first at the goal. Others faint when they stop to sign the registers along the road: they recover after a few minutes and then go on their way. It would seem that repose instead of improving, aggravates the conditions of the heart.

In order to ascertain the changes which the pressure of the blood undergoes when a march has been performed, I made a series of experiments on soldiers. Of these experiments I communicate one in detail:

On July 10th, Janetti, a soldier from Busto Arsizio, left the laboratory at 6.25 a.m., after breakfasting, for Baraccone on the Rivoli road, which is at a distance of 9 kilometres from Turin. His pulse was then beating at the rate of 80 to the minute, the rate of breathing being 16 per minute. Pressure of the blood measured with the sphygmomanometer, 80 millimetres of mercury. He carried arms and baggage, and these with his clothing gave a weight of about 22 kilograms. As the weather was warm, he was told to walk in the shade of the great elms which border the road.

At 11.47 a.m. he had returned from Baraccone. Pulse, 102. Breathing, 20. Blood-pressure, 100 millimetres of mercury. He rested, lunched, and started again at 2 p.m. to repeat the march.

He returned at 7 p.m. The pulse, on his arrival, beat 126 times in the minute. I introduced his fingers into the stalls of the sphygmomanometer and found that the pressure oscillated between 76 and 80 mm. Janetti was not standing still, he kept resting his body first on one leg and then on the other. As this restlessness moved the fingers and made it difficult to determine with accuracy the pressure of the blood, I begged him to stand still. Suddenly the pressure diminished. I looked first at his fingers but found that their position was not altered. Janetti then told me that he felt unwell; I looked at him and saw that he was pale and that he was leaning his head on his shoulder. I saw that he was fainting and immediately released his fingers. The pressure had sunk to 50 millimetres. We assisted him to bed, supporting him under the arms and then gave him some fresh water to drink. Shortly afterwards he had somewhat recovered. I then measured the pressure again which amounted to only 75 millimetres. The pulse was 106. At 7.28 p.m., about twenty minutes, that is, after the fainting-fit, he was perfectly well again.

The importance of this experiment lies in the observation of the change in the pressure of the blood during a fainting-fit. The subject did not completely lose consciousness, except perhaps in the moment in which we laid him on the bed. The pulse grew somewhat slower immediately before the swoon. Unfortunately I had not this time registered the pressure on the smoked cylinder as I nearly always do.

The diminution of the blood-pressure on the second return from Baraccone after the subject had walked 36 kilometres, is the most evident symptom of the fatigue of the heart, the beating of which was accelerated, the pulsations amounting to 126 per minute, but which lacked energy nevertheless to keep up the pressure of the blood.

To the reader whose indignation may possibly have been aroused by reading this second account of a fainting-fit, I owe the explanation that for many years I have been conducting researches on fatigue. Professor V.

Aducco, Professor Maggiora and my brother, had at their disposal whole companies of soldiers who performed forced marches. It is therefore not to be wondered at if in the course of these studies some cases of indisposition occurred. My brother and Professor Maggiora often walked till they were utterly exhausted and livid marks appeared on their legs. I mention this as a testimony to the enthusiasm and abnegation with which these researches were carried on.

These studies of the phenomena resulting from forced marches, and the experiments made on the soldiers of our expedition before the ascent was begun, enable me to assert that an identical degree of fatigue in the mountains and in the plain produces in the former instance more serious phenomena of cardiac fatigue than in the latter.

VIII.

When the walls of the blood-vessels are not perfectly elastic as in old and sometimes in young people (in whom, one may say, the arteries have become prematurely aged), fatigue causes still more serious circulatory disturbances. In order to form an idea of the injurious effect which the hardening and diminished elasticity of the arterial walls have on the heart we need only think of the pneumatic tubes of the bicycle. The importance of this invention consists in the diminution of the friction and the deadening of the concussion to which the bicycle is subjected on its course. These elastic tubes are now also applied to carriages, and it has been found that their use lessens the work of the horses by one-third. The heart in the old may be compared to a man riding a bicycle of which the pneumatic tubes are no longer intact.

This explains the circumstances which I have often had occasion to observe, that a walk on the mountains, even though not very fatiguing, produces irregularities in the cardiac rhythm of persons in whom the arterial walls are not perfectly elastic. These irregularities may last for three days, and are accompanied by a sense of prostration which only slowly disappears.

Even in healthy persons violent exertion produces irregularities of the pulse. During my sojourn on Monte Rosa I noticed that in nearly all, the marches over the glacier caused a slight irregularity in the beating of the heart.

In the guides I often found the pulse to be irregular and this even in the strongest persons, Zurbriggen, for instance.

The preceding observations explain why amongst mountaineers disease of the heart is much more frequent than in the plain, and why there is a greater percentage of men than women who suffer from it. In my journeys through the Alps I have often talked with the physicians on the French and Swiss as well as on the Italian side on this subject, and was invariably informed that the old people in the mountains nearly all die of heart disease.

A certain degree of development of the heart above the average size is necessary, and therefore we ought not to shrink from exertion, for only through exercise can this supernormal development be effected.

This is very apparent in the horse. Competent authorities affirm that the normal weight of the heart in a horse of ordinary breed is 3 to 4 kilograms; whereas the heart of a racehorse weighs on the average from

5 to 6 kilograms. In consequence of the excessive and continuous work of the races, the heart of an English thoroughbred may even attain the weight of 8 kilograms, without any circulatory disturbance resulting from a degree of hypertrophy such that the weight of the heart has become doubled.

So far as I know, no investigations have been made on the variations in the weight of the heart in different regions, but the exertions performed by mountaineers convince me that their hearts must even in youth be much more developed than those of the populations of the plain.

Shepherds' cottages on Monte Rosa.

CHAPTER VI

ACCIDENTS CAUSED BY EXCESSIVE FATIGUE AND NERVOUS EXHAUSTION

I.

THERE is only one kind of fatigue—nervous fatigue. This is the sole type, from which all forms of exhaustion derive, when the activity of the organism passes the physiological limits.

I have already studied this question in my book *La Fatica*. The subject is inexhaustible and will always lend itself to new researches. We must, first of all, distinguish fatigue from lassitude. We all know what fatigue is. It is a vague sensation which we cannot define, still less express its different degrees in words. To that minor feeling of fatigue, which lasts after we have rested, we give the name of lassitude.

Lassitude seizes us sometimes without any preceding work of brain or muscles, a phenomenon observable more especially in the hysterical and in persons of great nervous excitability. Favourable and unfavourable moods, good or bad temper, of which we so often speak, are not a caprice of the organism, but arise, like good and bad weather, from natural causes, and trouble the atmosphere of the nervous system.

One of the probable causes of these changes taking place in us, I believe to have found in studying the temperature of the brain in man. A young girl called Delfina Parodi, had a wound in the temple at the left side of the forehead which penetrated the skull. When it was healed an opening remained in the bone through which I was able to introduce a thermometer into the Sylvian fissure (a deep part of the brain and the most important for the study of psychic phenomena).[1] This was the first time that a physiologist was able to examine, with such exactitude, the temperature of the human brain.

The result of these researches [2] was the conclusion that there are two causes of the development of heat in the brain. One is psychic activity, that is, the chemical work necessary for the maintenance of consciousness; the other is the nutrition and denutrition of the brain which act independently of the functions of the intelligence and of movement. I have given the name of *conflagrations* to those augmentations of temperature which I observed during sleep untroubled by dreams, in the state of repose and complete unconsciousness.

I was able to measure with the thermometer the intensity of the consumption of energy which takes place in the brain without transforming itself into a sensation or a thought. "Can the brain then work idly?" it may be asked. I answer, "Yes." It is a serious affirmation but it is based on what I observed while the subject slept or was under the influence of absinthe. In order that the reader may understand this internal dissociation and increased rapidity of assimilation I suggest the analogy of a watch in which the wound-up spring runs without turning the pointers. This comparison gives an idea of this nervous energy lost in the brain without the index of the internal sensations showing that a transformation has taken place in the organ of consciousness.

Of late years physicians have rightly attributed great importance to dreams as a cause of lassitude. Tissié gave great attention to this study and showed that certain apparently accidental pathological phenomena which appear in the hysterical, arise from the fatigue of the brain caused by dreams.

This is not the kind of fatigue of which I here wish to treat. The conflagration is a dissociative process, a consumption of energy depending on processes other than the physiological ones of thought and motion. I mention these facts in order to convince the reader that our senses are imperfect and limited, and that we lack a special sense to warn us and, so to say, to control the loss of energy in every nervous action.

For animals and for men living in natural conditions, it is certainly an advantage not to be molested by a sense of the losses of energy continually undergone in the struggle for life. Our machine is so constructed that fatigue stops us only shortly before the scale loses its equilibrium. The pain which accompanies fatigue is like a safety-valve which only opens to emit the alarm-whistle: till that moment we may work on undisturbed. Unfortunately, as we shall shortly see, this safety-valve does not act always and equally well in all men. So long as it was believed that an act of the will was something immaterial, it was lawful to think that it passed, leaving no trace on the matter of the organism, but now all are convinced that thinking or sensing too much may alone produce nervous exhaustion. Every voluntary act is the effect of an internal combustion which, together with the residua of the substances destroyed, leaves behind it, as it were, a long train of soot in the organism.

In my book *La Fatica* I have shown that every act of the will, even that, merely, of forcibly clenching the hand is always accompanied by central fatigue; that this contraction of the muscles occasions a consumption of

---

[1] The thermometer which I made use of marked the thousandth part of a degree.
[2] A. Mosso, *La temperatura del cervello*. Treves, Milano, 1894. *Die Temperatur des Gehirnes*, Leipzig, 1894, S. 86.

force in the brain, and that a certain time is necessary for this organ to regain its former state and strength.

Mountain-climbing, bicycle races, boat-races, all the various sports, all the more serious exertions of working-men, all the intellectual toil of the student, are identical in their nature: they are nothing else than fatigue of the nervous system.

General ideas have this advantage, that they draw together things which seemed far apart, that they find connecting links between diverse phenomena. The work of science is precisely this: to group together under the same law the greatest possible number of phenomena.

II.

In mountain-climbing the one who is at the fore-end of the rope suffers sooner and more from fatigue than those who are behind him. It may be thought that this is owing to the greater mechanical work performed by the pioneer, who must plunge through the snow, while the others follow in his footsteps, cut steps in the ice, remove obstacles, etc. But this does not suffice. Even on the Matterhorn and on mountains where there is neither snow nor ice, the foremost man feels more fatigued than the others.

Those who performed the first ascent of Mont Blanc, Monte Rosa, or other mountains, suffered much more than those who came after them, because in them the nervous fatigue was greater.

It is attention which tires us. Few bodily exercises fatigue so much as fencing, because in no other is the effort of attention greater.

I remember that we once lost our way on a glacier. One of the party unroped in order to explore the crevasses round about, returning afterwards to show us the right road. He went forwards boldly, alone. This was our first attempt to proceed without a guide on the glacier. We walked on for a few minutes, then one of our band stopped, declaring that he had no strength to go further, not because he was tired, but from the emotion he felt at seeing our comrade walking on in front unroped, hopelessly lost should his foot slip. Even before he spoke I had noticed, for I came next to him in the line, that he was not walking so well as at first and had felt some apprehension as we were on a slope. This was a nervous effect of his anxiety; as soon as the line was re-formed his muscles regained their strength and certainty of movement.

In this case it was the fear for another which caused fatigue, but much more frequently it is the fear for our own safety which influences us. In ascents when the rope is a hindrance, because the way leads over stony ground, the novices immediately suffer more from fatigue, owing to the feeling of being alone, without a guide and without support. At other times even stronger climbers recognise the effects of fear in the fatigue they feel; as, for instance, when all have unroped, because of the difficulty of clambering in any other way round steep and uniform walls of rock, when the false step of one would inevitably drag the others to their doom.

A very evident case of exhaustion arising from fear came under my notice at Breuil, where the Matterhorn is, as it were, the touchstone of mountain climbers. A very strong porter, who had made several ascents of Monte Rosa and the Breithorn, having climbed half up the Matterhorn, was unable to go farther. He told me that he was quite well and that he was astonished at not being able to proceed, not feeling sure of either hands or feet.

In order to understand the nervous fatigue in mountain-climbing, we must remember that this form of movement must not be compared to that performed when we walk along a good road with only gentle ascents and descents, when we may even read without thinking of the work of our legs.

In an ascent we find again the two fundamental elements of every voluntary act. First selection, and then decision. This work is repeated at every step when the way becomes difficult. After the nervous work of choosing where to place hand or foot, comes the decision to accomplish the proposed movement and then the nervous effort of its execution.

Work of this kind would soon exhaust us if voluntary acts had not in us the tendency to become automatic. That nervous processes tend to become mechanical is a happy disposition which permits of a great economy of nervous force. The superior office is, so to speak, in the upper storey, in the cerebral cortex at the surface of the convolutions : here the more difficult decisions are taken. When some work must be accomplished several times in succession, the business is gradually transferred to the lower floor, where involuntary acts are effected by prompter means and with a lesser consumption of energy.

Only in this way can we understand why nervous work such as that of walking fatigues us so little, while exclusive brain-work has so much exhausted us after one hour that we are unable to continue. Even the greatest and most prolific writers, as, for instance, Zola, only write for one hour with perfect vigour. The mind then becomes less active and the work toilsome. From a medico-psychological inquiry recently made by Dr. Toulouse of Paris, it appears that Zola, who has written so many volumes, is absolutely incapable of continuing the work of production after three hours' application.

Many think that the pacemaker in bicycle-races is of use because he breaks the air, diminishing in it the resistance for the one who comes after him, preparing a furrow for him, as it were. This is not the principal advantage, because the distance between the pacemaker and his follower is often so great that it is nullified. The useful effect is that the latter is saved the expenditure of all that nervous energy which would otherwise be lost in the work of attention.

III.

All those who have taken long walks or climbed mountains will have noticed that they walk more easily after half an hour or an hour. The same thing happens when we ride the bicycle or when we sit down to our desk to write or study. This is due to an excitement produced in the nervous system by motion.

Our body resembles those complicated, heavy machines which require a certain time to be put into motion, and, again, a space of time before they can be stopped. This state of excitement is useful so long as it remains within physiological limits. When the man of letters has "warmed to his subject" he works better. The slight emotion of the nervous system which is of advantage in work of the imagination, may be generated by easy muscular exercise. But once the inertia of the nervous system has been overcome, long pauses are not favourable to work.

Inaction and repose are fatal in mountain-climbing. The climber who works, cuts steps, while the cold wind is blowing, is always stronger and more courageous than the comrade behind him who stands waiting to take a step forwards. The will is here of little use ; the machine must be kept warm, so

Panoramic view of Monte Rosa from Rimpfischhorn (alt., 4,217 metres) on the north side. [V. Sella.

that the pressure of the blood may not sink below that level at which discouragement and muscular weakness befall us.

Professor Kraepelin recently showed that a man who works for half an hour and then rests for half an hour or an hour, only succeeds once, after the first pause, in regaining his original mental vigour; a repetition of the pause increases fatigue and the disposition to work diminishes rapidly.

It is true, therefore, that a slight degree of exhaustion is occasioned by every expenditure of activity of the nervous system. This fact passes unobserved in robust persons; only the weak notice it. Any one who attentively studies himself will, however, immediately become aware of the diminution of energy and of the slow increase of fatigue. I myself, for instance, notice every year that I offer more resistance to intellectual labour after the rest and recreation of the vacation. The fatigue produced by an equal amount of work disappears sooner at the beginning than at the end of the scholastic year. The daily occupations of the laboratory, the delivering of lectures, the more restless life in town, exhaust all exuberant strength.

We notice amongst all peoples that work is interrupted from time to time; the reason of this is that there are many who feel the need of a short pause so that their nervous system may recover. The repose of the Sunday is indispensable, because the daily rest and sleep throughout the week do not suffice to make good the losses of energy incurred.

The first investigations made on man with the object of learning what length of time is necessary for brain and muscles to regain their strength after a certain amount of work, were begun in my institute by Professor Maggiora, who found that the periods of repose must be three or four times longer than the periods of work, and that the efforts which we make when we are tired, fatigue us much more than equal efforts performed when we are rested. That work, even though light, which demands prolonged attention, causes the greatest exhaustion of the nervous system. Instinctively men avoid such work, preferring an apparently more fatiguing manual labour, which, however, demands less intellectual effort.

Kraepelin [1] has shown that the effects of a night spent in study are long felt, the mind only recovering its former vigour after four days.

Nervous fatigue is not only an exhaustion but also a poisoning. After the consumption of an amount of nervous energy, scoriæ contaminate the tissues and give rise to the disagreeable feeling of fatigue. The organism requires after a time an interval of repose, in order to retrieve its losses and cleanse the tissues from the slag of the work performed.

Chomel, one of the greatest of French physicians, relates that one day a youth came to the hospital in a state of feverish prostration. Chomel examined him carefully, and then wrote this diagnosis on the tablet at the head of his bed :—

Typhus or incipient small-pox.

This boy had come on foot in two days from Compiègne to Paris, and feeling himself exhausted, had presented himself for admittance to the hospital. The day after, to Chomel's great astonishment, the fever had left him, and after two days' rest the patient had completely recovered his strength.

[1] Kraepelin, *Hygiene der Arbeit*, p. 18.

IV.

Physical fatigue may occasion an exaltation in the same way as mental fatigue generates hallucinations. We notice the first stage in the difficulty we have to fall asleep after a day of hard work.

Great workers do not write at night, rather may we say that they extinguish the fire in the machine at sunset. The pressure of the blood gradually diminishes, and sleep is rendered possible.

If, sometimes, after intellectual or muscular work we seem to feel ourselves stronger, we must remember that this is an illusion arising solely from an artificial excitement, from an incipient nervous inebriation, so to say.

On stormy days, when the whirling snow rendered the ascent more toilsome, guides and climbers arrived at the Regina Margherita Hut in so excited a condition, that they appeared to be drunk. They talked in a loud agitated voice, then grew quiet, assuming a behaviour so different to that customary with them that their character seemed to have undergone a change.

On the other hand I have twice seen persons enter the hut in an extremely fatigued condition, sit down, and then, after a few minutes during which we lent them assistance, rouse themselves as from a dream, looking around them and only becoming fully aware at that moment that they were with us. I thought at first that the extreme fatigue prevented them from noticing their surroundings; but one of them told me that on entering the hut he really could not see well, and begged me to examine his eyes as he was afraid the frost had affected his vision. A snowstorm was raging that day. When this man arrived at the hut he was unrecognisable; I saw him fall down before the door like a mass of snow, so white were his clothes with ice and rime. His hair and beard were full of icicles.

On Monte Rosa I saw a colleague of mine caper about in the snow, throw himself down on his back with outspread arms, laughing and talking in a manner so different from his usual serious behaviour, that we were all in anxiety on his account, as we knew that he had not drunk anything.

Lemercier relates in the preface to Zsigmondy's book that he saw two Englishmen fall on their knees on the summit of Mont Blanc, and sing with a loud voice: "God save the Queen."[1] Piachaud tells of mountain-climbers who, having reached the top of Mont Blanc, began to shed tears.

That the contraction of the muscles is not necessary to produce all the characteristic phenomena of fatigue is seen in the profound emotions, and in the exhaustion of the nervous system caused by voluptuous enjoyment. The temporary excitement during the first period hides the effects of fatigue which reassert themselves on the day following.

Every prolonged effort produces a slight degree of exaltation, even in the most robust men. Féré believes[2] that excessive fatigue causes attacks of instantaneous madness in the degenerate, the epileptic and the hysterical.

In May, 1894, there was in Italy the first national resistance race promoted by the Cyclists' Union. The route, 530 kilometres in length, began at Milan, passed through Brescia, Mantua, Reggio, Piacenza, Alessandria, and ended at Turin. I had here an opportunity of observing the effects of great fatigue, so I undertook with some of my colleagues to receive the competitors on their arrival in Turin. At the Cyclists' Club,

---

[1] E. Zsigmondy, *Les dangers dans la montagne*. Paris, 1886.
[2] Féré. *Comptes rendus de la Société de Biologie*, 1892.

rooms, beds, baths, shower-baths had been prepared, also everything necessary for the performance of massage. The two first who arrived, having accomplished 530 kilometres in twenty-seven hours were in fair condition. But the subsequent arrivals all convinced me that cycling carried on in this way is injurious. All of us, even the non-physicians, were struck by one circumstance in particular: the exaltation of some of the cyclists. One talked so loudly and created such a disturbance, perpetually repeating from his bed the account of his journey, that we had to isolate him so as to let the others sleep, for neither entreaties nor threats could silence him.

There has been recently at New York a bicycle race which lasted six days. A prize of 60,000 lire[1] was to be given to the winner. Two poor fellows who took part in the race were thought for twenty-four hours to be mad, such was their state of exaltation.

To such excesses are men led by the ferocious curiosity of the public who, by paying for these spectacles, encourage them.

V.

Giuseppe Maquignaz said to me one day that in dangerous places one must slacken the pace for many reasons, amongst others because in such places one immediately feels more fatigued. This sagacious observation, showing such an intimate acquaintance with the psychology of the mountain-climber, excited my admiration. And yet I think fear is one of the emotions which Maquignaz least knows. Tyndall in speaking of Maquignaz, writes:[2] " Joseph, if I may use the term, is a man of high boiling point, his constitutional *sangfroid* resisting the ebullition of fear."

The physiological idea expressed by Tyndall in these words is not so far from the actual fact as its imaginative form might lead one to suppose. There are really men whose point of ebullition is higher than that of others; they present more resistance to the fire of danger, only extreme peril can agitate them. Fear exercises a pressure on the blood which Maquignaz was able to resist.

The more intense the emotion of the nervous system, the longer is the duration of the fatigue it causes. Even the most intrepid climbers may find themselves suddenly paralysed when in mortal peril, worn out as they are by the accidents and risks of the ascent.

I read lately the description which Fitzgerald gives of his excursions in the New Zealand Alps with the guide Zurbriggen. At a certain dangerous part, when they were both tied together, a stone struck Fitzgerald on the chest. Zurbriggen had time to seize the rope which was coiled near his feet and check his companion's fall into the abyss. The weight was such that Zurbriggen had to let the rope run between his fingers in order to lessen the strain, at the same time endeavouring to gain a better point of support, and a position such as would enable him to hold Fitzgerald suspended and save him. The latter was then drawn up, and the danger was over. They then sat down to recover from the nervous shock, which had been so great that half an hour passed before they felt able to move.

Accidents may cause a fainting-fit, as was experienced by Güssfeldt who is yet one of the most intrepid of modern Alpinists. Those who have never been in the Alps cannot imagine the state of mental tension in Alpine travellers, the unusual muscular exertion which is requisite,

---

[1] £2,000.   [2] J. Tyndall, *Hours of Exercise in the Alps*, p. 289. London, 1871.

nor the perils which menace their lives for hours together. The accounts we read in Alpine journals give us a faint idea of this rapid exhaustion of strength. They tell of almost vertical walls of crumbling rock, in scaling which each traveller knows that it is beyond his power to save the comrades to whom he is tied should one make a false step, but that he and all will be precipitated into the abyss. And thus they march forward for hours in succession, imminent death before their eyes.

This continual consumption of energy produces a serious exhaustion of the nervous system which alters the character—not for the better. With due exceptions we are less gay and jovial after great exertion. Nervous persons suffer most.

Saussure noticed these circumstances when he made his first ascent of Mont Blanc. "It seemed to us that we were more irritable, changed, and decidedly for the worse."

Cyclists will render this change of character proverbial. We all know what invectives and abuse they shower along the course when they foresee some hindrance. Only sometimes do mountain-climbers sink to the cyclist's level of politeness, and that is, when they are disturbed in the huts after a laborious march: the troublers of their rest are then greeted with the same good grace and urbanity.

VI.

A few years ago there was discovered in a sepulchre in the Appian Way, a mosaic, representing in the centre, a skeleton lying upon thorns, and pointing with the hand to the celebrated motto: *Know thyself.*[1] This mosaic which is worked out in white and black stones has a deep meaning. The words, taken from the fronton of the temple of Delphi, acquire a different signification written under a skeleton from that which the old philosophers gave to them. This picture seemed to me the symbol of physiology. It is the office of physiology to penetrate beneath the exterior, to show how this fabric of our body is built, to analyse so minutely its functions that the most natural of their manifestations strike us with awe.

I have now come to the saddest pages of my book. More than all others does the mountain-climber need to know himself; these sorrowful pages are for his meditation. My friend's grief and mine in reviving mournful recollections finds consolation in the hope of thus saving some too intrepid traveller from a fatal catastrophe.

After the period of excitement more or less noticeable which I have described, depression follows. Indifference marks the beginning of this new state of the nervous system.

Tyndall[2] expresses with the greatest clearness this psychic condition, in relating his ascent of the Weisshorn. "At the commencement of a day's work one often feels anxious if not timid; but when the work is very hard we become callous, and sometimes stupefied by the incessant knocking about. This was my case at present, and I kept watch lest my indifference should become carelessness."

This indifference may even make us reckless of our lives. I remember once entreating the guides to leave me on the snow. The remonstrances and

[1] Ersilia Caetani-Lovatelli, "Thanatos," *Memoria dell'Accademia dei Lincei*, 1887. Vol. iii. p. 62.
[2] J. Tyndall, *Hours of Exercise in the Alps*, pp. 102-3.

threats of the colleagues who lifted me up seemed to me very cruel. I promised to go on if they would only leave me for a few minutes lying on the snow. At that moment death did not alarm me, on the contrary, I looked upon its approach as a relief. I have never forgotten that strange moment of my existence.

This profound indifference to one's own safety and that of others, is, I think, one of the most serious factors in mountain accidents. The deeds of heroism, the contempt of life which we often admire in soldiers engaged in fight, are much more the natural effect of fatigue than of bravery.

I convinced myself, by studying my comrades psychologically when we were roped together, that after great exertion even the most cautious showed less prudence. The guides in front do not sound the ground with the same care as in the morning. Although all know that there is more danger in descending, few show the same zeal as before in maintaining the tension of the rope.

Accidents do not always happen in the most difficult places, rather in those which are reached immediately after some great danger has been escaped. These casualties in places comparatively easy are due to the nervous exhaustion which the preceding peril has caused, and to the subsequent indifference which robs us of our prudence and our watchfulness.

In cycling, which has become a profession and a show, we see these phenomena of fatigue attain even a more alarming degree than in mountain-climbing. Indifference, apathy, is one of the first phenomena manifest in cyclists; a state resembling hypnosis then takes its place. In a recent work on a bicycle race Tissié says: "The psychic state of a racing cyclist has much resemblance to that of hypnotic sub-consciousness." It will not be difficult for any Alpine traveller to find traces of this phenomenon in recalling his mountaineering experiences. I had several times the opportunity of seeing my companions in a state of suggestion, as it were, when suffering from excessive fatigue.

This explains why, in spite of apathy, we continue to walk. Persons who have reached this stage do not stop, and often seemed to be awaked by a wave of cold wind, a dangerous or simply difficult passage.

Many will have read with wonder in journals that celebrated cyclists have been unable to walk on alighting from their bicycle, but that on remounting they proceeded with the same velocity as before. This fact alone suffices to show the profound modification which the nervous system undergoes through fatigue.

Let us consider for a moment this phenomenon of automatism which facilitates our motion in ascents by saving nervous energy. It has perhaps happened to some of my readers to sleep while walking. I remember having walked, as army-surgeon, several kilometres, asleep, with closed eyes, holding myself fast with the hand to an ambulance-cart. The longer we continue to perform a movement the easier does it become until at last it is accomplished quite independently of the will. After covering hundreds of kilometres on the bicycle the contraction of the muscles, having been so often repeated, is produced by a slight nervous stimulus. A very faint impulse transmitted from the brain to the centres of the spinal cord suffices to originate the movement. On the contrary, a stronger stimulus is necessary for the execution of other voluntary movements, when the nervous force is exhausted.

Automatism plays a much more important part in our organism than we think. The action of the brain must be depressed before we can discover that certain functions are performed unconsciously, when the power of the will is diminished or almost extinguished.

The mountain-climber must never forget that he may become an automaton from the effects of fatigue, when, no longer the brain, but a blind, unconscious power will impel him to walk onwards. Like Tyndall, he must fear that indifference which is no longer the offspring of courage, but the manifestation of a pathological fact due to nervous exhaustion which annuls the consciousness of danger.

VII.

In my book, *La Fatica*, I have already described the weakening of the memory during ascents, giving the instance of a colleague of mine, professor of botany, who, as he continued to ascend, gradually forgot the names of plants known to him, which, however, he recalled again in descending. The weakening of the memory is a constant phenomenon in the state of fatigue caused by an ascent. Saussure says that in descending from the Col du Géant he could no longer find the words to express his thoughts.

The diminution of sensibility in the hands is generally thought to be an effect of cold, and so, in great part, it is; but even though our hands were warm we should find on touching the points of a pair of compasses that the sensibility was diminished. I have experienced myself, and have been able to confirm Kraepelin's statement, that the sensibility is lessened not only by intellectual work but also by muscular contraction. This is a subject which invites further investigation, as also the study of the muscular sense in fatigue.

Kraepelin has made experiments in which he made his subjects add numbers together. Keller has made investigations with the ergograph; Griesbach has studied the sensibility with the compasses and found that the greater the mental strain the more enfeebled was the cutaneous sensibility.

There are times during an ascent when we are obliged to take off our gloves, because only with the fingers are we able to clutch the ledges of the rocks. In spite of the fact that cold diminishes the sensibility, if we have to detach an ice-crust with our fingers or thrust them into the snow to make sure of the resistance of the rock, they immediately give us pain. The nails break because the cold renders them more brittle. The force with which the nervous system acts on the muscles is so great that contracture is caused, the will no longer succeeding in relaxing the fingers which remain contracted after every exertion, unable to extend themselves with the required promptitude.

Fatigue also causes a change in the muscular sense. These are phenomena which till now have been little studied. The heavy gait characteristic of very tired persons, which I described in a chapter on marches in my book on physical education,[1] depends partly on the circumstance that we do not feel the ground so well. I have often paid attention to this and have noticed that the inequalities of the ground are no longer felt by the foot with the same distinctness. In the morning when one is fresh one judges instinctively in a moment of the resistance of the rock, of the firmness of one's foothold. In the evening, when we are tired, we are confronted by a new and sometimes fatal difficulty in the slipping and sliding of the feet, owing to their insensibility and to the blunting of the muscular sense.

The mechanism which enables us to stand upright and walk is one of the most complicated problems in physiology. I have already remarked that

[1] *Die körperliche Erziehung der Jugen*, 1894, S. 135.

many wheels of this machinery act independently of the will. Their independent action is so pronounced that the will cannot even modify the course of these movements. We may convince ourselves of this if we watch any one walking after cycling for even a comparatively short space of time only. The manner of moving the legs and of stepping is different from what it usually is, nor does he succeed, in spite of efforts, in recovering his normal gait. If, after an ascent, we could banish immediately every trace of fatigue from the muscles, we should notice that we no longer have our habitual gait. This modification is caused by cutaneous sensations, but more especially by sensations in the tendons and joints.

We designate as motor hyperæsthesia the performance by the joints of a movement out of proportion to the object. When the sensibility of the skin is diminished, the sensibility of movement decreases also, a proof that the sensation of movement is peripheric and not central. There is no innervation of central sensibility accompanying the motor impulse from the beginning. As soon as one's foot slips, the ability to preserve an upright position and escape the danger is diminished.

This obtuseness extends gradually to all the sensory nerves. Even the eye no longer distinguishes the form nor appreciates the distance of objects with the same nicety.

Parrot made this observation at the beginning of the century in his journey through the Caucasus, and Tyndall, in describing his ascent of the Matterhorn, makes similar remarks.

The acuteness of vision decreases, and also the sense of light. When the sun is going down, to any one who is very tired it seems darker sooner than to another who is unfatigued. This obtuseness of the sense of light, by limiting the peripheric field of vision, prevents the walker from seeing his feet as well as before, if he does not pay greater attention.

Sight is certainly altered after an ascent. I have myself experienced that white objects appear nearer, black ones more distant. The appreciation of the relief is less accurate. A field of snow, a white stone, a stratum of a lighter tint assume a prominence which is not real.

VIII.

Excessive fatigue may cause death.

From our childhood we have heard about the soldier who, after the battle of Marathon, ran at such speed to announce the victory to Miltiades that he dropped down dead before the gates of Athens. A similar case occurred not long ago in a race amongst tourists.

In the Alps the effects of exhaustion are more to be feared, because to them are added the rarefaction of the air and the inclemency of the weather. Compared to the tourist, the mountain-climber has this disadvantage that he cannot stop when and where he will, when he notices that his strength is beginning to fail him.

There are two difficulties which render the study of exhaustion in nervous persons uncertain. The first is that we do not know what amount of energy is at their disposal. They are like people who set off on a journey without knowing what funds they have in their purse, to make use of an imaginative simile. The second is the difficulty of estimating their expenditure of force during the expedition. It is not to be wondered at if even on short tours they meet with various mishaps.

Let us examine these facts, apparently contradictory, which often lead the hysterical, the nervous, the weak, and the fatigued, into fatal errors in their physiological reckoning.

Fatigue produces, as its first effect, an excitement which gives a misleading feeling of increased strength. The inebriated think themselves stronger when excited by alcohol, whereas they are weaker and less resistant to fatigue. Nervous persons may often be recognised from their passion for sports ; the physiologist maintains that in them the excitement of fatigue is more intense and more easily originated than in robust persons. When the physician hears some one say, "I need a great deal of movement to feel well," he does not immediately accept it as a good sign, but reflects first whether the sought-for sensation of well-being is within physiological limits. Unfortunately this is an obscure domain in medicine, because our machine only creaks and stops when it is wearing out.

The excitement produced by the scoriæ of fatigue prevent our knowing how much potential nervous force we still possess. The most serious circumstance is that in working we break into provisions of energy and consume them day by day, without knowing what quantity remains, nor how much rest restores to us. Those persons who are nearest bankruptcy are unfortunately those who most enjoy the nervous excitement produced by fatigue. They seek it eagerly, like the morphiomaniac who uses morphia, not as a narcotic, but as an excitant. If we recall our acquaintances we shall all remember certain persons, more especially of the nervous and hysterical class, who, although of slender build, boast that they have never known fatigue.

Tissié has recently studied fatigue in tired, weak persons.[1] He mentions that physician and patient are often misled by the physiological paradox explained above, on which account the patient is encouraged to physical exertion as a means of consuming his superabundant strength, whereas the ration of bodily exercise is already excessive, and repose should be prescribed. Féré[2] has shown that nervous fatigue and profound emotions render us more vulnerable to the effects of poison. Muscular fatigue is also a poisoning.

A strange and fearful condition is that of the weak. Their body resembles a commercial house in which the cashier, who is the nervous system, does not keep the head of the firm informed either of the funds in hand or of the continual losses which the house suffers. Affairs proceed without a balance being struck, the fatal waste increases the nearer the approach of bankruptcy.

IX.

As an instance of this fatal error in the appreciation of strength, I here relate the death of Raffaello and Alfonso Zoja, sons of the Professor of Anatomy in the University of Pavia, which took place last year at a height of 2,100 metres. Although young, Raffaello was already known as an eminent biologist, an enthusiastic investigator who, full of the new possibilities of science, had found out new paths for the research of truth. Alfonso, a youth of a gentle nature, lived apart from the world, studying at the laboratory of

---

[1] Ph. Tissié, *La Fatigue chez les débiles nerveux ou fatigués*. Revue scientifique, Novembre et Decembre, 1896.
[2] Féré, Société de Biologie, 25 Juillet, 1885, p. 497. *Influence des agents physiques et des chocs moraux sur l'intoxication*. Société de Biologie, 19 Oct., 1895.

Professor Golgi, absorbed in the contemplation of Nature, ambitious to revive in himself the fame of his grandfather, the celebrated anatomist, Panizza.

In relating the manner of their death which will always be recorded with horror in the annals of mountaineering, I feel all the grief of a friend who would fain pay a tribute to the memory of these two dear youths on whom the University of Pavia and science had set such great hopes.

Dr. Filippo De Filippi, a pupil of mine, and assistant in the surgical hospital of Bologna, who was their companion on that sad day, wrote me a letter which I quote as a token of our common grief.

"BOLOGNA, *December 3rd,* 1896.

"DEAR MASTER,—I have allowed some time to elapse since the accident which you ask me to analyse for your book, in the hope that the poignant moral suffering, experienced at the time, and afterwards at the sight of the anguish of the afflicted family, might become dulled. But even now, when I think of those hours, my emotion is such that it cannot but prove prejudicial to a just appreciation and rigorously critical analysis of the facts.

"I shall begin my narrative by a few preliminary remarks on the physical conditions and past life of the two young men furnished me by their brother, Dr. Luigi Zoja. The elder, Raffaello, was twenty-seven years of age, tall, thin, fair, with a rather emaciated, almost ascetic face, fine features, and a sweet, serene expression. His head was that of a student, his body not much developed although one could not say it was of weakly build. He did not suffer from cardiopathy in 1892–93: he had been troubled by a gastro-intestinal dyspepsia accompanied by nervous phenomena manifested in rapid cerebral exhaustion which rendered any prolonged mental work impossible. These phenomena disappeared when the digestive disturbances were rectified, and in 1894 his health was good. Nevertheless he suffered in this year from a gastro-intestinal poisoning of unexplained origin, which broke out in an acute form with vomiting and accompanied by alarming phenomena of syncope, lasted a few days, and was followed by a prompt recovery. In 1895 the three brothers had an attack of scarlatina in a mild form, and without renal complications. For years Raffaello had made Alpine excursions with his brothers, had repeatedly ascended to the height of 3,000 metres, once even as high as 3,600 metres, without experiencing any ill effects. Only during one ascent undertaken after having danced till 2 a.m., and without any night-rest at all, he was seized at a height of 2,400 metres with general physical adynamia with pronounced mental apathy. He was able, however, to accomplish the remainder of the ascent, and recovered at once on descending. His brother Luigi is of opinion that this was an attack of mountain-sickness. This year we ascended all together two peaks of the Valle Vigezzo, a few metres higher than the peak Gridone, without any one's suffering in the least. In no ascent had the Zojas experienced bad weather or snow-storms. I may add that Raffaello was particularly sensitive to cold.

"The younger brother, Alfonso, nineteen years old, of rather weakly build up till his seventeenth year, had developed rapidly since that time. He was a well-formed lad, lean but wiry in appearance, very active, with the general air of an athlete. He had never had any other illness than the scarlatina already mentioned. For two years he had accompanied his brothers on their Alpine tours, had reached the height of 2,800 metres without any physical disturbance resulting. In spite of his leanness, perhaps in consequence of his rapid development, he used to eat a great deal, a circumstance about which we often joked.

"On the evening of the 25th of September, everything being arranged for the expedition, Raffaello and Alfonso went to bed at 9.30 in order to rest for a few hours. For several days no ascents had been made, and on this day they had only taken an ordinary and not fatiguing walk. At midnight, after the usual breakfast, we started, the weather being beautiful. For four hours and a half we walked by the side of the torrent, almost on level ground, all in our usual cheerful humour, carrying our well-furnished knapsack in turn as we had always done. In an ascent, not toilsome, of an hour and a half we reached the last alp (1,200 metres high). It was 6 a.m., and we took our first snack: bread, eggs, cheese, with which we drank tea. We had no wine with us; the Zojas were total abstainers, and in the mountains I, too, prefer tea or coffee. After half an hour we went on our way. At 8 o'clock we were at the foot of the steep to which we had looked forward as the most enjoyable part of the expedition. I took the knapsack and from this moment I kept it, not because my companions seemed tired, but to relieve them of the feeling of unequal poise which it occasions during the climb, and to render the latter less difficult. The ascent was almost a delusion, certainly it was not more difficult than the others we had accomplished together that year, and we remarked that it was scarcely worth while coming so far for so little. The weather was still fine. A few clouds rested on the more distant chains, and a light, not unpleasant breeze blew from the north. Towards 11 o'clock a sudden gust of wind enveloped us in a transparent mist, and a fine hail began to fall at intervals. This was a freak of the wind which lasted for about fifteen minutes, after which the sun shone out again. We were already near the summit and paid no heed to this occurrence. A little before midday we were on the last crest of the Roccie di Gridone (about 2,100 metres in height). We might consider the ascent as accomplished, and we sat down comfortably to lunch, and to enjoy the panorama. We knew that we had only to climb three easy peaks little higher than the crest, in order to reach the path Bocchetta di Fornale and the lower alp-huts of Val Cannobina—a walk at the most of four hours' duration. We all three ate, but I cannot say whether the Zojas ate less than usual. Certainly they were in their customary good humour, nor had they seemed tired to me, not even during the last climb; I had not till then the faintest suspicion that they were in an abnormal condition. You know already that a sudden thunderstorm from the north overtook us as we sat, before we had time to notice that the weather was changing. In less than ten minutes we were enveloped in a dense cloud which obscured the view at the distance of a few metres, and the snow began to come down thickly in great flakes which rapidly whitened the rock, covering it in a quarter of an hour with almost a hand's depth of snow. The wind, which had become strong, drove the snow furiously before it. Such a storm was new to me at that height, and certainly, considering the situation, it was of exceptional violence. It did not occur to one of us to climb down again by the same steep rock which we had clambered up. I shouldered the knapsack and we went on. At once, at the first cautious steps taken, I noticed that my companions were walking feebly and uncertainly; I imagined it must be the effect of the wind which renders the passage of the crest awkward to any one unaccustomed to it, and counselled Raffaello who followed me first, to go on all fours if he did not feel sure of himself. At that time I took more notice of the rope than of them, so as not to let them slip. Before the lapse of half an hour even, Raffaello asked me to stop a while because the wind was taking away his breath. I then noticed that both were unwell, and that their laboured gait did not arise merely from a mental depression caused by the storm. They were pale, their teeth were chattering, they complained of nausea and of slight headache, were apathetic, irresponsive alike to my jokes and entreaties, their gait and movements were weak, without energy; they said they were not frightened but tired, if I let them rest a little, they would be able to walk better afterwards. Then began a long struggle, I endeavouring by every means in my power to draw them onwards and prevent them from stopping every moment; the forward march became a torment to all three. The walls which fell away at right and left were steep, we had to walk in single file as I had to watch my companions' every step. We only went on abreast at those parts in which I could walk on the one side of the mountain, they on the other, the rope passing over the crest.

"At 4 p.m. I had lost all hope of reaching the col before night-time. The weather continued bad, we had covered little more than a third of the crest, and although I did not foresee the catastrophe which hung over us, I knew that my companions, ill, in a state of physical and mental inertia, were in the worst of conditions for spending a night in the snow. I then decided to attempt a direct descent through a gully in the Val Cannobina wall. We sank up to our knees in the snow and descended slowly, the Zojas first, I after, holding them up by the rope, because they were sliding downwards rather than helping themselves with hands and feet as the place required one to do. In half an hour when we were 60 or 70 metres below the crest, a vertical descent of rock stopped us. I unroped, and for a quarter of an hour I sought a passage through the gully and on its lateral walls, but in vain; not even the foolhardy could have found a means of descent, and we had to return to the crest. The gully was steep, and if my companions walked with difficulty now, what was to be expected after the night which was awaiting us? Yielding to my prayers they tried to eat something, but nausea made them spit out the half-chewed morsels; they sipped a little tea and then very unwillingly recommenced the climb. It lasted little more than an hour, but under the circumstances it seemed eternal. It was already night (6 p.m.) when we reached the crest at a point about 2,100 metres high. In a few minutes I found a level of rock a few square metres in area, a little below the crest, sheltered from the wind but not from the snow, and there we halted. One could read in their eyes the satisfaction of the Zojas at not having to walk any more.

"I began to feel very anxious about Raffaello. He sat motionless, with open, fixed eyes. He did not tremble, nor did his teeth chatter, as was the case with Alfonso and with me, he did not speak unless questioned; he said he felt well now, and *did not feel the cold any more*. He breathed regularly, his pulse was rather rapid, rather low, rhythmic, and moderately compressible. Alfonso appeared tired, apathetic, too, but he was evidently not in the exhausted condition of his brother. They drank the little tea we had left. Our matches had become damp in our pockets so that we could not light the lantern, nor make use of our coffee-machine. Again I tried, but in vain, to make them eat something. Almost immediately we began to massage Raffaello, Alfonso the joints, and I the trunk, forcing him to speak, so that he might not fall asleep. It continued to snow with the same violence, every now and then Alfonso and I shook the flakes from our shoulders. The temperature must have been 1–2 degrees above zero. Raffaello was gradually growing worse, I became aware of it from his tardy answers, from the necessity of repeating more than once the same question; his pulse was becoming more rapid. At a certain moment, after I had asked him something several times in a loud voice, he looked at me with wide-open eyes, and said softly—'*I do not understand.*' I then began massaging him with snow again, applying energetic friction to chest and back. Every now and then Alfonso and I paused, worn out. I took little notice of Alfonso, his teeth were still chattering from the cold, and he spoke little; he appeared perfectly conscious but did not perceive the gravity of his brother's condition. At midnight the storm subsided with the same rapidity with which it had risen, and in a few minutes we saw a starry sky and a splendid moon. It immediately began to freeze, and the temperature must I think have been rather low from the rapidity with which icicles formed on the rock. There were perhaps 6–7 degrees of cold, but it is difficult to form a correct idea when one is drenched, tired, and in the midst of frozen snow. After a while Alfonso noticed that his brother no longer gave any reply to our questions, I told him that Raffaello was falling asleep, and that he must continue to massage vigorously. This was now of little use at the joints, but it was a means of keeping Alfonso awake, and enabled him to withstand the cold. Raffaello was, I think, at this time completely unconscious; his pulse was filiform, rapid, his breathing still regular; there was no convulsive movement; when the arm was raised it dropped again as in flaccid paralysis, there was no reaction on external stimuli, the gaze was fixed, almost glassy. He began to say a few words without sense, articulated with difficulty in a quiet delirium which lasted only a short time. Towards one o'clock the breathing seemed to grow slower and less regular. We then laid him on his back (till now he had been in a sitting posture, leaning against the rock in order to be better sheltered from the snow), and began to induce artificial respiration, still continuing the friction of the thorax. Alfonso was silent and I did not dare to look him in the face—but he did not understand as yet. . . . Another hour passed thus. Suddenly I felt the skin of the patient become covered with perspiration and almost immediately I noticed the complete relaxation of death; the heart had first ceased to beat, I still felt afterwards the thorax rise and fall in active inspiration. It was about 2 a.m.

"Alfonso had not noticed anything, and made a few more movements for artificial respiration. Then he felt his brother's arms stiffen in his hands, and letting them fall he asked suddenly, in a frightened tone: '*Is he dead?*' I bowed my head, and he began to weep silently without sobbing, repeating every now and then: '*Poor Jello!*' With difficulty I replaced the already stiffened body against the rock, sheltered in part by a little opening, and then endeavoured to subdue my own awful anguish, and take thought for the survivor. His immobility had made him feel the cold acutely at once, he nestled close up to me and I beat and massaged his body. I could not persuade him to make any active movement. His consciousness was not continuous nor complete. At intervals he repeated his brother's name weeping, without, however, that violent grief which he would have exhibited under normal conditions. He cried almost like a child, in a resigned way; it was more distress than despair. Then the cold began to trouble him again, he trembled and cowered close to me telling me to continue the friction. The moon shed a brilliant light all around, there were more than three hours before dawn; I thought it would be well to escape the agonising sight of the corpse, and to warm ourselves by walking on again, however slowly, but it was impossible to make Alfonso stand up. When he tried to rise, supported by me, his legs gave way under him as though paralysed. I had to resign myself to the long inactive waiting. I was not very anxious; I saw that he was very tired, with the moral inertia of mountain-sickness on him, half-stupefied by our awful misfortune, benumbed with cold, but I hoped that within a few hours day and the tepid warmth of the sun would enable him to move on; we should then little by little reach the path which would be our salvation. At 6 o'clock it began to dawn, but Alfonso was still in the same condition. As a last attempt I then swept the snow from a part of the rock as well as I could, made him lie down and told him to try to sleep a little. With the dawn the cold had increased, so I stretched myself upon him, attentively watching him. He fell almost at once into a normal sleep, not lethargic but fairly deep, in spite of the uncomfortable position and the hindrance which my weight opposed to his breathing. He slept nearly an hour and awoke of himself towards 7 o'clock, when it was fully daylight. I persuaded him to eat two eggs, and at 7.30 he was able to stand, and we set off. He walked like a drunken man, slipping at every step. I myself was not very steady on my feet, but with the movement I soon regained elasticity and certainty. But Alfonso appeared still exhausted, and I did not notice that the mild temperature produced any amelioration of his condition. Every few minutes I had to allow a halt, and these pauses continued to grow longer, so that in two hours we had only got over the same ground as one would cover usually in a quarter of an hour or little more. We were scarcely 20 metres below the last peak which rose between us and the col, Alfonso had been sitting down for a few minutes and resisted all my entreaties to make a last effort. His teeth were chattering again; for a while he replied to my prayers by telling me to let him rest a little longer, then he spoke no more although he understood what I said to him. He felt tired, that was all. I sat down near him and talked to him of his brother, trying to shake him out of his inertia. He said to me then: 'When we come to Finero (a market-town in Val Cannobina), we will telegraph to Gigi and I shall wait and go home with him'—a sentence which shows better than any description his complete unconsciousness of his own state. I was anxious, the tardiness in replying was beginning, a serious physical languor was apparent, I saw that he was so exhausted that I asked myself if he could possibly hold out for two hours longer. I began again to beg him to move on, but soon I noticed with anguish that he could not. Only one resource remained: to let him slide down by a narrow rocky path covered with snow, which fell very steeply downwards at two paces from us. Alfonso was still conscious, so I persuaded him to drag himself to this spot, I helping him. I then began to let him slide downwards, seated on the snow, telling him to steer himself as well as he could with his arms. When the rope had run out (we were tied together at about five metres' distance) I sat down likewise on the snow in the narrow path, and began to let myself slide. Alfonso hung with his whole weight at my waist, for I had fastened the rope round my body, needing, as I did, both hands to keep up myself and him, by grasping the rocky prominences of the side walls which, fortunately, were solid and abundant. In this way we descended cautiously 50 metres; suddenly, at a moment when I was sliding down sideways, I felt the tension of the rope slacken, and turning, I saw Alfonso on hands and knees, almost lying down, burrowing with his hands in the snow. I called to him without result; I unroped, fastened the end of the rope to a jutting rock, and hurried down to him. He was unconscious, his breathing was slow, his pulse small and rapid. It must have been about 10 a.m. I rubbed him with snow, half stupefied by the fatality which pursued us. After about an hour he died quietly, without a struggle, with a progressive slackening of the breath, while the pulse became gradually weaker and more rapid. I felt exhausted and climbed up almost at once to the crest whence in half an hour I reached the path."

X.

So long as there is a physiology of fatigue, these pages of Dr. De Filippi will be remembered. Amongst accounts written by mountain-climbers, few equal this one in the sagacity and presence of mind to which the accurate and faithful observation of facts bears witness.

The process which terminates in sudden death is perhaps one of the least known in the science of disease; many difficulties stand in the way of its investigation, for which reason, too, the above faithful account will be of interest to the pathologist.

Sudden death is often, as in the case related above, caused by paralysis of the heart. We all know that the heart beats more violently and frequently when we undergo some deep emotion. In the depression of a great misfortune some feel an oppression as though their breath were taken away. The sigh is a profound inspiration which we execute when in sorrow in order to compensate for inadequate breathing. When we place animals under the pneumatic bell and rarefy the air they become sleepy, drawing from time to time deeper breaths. I have already remarked that during my sojourn in the Regina Margherita Hut I noticed some persons and a dog breathing deeply the whole day.

There are women who often faint merely on hearing of an accident, at the sight of one or at an unexpected noise. It is probable that in these cases the heart is paralysed owing to a defect of central innervation, arising from the rapid exhaustion which the emotion has caused in the nerve-centres.

A lamented death in my own family gave me, a few years ago, the occasion to experience personally the weakening action of emotion on the heart. In ascending the stairs of my house, I felt myself for the first time obliged to slacken my pace and to stop because my breath was gone. The pulse had quickened and I felt my heart palpitating. This was a phenomenon such as is often noticeable in mountain-sickness. The heart, owing to central exhaustion arising from emotion or fatigue, no longer contracts completely but remains somewhat dilated; the circulation in the lungs proceeds more languidly and the gaseous interchange in these organs becomes insufficient. This is the first cause of laboured breathing; the heart beats more frequently in order to make up for its incomplete contractions. When the defect of innervation becomes more serious, a paralysis of the heart ensues and is always followed by immediate death. This explains why old or weak persons sometimes succumb in consequence of a psychic emotion.

Profound emotions and the effects of fatigue are more to be feared if the outside temperature is low and become fatal when, owing to the depression of the functions of brain and spinal cord, those centres which regulate the temperature of the body and the tonicity of the blood-vessels are paralysed.

The drunken are much more liable to death from cold than other persons. The death of those who have succeeded in killing themselves with alcohol or absinthe must be explained in this way, because alcoholic liquids alone would not cause death. The paralysed vessels dilate and the blood cools, no longer finding in a state of activity within the organism that automatic machinery which otherwise reinvigorates the vital processes and reinforces the combustion in the tissues at the first lowering of the temperature of the blood. Little by little the heat of the individual is lost, consciousness is extinguished, the heart ceases to beat, the breathing stops and death ensues.

In the last part of his letter Dr. De Filippi expressed his opinion as to the cause of death of the brothers Zoja, an opinion in which I fully concur. "Perhaps the predominant factor was a progressive weakening of the heart and a vaso-motor paralysis. Certainly it was a form which one cannot satisfactorily enter under any of the heads of classified diseases. It is also possible that there was an actual intoxication with fatigue poisons, which may be a factor in all deaths from exhaustion after great muscular overstrain. Perhaps individuals in whom the metabolic processes are slow, organisms with incomplete combustion and tardy elimination of residuary products may be specially predisposed to this form of poisoning, more particularly if the cold still further dulls the activity of the organic chemistry. Raffaello's antecedents show that his nervous system was exceedingly susceptible to toxic infections; Alfonso, on the contrary, was apparently in normal physiological condition. It is possible that the emotion excited by the death of his brother was too violent for his wearied organism, tormented for hours by mountain-sickness, exposed for a long time to an unusual loss of heat, for, during about twenty hours he had scarcely tasted food. Certainly all these factors were implicated. Our ignorance as to the modifications of the metabolic processes during mountain-sickness prevents our saying whether that malady favours the accumulation of fatigue-poison in the organism, and we are obliged to grope about on the uncertain ground of hypothesis."

Gressoney St. Jean.

CHAPTER VII

ASCENTS—OUR CAMPS—GNIFETTI AND REGINA MARGHERITA HUTS

I.

THE establishment of the rules to observe during an ascent and the acquirement of the technical knowledge necessary to overcome difficulties and avoid dangers, are the results of long and successful Alpine experience. The name of Güssfeldt[1] alone recalls a whole class of distinguished Alpine writers.

But this is not the subject of which I wish at present to treat. After having rapidly reviewed the more serious changes taking place in man on the Alps from the effects of fatigue and rarefied air, I now propose an analytical study of ascents.

I have already mentioned that during an ascent we are not always the same, and that the organism responds to stimuli in various ways according to the stage of fatigue at which we have arrived. My intention was to keep those phenomena observable during the first part of an ascent distinct from those due to fatigue which manifest themselves later and which are more serious, almost morbid.

[1] P. Güssfeldt, *Das Wandern im Hochgebirge.* Anhang 299. In den Hochalpen.

Near the inn of Gressoney la Trinitá, to the left of the Lys, I selected a stretch of ground rising from the flat meadow near the waterfall up the side of the valley and intersecting the pathway of the Netscio. Assisted by the engineer Bellini I measured off a height of 100 metres at a point where the gradient of the meadow was 50 in 100. The first part of the slope was, however, somewhat steeper. Here I made a series of experiments on many persons whom I caused to ascend the slope at an ordinary pace, at a rapid pace, or, finally, running.

The following is an example of one of these experiments performed on myself in August, 1895. Temperature of the air 13°:—

Time.	Pulse.	Breathing.	Rectal temperature.	Observations.
9.40 a.m.	60	15	37·2	
9.42 ,,				I start from the foot of the slope and take 6 min. 55 sec. to reach a height of 100 met.
9.53 ,,	114	30	37·7	
9.55 ,,	88			
9.56 ,,	84	21	37·8	
9.58 ,,	84	20		
10.3 ,,	84		37·8	Repeated coughing.
10.5 ,,	—	17	37·7	
10.7 ,,	79	17		
10.12 ,,	80	16		
10.15 ,,	—	16	37.6	
10.20 ,,	74	15	37·55	
10.25 ,,	73	15		
10.40 ,,	63		37.2	
10.45 ,,	60			

These figures show the increase in the frequency of pulse and breathing, and the rise of the internal temperature consequent on the raising of my body, 74 kilograms in weight, to a height of 100 metres, my age being forty-nine years. The pulse, after having attained 114 beats in the minute, began to diminish; while the temperature remained high, increased slightly during repose, and regained the normal a little before the pulse.

The thermometer which I made use of was a Baudin maximum thermometer with a very small bulb, which attained the temperature of the body in less than two minutes. I read the indication for the first time at 9.53 a.m. after more than four minutes', the second time after three minutes' application.

The breathing first regained its normal frequency, slackening in a more rapid proportion than the pulse, whereas the temperature only began to decrease much later. We may therefore say that of the three phenomena here studied the respiratory activity first diminishes, then that of the pulse, and finally the internal temperature. I had to remain for one hour lying on the grass before every trace of this little ascent had disappeared from the organism.

I have noted an attack of coughing. This, as I think, indicates an accumulation of blood in the lungs. I cannot assert this positively, but I know of no other explanation for the cough so often observable in ascents, especially in weak persons or in those who are beginning their training, as I was in this case.

II.

To ascend 100 metres in three minutes and a half is said to be the maximum rate. In order to ascertain the strength of certain mountain-climbers I instituted up-hill races. The engineer Bellini, with whom I had exactly measured the ground to be gone over, stood below, I at the goal at the top; the former counted before the start the pulse and breathing of each runner, to whom he gave a paper on which he had written the resultant figures, giving me a sign with the hand at the moment the race began.

Sig. Mario Borsalino, student, 18 years of age and weighing 58 kilograms, ran 100 metres uphill, the gradient being 50 in 100, in 4 min. 33 sec. The table given as foot-note [1] shows the data resulting from this observation.

We made eight experiments in order to ascertain the velocity of ascent. Those in which the speed was greatest are here given.[2]

[1] *Mario Borsalino.* 18 years of age. Weight, 58 kilograms.

Time.	Pulse.	Breathing.
3.20 p.m.	76	21
3.34 ,,	66	
	70	
	68	
Starts at 4.0 ,,	70	19

Arrives in 4 min. 33 sec. For about a minute I was unable to count the pulse as it was too weak and filiform.

4.6 ,, I count for only 30 sec.	150	31
	140	27
4.8 ,,	120	26
4.11 ,,	120	24
4.23 ,,	108	
	106	22
Coughs several times.		
4.43 ,,	90	18
4.45 ,,	94	18

The breathing has therefore recovered a rate below the normal before the pulse.

5.5 ,,	93	17
5.20 ,,	87	17
5.40 ,,	80	16
5.43 ,,	72	17

After one hour and forty minutes the heart had still not recovered its normal rate.

[2] *Julius Lochmatter.* 28 years of age. Weight, 75 kilograms. Guide.

Time.	Pulse.	Breathing.
3.18 p.m.	71	13
3.20 ,,	82	15
3.30 ,,	88	

Noticing that the pulse was so rapid we told the subject to sit down and rest.

Starts at 4.13 ,,	98	20

Arrives in 3 min. 45 sec. For about two minutes the pulse is too weak and filiform to be counted. Breathing 38.

4.18 ,,	140	33
4.20 ,,	132	28
4.22 ,,	130	26
Coughs a little.		
4.25 ,,	124	26
4.27 ,,	120	20

The breathing becomes normal before the pulse.

5.2 ,,	106	20
5.12 ,,	104	19
5.20 ,,	102	17
5.35 ,,	96	18

After an hour and a half both the breathing and the beating of the heart become less rapid than before the start.

The guide, Lochmatter, performed this ascent of 100 metres in 3 min. 45 sec. He told me that this was the maximum rate and that it would be impossible to cover double the distance at the same speed.

During the first two minutes the pulse seemed to me to beat nearly 160 times in the minute. When I laid my hand on his chest I felt a strong palpitation, but even here I could not count the pulsations well. It is probable that in such cases the heart does not quite empty itself, thus resembling the piston of a pump which does not run its course when the work to be accomplished becomes heavier.

In the experiment made on the guide Lochmatter we see how the beating of the pulse may be accelerated merely in consequence of an emotion. After lunch, at 2 p.m., its rate was 73; when we went into the meadow near the slope and the others began to race, the pulse rose to 82. In spite of repose it was not possible to effect a diminution of the cardiac pulsations, they increased, on the contrary, from 88 to 98. His pulse betrayed his emotion and his desire to beat the other guides whose data I have omitted for the sake of brevity.

After dinner, at 8.30 p.m., when the pulse should have beaten at a greater rate, I counted only 74 pulsations in the minute.

While engaged on these experiments I came across a young mountaineer, a very strong porter, thirty-three years of age, who had an irregular pulse; after this ascent of 100 metres performed in six minutes this irregularity disappeared.

That the pulse in such cases becomes regular after exertion was a fact known to Christ and to others who have occupied themselves with studies of this kind. During fever also, those irregularities of the pulse which some people have and which are not in themselves a symptom of disease, often disappear. Smokers often exhibit these irregularities of the pulse which cease when they give up smoking.

III.

It does not suffice, in order to determine the respiratory activity during ascents, to count the number of inspirations per minute, one must, further, measure the quantity of air which we introduce into the lungs.

In order to ascertain the respiratory increase for an ascent of 100 metres I placed one gas-meter at the foot of the slope and another at the goal. The person on whom the experiment was to be made adjusted the mask on his face, lay down on the ground and breathed through the valves and meter, then performed the ascent at an ordinary pace, again put on the mask when he had reached the goal and breathed into the second gas-meter, lying down on the ground as before.

In a foregoing chapter I have already explained the disposition of the valves for the measurement of the air we breathe. As an illustration of the augmentation which the breathing undergoes even when one ascends slowly, I communicate an experiment which I made on a porter of Gressoney, thirty years of age. I first determined how many litres of air he introduced into his lungs while in the meadow below, after he had lain on the ground for five minutes with the mask, in communication with the meter, on his face. The following are the numbers of litres breathed which I read every two minutes on the meter:—

$$7\cdot9300 - 8\cdot4185 - 8\cdot0352 - 7\cdot8400 - 8\cdot1250.$$

He then rose and, holding the gutta-percha mask to his face, slowly ascended the mountain side. In seven minutes he raised the weight of his body, amounting to 67 kilograms, to a height of 100 metres; immediately on reaching the goal he lay down, and I at once began to note the quantity of air inspired every two minutes, obtaining the following values:—

14·6400 — 11·9064 — 10·9800 — 9·9308 — 9·0280 — 8·1300.

From this experiment we see that the respiration became twice as deep in consequence of the ascent of 100 metres in seven minutes. A greater speed in the ascent may, as I have observed, quadruple the volume of air inhaled. In the last case, I must add that the action of the valves of the apparatus was not perfect, the breathing being too rapid and deep.

IV.

That it is not lack of breath which causes us to halt during an ascent is shown by the fact that some, as, for instance, Lortet, recommend walking with the head down in order to diminish the opening of the respiratory passages.

"Those who know how to walk on high mountains keep their head down in order to diminish the opening of the respiratory passages, and breathe only through the nostrils, the mouth being kept shut, while they take care to suck some small unyielding body, such as a nut or a stone, which augments the salivary secretion."[1]

Recently I had the pleasure of making the acquaintance of the celebrated mountain-climber, M. Charles Durier, president of the French Alpine Club. I remembered having read, in his story of Mont Blanc, a sentence which had made an impression on me. In speaking of the advantages which certain little indulgences may procure us on the summit of Mont Blanc, Durier wrote: "If one is a smoker, one has a little stove at which to warm one's fingers."[2] This sentence alone convinced me that in M. Durier the respiration must undergo little alteration, but it was the first time that I had heard the pipe praised as a means of warming one's fingers on the summit of Mont Blanc. I begged M. Durier to give me some information as to his mode of breathing, upon which he kindly wrote the following in my note-book:

"A little below the summit of Mont Blanc, not feeling any shortness of breath, I halted, filled my pipe and lit it in order to see whether I should suffer from oppression. I was not troubled in the least and arrived at the top with my pipe alight (1869, at the age of 39). Since then I have never reached any summit without my pipe in my mouth and have never felt the slightest discomfort. Judging by my personal experience, I should even say that it renders the breathing regular and prevents shortness of breath."

If mountain-climbers were to be divided into two classes, the one resembling M. Durier, the other composed of those who, on great ascents, stretch their necks and protrude the tongue, I confess that I should belong to the last category; I should find myself, however, in good company, nevertheless.

Whymper says that on Chimborazo he had fever and headache, and breathed hurriedly with his mouth open.

[1] Lortet, *Perturbations de la respiration, de la circulation et surtout de la calorification à de grandes hauteurs sur le Mont Blanc.* Comptes rendus, tome 69, 1869, p. 708.
[2] Charles Durier, *Le Mont Blanc.* Paris, 1877, p. 236.

I do not consider it of use to give rules for the mode of breathing; each one ought to breathe as he feels inclined. In no other sort of exercise should unconsciousness and automatism have greater weight. In a recent writing on training, Tissié says: "Very few persons know how to breathe. In out-of-door exercise the inspiration should be by the nose, the expiration by the mouth."[1] I willingly recognise Tissié's great competency respecting the study of fatigue, but I do not share his ideas as to the mode of breathing. The reason of this difference I shall show further on in speaking of the influence which the wind exercises on the respiration.

V.

On the march the soldiers halt ten minutes for every hour of walking. Alpinists would do well to adopt this rule on their marches in the mountains.

I have not made special observations on this subject, already touched upon in my book on fatigue. It is a difficult study which cannot be pursued satisfactorily on the Alps. I here mention the sole fact that the work of the muscles is subjected to the same laws as that of thought.

While writing this book I have several times had the experience, that if I remain at my desk for an hour, or an hour and a half, and then make a pause of fifteen or twenty minutes, during which I rest or walk about, I can perform satisfactory work of eight or nine hours per day for several weeks in succession. If I, inadvertently, let myself be carried away by working zeal from 7 to 11.30 a.m. without resting, I feel less well in the afternoon and often have a headache.

When I am merely copying, I do not notice whether the pauses are long or short, and take up my work again with equal facility. But if I am busy with some chapter which requires more concentrated attention, and rest for half an hour, this prolonged pause hinders the continuation of the work. I notice, in taking up my pen again, that the train of thought is interrupted. I believe that all, more or less, feel the same difference also during the exertion of an ascent.

The fatigue of the legs is likewise a nervous phenomenon, and I have already shown the close connection between work of the brain and of the muscles on an ascent.

In order to understand the phenomena consequent on fatigue we must remember that all intense work of the brain or of the muscles profoundly modifies the state of these organs. These changes, which till now it has not been possible to study in the brain, may be observed in the muscles, and every one may convince himself of the material alterations taking place in these after unusual exertion, by observing, for instance, the flexor muscles of the arm after they have been vigorously exercised. If, for example, we take a dumb-bell weighing 5 kilograms and execute a series of 25 contractions with the arm in one minute, we see, after the work is finished, that the biceps muscle has become thicker. At first, while resting, we feel no discomfort, but after a few hours, even a slight pressure on the muscles produces a painful sensation. A stiffness of the muscle becomes manifest, the arm remains bent, and we cannot extend it without feeling great pain. After four or five days every trace of stiffness has disappeared, and the movements of the biceps become untrammelled once more.

At Gressoney and at Indra Camp I made some observations on the changes

[1] Tissié, *L'entraînement physique.* Revue scientifique, 1896, W. 17.

in the tonicity of the muscles during ascents. For this purpose I made use of an instrument to which I have given the name of myotonometer. With the aid of this apparatus I saw that the muscles forming the calf of the leg are more easily lengthened by an equal weight when we are tired than when we are fresh. An ascent of three or four hours' duration is sufficient to modify the tonicity of the muscles. We do not become aware of this until the exhaustion of strength is great, but the fact that we drag our feet when we are very tired is in part due to the above inconvenient circumstance. The nervous system acts on muscles which yield more easily to the stretching influence of the weight of the body. Their contraction is slower and less efficacious. I pass on, however, as a further explanation of this subject would necessitate too lengthy a digression.

The apparatus which I made use of on the Monte Rosa expedition was in the primitive form in which I exhibited it at the tenth International Congress of Medicine in Berlin, in 1890.[1] I improved it afterwards,[2] when it was also made use of by Dr. Benedicenti in his investigation of fatigue.[3]

It is known to all that the legs become stiff if we make too long a halt during a march. Lagrange attributes this stiffness to a flagging of the circulation, and says that when the muscle ceases to contract the muscular fibre is no longer adequately washed by the blood.[4]

In the tired muscle the circulation of blood and lymph becomes altered, and this may tend to the production of a less perfect physiological condition of the muscle, but I maintain that it is other causes which give rise to the annoying sensation which we have all experienced after a long walk, when we have rested for a time and then wish to contract our muscles again.

In the position of repose the heel of the foot is on a higher plane than the toes. We shall notice this if we observe a person sitting on a table with the legs hanging down. When we put the foot to the ground in order to walk and compress the sole with the weight of the body, heel and toes are held on the same horizontal plane, and the muscles in the posterior part of the leg are stretched. On measuring the force necessary to make the sole of the foot form a right angle with the vertical line of the body I found that a weight of 11 kilograms must be applied to the tendon of Achilles. This weight, which we must imagine as stretching the muscle whenever the weight of the body is thrown on to one leg, produces the annoying tension which we feel in the so-called stiffness of the legs. We have in the muscles sensory nerves which in consequence of fatigue and of the circulatory changes thence resulting, become more susceptible to irritation. The pains of muscular rheumatism arise from the irritation of these nerves when we stretch the muscles of the calf in putting the foot to the ground.

The tired muscle becomes in repose œdematous. Many persons on rising in the morning have a feeling of fullness in their hands, or their eyelids are slightly swollen. A similar phenomenon is, in all probability, originated in the muscle after intense work, because the dilated blood-vessels allow the lymph to ooze out in greater abundance.

It must first be demonstrated, however, that the muscles are œdematous.

---

[1] A. Mosso, *Verhandlungen des X. internationalen medicinischen Congresses.* Berlin, 1890, Bd. ii. Abth. ii. p. 10.
[2] A. Mosso, *Description d'un myotonomètre pour étudier la tonicité des muscles chez l'homme.* Archives italiennes de Biologie, tome xxv. p. 349.
[3] A. Benedicenti, *La tonicité des muscles étudiée chez l'homme.* Ibidem, p. 385.
[4] F. Lagrange, *Physiologie des exercises du corps.* 1888, p. 103.

The following experiment will show why I consider this hypothesis very probable.

The soldier Chamois left Gressoney St. Jean early in the morning and reached Indra Camp after four hours' march. As soon as he arrived I made him sit down on a table with his legs hanging down. I let the right leg hang down naturally, while under the left I placed the stirrup of the myotonometer, which kept the point of the foot raised about as high as it can be lifted by means of a voluntary movement.

After the left foot had been in this position for forty minutes I took away the myotonometer, but the point did not immediately return to its natural position, it remained for more than ten minutes higher than the point of the right foot. This proves that the elasticity of the muscles was altered and that, after exertion, the muscle assumes a pasty consistency which it has not when in repose.

On walking, after the removal of the instrument, the subject said that there was a greater stiffness in the right leg, that is in the leg left in repose. This, I imagine, was due to the circumstance that the traction must have been stronger in this muscle, which became œdematous and swollen with the foot in a different position from that which it assumes when we throw our weight upon it in walking. The sensory nerves of this muscle suffered a painful irritation, because the deformation which the muscle had to undergo, when the foot resumed the horizontal position, was greater.

Œdema alone is not, however, a sufficient explanation of these phenomena. The sensitiveness of the nerves in the muscles increases after exertion, a fact which is much more apparent in persons weakened by illness who begin to make use of their muscles again after long repose, than in robust individuals.

I here communicate an observation made on himself by Professor Forlanini, director of the hospital at the University of Turin.

"In 1881 I had a pleurisy with an effusion at the left side. Two incisions were therefore made, one ten days after the other, four and a half litres of liquid being extracted. The fever lasted for a long time after the evacuation, and convalescence was also long.

"I went into the mountains at the beginning of July and suffered from fever for several days again. At the end of July I accomplished an ascent: starting from a height of 1,200 metres I reached an altitude of 3,000 metres. It was an exceedingly fatiguing expedition for me, especially at first, when I was often obliged to sit and even to lie down, as I could not stand upright, and was also seriously troubled with dyspnœa and palpitation of the heart. Beyond the altitude of 2,000 metres these disturbances diminished considerably. I walked on thus from six in the morning till eight in the evening, with two halts for lunch and dinner.

"I was very tired on my return. I ordered a bath, and while it was being prepared I stretched myself on my bed and waited. Ten minutes later when the bath was ready I could not rise. I had a feeling as though the muscles of the lower extremities were in a state of pasty stiffness, and even the muscles of the trunk and arms were stiff. Every muscular movement, stretching, even the gentle pressure of a muscle caused me great pain. Two persons had to assist me to undress, a process which took a great deal of time and caused me much suffering. I fell asleep at once and passed a quiet night. In the morning all these phenomena had vanished, leaving only a stiffness such as one is accustomed to after a long walk in the mountains."

Camp near Linty Hut (alt., 3,047 metres).

Carefully performed massage after a march prevents the appearance of those pains in the muscles which the French call *courbature*.

This proves that the stiffness is a peripheric phenomenon: to cure it, it suffices to squeeze well the muscles and promote an abundant circulation of blood and lymph by means of passive movement. For further particulars I refer the reader to two studies by Dr. Maggiora on the physiological action of massage.[1]

VI.

The matter of which I have to treat is so complex that I have renounced the hope of being able to follow a methodical mode of procedure. Nor would it be possible to select a function and to study it without considering its relations with other functions of the organism. As the surroundings in the Alps exercise a great influence on the organism, I shall give a brief description of the places at which we halted on the slopes of Monte Rosa.

The first series of observations in Turin had lasted about a month. On July 18, 1894, we pitched our laboratory-tent at Gressoney la Trinità on the banks of the Lys, in a meadow, at an altitude of 1,627 metres, at a short distance from Thedy inn, and began the second series. In a few days we had arranged everything. We studied the quantity of air inhaled, the form of respiration, the amount of carbonic acid eliminated, the pressure of the blood, the force of the muscles, &c. In the morning before the soldiers rose, temperature, rate of breathing and of the pulse were ascertained in all.

A week later, on the 25th of July, we packed our baggage on to five mules and moved our camp to Indra, leaving at Thedy inn provisions and various things which we had fetched later, as need arose.

The Indra encampment was at a height of about 2,515 metres, at a little distance from the ruins of a mill which was once made use of for gold-mining purposes. The temperature, especially at night-time, sank very low, so that in the morning the water in the pails was covered with a crust of ice two or three centimetres thick, and the meadows were bedecked with hoar frost.

At Gressoney, in order to protect one of our thermometers from the sun and measure the temperature of the air, we had had a perforated box constructed, the inside of which was blackened and which was fixed on to a pole a metre and a half high. During the whole of our sojourn on Monte Rosa we continued these observations with regularity. The most important of them are given at the end of the book. Here I need only mention that the maximum temperature which we observed at Indra was 14° at 3 p.m. on July 27th.[2]

A characteristic of the Alpine climate already noted by meteorologists is the rapid rise of the temperature in the morning.

Within one hour the temperature may rise 10 degrees. The earth cools greatly during the night, because the air is drier and less dense. In the morning the bottom of the valley remains in the shade while the sun is already far above the horizon; the direction of the rays being more vertical in the morning the earth and surrounding air become rapidly warmed. These differences disappear in proportion as one rises above the valleys; on

---

[1] A. Maggiora, *De l'action physiologique du massage sur les muscles de l'homme*. Archives italiennes de Biologie, tome xvi. p. 225.—*Influence du massage sur la contraction musculaire*. Ibidem, tome xiii. p. 231.

[2] J. Vallot, *Annales de l'Observatoire météorologique du Mont Blanc*. Paris, 1893, p. 20.

Parrot Peak (alt., 4,463 metres).

the summit of Monte Rosa we shall see the diurnal variations of the temperature reduced to a minimum of a few degrees.

On the 31st of July we removed again and encamped near Linty Hut, at an altitude of 3,047 metres, where H.M. Queen Margaret had encamped the year before on her expedition up Monte Rosa. In the adjoined illustration our tents are seen. Dr. Abelli slept in the laboratory-tent, the soldiers' quarters were at a little distance from the place where had been the kitchen of her Majesty and where the suite had encamped. The illustration showing the Vincent Pyramid in the second chapter gives a view also of this rocky level as one looks towards the glaciers Indren and Garstelet. At a few metres from the camp, the snow accumulated between the rocks provided us with water.

On the night of our arrival Dr. Abelli suffered from hemicrania with an attack of vomiting. These were the first symptoms of mountain-sickness which appeared. Dr. Abelli recovered and had no repetition of the attack.

The weather, which had at first been fickle, had become fine and favoured our settling. The warm rays of the sun cheered us in the midst of this desert spot whence every trace of vegetation had vanished. Around us roared the torrents and the glacier of Garstelet. At 10 o'clock an immense avalanche broke off from the front of the glacier and rushed stormily downwards like a wave of foam, while behind it rose a cloud of dazzling whiteness. It was a new life for us, and often did we pause in our work in order to contemplate the majestic sweep of the glacier, with its abysses, its rocking crests, the smooth walls of ice reflecting the rays of the sun and the sparkling brooks issuing from azure caves at its base.

On August 2nd the weather was very bad. Towards evening we had a thunderstorm with hail. During the night the snow continued to fall, and all through the next day it rained. The water from a little torrent inundated the laboratory, taking its course straight through it. We were obliged to clear the tent and move instruments and provisions elsewhere. Our tents withstood both wind and snow well. We had taken oilskin covers with us, which formed the floor of each tent, and on which our field-beds stood.

On August 4th the weather had cleared again. At 2 p.m. the thermometer in my tent marked 19·5°.

I had taken books with me, lest time should hang heavily on my hands, but the hours fled unnoticed. Of the days spent in our encampments I retain the pleasantest of memories, as of a well-being hitherto unknown. It was a time of my life full of an emotion which words fail to express. The poetic charm of my surroundings, the religious sentiment which Nature awakes in us, subdued me, held me captive.

In the evening I used to sit down, tired, before the tent and gaze at the golden glory in the west, at the purple-hued clouds and the Vincent Pyramid lit up by the last rays of the sun. Far away in the plain the grey curtain of night was already drawn, and I could scarcely realise that I was on that mountain which at eventide stands out in fiery majesty against the blue sky, on that glacier pile whence the sun, when day is dying, sends a farewell greeting to Italy.

Then suddenly night spread its mantle over all. The glittering stars rendered the darkness more solemn and more pitiless. Nature seemed grander, more mysterious in that stupendous solitude.

The two Gnifetti Huts (alt., 3,620 metres).

VII.

In the second chapter I have introduced an illustration in which the Vincent Pyramid is seen; to the left on the horizon is a black crest in the midst of glaciers. On this rock Gnifetti Hut was constructed, at an altitude of 3,620 metres, by the Varallo section of the Alpine Club. A mountain ridge running from the encampment near Linty Hut in the direction of the Vincent Pyramid separates the Lys glacier from the glacier Garstelet. A walk of two hours in this direction brings one to Gnifetti Hut.[1] The road is easy but tiring, because before reaching the glacier we must cross snow fields and rugged, rocky tracts. An illustration at the end of the book (see p. 224), shows our party on the descent from Monte Rosa. In this picture the glacier Garstelet is seen stretching below Gnifetti Hut after winding round the slopes of the Vincent Pyramid. It is an immense inclined plane of ice, the surface being uniform, without crevasses.

I took a photograph of the little and the big Gnifetti Huts as they were in 1894. Now there is a larger and more commodious hut, fourteen metres in length, and composed of four rooms in communication with each other.

On August 4th the porters carried the greater part of our instruments into the two huts. On the 5th my brother, Bizzozero, and I arranged the little hut as a temporary laboratory. Unfortunately it was only three metres long and two broad, but the shelter it afforded, compared to the tents, was a great relief. We had gradually accustomed ourselves to the cold and frost in our camps, but when at last we were able to warm ourselves at the stove the sense of comfort and luxury was such that we came to the conclusion that the most trying time of our expedition was past. Here, too, however, we were troubled with the snow, as may be seen in the illustration showing the smaller hut.

VIII.

On August 9th, in company with Bizzozero, the guide Simon, the soldiers Jachini and Sarteur, and two porters, I went to the Regina Margherita Hut. The next day my brother followed with others of the party, and on the third day Dr. Abelli arrived with the rearguard and the stores.

The path which leads from Gnifetti Hut to the summit of Monte Rosa is at first rather steep. When one has reached the spurs of the Vincent Pyramid a level stretches out before one, and after a steep climb of about 600 metres one arrives at the Col du Lys, whence the valley Grenz descends. At the bottom appear the Görner glacier and the imposing peaks of Zermatt, and towering above them the Matterhorn. To the left rise the formidable brown rocks of Lyskamm. A little further forward extends the immense ice plain overlooked by the stately heights of the Monte Rosa.

The difference in level between Gnifetti Hut and Regina Margherita Hut is less than 1,000 metres. It is a walk of four hours' duration. In no other part of the Alps is there a grander view of snow and glaciers. The illustration (reproduced from a photograph taken by Vittorio Sella), which shows Parrot Peak from the upper plateau of Lysjoch, gives us an idea of this sublime landscape, which rivals the polar regions in its imposing grandeur. In front is the Regina Margherita Hut as it is seen from the Swiss side.

---

[1] This name was given to the hut in remembrance of the parish priest of Alagna, Don Giovanni Gnifetti, who in 1842 was the first to set foot on the summit where the Regina Margherita Hut has since been erected.

The little Gnifetti Hut which served as a laboratory (alt., 3,620 metres).

On our arrival here my thoughts turned towards Alessandro Sella, who had so energetically promoted the construction of this hut for scientific purposes as well as for a shelter, and towards his father, Quintino Sella, the founder of the Italian Alpine Club, who had initiated me into the study of the Alps, and I felt myself animated by a lively sense of gratitude to this family so untiring in the service of their country.

The construction of the Regina Margherita Hut was the most daring achievement of the Italian Alpine Club; it formed a worthy close to the work of half a century devoted to the conquest of the Alps.

View of Regina Margherita Hut from Col Gnifetti (alt., 4,560 metres).

CHAPTER VIII

ALIMENTATION AND FASTING

I

AN ascent of the Faulhorn accomplished by Fick and Wislicenus altered the ideas of physiologists about the origin of muscular force and the chemical value of alimentation.

Justus von Liebig had divided foods into respiratory or heat-producing foods, because, according to him, heat was developed by their combustion, and plastic foods (such as albumen, caseine, and all other substances containing nitrogen), which, in his opinion, built up the muscles and tissues. This theory, which seemed the greatest triumph of chemistry applied to the organism, was so simple that it was accepted by all. When we read the chemical letters of Justus von Liebig[1] we are even now astonished at the literary talent which enabled him to popularise his great discoveries.

Unfortunately the origin of the force and heat of our organism is not so simple as Liebig thought.

[1] Justus von Liebig, *Chemische Briefe*, 6 Auflage, p. 256.

In 1865 Fick and Wislicenus performed an ascent in order to test the truth of Liebig's theory. Granted that the force of the muscles is due exclusively to the combustion of their substance, the azote of the muscles ought then to pass into the urine, producing an augmentation of urea.

The two investigators started from Lake Brieg and climbed the Faulhorn, which rises to a height of 1,956 metres above the level of the lake. During the ascent and for twelve hours before they took no food containing nitrogen, restricting themselves to a diet of starch, fat, and sugar. They collected the urine during the six hours of the ascent and six hours following, and determined the amount of nitrogen contained in it, finding that the destruction of albumen which had taken place in their bodies during the ascent was so inconsiderable that it could not be looked upon as the cause of the mechanical work accomplished.

This statement is probably no longer reliable when a great ascent is performed, because, as I have already shown in another work, the physiology of tired man is different from that of man when rested.

Zuntz, who has devoted much attention to this problem, recently said: "When the work is intense and the organism reaches the utmost limits in the manifestation of its strength, and especially when the respiration is not complete or sufficient, a much more abundant destruction of albuminous bodies takes place."

II.

When Dr. Paccard and the guide Balmat started for the first ascent of Mont Blanc they took their alpenstocks and two woollen rugs, but scarcely any provisions with them.

I have performed ascents while fasting, and others when I have eaten, and have never noticed any difference in the fatigue experienced.

When I ascended the Vincent Pyramid in winter I filled my pockets with dried prunes and ate nothing else the whole day. The sour-sweet taste was agreeable to me and the stone, which I kept in my mouth, excited a secretion of saliva which prevented me from feeling thirsty.

It is a popular idea at the present day that our body may be compared to a locomotive which, by means of burning coal and the vapour of heated water, accomplishes mechanical work. The tender which carries the supply of coal is represented by the nutritive material stored up in our body in order to sustain the work of the muscles. In the next chapter I shall examine this comparison more closely, here I only remark that the tender of our machine cannot be loaded only a few hours before the start, but must have its stores in readiness at least twenty-four hours before, and that during the journey the supply of fuel in the tender cannot be renewed. In other words, during the day on which we accomplish an ascent, we work with the accumulated force of the days before.

Paul Güssfeldt thus describes his condition after a nocturnal march during his ascent of Aconcagua, when a height of 6,200 metres had been reached:

"Between eight and nine o'clock in the morning our little tea-machine was set a-going; having melted a little snow I threw in some leaves of tea, added a few pieces of bread as hard as stone, and then swallowed the whole, my people partaking likewise. This was the sole food which I had taken during twenty-four hours, and yet I had not suffered from hunger. And, strange to say, although the air was very dry, I was not even troubled by thirst."

Regina Margherita Hut on Gnifetti peak (alt., 4,560 metres).

That it may not be thought that Güssfeldt[1] had fed well on the preceding days I must say what his provisions were when he made the daring attempt to ascend Aconcagua without having any European guide with him. Having ridden to a height of 4,500 metres, there remained 2,500 metres to be covered on foot. He took with him a handful of tea-leaves, some ship-biscuit, raw onions, and a little *charqui*. Charqui is dried ox-flesh, fibrous and of a reddish-brown colour. "The best dish which I had eaten for several days was called *baldiviano*, prepared by putting water on the dried flesh and then mixing in onions, red pepper, biscuit or potatoes." "This was," says Güssfeldt, "my sole food, and the dinner-hour was rendered the most disagreeable hour of the day by this baldiviano."

III.

The alimentary substances which we put into our mouths become living substance of the body. How this assimilation is effected, how the cells extract the material peculiar to them from the foods we have digested, is a mystery. Our wonder is the greater when we see that from the most diverse foods material is extracted for the brain, the muscles, and the endless variety of elements constituting a living being.

The changes which take place in our strength when we work without eating is a subject which has engaged the attention of physiologists. As, at present, there is no hope of learning in what manner the assimilation of nutriment is accomplished, we should like at least to determine the time which is necessary for the completion of the process. The first researches with the aid of the ergograph I made together with Professor Maggiora. We found that the latter was very sensitive to the lack of food. The resistance of his muscles to work rapidly diminished during fasting,[2] and rapidly recovered the normal during alimentation.

In a company of many persons travelling together, who must perforce observe the same regimen, one may easily notice the great individual differences which exist in the resistance to fasting, when a meal is by chance delayed for a considerable length of time. In spite of the numerous publications on this subject, we do not, however, know the cause of these individual variations. Dr. G. Manca conducted an investigation of this question in my laboratory.[3] I can here merely mention this problem, which is too complex to admit of adequate treatment in this work.

The curves which we obtain with the ergograph give us a partial idea of fatigue only, as the prolonged exercise which modifies the activity of the heart and the breathing is lacking in these experiments. I hope that other physiologists may soon make a more complete study of the influence of fasting during ascents.

One thing only I wish to mention which at first seems a paradox. There are persons who become stronger after fasting completely for a day or two. This is a curious nervous effect, showing that the lack of food produces

---

[1] P. Güssfeldt, *Reise in den Andes.* Berlin, 1888, p. 295.

[2] For the sake of brevity I do not further enlarge on Professor Maggiora's researches published under the title of *Influenza del digiuno e del nutrimento sulla fatica muscolare* in the Memorie dell' Accademia dei Lincei, 1888, and in my journal, Archives italiennes de Biologie, tome xiii. p. 226.

[3] G. Manca, *Influence du jeûne sur la force musculaire.* Archives italiennes de Biologie, tome xxi. p. 221.

in these persons a morbid excitement which manifests itself in the temporary increase of vigour. This explains the resistance observed in many individuals, who after having fasted for twenty-four hours have been astonished to find themselves less weak when walking than they had thought would be the case.

Professor Aducco wrote with the ergograph the tracing A with the left

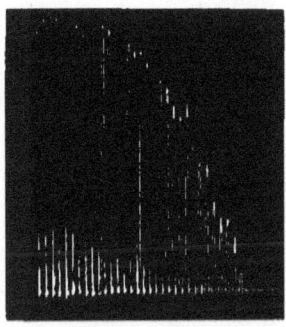 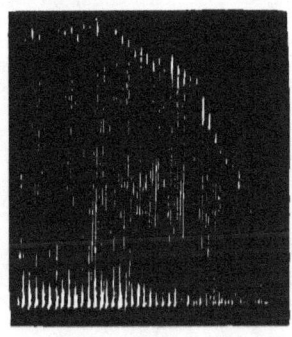

FIG. 39.—Professor Aducco.—Ergographic tracings.
A. Normal fatigue-curve.　　　　B. Fatigue-curve after a fast of 26 hours.

hand, raising a weight of three kilograms every two seconds (Fig. 39). After twenty-six hours of rigid fasting he wrote the second tracing B, the same weight being raised. The form of the curve is not changed but the mechanical work accomplished is greater. About seven contractions more are per-

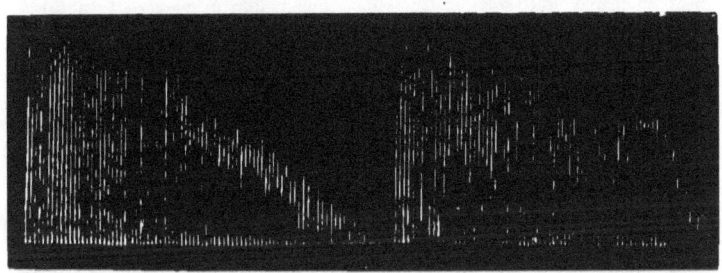

FIG. 40.—Dr. Colla.—Ergographic curves.
A. Normal fatigue-curve.　　　　B. Fatigue-curve after 41 hours' fast.

formed at the beginning of the second curve without any sign of diminution manifesting itself, whereas the normal fatigue-curve exhibits less vigour.

Dr. Colla raised three kilograms with the middle finger on the left hand every two seconds, tracing the normal curve A of Fig. 40. After fasting for forty-one hours, the curve B of the same figure was written. Here, too, there appears an augmentation of strength at the beginning and at the end of the curve. These tracings have been reduced by one-third in the process of reproduction.

The first symptoms of hunger are the most painful. These disappear after a while and one feels better. I, too, have often fasted by way of experiment for twenty-four hours, and have, at the end of that time, felt myself in a better condition than I had thought possible.

The resistance to fasting being of such individual diversity, it follows that each one, before undertaking an expedition of any length in the mountains, must find out for himself what are the capabilities of his organism. Further, we must bear in mind that as the fatigue of an ascent weakens the activity of our digestive organs, we must be careful never to overload the stomach on mountaineering excursions.

IV.

Amongst all the organs of the body the stomach presents perhaps the greatest variations in its activity. To hide our ignorance we say that the stomach is a capricious organ. This explanation may satisfy a patient, but for the physiologist no such caprices of the organism exist. There is a reason for everything and every phenomenon is the effect of a cause. But as we do not know these causes we must resign ourselves to look upon these phenomena as upon the changes of the weather, convinced in both cases of the existence of causes which we have not yet discovered.

All know that the healthiest and strongest men nourish themselves in various ways and that what agrees with one, may cause suffering to another. As a rule we eat too much, much more than is necessary; accustomed as we are to feel better after eating the distension of the stomach becomes at length a factor in our well-being.

The Irish, who live principally on potatoes, cannot satisfy themselves with meat when they go to work in England. This is due to a nervous sensation in the stomach, consequent on the previous exaggerated dilation of this organ, which gives rise to the belief that it is not full. During famines whole populations are known to eat substances certainly without nutritive properties and which yet soothe the distressing sense of hunger, because they mechanically distend the stomach. Similarly, nervous persons feel from time to time the need to eat.

The stomach is not only important on account of its nerves and its digestive function, but also from the point of view of the circulation of the blood. Many phenomena which are attributed to the digestion, are due, on the contrary, to a different distribution of the blood in the inner parts of the body. As a proof of this I communicate an experience which doubtless many have had. When we chance to smoke too strong a cigar, we feel ill —this is at least the case with moderate smokers such as I am. Sometimes we feel a little nausea and dizziness. If the smoker then drinks a glass of fresh water, the indisposition immediately disappears. My opinion is that this phenomenon has its origin solely in the blood-vessels. The augmented pressure of the blood is due to the contraction of the vessels of the stomach and intestines, and I have proved by means of the sphygmomanometer that when one smokes a strong cigar and begins to feel indisposed, the pressure of the blood diminishes, increasing immediately when one drinks a glassful of fresh water.

Even when a wine-glassful of cognac is drunk I have seen the pressure of the blood augment for a few minutes. The temporary feeling of well-being which alcoholic liquors produce in some individuals would therefore appear to be a reflex phenomenon, that is, a contraction of the blood-vessels which, in augmenting the pressure of the blood for a few minutes, makes us feel better. The use of aromatic vinegar or ammonia in cases of indisposition or fainting has the same physiological reason.

The influence of food on the pulse I made the subject of one of my earliest investigations.[1] I make mention of this because of the intimate connection of those researches with the question at present under consideration. In studying the pulse of the forearm with the hydrosphygmograph, I

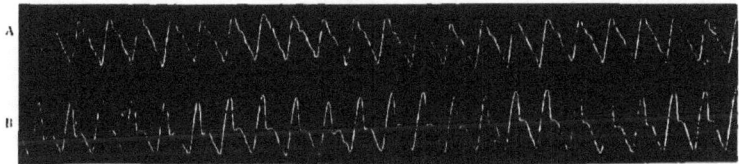

FIG. 41. - Professor Albertotti. A. Pulse-curve during fasting. B. Pulse-curve immediately after eating.

saw that the tracings after lunch were quite different to those taken in the morning before the subject had broken his fast.

The two subjoined tracings (Fig. 41) show Professor Albertotti's pulse at 11 a.m. before, and at 2 p.m. after lunch. The rate of the pulse which was 68 to the minute while the subject was fasting, has risen in the second curve to 86.

This suffices to show that even a light lunch exercises an influence on the heart and tone of the blood-vessels.

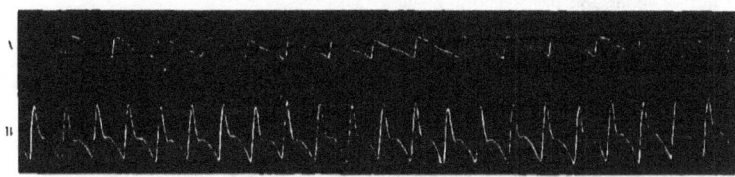

FIG. 42. - Professor Luigi Pagliani. A. Pulse-curve during fasting. B. Pulse-curve immediately after eating.

Curve A of Fig. 42 is Professor Luigi Pagliani's pulse-curve before lunch, B the pulse-curve after lunch, which was taken in company with others at the laboratory, so as to exclude the possibility of the pulse being altered by walking.

The change which food produces in the form of the pulse is similar to that caused by fatigue. This resemblance arouses surprise; it seems at first as though the effect should be the reverse. If we compare the tracings B,

[1] A. Mosso, *Sulle variazioni locali del polso.* R. Accademia delle Scienze di Torino, Novembre 1877. *Die Diagnostik des Pulses.* Leipzig, 1879.

Fig. 41, and B, Fig. 42, taken after breakfast, with my pulse-curve taken after the ascent of the Vincent Pyramid, which was performed fasting (see Fig. 25, p. 53), we see that in both cases the pulsations become higher, and that towards the middle of the descending line a secondary so-called dicrotic elevation appears. As fatigue dilates the blood-vessels in the muscles and produces a certain degree of anæmia, due to the congestion of these organs, so during digestion there is a similar withdrawal of the blood, which flows more copiously to the stomach and intestines, and thus the same effect on the pulse is produced.

This is one explanation of the resemblance of the pulse-curve during digestion and fatigue. But again, the products of the substances digested generate effects similar to those due to fatigue when they penetrate into the blood. The problem is still more complicated by the fact that nervous phenomena, more than all others, modify the circulation of the blood. In fact the variations of the pulse, like the increased muscular force observed in Professor Maggiora, appear immediately after eating, before the liquids and substances introduced into the stomach have had time to become absorbed. This observation leads us to think that we have here to do with an essentially nervous phenomenon, and with a change in the circulation of the blood which modifies our sense of bodily well-being or indisposition, without a corresponding chemical alteration, or a change in the nutrition of the tissues.

V.

Fatigue alone suffices to influence the activity of the stomach. Professor Lauder Brunton in a valuable work on disorders of the stomach[1] says that there are some ill-advised persons who think that exercise after a day of hard brain work does them good, and who, therefore, instead of resting when they have a little free time, take a three or four mile walk or a long ride on their bicycle before dinner. The consequence of this is, Professor Brunton concludes, that overstrain of the muscles being added to that of the brain, digestion is spoilt and indisposition ensues.

Zsigmondy says that "in the majority of cases mountain-sickness is solely due to gastric obstruction, because the tourist coming from the town has not yet accustomed himself to mountain regimen."[2]

This opinion of Zsigmondy, shared by the majority of Alpinists, will undergo a gradual modification in proportion as bicycle races render the fact more generally known that stomachic disturbances, nausea, and vomiting are produced in the plain as well after a race of six or seven hours' duration. Fatigue is the cause of these disturbances; and it is scarcely necessary to remind the reader that not all individuals suffer in the same degree from fatigue.

Dr. J. Salvioli made a series of researches in my laboratory on the influence which fatigue exercises on digestion.[3]

The results of this investigation were: That fatigue produces a diminution in the quantity of the gastric juice; that the gastric juice secreted loses much of its digestive properties; that the alimentary substances pass from the

---

[1] T. Lauder Brunton, *On disorders of digestion, their consequences and treatment.* London, 1886, p. 66.
[2] E. Zsigmondy, *Les dangers dans la montagne*, 1886, p. 180.
[3] I. Salvioli, *Influence de la fatigue sur la digestion stomacale.* Archives italiennes de Biologie, tome xvii. p. 249.

stomach into the intestines before being digested. Fatigue therefore produces a series of alterations in the stomach, and recently Cohn has confirmed the statement that tiring movement hinders digestion.[1]

We must not, therefore, follow too readily the advice of the guides, still less so that of the Swiss guides, who are accustomed to eat every three hours. We must eat only when we are hungry, and pay no heed to others in this respect. Above all, we must not allow ourselves to be persuaded by the guides to drink too much. For the latter it is an occasion for rejoicing when they find liquor and wine in abundance. Zsigmondy, who had had great experience of guides, has left the following warning in his writings:—

"I believe that alcohol is a factor in the deplorable accidents on the mountains. The sense of well-being produced by alcohol is exceedingly brief. The potato which we eat gives more heat and more strength than the alcohol which is distilled from it."[2]

I have seen persons suffer from mountain-sickness whose stomach was quite empty, and who had eaten with good appetite the day before. While I was at Gnifetti Hut some travellers arrived from the Col d'Olen, fasting and in good condition. They went as far as the Col du Lys, where they halted because of stomachic disturbances and nausea. They returned in the evening, ate with us, and in the morning, without having been in the least troubled by digestive disorder, started in high spirits for Gressoney.

One need not be a physiologist in order to convince one's self that fatigue influences digestion. In consequence of an ascent or prolonged walk the quantity of intestinal juices continually secreted by the glands becomes less. If an intense cold does not produce intestinal disturbances one generally suffers from constipation during an ascent. Attentive observation will confirm the statement that the greater hardness of the fæces is not due to their remaining longer in the rectum, nor yet because less liquid has been drunk. Even without having any special knowledge of the processes of decomposition taking place in our body, we often become aware of an abnormal state of the digestive system from the characteristic and unusual odour of the intestinal gases.

It may be thought that the loss of appetite is due to fatigue fever, but this is not the case; for on Monte Rosa I have found an almost normal temperature in persons whose loss of appetite was such that they felt a repugnance to food.

VI.

All those who have performed ascents will have noticed that taste alters when the mountain summits are reached. Professor Ulrich in his description of his ascent of Monte Rosa remarks that at a certain height a greater quantity of salt must be added to the food, which is otherwise insipid, and suggests taking only salted or smoked meat on mountaineering expeditions.

The proverb says, "There is no accounting for tastes," and were I to relate all that Alpinists have told me which bears out the dictum, the dissertation would be lengthy. All, however, are agreed that taste changes, and that it must be stimulated by piquant flavours. This, too, is an effect of over-exertion. We did not experience this change during our sojourn in the

---

[1] F. Cohn, *Ueber den Einfluss mässiger Körperbewegungen auf die Verdauung.* Deuts. Arch. f. klin. Med. xliii., 239, 250.
[2] *Op. cit.*, p. 179.

Regina Margherita Hut when we were well rested. Only at first some of us lost our appetite, but it returned when we had recovered and acclimatised ourselves.

Saussure had a similar experience during his sojourn at the Col du Géant, where he stayed for sixteen days. He says that when he and his party arrived, all suffered from absolute loss of appetite, whereas afterwards the process of digestion was perfect. "Hunger seemed to us much more distressing and imperious, and yet we were more easily satisfied, and digestion seemed to proceed with greater promptitude than in the plain."[1]

They were, it is true, at an altitude of only 3,365 metres, where, a century later, the Queen of Italy, overtaken by a violent storm, was obliged to pass the night, and did not experience the least suffering.

A year before we undertook the ascent of Monte Rosa, my brother and Dr. Paoletti[2] found that sugar has the property of augmenting muscular force. The researches with the ergograph show that a greater manifestation of energy may be obtained from the tired muscle if the subject drinks a glass of sugared water. The most advantageous solution would appear to be that of one part sugar to ten parts water. This dynamogenic property of sugar explains the usually greater consumption of honey and saccharine substances in the Alps than in the plain.

The examination of the dynamogenic action of sugar during ascents was in our programme of investigations, and my brother made several experiments, which, however, were interrupted by bad weather, and by our other researches on the chemistry of respiration.

I have seen Alessandro Sella, who, as a rule, never took sugar, even in coffee, eat it in abundance in the mountains. His father, he told me, used to do the same, even keeping a supply of pieces in his pocket. In this imperative desire we recognise the voice of nature indicating the regimen to be followed during exertion, for I have never made similar observations with respect to meat and other albuminous foods.

Before me lies the provision list of our expedition: its items are in no way remarkable, being such as are usual on similar excursions. We took with us a goodly store of Naples macaroni, of which we partook almost every day, rice, dried pulse, numerous canisters of preserved fruits and vegetables and boxes of biscuits. In drawing up the culinary list before the start we took care to provide for the variation of the dishes, in view of the probable diminution of appetite. As it was my intention to maintain as far as possible the same regimen on the heights as in the plain, we took means to provide ourselves continually with fresh meat, even while we were in the Regina Margherita Hut. At an altitude of 2,515 metres, at Indra Alp, we began to kill sheep, which we bought from the shepherds, for our daily use. Like good Piedmontese, we often ate polenta.[3] We had been told that at a height of 4,000 metres it is not possible to cook it properly, but this is not the case. The boiling-point of water on Monte Rosa is at 85°, and this temperature more than suffices to cook the polenta excellently.

Should any one be inclined to think that the stomach no longer performs its functions with regularity at an altitude of 4,560 metres, I need only say

---

[1] Saussure, *Voyages dans les Alpes.* Tome iv. p. 318.
[2] U. Mosso et L. Paoletti, *Influence du sucre sur le travail des muscles.* Archives italiennes de Biologie, tome xxi. p. 293.
[3] Ground Indian corn boiled in salted water to a stiff porridge. It is usually eaten with butter and grated Parmesan cheese. Cold polenta may be fried in slices in butter.—Trans.

that I ate double rations at dinner, as, for instance, one day, a large portion of tinned lobster seasoned with oil and lemon and eaten with three or four slices of fried polenta, some boiled meat with salad of preserved French beans and cucumbers, cheese and dried fruits.

I could scarcely have subjected my stomach to a severer test, and yet I had no subsequent reason to regret the experiment. Later in the evening we took coffee or tea, while the soldiers sang and played on their instruments. It was, I believe, very good for our health that we always ate warm food. In the morning as soon as we were up we drank plenty of coffee, milk, tea, or chocolate. As far as Gnifetti Hut we always had fresh cow's milk, which was brought to us from the meadows beneath; afterwards we made use of condensed milk. At midday and in the evening we also ate warm food. I consider it of rigorous necessity on the Alps to avoid withdrawing too much heat from the organism by eating and drinking cold foods and liquids.

Senator Perazzi, a noted mountain climber, once told me that he never suffered from mountain-sickness but once, and that was at Mont Combin, where he had passed the night in an Alp hut, and where, on leaving in the morning, he had not been able to get anything warm to drink.

Our rule was to eat and drink as usual. Each of us in turn presided over the culinary operations. Marta and Cento were very fair cooks; their efforts reconciled me to eating mutton, to which I was not accustomed, and which I digested, although I disliked its odour.

A sure proof that our regimen was normal is given by the table showing the weight of members of the party (see p. 271). Beno Bizzozero gained in weight, and none of us lost, in spite of the more active life.

VII.

Our excellent state of health at an altitude of 4,560 metres contrasts strangely with the sufferings undergone by Dr. Egli-Sinclair and Dr. Guglielminetti at a height of 4,365 metres (about 200 metres lower) in Vallot Hut on Mont Blanc. A still more striking contrast is furnished by a comparison of Lewinstein's recent observations on rabbits[1] and our own experiences. These animals died from fatty degeneration of the heart and other organs, when they were kept for only two or three days in an enclosed space in which the pressure of the air was reduced to only a little less than one-half.

This observation merely serves to show, I think, that experiments performed under the pneumatic bell differ too widely from the life on the Alps to ensure reliable results. Indeed, we know that rabbits kept in the Observatory of the Pic du Midi at a height of 2,877 metres throve so well that they littered.[2]

I have often seen guinea-pigs eat with appetite at a pressure corresponding to a height of 6,400 metres. Dr. Scofone, assistant of Professor Giacosa, took some cocks up to the Regina Margherita Hut, and found no difference in their organic change at that height. I found rats in Gnifetti Hut (alt., 3,647 metres) that remain there all the year it seems, and multiply. Lewinstein's experiments are too complicated to permit of the positive conclusion that rabbits succumb when the atmospheric pressure is diminished by one-half.

[1] Lewinstein, *Archiv. für. gesam. Physiologie*, vol. lxv.
[2] Regnard, *La cure d'altitude*, p. 125.

Before we started on our expedition I had made arrangements for the supplies of fuel to be taken. A friend recommended our taking coal-bricks, as wood makes too much ash. It is true that for the production of the same degree of heat wood costs more than coal and is less easily carried, but once we had reached the heights I became convinced that wood is the best kind of fuel for those regions. On stormy days, such as we experienced several times, we should, I think, have been obliged to extinguish the stove in order to escape suffocation had we made use of coal or coke.

All who suffer from mountain-sickness become extremely sensitive to kitchen odours. Some suffered to such a degree that they preferred to go out of the hut while we others were eating, or else they went into the other rooms in order to escape fumes which, if not precisely agreeable to us, certainly did not sicken us as they did the sufferers.

I did not make any special researches on the quality and quantity of foods hygienically most advisable during ascents and living in the mountains. As a physician I must, however, say a word or two on the opinion of certain Alpinists who think it necessary to eat a lot of meat and fat foods in order to protect themselves from the cold and increase their strength. The only advantage of a meat diet is that a lesser volume of food is sufficient for our needs.

A proof that it is not necessary to eat meat in order to be strong is furnished by the Italian labourers, especially the peasants of Lombardy, who are most industrious and whose diet consists of little else but polenta.

In England I noticed that the hardest work in the ironworks was performed by Irishmen, who eat little meat. One of the heaviest tasks is that of the metal-carriers. These workmen, who wear leather aprons reaching to the knee, and whose hands are similarly protected with leather, seize iron bars weighing over sixty kilograms and often still hot, raise them high up and break them by bringing them down with a crash upon a stone or one upon another. I talked to these workmen and learnt that their diet is more vegetable than animal.

I conclude, therefore, that one should not alter one's regimen when living on the Alps. Even when one proposes to undertake great exertions, it is better to adhere to the diet to which one is accustomed.

All travellers in Central Asia acknowledge that the coolies, who eat only rice, are as strong as Europeans, and oppose as great a resistance as we do to the cold and rarefied air of the Himalayas. The Goorkhas carry four myriagrams on their backs with the same ease as Europeans carry two. Conway performed the ascent of Mont Viso with two Goorkhas, to whom he gave a load of thirty kilograms each. They climbed to the summit with this weight, and an eye-witness told me that they ascended tranquilly without perspiring.

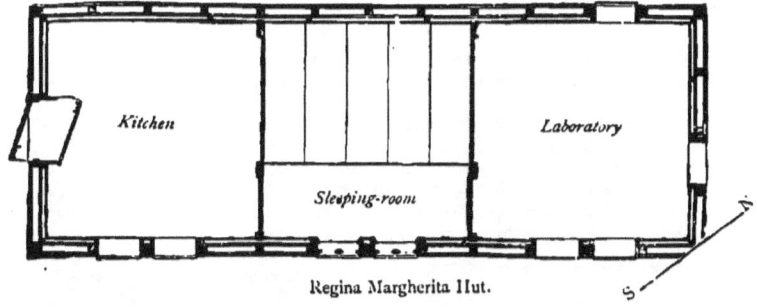

Regina Margherita Hut.

CHAPTER IX

THE TEMPERATURE OF THE BODY—CLASSIFICATION OF MOUNTAIN-CLIMBERS

I.

IT was formerly thought by physiologists that the chemical energy of the muscles was first transformed into heat and then into mechanical energy, a process resembling that in steam or gas engines. Since the researches of Pflüger and Fick it is now usually admitted that chemical energy is transformed directly into the mechanical work of the muscles, producing their contraction.

To use a technical word (now entered into common use) we may say that the muscles do not resemble a *thermodynamic* but a *chemodynamic* machine.

The chemical energy contained in food accumulates little by little as nutrition proceeds, in the nerve-cells, the muscular fibres and in all the tissues of the body in the form of organised matter. This chemical energy which was in the food and has subsequently become substance of our body, remains inert for a greater or lesser length of time, in a state of latent power, enclosed, as it were, within the tissues in a state of tension. Under the impulse of the nervous system, at a given moment, the organic matter of the muscles and of the brain itself becomes disintegrated, giving rise to a physiological activity, to the force of the motor centres and of the muscles.

One part of this energy is dissipated in the form of heat, and diffuses itself through the organism, which is thus warmed. Scarcely any one now holds the opinion that the heat of our body is transformed into mechanical work. Physiological work leaves heat behind it as a residuum; but this is not the cause of the nervous functions, rather the last manifestation, the soot and scoriæ, so to speak, of the physiological work.

We have two means of studying the transformations which take place in our body during an ascent. We may collect the scoriæ and disintegrated substances as did Fick and Wislicenus. The substance of our cells becomes transformed and similar to inorganic matter in proportion as life and movement are developed out of them. The blood itself becomes wasted, as is shown, during ascents for instance, by the more reddish colour of the urine. The other method of study consists in the measurement of the internal heat accompanying the work of the ascent. The first method has been adopted by Professor Zuntz and his son, Drs. A. and F. Loewy and Schumburg, whose recent investigations on Monte Rosa on the residua of the human body have contributed a new chapter to the physiology of man on the Alps.[1] By the second method I performed several experiments, with an explanation of which I shall detain the reader for a few moments.

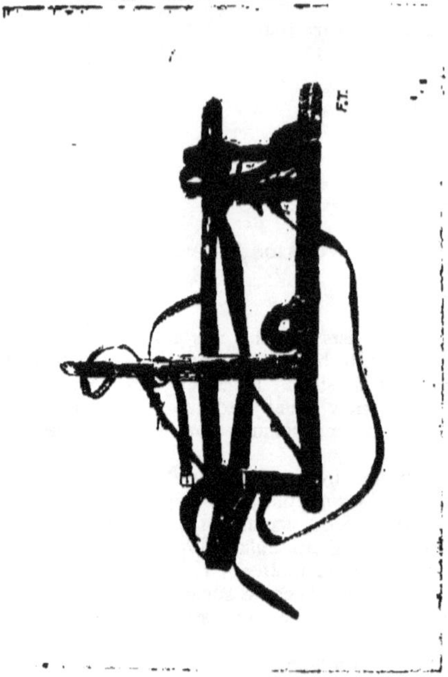

FIG. 43.—Carrying-frame on Sella model.

It is a law that the production of heat accompanying the transformation of energy during an ascent, is not proportional either to the duration or to the intensity of the mechanical work accomplished by the muscles. As a demonstration of this I communicate the following experiment.

At Val Tournanche I selected a sturdy porter of whom I had already made use in other researches on the Breithorn. I determined to study the change of temperature in this man at the end of September, when he was in good training, and then again at the end of the winter.

I went to Breuil and measured off a height of 400 metres between Avuil and Chapellette. For the sake of brevity I communicate one only of the repeated experiments then made. The subject weighed 74 kilograms and carried a load of 40 kilograms in a carrying-frame[2] on his back. In this experiment, performed in the morning, his internal temperature rose from 37·1° to 37·5°. The temperature of the air was 12°, the sky cloudy and a light wind blowing.

[1] A. Loewy, F. Loewy and Leo Zuntz, *Ueber den Einfluss der verdünnten Luft und des Höhenclimas auf den Menschen.* Pflüger's Archiv f. d. ges. Physiologie, Bd. 66, p. 477.

[2] I insert an illustration of this carrying-frame, which I consider indispensable to all those undertaking expeditions over the glaciers. The model is that of V. Sella, and has been tested by him with satisfactory results on the most difficult ascents in the Alps and Caucasus Mountains. This carrying-frame surpasses all other means I know of for the transport of instruments and provisions to great heights. The weight of the whole frame with the leather thongs for strapping on, &c., is 1,800 grams. (V. Sella, *Nel Caucaso Centrale*, Bullettino del Club Alpino Italiano, 1889, p. 314.)

In May of the following year I wrote to the man, who thereupon came to Turin. We went by rail to Sassi, distant 400 metres in a vertical line from Superga. The road which unites these two points is 3,900 metres long, easier and less steep therefore than that between Avuil and Chapellette, the height remaining the same. The temperature of the air was 20°. We started at 4.7 p.m., and arrived at Superga at 5.21, the subject carrying the same weight of 40 kilograms. His rectal temperature, which was 37·2° at Sassi, was 39° when we reached the Superga Hotel.

The exertion of this ascent produced therefore a feverish condition, whereas eight months before the same weight being carried and the same mechanical work accomplished, the internal temperature had remained within physiological limits. The efficacy of the chemical consumption and of the mechanical work executed by our machine, is a value which varies greatly according to the conditions in which we are situated.

Training is an unconscious instruction which we give to the nervous system, which is thus taught to effect the contraction of the muscles without any unnecessary expenditure of chemical work.

II.

It is certain, therefore, that the same person, accomplishing the same amount of work does not always produce the same amount of heat. Further, different persons performing the same amount of work at the same time and under the same conditions, do not produce the same amount of heat.

Three medical students, the Signori Chiesa, Forni, and Ventrini, assisted me in these investigations. I gave to each of these gentlemen a maximum thermometer [1] which had been compared with a Baudin thermometer, and for three days in succession they took their temperature five times daily. The averages of these observations are given in the table below.[2]

The normal temperature at various hours of the day being thus ascertained, the subjects began a series of walks from Sassi to Superga on the high road

---

[1] For my first physiological investigations on the Alps I constructed an apparatus for measuring the temperature of the urine.[*] This method may be advantageous in certain circumstances; I followed it in determining my internal temperature during an ascent of Mont Viso. The results agreed with those obtained by measuring the temperature of the organism in the rectum. The methods often followed by Alpinists of placing the thermometer under the tongue or in the arm-pit are unreliable. In order to give an idea of the errors incurred in the study of the temperature during ascents, I instance Lortet and Marcet who found that the body cooled during an ascent of Mont Blanc. If the temperature had been measured in the rectum instead of in the mouth, an increase would certainly have been found. The cold air passing through the nose, and the more rapid breathing had produced a cooling of the mouth, although the temperature in the deeper parts of the body was certainly greater.

[*] A. Mosso, *Sopra un metodo per misurare la temperature dell' orina.* R. Accademia dei Lincei, 3 giugno, 1877.

[2] AVERAGE TEMPERATURE OF THE STUDENTS CHIESA, FORNI, VENTRINI.

Names.	Time.						Weight of Body.
	5 a.m.	9 a.m.	12 a.m.	3 p.m.	6 p.m.	9 p.m.	
Chiesa	36·9°	37·2°	37·2°	37·6°	37·5°	37°	65 kilograms.
Forni	36·6°	36·8°	36·9°	37°	37·3°	36·8°	60·90 ,,
Ventrini	36·9°	37°	37°	37·3°	37·1°	37°	61·40 ,,

which, as I have already mentioned, rises 400 metres per length of 3,900 metres. From the following table of observations we see that even short walks may cause a considerable augmentation of the internal temperature when we are not in training. In Ventrini the temperature rose from 37·3° to 39·5°. There was thus an increase of 2·2° which amounted to actual fever, and this notwithstanding that the pace kept had been moderate, no weight carried, and that the temperature of the air was only of 20°–22°. On the 14th May the same walk produced less heat in the same subject, his temperature being only 38·5°, on May 16th it was less again, amounting to only 38·3°. We see thus that training gradually lessens the increase of temperature after exertion.

CHANGES PRODUCED IN THE TEMPERATURE OF THE BODY, IN THE RATE OF BREATHING AND PULSE BY AN ASCENT OF 400 METRES.

Date	Time		Temperature			Breathing			Pulse			Temperature of the air.
			Chiesa	Forni	Ventrini	Chiesa	Forni	Ventrini	Chiesa	Forni	Ventrini	
May 12	7.35 a.m.	Departure from Turin										
	10.0 „	Arrival at Superga	38·15°			20			100			16°
	11.25 „	After resting	37·4°			18			87			
	1.30 p.m.	Arrival in Turin	38·0°			20			96			
13	4.7 p.m.	Departure from Sassi										
	6.10 „	Arrival at Superga	38·8°	38·5°	39·5°	29	38	34	135	99	103	20°–22°
	7.49 „	After resting	37·4°	37·2°	37·5°	22	22	26	95	79	75	
	8.49 „	Departure from Superga										
	9.0 „	Arrival at Sassi	37·5°	37·6°	38·3°							
	10.0 „	Arrival at Superga	38·0°	37·8°	38·8°	20	26	19	109	102	110	
	11.10 „	After resting	36·9°	36·9°	37·7°	20	20	24	86	88	90	
14	1.40 a.m.	Arrival in Turin	36·9°	37·3°	37·1°	18	19	20	88	78	75	
14	5.10 a.m.	Departure from Sassi										
	6.10 „	Arrival at Superga	38·5°	38·2°	38·5°	20	22	20	118	87	112	–20°
	7.16 „	After resting	37·1°	37·4°	37·8°							
16	7.26 a.m.	Departure from Sassi										
	8.26 „	Arrival at Superga			38·3°		23			90		16°

In a series of similar experiments which I made with soldiers there was an average increase of the internal temperature of 0·3° to 0·5°, but it is needless, after the example given at the beginning of the chapter, to make further statistical communications for the purpose of showing the efficacy of training. The mountain-soldiers who were with me on Monte Rosa performed maximum exertions during the ascent almost without any accompanying change in the temperature of their body, so different is the influence which the nervous system exercises on the chemical processes of the organism in different individuals, though the amount of mechanical work remains the same.

Forel, professor of general physiology at Lausanne, is the author of two memoirs on the changes of the human temperature during mountain-climbing.[1] Further on I shall have occasion to quote from this work, certainly one of the most valuable contributions to Alpine literature. In studying the influence of the nervous system on the animal temperature [2] my brother observed that

[1] F. A. Forel, *Expériences sur la température du corps humain dans l'acte de l'ascension sur les montagnes.* Genève et Bâle, 1871, 1874.
[2] U. Mosso, *Influenza del sistema nervoso sulla temperatura animale.* Accademia di medicina di Torino, 1885. *Einfluss des Nervensystems auf die thierische Temperatur,* Virchow's Archiv, vol. cvi., 1886.

when we perform a march the temperature first rises and then, though the exercise is continued, progressively diminishes, notwithstanding that we are still accomplishing the same work. We see this from the foregoing table. In all three subjects, on the return to Superga, the temperature remained lower by 0·7° and 0·8° than it had been during the preceding ascent performed four hours earlier. This is another proof that the heat produced does not correspond to the work accomplished by the muscles. There is a nervous excitement which, almost like an emotion outside the threshold of consciousness, accompanies every manifestation of nervous activity, and renders every calculation of thermodynamic equivalence impossible.

The manifestation of the chemical energy in the muscles is the more perfect the less the latter become heated, and the greater the work they accomplish. The following example will surprise physiologists, for no one would have supposed that a man could perform an amount of work so far surpassing the average, almost without the least modification of the internal temperature, nor that at an altitude of 4,500 metres, such muscular exertion could be accomplished with impunity. I refer to Corporal Jachini whom I hold to be one of the strongest men, and the most perfect piece of living mechanism I have ever known.

On August 10th he left the encampment near Linty Hut (alt., 3,047 metres) and went down to Gressoney St. Jean (alt., 1,375 metres), to meet the party of soldiers coming from Ivrea in order to accompany them, together with another guide, to the Regina Margherita Hut. At 7.0 a.m. on the next day he had returned to Gnifetti Hut (alt., 3,620 metres). On the 12th he left with his companions at 5.40 a.m. and arrived at Regina Margherita Hut at 9.7 p.m. He had left Gnifetti Hut with two myriagrams of wood on his shoulder. When he and his party had reached the foot of Gnifetti Peak, a soldier called Chamois began to feel ill, so Corporal Jachini relieved him of his knapsack weighing 18 kilograms, which he placed on his own carrying-frame. He then left his companions to support the sufferer, and climbing the steep glacier of Gnifetti Peak in a zig-zag line, he reached the hut before the others with a load of about 40 kilograms on his shoulder, including the weight of the carrying-frame.

He knew that I was desirous of ascertaining the temperature after the greatest possible physical exertion, and so I examined him at once.

At 9.10, three minutes, that is, after his arrival at the hut, the rectal temperature was 37·4°. Pulse, 85. Breathing, 26.

At 9.24, after having read a letter which had arrived at the hut the day before, and which he had been eagerly expecting. Temperature, 36·5°. Pulse, 74. Breathing, 18.

At 9.38. Temperature, 36·5°. Pulse, 73. Breathing, 18.

Notwithstanding the extraordinary exertion the temperature of his body had risen only a few lengths of a degree, and after a quarter of an hour, in spite of a slight emotion, it had returned to the normal, which in him is 36·5°.

The effects of training do not alone explain this case. There must be besides a constitution of such perfection as physiology rarely meets.

III.

Were I called upon to classify a party of mountain-climbers according to their strength I should repeat the above experiment. There is, I think, no better method of ascertaining the relation between nervous activity and muscular work. The thermometer is in this case a reliable instrument wherewith an estimate of the working fitness of our body may be obtained. The new ideas set forth at the beginning of the chapter on the origin of animal heat convince us that an organism is the more perfect, the less it becomes heated in accomplishing a given amount of work.

I do not place much reliance on the determination of the vital capacity as a means of furnishing a computation of the physical powers of Alpinists, or rather I should say, I do not attribute to the statistical results obtained with the spirometer that exclusive value which it is the present tendency to do. I have already said that man inhales a quantity of air which is more than sufficient for his needs. On the mountains where the air is rarefied it is not of much advantage to have lungs of more than average size, if the heart grows languid and the circulation of the blood slower.

We know that mountain-sickness is not due solely to a lack of oxygen. Well-developed lungs may be of some advantage, but this condition alone does not suffice to constitute a good mountain-climber.

Another time the soldier Sarteur carried 20 kilograms on his back from Linty Hut to Regina Margherita Hut. On his arrival I immediately took his rectal temperature, which I found to be 37·3° (that is scarcely two-tenths above the normal of that hour on days when no exertion was called for). I felt full of admiration for the perfection of this living machine. The physiological ideal of human strength is not that of the vulgar whose applause in the circus greets athletes deformed by the hypertrophy of the muscles.

Typical beauty in muscular contraction is not the momentary manifestation of excessive strength, but the execution of heavy and prolonged work in which the nervous system and the muscles act so perfectly that no force is wasted, only that exact amount of chemical transformation taking place in the organism which the work to be accomplished demands. It is the calm—the silence, so to speak—with which our machine acts which we most value. My enthusiasm during these experiments was so great that in this marvellous economy of energy I seemed to recognise a moral sentiment of nature and, imbued with the poetry of my surroundings, the idea that I had discovered an ethical perfection resulting from exercise fascinated me.

IV.

A classification of mountain-climbers has already been attempted by several authors of repute.[1] Conway after having spoken of the scientific, artistic, and inquisitive types, describes two other types which have special physiological characteristics. The one is the *mountain-climber*, the other, the *mountain-gymnast*. Conway says that till now the gymnast type has prevailed, but that now the turn of the climber has come. "The future of Alpine literature depends upon the climber, but the prosperity of climbing as a sport depends upon the gymnast."[2] He adds that the climber hates civilisation, and is usually a dark, dolichocephalous man.

I have some doubt as to the correctness of this statement that the mountain-climber has a long, narrow skull. Conway does not mention having taken measurements; these, I am convinced, would furnish a contrary result.

---

[1] W. Marcet, *Climbing and Breathing at High Altitudes.* Alpine Journal, 1886, p. 1, xiii. W. M. Conway, *Centrist and Excentrist.* Alpine Journal, 1891, p. 397. W. M. Conway, Alpine Journal, 1891, p. 108.

[2] W. M. Conway, *The Dom from the Domjoch.* Alpine Journal, 1891, p. 110.

Men with a long skull, and those with a roundish skull are distributed in zones in which sometimes the one and sometimes the other form is predominant. Amongst the populations living near the Alps Calori and Virchow have found that on the German side as well as on the Italian the prevailing type of skull is not dolichocephalic but brachicephalic. The Piedmontese who, it cannot be denied, are good mountain-climbers, have the skull of the ancient Celts which is roundish or brachicephalic. The populations further removed from the Alps are dolichocephalous.

The more usual classification is that into rock-climbers and icemen, based on a constitutional difference of the body and on training. The Italians show greater aptitude for rock-climbing, because the mountains on the southern side of the Alps to which they are accustomed are more precipitous. On the northern side where there are greater stretches of snow the icemen abound. But even in one region both species may be found. We notice this when on a mountaineering excursion a choice must be made between two paths presenting about equal difficulties and facilities. Some prefer the rocks, others the glacier. In such cases, however, I have generally seen that the path over snow and ice is preferred.

One important requisite to an Alpinist is to have long legs like Maquignaz, Lauener, and Cupelin, and for the following reasons. In climbing, long legs enable us to raise the foot high without effort, and further, at the end of a march or of an ascent a smaller number of steps will have been taken than by short-limbed individuals.

Fatigue being a process of a nervous nature, it is the more intense the greater the number of stimuli which the motor centre has had to transmit to the muscles executing the steps ; on this account short people who must take a greater number of steps, or else must take unaccustomed strides, become more tired.

In selecting guides or porters for an Alpine campaign the preference should be given to tall persons for still another reason. The functions of a small animal are performed with less economy than those of a bigger animal. The greater the volume of an organism, the slower is the beating of the heart and the lower the rate of breathing. The small animal eats more in proportion to the bigger one, because a greater quantity of fuel is needed to keep up its heat. A small mass of matter cools more rapidly than a larger mass, and the same law holds good for the body of animals ; the smaller the latter, the greater must be the rapidity of the metabolic processes in order to ensure the continuance of the vital functions.

V.

Celebrated guides when together recognise without hesitation the superiority of each in his own peculiar department. Rey's forte was glacier climbing, Maquignaz and Carrel excelled on the rocks. Maquignaz, a guide of authority and repute, would never have thought of heading a file on a dangerous ice slope, if Rey were also of the party.

I often admired the natural discipline which in these mountaineers prompts the recognition of the skill of their colleagues and even the superiority of their rivals. The spirit of subordination has become an instinct as it were, because in no other kind of life is the responsibility so great, the danger more continuous and success more uncertain.

When making excursions with celebrated guides I profited by their company, in order to ascertain the limits of human strength in its resistance to work. In my notes of 1880, I find the following, which I communicate as an instance of the degree of excessive exertion which man can bear. Maquignaz started on July 21st from Val Tournanche, crossed the Col du Théodule and descended at Zermatt. The next day, having undertaken to conduct two Englishmen up the Matterhorn, he passed the night at the Swiss Hut. This was the first ascent which he had performed that year and he felt more tired than usual. On the 23rd he went down to Breuil. On the 24th he left again with a lady and gentleman with whom he ascended the Breithorn, returning afterwards to Breuil again. On the 25th he left once more for Zermatt with other Alpinists. On the 27th he again crossed the Matterhorn, and after sleeping at the Swiss Hut, descended to Giomein. For seven days in succession he had not been able to take his usual amount of sleep as he went to bed late and rose early in the morning. On arriving at his home after this extraordinary exertion, he remained for twenty-four hours in bed without being able to sleep or eat. Only on the second day he fell asleep, still fasting, and after a long sleep woke up fully restored.

If I have spoken often of the guides, those humble sons of our valleys, whose names are so indissolubly connected with the story of their Alps, it is because to these, our masters, a meed of praise is most justly due. Nor do I mean that honour is theirs merely on account of their physical strength: the character, the moral rectitude of the old guides of the Italian school are still more worthy of our emulation.

In the story of the Alps there are instances of love of country which claim from us the tribute of remembrance and the recognition of that virtue and abnegation which form the basis of the glory and strength of a people. When Giuseppe Maquignaz had discovered a path up the Dent du Géant, which till then had been thought inaccessible, he refused to conduct certain foreigners first to the summit, although they offered him a far greater sum than the Italian climbers were able to give.

Such idealism ennobles all of this humble shepherd-race who, in their lonely valleys, are animated by the thought of their country's greatness.

Noble souls they are, under a rough exterior, upright men, excellent comrades, often taciturn, but of a marvellous presence of mind when confronted by danger, of an undaunted promptitude of decision when face to face with death.

Seila Hut.   V. Sella

CHAPTER X

INDIVIDUAL DIFFERENCES

I.

IN Gartok, at an altitude of 4,598 metres, on the slopes of the Himalayas, towards Thibet, a fair is held every year in August, which draws thousands of individuals together from all parts of Central Asia. As there is not sufficient house-room for all, they bring black tents with them under which they spread out their wares and the fair begins. This is certainly the highest point in the world at which a market is held. At Hánle in Ladak and round about the lakes Mansaraur and Rakus, there are monasteries in still more elevated situations (4,619 metres) and which are inhabited all through the year by Buddhist monks. Shepherds with their flocks and wild sheep are to be found at still greater heights in the neighbourhood.[1]

The brothers Schlagintweit, who have given us a minute description of the populations living in the elevated regions of Asia, do not say that they are in any way different from us. Jourdanet, after a careful study of the thorax in the Mexicans concludes "that in men whose whole life has been spent in the midst of an atmosphere exercising only three-fourths of the usual

---

[1] Hermann, Adolph and Robert Schlagintweit, *Results of a scientific mission to India and High Asia.* Leipzig, London, 1862, vol. ii.

pressure, the thorax has not acquired any greater development than at the sea-level."[1]

In Europe, at a height of 3,000 metres many persons begin to suffer from mountain-sickness. In America, on the other hand, we have, at an altitude of 3,960 metres the city of Potosi celebrated for its silver mines, and which once numbered 160,000 inhabitants.

In this region, situated below the equator, Alexander von Humboldt attempted the ascent of Chimborazo in the last months of the eighteenth century. When he had reached the region of perpetual snow which begins there at a height a little above the summit of Mont Blanc, the natives forsook him.

"The Indians, with one exception, abandoned us at an altitude of 15,600 feet. Prayers and threats were alike vain; they declared that they were suffering much more than we." When the height of 5,800 metres was reached, Humboldt thus describes the condition of the party: "By degrees we all began to feel very ill at ease. The inclination to vomit was accompanied by slight dizziness and was much more distressing than the difficulty in breathing. Our gums and our lips bled. The conjunctiva was bloodshot in all of us without exception. At the time of the conquest of the equinoctial region of America the Spanish warriors did not go beyond the lower boundary of the region of perpetual snow, which corresponds to the height of Mont Blanc, and yet Acosta in his *Historia natural de las Indias* gives a detailed account of 'the discomfort and stomachic cramp, painful symptoms of *mountain-sickness*' which may be compared to sea-sickness."

I quote this passage from Humboldt because many ascribe great importance to cold as a factor in mountain-sickness. Here we see that in equatorial regions while the temperature was above zero, the symptoms of mountain-sickness at a height corresponding to that of Mont Blanc were as serious as in our hemisphere and that the natives, far from being exempt, suffered more than the Europeans.

The physiologist Alphonso Borelli, in describing his ascent of Mount Etna (alt., 3,310 metres) in 1671[2] mentions the serious state of lassitude which obliged the strongest men to sit down after only average exertion and gather strength by frequent breathing.

II.

The guide Mattia Zurbriggen of Macugnaga is, at the present day, the man by whom the greatest height has as yet been reached. Immediately after his return from the Himalayas I went to visit him, and, after making a little excursion with him on Monte Rosa, begged him to come to my laboratory for a few days in order that I might study him with greater convenience. A more accurate knowledge of this man who presents such resistance to rarefied air seemed to me a matter of importance to the study of the physiology of man in the Alps. Zurbriggen was with Conway on Pioneer Peak, which is 6,888 metres high. At this point Conway says: "All felt weak and ill, like men just lifted from beds of sickness, but Zurbriggen was able to smoke a cigar."[3] Zurbriggen still felt pretty well at this height, although, as he told

---

[1] Jourdanet, *Influence de la pression de l'air sur la vie de l'homme*. Tome iii. 321.
[2] *De Motu animalium*, Rome, 1681, p. 242.
[3] W. M. Conway, *Climbing and Exploration on the Karakoram-Himalayas*. London, 1894, p. 522.

me, any movement immediately caused a feeling of discomfort, and no one was able to tie on both shoes without pausing in between to draw breath, but in spite of this he was of opinion that at a slow pace it would have been possible to climb two thousand metres higher. Zurbriggen therefore entertains no doubt but that man is able to reach the loftiest peak on this earth which is 4,000 metres higher than the summit of Mont Blanc.

In 1895 Zurbriggen went with Fitzgerald on an expedition to the New

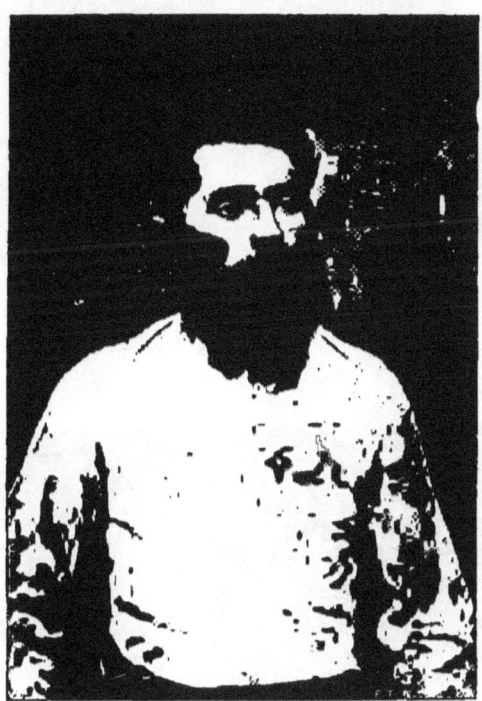

Mattia Zurbriggen.

Zealand Alps, and in January of last year he climbed the Peak of Aconcagua in Chili, the ascent of which was first attempted by Güssfeldt. Fitzgerald was obliged to stop a few hundred metres lower down, but Zurbriggen, who was accompanying him, reached the top of this volcano, 6,970 metres in height. This is the greatest height which has as yet been reached by man on the mountains. Fitzgerald is of opinion that Aconcagua has an altitude of over 24,000 feet.

Zurbriggen was, in 1894 when I examined him, thirty-eight years old, weighed 67 kilograms and had a stature of 1·68 metres. I ascertained his muscular force by means of the ergograph. With his middle finger he raised a weight of 4 kilograms, the curve given in Fig. 44 resulting. From it we see that the strength of his hands does not surpass the average but that he has a supernormal resistance to fatigue. This reproduction of the curve is smaller than the original by two-tenths.

Zurbriggen's pulse is somewhat irregular, I counted it for four minutes in succession, the number of pulsations being different every time: 55, 60, 63,

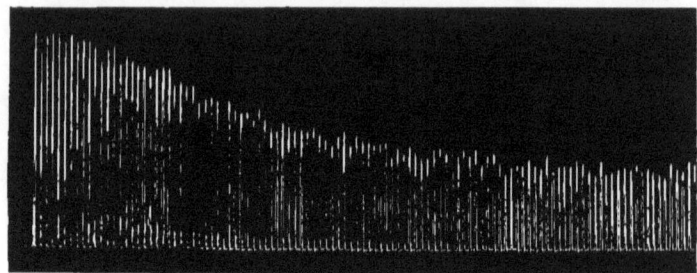

FIG. 44.—M. Zurbriggen. Ergographic-curve. A weight of 4 kilograms is raised every two seconds.

66. His heart is normal. I took the respiratory curve with Marey's double pneumograph which was simultaneously applied to thorax and abdomen. In Fig. 45, the upper curve shows the thoracic respiration, the lower that of the

FIG. 45. Zurbriggen. T. Thoracic respiratory curve. A. Abdominal respiratory curve written at the same time.

abdomen. Here, too, I found the usual rhythm and depth of breathing. Further on I shall mention other observations which I made on Zurbriggen; at present I need only add that he presents no peculiarities such as would lead one to expect his remarkable resistance.

Some physiologists have attributed immunity from mountain-sickness to a preponderating development of the thorax. Zurbriggen's vital capacity is 3,800 cubic centimetres, that is, a little above the average, which for a man of his stature (1 m. 68) would amount to 3,500. A glance at his photograph will, however, convince the reader that his chest width is not exceptional. The chest-girth is 0·91 metres.

I have carefully studied the body and functions of the nervous system in other guides and celebrated climbers, and have never found any difference between them and the average of men. One usually thinks the excellence of a guide or climber depends on the force of the muscles. The foregoing ergographic curve proves that this greater muscular energy is non-existent. I compared likewise Zurbriggen's legs with others and found that they were not more developed than those of the laboratory servant Giorgio Mondo, or of several other frequenters of the laboratory who had suffered severely from mountain-sickness. I know, moreover, celebrated Alpinists and guides who have slender legs. I did not, in fact, succeed in establishing either a physical or functional difference between Zurbriggen, the man who has broken the record in mountaineering, and other men.

III.

In the resistance to compressed air we find similar individual differences to those which manifest themselves under the influence of rarefied air. I noticed this in the diving-school in Spezia. Some sailors dived to a depth of 40 metres, a distance equal to four atmospheres. Others began to feel distress before they had reached a distance of 8 metres. They then shut the valve, the diving-apparatus filled with air and rose again to the surface. As it is an advantage for the sailors of the torpedo-boats to be certificated as divers, they being then paid by the hour for work under water, the fear that these exercises are compulsory, is excluded. I saw a soldier try to descend several times but he always returned to the surface before reaching a depth of 10 metres, although he endeavoured to accustom himself to the augmented pressure by a gradual descent.

My opinion is that the cause of these individual differences must be sought in the nervous system rather than in the blood. Paul Bert saw that mountain-sickness could not be attributed merely to lack of oxygen, as there are men who spend their whole lives at heights where others suffer intensely. He maintained, in order to remove this objection to his theory, that the composition of the blood must become altered, the adaptation consisting in the production of a greater number of red corpuscles and in a modification of the hæmoglobin.[1]

Facts have not supported either of these hypotheses. Jourdanet affirms that in elevated regions men are generally anæmic. I examined Zurbriggen's blood only a few months after his return from the height of 6,888 metres and found that it was normal. The number of corpuscles, the density, the colouring substance of the corpuscles were as in the majority of men.

It is singular that some persons who have survived very strong depressions, suffer from mountain-sickness at inconsiderable heights. I instance Gaston Tissandier.

The profound impression created twenty years ago by the catastrophe of the balloon "Zenith," in which Sivel and Croce-Spinelli met with a tragic end, will still be remembered by many.

As an instructive illustration of the action of rarefied air I quote a passage from the account which Tissandier published in his journal *Nature*.

[1] P. Bert, *Op. cit.*, p. 1,108.

"At a height of 7,000 metres Sivel, who had unusual physical strength and a sanguine temperament, began to close his eyes at intervals, to doze even and to lose colour. But his valiant spirit refused to give way to these movements of weakness for any length of time; he recovered himself with an expression of firmness, bade me empty the liquid contained in the exhauster after my experiment, and threw ballast overboard in order to reach more elevated regions.

"At 7,500 metres the numbness which comes over one is extraordinary. Body and mind grow gradually, imperceptibly weaker without our becoming aware of the change.

"Presently I wished to take hold of the oxygen tube but found that I could not raise my arm. My mind was, however, still quite lucid. I kept my eyes fixed on the barometer.

"I tried to call out: 'We are 8,000 metres high,' but my tongue was as though paralysed. Suddenly my eyes closed and I fell down like a log, completely losing consciousness. It was about 1.30 p.m.

"At 3.30 p.m. I re-opened my eyes feeling dazed and exhausted, but gradually my mind grew clear. The balloon was descending with frightful rapidity. My two companions were cowering down in the boat, their heads hidden under their travelling rugs. I gathered all my strength together and tried to raise them. Sivel's face was black, his eyes dull, his mouth open and filled with blood. Croce's eyes were half closed and his mouth covered with blood. . . .

"When I touched the ground again I was seized with a feverish excitement and fell down, while my face became of a livid hue. I thought I was about to join my friends in the next world."

The "Zenith" had reached a height of 8,600 metres. Three persons had taken part in the ascent and only Gaston Tissandier escaped death.

Our first idea is that Tissandier must have been more robust than his two companions. But this explanation would be incorrect. He survived, on the contrary, because he offered less resistance to the action of the rarefied air. He was the first to fall into a stupor and this sleep saved him. For the sake of brevity I have not quoted that part of the account which relates that Tissandier's companions were still in movement, working actively, while he was already so weak that he could not even turn his head to look at them. The profound sleep into which he fell, dulled the vital functions for some time, so that his passage through those elevated regions of the air left him unharmed. The other two utterly consumed their share of energy and perished from exhaustion due to the rarefaction of the air and cold. Similarly, we have seen that the brothers Zoja died in consequence of a much less considerable rarefaction of the air but a much greater degree of fatigue. I shall return to this subject later when speaking of sleep.

It became evident later, when Tissandier endeavoured to reach the summit of Mont Blanc, that he was not constitutionally a good Alpinist, in spite of his ascent to 8,600 metres. I extract these notes from a writing of M. Vallot, in which he describes the construction of his observatory on Mont Blanc.[1] While residing in his hut on the summit of Mont Blanc in the summer of 1890, M. Vallot learnt from his wife, who was in Chamonix, by means of the optic telegraph, that M. Gaston Tissandier was leaving to pay him a visit on Mont Blanc. I prefer, however, to relate the incident in Vallot's words in order that it may preserve all its Alpine colouring.

[1] I. Vallot, *Annuaire du Club Alpin Français*, vol. xvii., 1890.

"Towards 2 a.m. we were suddenly roused by a violent knocking at the door. It was two of my porters furnished with lanterns who had arrived with their loads. On my asking them, not without astonishment, what odd fancy had induced them to come at that hour, they handed me two letters: one was from M. Gaston Tissandier telling me that he had had a sunstroke on climbing up to the Grands-Mulets and that he would not proceed further, the other was from his friend M. Launette who informed me that M. Tissandier's condition had grown worse, that he was suffering not only from sunstroke but also from fever and mountain-sickness, and that the writer, a prey to the most lively anxiety, solicited my advice and my help.

"Six hours must be reckoned for the climb from the Grands-Mulets to the Bosses, but this is compensated for by the rapid descent: in one hour we had arrived at the hut. Happily M. Tissandier was much better; we chatted a long time together while he inhaled the oxygen which I had brought and then, completely restored by the vital gas, he rose and walked down with a firm step to Chamonix."

IV.

The mountain-climber who crosses the Alps by the Great St. Bernard, Mont Cenis, and elsewhere, looks with admiration on the roads constructed at this height and deems them a triumph of modern civilisation. And yet, many centuries ago, finer roads had been already made at still greater heights. In Peru the Incas constructed roads more than six metres wide at altitudes superior to all our Alpine passes.

Humboldt[1] in his *Ansichten der Natur* describes these ruins as follows:

"The Roman roads which I have seen in Italy are certainly not more imposing than these works of the ancient Peruvians, which I have come across at a height of 12,440 feet, at which height also I found the ruins of the palace of the Inca Tupac. These roads extending for forty-six geographical miles, some paved with level stones, others macadamised, crossed the Andes from the sea."

It is with a feeling of wonder and profound commiseration that we think of the ruins of those gigantic works carried out by an industrious people in the most elevated regions of the earth before Europeans carried extermination and desolation into their midst.

One road which rivals those described by Humboldt is the Great Pacific Railway, which, on the plateau of the Rocky Mountains at Evan Pass rises beyond 2,500 metres.

Thinking there might be racial differences as regards the resistance to rarefied air, I determined to gain some information on the life of the workmen and engineers who were engaged in the construction of the Great Pacific Railway. Dr. Paolo de Vecchi of San Francisco, once a fellow-student, kindly sent me some observations obtained from Mr. George Davidson and other engineers, who constructed the most difficult part of the railway.

I communicate a few passages from Mr. Davidson's letter[2]:—

"The highest summits of the Californian mountains, where I have been for weeks and sometimes for months together, are those situated along the

---

[1] A. Humboldt, *Ansichten der Natur*. Das Hochland von Caxamarca.
[2] Re-translated from the Italian.

Central Pacific Railway, which rise to a height of 4,000 metres. At an altitude of 3,000 metres I was able to perform a great deal of physical work in spite of the most varied conditions, and was scarcely aware of the elevation. At Mount Lola, 3,090 metres high, one of my friends who was visiting the station could not remain in my tent. He was obliged to eat and drink outside, because, as he said, when shut up he had a singular feeling of indisposition. He complained more especially of his head, and could not overcome his anxiety that some danger was threatening his mental faculties. This feeling of indisposition was greatly relieved when he was able to look around at the plants, animals and rocks outside of the tent. And yet we were a party of twenty men at work, and not one of us suffered. Ten of us stayed there for two months and a half without any inconvenience, and I worked even fifteen hours a day.

"At San Bernardino, 3,900 metres high, the last climb is so steep that it is impossible to scale it on donkeys. Here I had to halt every thirty metres, because my heart was beating 137 times in the minute, my breathing was 60, and I had to keep my mouth open. During the ascent I took a spoonful of brandy with a little snow at every halt. All the same I had twice a sudden and violent pricking pain in my heart. I reached the top, and after a few minutes' rest I walked along the crest of the rock without any further disturbance.

"I have always been a worker with great powers of resistance, and I may say that for about fifty years I have worked on the average fifteen hours a day, without even resting on Sundays.

"In 1885, in consequence of a strong emotion, I found my heart intermittent and irregular. At the end of a year, however, my normal condition had returned, and until now I have always been quite well.

"GEORGE DAVIDSON."

I have collected other documents relating to American mountaineering, but all know now that the Anglo-Saxon race does not present a superior resistance to fatigue, although it has furnished the greatest number of sturdy Alpinists. The Italian guides are, as a matter of fact, those which have best stood the trial of great ascents in every clime.

V.

The mode of reaction to stimuli presents the greatest individual variations.

I once stayed for several days at the Great St. Bernard Hospice (alt., 2,472 metres), and one week on the Little St. Bernard (alt., 2,513 metres), and observed that many persons show symptoms of mountain-sickness even at these inconsiderable heights. Some stop from time to time during the last part of the climb, and arrive panting. They are unable to eat, cannot sleep at night, and have a feverish feeling. Some of these feel quite restored on rising the next day, others, on the contrary, express the wish to return at once. It was doubtless only a chance occurrence that during my sojourn the two persons who suffered the most had come from Martigny, while of the large parties arriving from the Aosta side not a single member showed symptoms of indisposition.

Dr. Courten of Zermatt told me of a lady who had had an attack of mountain-sickness on the Riffelalp (alt., 2,127 metres), and of another who had suffered from the malady at Görnergrat (alt., 3,136 metres). He examined these ladies, but found no defect of the heart in either of them.

At Gressoney la Trinità (alt., 1,627 metres), where I have spent a month every summer for several years, I have noticed that fat persons more especially complain of the thin air during the first few days. This is comprehensible, as they have a greater weight to raise when they walk up the mountain. I have, however, also seen thin people suffer immediately on their arrival. These generally complain of headache, do not sleep well, suffer from oppressed breathing, especially at night time, and are apathetic. One young lady suffered from nausea and vomiting for almost two days.

Still lower even, at Gressoney St. Jean, some persons have a difficulty in breathing, and complain of sleeplessness. And yet at Gressoney la Trinità there is a group of houses at a height of 2,037 metres inhabited all through the winter. Moutei is in fact one of the highest inhabited places in Europe. I told this once to a rather corpulent friend while walking with him a little below Moutei. "I daresay," he replied, "but as for me, the first day that I was here everything swam before me, and I felt my legs give way beneath me simply owing to the rarefied air. Otherwise I was perfectly well, and accustomed myself in a few days to climb higher."

Professor G. Pisenti, in an article on mountain-sickness,[1] writes that when he was at Abetone in the Tuscan Apennines as physician, he suffered from mountain-sickness, although the altitude was inconsiderable.

"The climatic establishment," he writes, "is at a height of 1,380 metres, I, who usually sleep soundly for ten hours in succession, suffered from sleeplessness the whole of the time that I was up there, lost my appetite and became thin. One day, having attempted to climb the Libro Aperto (alt., 1,800 metres), I was utterly unable to reach the summit, so irresistible was the sense of fatigue which had come over me, to say nothing of laboured breathing and oppression on the chest."

I wrote to Professor Pisenti in order to have further information as to his condition, and he replied as follows: "I was at Abetone in the month of September, when the affluence of visitors had ceased, on which account there was very little to do, all the more so as almost everybody was in the best of health. I remained there for only ten days, as my sufferings had increased to such a pitch, from insomnia more especially, that I was compelled to give in. As soon as I had left Abetone and gone to Bologna, my tranquil rest returned, the wakefulness disappearing as though by magic. During the last days at Abetone I was troubled greatly by the loss of appetite which was such that with the exception of milk every food was repugnant to me."

The pains which some persons feel in old wounds when the barometer falls and the indisposition which warns nervous persons of the approach of a storm, are examples of the great susceptibility of certain individuals to the rarefaction of the air.

It is a law of life that physiological functions never correspond to an exact quantitative formula.

VI.

Giovanni Antonio Carrel once told me about an Englishman whom he conducted from the Riffel to the Breithorn. When they had reached the Breithorn Plateau, the Englishman fell to the ground as though dead.

[1] *In alto.* Cronaca bim. della Società Alpina friulana, 1895, p. 68.

This climber, knowing by experience that he would become ill, had taken with him two guides and two porters, whom he assured that the state he might fall into need cause them no anxiety, ordering them to take him to Breuil, even though they had to carry him. On the glacier he staggered like one drunken. His companions had to support him under the arms as he fell asleep from time to time and then fell down. They spent the night in the Théodule Hut, and then went down to Breuil. Here the guides learnt to their astonishment that the gentleman meant to attempt the ascent of the Matterhorn. All in chorus tried to dissuade him, but he was not to be moved. He said that he was accustomed to these sufferings of the first day, and averred that he would be perfectly well on the morrow, and, indeed, the next day he began the climb up the rocks of the Matterhorn with firm and sure foot.

I know no other instance of so speedy an acclimatisation. If disturbances so serious disappear in a time so brief, we must conclude that mountain-sickness does not depend on the blood, for the number of red corpuscles and the quantity of iron or hæmoglobin which they contain cannot sensibly change in the space of two days. Only the nervous system is capable of so prompt an adaptation.

Not all have, however, the same facility of acclimatisation. In this respect the instance of Professor Pisenti is very instructive. I have seen very robust persons who, even after four or five days spent in the Regina Margherita Hut, were not yet acclimatised; they still were awaked through the night by oppression on the chest, and had to rise in order to obtain relief. As soon as they had descended to an altitude of 2,500 metres they slept profoundly the whole night.

It has been maintained in support of the hypothesis that mountain-sickness is caused by lack of oxygen, that persons living at an altitude beyond 3,000 metres have lungs which from birth are adapted in development and structure to the rarefaction of the air. But this is not the case, because even amongst the natives of Asia and America born on the slopes of the highest mountains, there are some who suffer from mountain-sickness if they ascend further, whereas amongst those born at the sea level there are some able to resist very high degrees of rarefaction. I venture, therefore, to affirm that a great part of mankind is born with lungs and nervous system adapted for living at great altitudes. We have an instance of this in the recent memorable journey of Mr. George R. Littledale,[1] who, in 1895, travelled across Tibet from north to south. He was accompanied by Mrs. Littledale and by a nephew, the party remaining six months (from April 26th to October 16th) at or above an altitude of 15,000 feet. They encamped for four weeks above the height of 4,600 metres. One hundred horses were lost on this journey, and Mrs. Littledale became seriously ill at a height above that of Monte Rosa.

[1] George R. Littledale. *A Journey across Tibet.* The Geographical Journal, May, 1896, vol. vii. p. 478.

FIG. 46.—Field-bed set up. Another to the left is packed up ready for transport.

CHAPTER XI

TRAINING—VITAL CAPACITY—MOUNTAINEERING

I.

THE object of training is to increase the strength of the body. The law in accordance with which the augmentation of strength through exercise proceeds, becomes apparent during the performance of ascents, but a more satisfactory explanation of it can only be obtained by means of simple experiments continued for a considerable length of time, which furnish constant terms of comparison.

Dr. G. Manca determined, in my laboratory, the manner in which the strength of the arms increases through exercise. The dumb-bells which he made use of for this investigation weighed five kilograms each, like those which we used later on Monte Rosa. During the experiment, repeated daily at the same hour, a metronome beat the seconds. The dumb-bells were raised from the position of repose to the height of the thorax, then above the head, lowered again to the height of the thorax, and then to the original position. One second was allowed to elapse between each movement, and this exercise was continued until, as I mentioned before in the first chapter, the subject became tired. Dr. Manca continued this exercise for seventy days in succession, Dr. Cao for thirty-five days.

Fig. 47 shows the results of training in Dr. Manca. The progressive augmentation of the quantity of work performed every day appears evident from the rapid ascent of the line which begins in the lower corner of the left hand and finishes at the upper right-hand corner. The numbers below indicate the days of exercise, those in the margin to the right and left mark the number of times which the dumb-bells were raised every day. There are variations from one day to another, we see sometimes that strength has diminished or has remained the same as on the preceding day, but the training-curve is nevertheless an ascending line. On the seventieth day Dr. Manca raised the dumb-bells 126 times, thus accomplishing an amount of work five times greater than on the first day. The training-curve is therefore not a straight line, nor yet a parabola, nor any one of the many regular geometrical curves.

In order to discover the fundamental type amongst the daily irregularities, Dr. Manca took the average of the daily increase of every fifteen days. The smaller figure in the higher left-hand corner gives a graphic representation of the average augmentation of strength calculated in this manner. The numbers below and above the figure indicate the successive periods of exercise of fifteen days each, the numbers to the left hand, the average daily augmentation. Thus we see that in the first fifteen days Dr. Manca's daily average increase of strength amounted to 1·28, in the second to 2·62, in the third to 3, in the fourth to 3·53, in the fifth to 5.

Taking into account Fechner's studies on this subject, Dr. Manca concluded that "muscular strength increases during prolonged exercise in an irregular geometric progression."[1]

II.

The above is an exposition of the fundamental law in accordance with which strength increases through exercise; it must, however, be confessed that we are but at the beginning of these investigations; no study has yet been made, by means of exact methods applied to other muscles, of the effects of that severe training to which superiority in the various physical exercises is due.

On the occasion of a visit to the University of Oxford I asked one of the celebrated trainers for the boat-race what was the object of the course of training, which is there of the duration of one month. He extended the fingers of one hand and closed them one after another as he replied:—

"1stly. To get rid of fat and superfluous water.

"2ndly. To increase the force of the muscular contractions.

"3rdly. To increase the resistance to fatigue.

"4thly. To train the breathing.

"5thly. To regulate the heart's action."

This answer convinced me that the trainer was fully master of his vocation. "To any one who is not properly trained," he added, "exertion gives a feeling of suffocation, owing to the difficulty of drawing breath deep enough." This is also the opinion of mountain-climbers and of all those who have felt what it is to be "out of breath" during a rapidly performed ascent. We shall see, however, that just the opposite is the case. Training accustoms us to breathe less during the same or even greater exertion.

All who have observed recruits running, or youths who are beginning their training for a race, will have noticed that they cannot hold out for five minutes without their breathing becoming laboured. After several months of training they are, on the contrary, able to run for half an hour unhindered by oppressed respiration, palpitation, or pain in the spleen. A part of the

---

[1] G. Manca, *Études sur l'entraînement musculaire.* Archives italiennes de Biologie, tome xvii. p. 390.

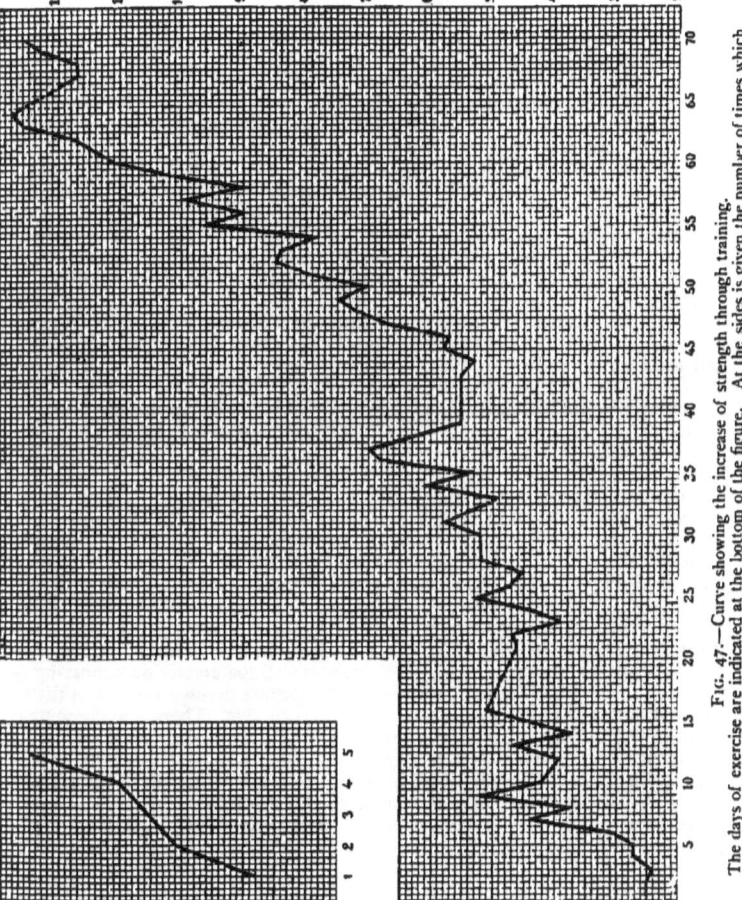

FIG. 47.—Curve showing the increase of strength through training. The days of exercise are indicated at the bottom of the figure. At the sides is given the number of times which the five-kilogram dumb-bells were raised by Dr. Manca at four-second intervals.

resistance thus gained is always lost during the winter when we give ourselves up more to repose.

The effects of training vary greatly in different individuals. During repeated sojourns at Alpine stations I have seen the less robust persons suffer from every little exertion during the first few days. A walk which occasioned the least fatigue, a steep path, a series of steps, such as one often meets with on short cuts, caused palpitation and coughing. The latter is a momentary irritation of the bronchia due to the accumulation of blood in the lungs. The heart becomes sooner tired and the lungs, in consequence of the deep inspirations, swell and become hyperæmic. After a few weeks of exercise the heart and the whole body are so much strengthened that these same persons are able to perform much greater exertions and even to attempt ascents.

Even very strong individuals may experience mountain-sickness if they are not trained. I instance two mountain-climbers by whom very great heights had already been reached—Conway and Fitzgerald. The former, in describing his journey through the Alps from the Col de Tende, writes [1] : "When we started walking in June it is probable that none of us were in very good condition. Our early ascents were made in a region which nowhere rises to a high level, and for some days we did not reach an altitude of 10,000 feet. At this time we frequently experienced discomfort from the effect of diminished atmospheric pressure. The fact appears to be worth record, for I do not remember ever before noticing any similar sensations in Europe at so low an elevation. I shall describe only my own experiences, but they were similar to those of the rest of the party. I have said that we were not in good mountaineering condition, but I was not in bad condition either. I had been taking two hours' exercise with daily regularity for several months and could walk twenty miles, at any rate, without inconvenient fatigue. I was, in fact, distinctly pleased with myself the first day in the hills, and thought I had never begun an Alpine season so well. My disgust was all the greater next morning, when, at about 7,000 feet, all the symptoms overtook me in a mild form that we used to feel at about 19,000 feet in the Karakorams. There was the same peculiar fatigue, the same discomfort if the regularity of the breathing were interfered with, the same disinclination to stoop or permit the arms to press against the sides. I should probably not have noticed these effects in detail if Himalayan experience had not familiarised me with each of them in an acute form. The faintest suggestion of them was therefore immediately perceived and recognised for what it was."

III.

" The first lovers of the Alps were all scientists, hence one understands that mountaineering took first an essentially scientific direction. Perhaps now that the exploration of the Alps is complete is the favourable moment for a return to those early ideals."

These words of one of the most intrepid and esteemed colleagues of the Alpine Club recurred to me when, from the Regina Margherita Hut, I had a nearer view of those dangers which he overcame in company with Vaccarone and Zurbriggen, when ascending Gnifetti Peak from the Macugnaga side.[2] I repeat them now that I am about to write a few lines on the

[1] W. M. Conway, *The Alps from End to End.* London, 1895, p. 12.
[2] Guido Rey, *Il Colle Gnifetti.* Boll. Club alpino italiano, vol. xxvii., 1894.

future of mountaineering with the conviction that their author would be better able than any other to give a rational and hygienic direction to the scholastic excursions (*carovane scolastiche*).

The physiological study and practical following-up of training have scarcely even reached an elementary stage, notwithstanding the numerous publications on the subject. Whatever part of our organism physician or dilettante may set himself to study in order to ascertain the laws in accordance with which its functions become invigorated by exercise, he will find untrodden ground before him.[1]

Dr. Gruber[2] and Prof. H. Kronecker made a series of researches on training, and found that a man, walking on level ground, produces double the amount of carbonic acid which he produced when in repose. Another experiment was then made. The subject was made to ascend the tower of Berne cathedral from the level of the Aar, a height of eighty metres. During the first days he produced four times more carbonic acid than when in repose. When he was trained to the exercise he only produced three times more carbonic acid than when in repose. These researches are important as they confirm the use of training with statistical accuracy. They show that the production of carbonic acid is not a function indissolubly connected with muscular work. Through exercise we learn to make our muscles work with a smaller quantity of fuel. Prof. Zuntz of Berlin obtained the same results almost at the same time.

It is, however, more especially with regard to the training of the nervous system that modern physiology shows the greatest gaps. As an illustration of this I need only mention dizziness. Goethe,[3] in speaking of the years which he spent at the University of Strasburg, wrote as follows:

"My state of health was such that I felt able to carry out successfully any necessary or desired undertaking; I retained only a certain sensitiveness which sometimes disturbed my equability. More especially was I distressed by dizziness which attacked me whenever I looked down from a height. I mounted alone, the highest tower of the cathedral and sat for about a quarter of an hour in the so-called neck, under the corona as it is termed, before I dared step out into the fresh air again, on to the platform which is scarcely one yard square and offers small means for holding fast. Standing here one sees an endless expanse of country before one. . . . One has the feeling as though one were floating through the air in a balloon. I imposed a frequent repetition of this terror and suffering on myself, until at last I became quite indifferent to the former impressions. These preliminary exercises proved later of great advantage to me on journeys through the mountains, during geological studies, on visiting large edifices in building, when I emulated the carpenters in running over the rafters and cornice, in Rome also where the closer inspection of important works of art necessitates such feats."

The high temperature of the body, the palpitation of the heart, the muscular changes, the oppressed breathing resulting from exertion, all diminish when we train the body.

The oldest writer on medicine, Hippocrates, expressed the fact in the words, *Motus roborat, otium labefacit.*

[1] Those who wish to know the titles of works and articles on this subject I refer to Billings' *Index Catalogue*, where, under the heading "Exercise as a Remedy," they will find over two hundred publications; those, equally numerous, by the trainers of race-horses are not included, nor the books and articles designed for the use of the students preparing fo foot-races and boat-races. The recent publications of F. Lagrange are worthy of notice.

[2] Max Gruber, *Ueber den Einfluss der Uebung auf den Stoffwechsel.* 1888.

[3] Goethe, *Aus meinem Leben*, ix Buch.

IV.

The greater development of the chest compared to that of the rest of the body has always been a sign of strength. Helbig remarked that the statues of classical Greek art are all in an inspiratory position, the chest thus attaining its greatest breadth.

To the English physician, John Hutchinson,[1] we owe a practical method for the measurement of the amount of air which an individual introduces into his lungs. The instrument which he invented for this purpose, and to which he gave the name of spirometer, is often seen in gymnasia, in hospitals, and in those rooms of life insurance societies set apart for the medical examination of clients. The capacity of the lungs is indeed an important item in the physical valuation of a person. It is not, however, the only thing to be considered, nor is it, perhaps, the most important characteristic, as we shall presently see.

Hutchinson's spirometer cannot be conveniently carried on Alpine expeditions. Even in the plain, if one has not had much practice, so as to be able to rectify it, serious errors may be incurred by its use. I made use of the gas-meter described in Chapter III., p. 39, and by its aid ascertained the vital capacity of all those who had accompanied me, and of all chance visitors during our sojourn on Monte Rosa. The vital capacity in each case was measured three times and an average then drawn from the resultant figures. As fatigue decreases the depth of the inspiration when three full breaths are drawn one after the other, I allowed for this and other reasons presently to be mentioned several minutes to elapse between the measurements.

The apparatus was placed on a rather high table, and in order always to ensure a horizontal position it was supported by a board of wood furnished with three pressure screws. An air-level completed the arrangement, as elsewhere stated. The subject stood upright, with vest unbuttoned (so that the deep inspiration he was about to make might encounter no obstacle), slowly and forcibly filled his thorax with air, and then, having introduced the india-rubber tube between his lips, exhaled the same slowly, as completely as possible emptying the lungs.

Let us now see whether a person at an altitude of 4,560 metres introduces a greater or lesser quantity of air into the lungs than in the plain.

A similar experiment made by Paul Bert[2] in the pneumatic chamber showed a diminution by one-half of the vital capacity at a pressure of 420 mm., which corresponds to the height of Monte Rosa.

Other physiologists who have measured the vital capacity in rarefied air have found smaller, but still considerable differences. Vivenot says that two strong persons inhaled, the one 494 cubic centimetres, the other 394 c.c. less than at the ordinary pressure, when breathing air rarefied to correspond to a height of 4,470 metres, one maximum inspiration and expiration being executed.

I restrict myself to the communication of a few observations made on Monte Rosa, for which I refer the reader to the table at the end of the book (Table X.). From the series of measurements taken we see that at an altitude of 4,560 metres the vital capacity was always less than it was in Turin.

---

[1] John Hutchinson, *Von der Capacität der Lungen.* Braunschweig, 1849.
[2] P. Bert, *Pression barométrique,* p. 716.

V.

If instead of studying the pulmonary capacity of man when in repose at varying altitudes above the level of the sea, we do so during a march or after the accomplishment of an ascent, the problem becomes much more complicated.

In Chapter III. I have mentioned that the force of inspiration diminishes when fatigue becomes general; besides this, it is possible that laborious ascents give rise to an accumulation of blood in the lungs. If this be the case, we can understand why a few minutes' rest is sufficient to restore strength. Without taking into account all the causes which awaken a sensation of well-being in repose, let us examine this hypothesis of a stagnation of blood in the lungs. Many persons feel dizzy after blowing up a fire or drawing a succession of deep breaths. This slight sensation of vertigo I have shown (by means of an instrument which I need not here describe) to be produced by an accumulation of blood in the lungs.[1] At every inspiration a greater quantity of blood is collected in the lungs than is expelled by the expiration following. This sudden withdrawal of blood from the heart and circulatory apparatus gives rise to anæmia of the brain.

If, at the end of an ascent, the blood-vessels which line the surface of the alveoli and bronchia are dilated and contain an overplus of blood, there will be less space for the air inhaled. Let us therefore see what results are obtained with the spirometer.

Sarteur and Solferino, two of the strongest men of our party, left Gnifetti Hut at 4.30 p.m. without loads, and arrived at the Regina Margherita Hut at 7 p.m., fasting, but in excellent condition. Temperature, —13°.

Immediately after their arrival we measured their pulmonary capacity. They each executed alternately three inspirations, the measurement being repeated after 1 hour and 35 minutes.

Sarteur...	3,806 cubic centimet.	3,952 c.c.	4,099 c.c.
After 1 hr. and 35 min.	4,666 c.c.	4,904 c.c.	4,782 c.c.
Solferino	4,123 c.c.	4,148 c.c.	3,928 c.c.
After 1 hr. and 35 min.	4,489 c.c.	4,489 c.c.	4,392 c.c.

If we take the average of the three first observations made by means of the spirometer on the soldier Sarteur immediately after the ascent, and compare it with the average of the three observations made after the lapse of one hour and thirty-five minutes, we see that in this space of time the vital capacity increased by 832 cubic centimetres. In Solferino the augmentation was only 390 cubic centimetres. I consider it probable that these figures partially represent the quantity of blood from which the lungs had in the interval freed themselves, but the conditions of this experiment prevent a positive affirmation.

Other and more minute researches than we were able to make during our brief stay on Monte Rosa are necessary. We know that the heart, too, dilates during ascents in consequence of fatigue. After an hour and a half

---

[1] A. Mosso, *Sulla circolazione del sangue nel cervello dell' uomo.* R. Accademia dei Lincei, 1879. *Ueber den Kreislauf des Blutes im menschlichen Gehirn.* Leipzig, 1881 p. 139.

this organ must have diminished in volume, thus permitting of the entrance of a little more air into the thorax by means of the lungs. Again, we have the fatigue of the inspiratory muscles, and a still more serious complication in the paralysis of the vagus nerve, all of which factors contribute to produce the dilatation of the pulmonary blood-vessels. This enumeration makes the difficulty of the investigation apparent.

The idea had occurred to me that mountain-sickness was perhaps due to a circulatory disturbance, the immediate cause being the accumulation of blood in the lungs.

In several persons who suffered from mountain-sickness with the annoying phenomena of vomiting, sleeplessness, and headache, in Sig. Bertarelli and Sig. Bizzozero, amongst others, I measured the pulmonary capacity while the symptoms were most pronounced, and again on the day when they had disappeared, and found no difference after the cessation of the indisposition. Sig. Bertarelli's average vital capacity remained at 3,480 cubic centimetres, and Bizzozero's at 4,200 cubic centimetres with small variations.

If we compare the vital capacity of the two keepers of the Regina Margherita Hut with that of travellers who arrived there suffering from mountain-sickness, the conviction forces itself upon us that the quantity of air which we introduce into the lungs has a lesser efficacy than is generally thought.

Francioli and Quaretta, the two keepers of the Regina Margherita Hut, are, amongst all the inhabitants of Europe, perhaps those who remain for the greatest length of time at an altitude of 4,560 metres every year. They go up at the beginning of July and stay till the end of September if the weather permits.

In spite of their continually ascending and descending the glaciers of Monte Rosa with their provisions on their shoulders, their vital capacity is in proportion to their stature and weight.

Francioli, whose photograph is reproduced in the next chapter, is 1 metre 74 centimetres in height, weighs 77 kilograms, and has a vital capacity of 4,017 cubic centimetres. Beno Bizzozero, whose stature is 1 metre 78 centimetres, and weight 59 kilograms, has a vital capacity of 4,200 cubic centimetres. Francioli has never suffered from mountain-sickness; Bizzozero had rather a severe attack immediately after his arrival at the Regina Margherita Hut, although his vital capacity surpassed that of Francioli.

Quaretta is 1 metre 64 centimetres in height, has a weight of 70 kilograms, a pulmonary capacity of 3,790 cubic centimetres, and never suffers from mountain-sickness.

I might here add a long list of persons who suffered from mountain-sickness, although their pulmonary capacity, in proportion to their stature and weight, surpassed the average.

VI.

It is indubitable that the exercise of the legs produces an augmentation of the thoracic capacity. Marey's[1] researches on this subject alone afford a sufficient proof. In my book on physical education I have written a few pages in order to show that the use of the gymnastic apparatus is not essential to the enlargement of the thorax, the same effect being produced by walking

---

[1] Marey, *Modifications des mouvements respiratoires par l'exercice musculaire.* Comptes rendus, 1880, p. 145.

and athletic sports. Prof. Ziemssen recently held a lecture in Munich on the importance of sports in the open air for young people, communicating the results of the observations made by himself and his assistants for many years in the schools. On comparing the values obtained with the spirometer he found that when the pupils return after the autumn holidays their vital capacity is greater than when they leave school at the end of the summer. Prof. Ziemssen attributes this augmentation to the free movement in the open air.

It is generally believed that a sojourn in the Alps effects an enlargement of the thorax. Experiments on the members of our expedition did not enable me to confirm this, although we remained for more than a month on Monte Rosa, owing to the fact that we were already trained before starting. Marches in the plain also effect a maximum expansion of the thorax, which cannot be augmented even by a sojourn in the Alps.

Before me lies a statistical register of the vital capacity, height, weight, and age of my colleagues of the Turin Section of the Alpine Club. These figures which I determined with the utmost accuracy would doubtless please lovers of statistics, and might not be without use in anthropometrical investigation, but I fear their insertion would render this work too voluminous, I therefore restrict myself to a summary of the results.

Some mountain-climbers with a pulmonary capacity above the average, suffer nevertheless from mountain-sickness.

Two excellent climbers who have accomplished the most difficult ascents have a pulmonary capacity below the average.

These results show that current opinion on this subject is not very reliable. Small lung volume is therefore no obstacle to our becoming good climbers and enduring exertion and the rarefaction of the air on ascents. It is not true that a pulmonary capacity surpassing the average ensures immunity from mountain-sickness.

VII.

Nearly every year when I go into the mountains, I take note, during my first walks, of the rate at which the muscles of the legs resume their working fitness.

I shall illustrate my meaning by an example. If I take a first walk from Gressoney la Trinità to Lake Gabiet, passing by Orsia, and returning by the Netscio Valley, walking slowly, I am four or five hours on the way, ascending during this time from 1,627 metres to 2,339 metres, a height, that is, of 712 metres. The next day, and even two days afterwards, the muscles have not yet returned to their normal state, and in stretching them by putting the foot to the ground I feel a slight stiffness and pain. This pain is due to the effort made during the descent to counterpoise the weight of the body by means of muscles not yet inured to the work.

After a week's exercise I go on foot to the Col d'Olen, stay there for lunch, and return in the evening. The exertion is in this case double the former, the ascent being from 1,627 to 2,865 metres, and yet the day following I feel not the least pain in the legs.

Until now, so far as I know, no methodical investigations have been made of the time necessary to cancel the effects of training. In my book *L'educazione fisica della gioventù*,[1] I have touched on this subject, showing

[1] Chap. vii. section iv. p. 145.

that the augmentation in the volume of the muscles due to exercise soon disappears, whereas the inurement of the nervous system is more persistent. "From these first experiments it appears that the effect of exercise on the nervous system, the internal effect so to speak, lasts longer than the peripheral or muscular effect."

Respecting the change in the capacity of the lungs, I made an important observation on Dr. A. Ferrari, one of the most active members of our Alpine Club. Last year, in the month of September, he had a vital capacity of 5,040 cubic centimetres and a weight of 71·4 kilograms, his age being twenty-seven years and his height 1·82 metres. The measurements were taken while he was in good training, having performed a considerable number of ascents. During the first few days the figure 5,040 c.c. was almost constant.

After the repose of a month his vital capacity had diminished, and he was unable in spite of effort to pass the limit of 4,630 c.c. We see from this experiment how brief is the effort of training on the capacity of the lungs.

It is my opinion that the adaptational improvements acquired through exercise disappear in the same order in which they became manifest. Future research will probably show that the expansion of the lungs and the augmentation of the volume of the muscles are the first phenomena to disappear during the repose of a few weeks, then the heart will diminish in volume, and lastly, the acquired capabilities of the nervous system will be lost. Some of the latter will, however, hold their ground notwithstanding the rapidity of their acquirement. Cycling, for instance, establishes in us a nice sense of equilibrium which remains with us throughout life, although the co-ordination of the movements called for was developed in a few days in the spinal cord and brain which immediately adapted themselves to this new function.

Mountain-sickness decreases as the training of Alpinists becomes more complete, and as the Alpine refuge-huts increase in number and comfort.

Whymper remarks that had he to chose between rendering the Alps less laborious, or mountain-climbers more robust, he would prefer the latter. All are, I think, of his opinion. Nevertheless it is indispensable to the progress of mountaineering that the Alpine refuge-huts should be multiplied and, as much as possible, improved.

The conquest of the highest summits is now complete, the most adventurous and dangerous epoch in the history of ascents in Europe. Mountaineering will now return to its normal lines: the serene contemplation of the Alps, without the morbid enthusiasm for exhausting marches or the mad appetite for dangers, will once more hold sway.

Doubtless others have had the same experience as myself, and have found that bird's-eye views of great panoramas from the loftiest peaks of the Alps have scarcely left a trace in the memory. The most vivid impressions of my Alpine life are those of days spent in encampments at an altitude between 2,000 and 3,000 metres, contemplating the grand profile of the Alps, admiring the perpetually changing effects of light in the valleys or gazing with wonder at the glorious sunsets. Far from civilisation and social annoyances, the fever of care subsides, existence, viewed with more humility and more sincerity, assumes a poetic aspect of unspeakable charm.

It is my hope that mountain-climbers, renouncing the vain glory of foolhardy ascents, may find their delight in travelling through the Alps, inspired with enthusiastic affection for these grandest of our mountains.

A mountain-loving youth, to whom a tent at the height of the last pastures is the fulfilment of their desires, would be an ideal outcome of mountaineering. A people who love their mountains will certainly become not only stronger physically, but will acquire likewise a greater moral force of character.

VIII.

In the neighbourhood of Oxford I once had the pleasure of coming across an encampment of students in a wood. When the University term is over these young men set off in companies for a boating party of a few weeks' duration. In the evening they cease rowing, pitch their tents under the trees on the banks of the river, begin cooking operations, and rest from the labours of the day. In the morning they take to the boats again at an early hour, or else make a longer halt in order to fish, draw, shoot, or read.

Camping-out is a dream of happiness to the sturdy English youth. On the Alps nomadic life is still more delightful and salutary. Amongst the pleasantest recollections of younger years I count two excursions which I made in the mountains with my knapsack on my back. I still preserve the diary of a journey in Savoie undertaken with a few friends in 1868. These were the first pages which I wrote on the Alps and now, thirty years later, I still re-read with pleasure those youthful impressions and first botanical notes on the Alpine flora. Of another excursion to the Gran Paradiso, the Little and Great St. Bernard, with other students, I shall have occasion to speak later.

I am convinced that in a great measure I owe my physical strength to my love for outdoor life, to my predilection for walking, for exertion, to a cheerful indifference to ease and to a contempt for idleness—in a word, to the virtues of the mountain-climber. I would never advise any youth to stay at large hotels unless obliged to do so. The centres which offered the greatest attraction to Alpinists are gradually being transformed into vast hospitals filled with the germs of phthisis owing to the great influx of consumptive invalids. The most elementary caution warns us to avoid living or coming into contact with these sufferers. Any one who is free to do so, all leaders of Alpine excursions should always choose those regions less frequented by visitors and flee all hotels which offer the greatest luxury and ease. Young climbers who wish to become strong and hardy should sojourn at considerable heights, and for shelter give preference to Alp huts and shepherds' cottages.

For the sake of greater independence, camping is preferable to all. With a tent and a bed one is provided with a house of one's own on the Alps, nor is the expenditure necessitated great. If two Alpinists club together, take with them one guide and two porters, an expedition is easily organised and sufficient comfort ensured. The field-bed, of which I give a drawing in Fig. 46, weighs ten kilograms altogether when packed into the waterproof bag furnished with straps for carriage, as may be seen to the left of the illustration. When the bed is set up the wadded waterproof cloth serves as a mattress. By means of a chain the head-end may be raised or lowered at pleasure. Many consider a woollen or india-rubber cushion unnecessary. On our expedition we each had two sheets; but this, too, is luxury, for the rugs suffice. An india-rubber basin and a folding-stool, such as are seen near the foot of the bed in the illustration, completed the furniture of our tent.

Until free excursions have become an institution amongst climbers, I fear those will be few in number and only of the wealthier classes who will be able to grant themselves the luxury of camping-out on the Alps. Any one who has experienced the charm of this mode of life will certainly prefer the tent to furnished apartments at hotels. I hope the time is not far off in which the different sections of the Alpine Club will interest themselves in making it possible to hire the necessaries for expeditions of this kind. The progress of hygiene and mountaineering is drawing us onward to these new ideals of an open-air life. Co-operation will doubtless solve all difficulties.

It is difficult to predict the future of mountaineering. Since it has become an art, "the true Alpinist," as Vaccarone said, "loves art for art's sake." The mountains offer ever new difficulties to the climber, and spur him on to new deeds of daring. Some thought that mountaineering would die a natural death when man had set his foot on all hitherto untrodden summits. But this is not the case. The most daring form of mountaineering will survive so long as there are men who feel the need of strong emotions. Even a superficial examination of the social psychology of our day will convince us that the keynote of our emotional gamut is assuming a continually higher pitch. The more modern nervousness blunts sensibility, the more imperatively does it demand an increase of intensity in stimuli. This, too, is a physiological law.

IX.

It is a fatal error of the ruling classes to diminish more and more the time destined to physical exercise in schools. Another prejudicial effect of present education is the distressing uniformity it aims at, which suffocates all initiative in the young. Against an excess of this kind there is no other remedy than the promotion of vigorous but scientifically directed physical training. Mountaineering is therefore, above all else, to be recommended to young people; no other exercise gives perhaps a greater impetus to individual activity or more effectually strengthens the character and enlivens the intelligence. The most simple and most natural mode of life gives the most satisfactory development to both body and mind.

All sports are useful according to surroundings and individual inclination, and all serve to invigorate and straighten the present generation, growing round-backed over its books. But all may become injurious if followed to excess. Cycling had the merit of having given a powerful impulse to muscular exercise and to have rendered exertion popular. Now, however, we are near pursuing the diversion to a vicious excess.

Ch. du Pasquier, in a psychological article on the pleasure of cycling, published in the *Revue Scientifique* in August, 1896, wrote the following memorable words:—

"It is comprehensible under these circumstances that immoderate bicycle exercise brings about a state in which activity of the nerves is reduced to a minimum and the individual deprived of his personality, just as machine labour and the division of labour rob the workman of all initiative and reduce him to the level of an automatic machine."

Cycling is not actually a sport, it is a means of locomotion, of which an abuse has been made by professionals whom the public encourages by paying them. The most serious injury produced by bicycle races is the hypertrophy of the heart. The most celebrated champions remain at their best only for a few years, they soon attain their maximum of velocity and resistance, and then become victims to cardiac hypertrophy. Whereas the

Alpinist increases in strength and continues to perform difficult ascents even at sixty years of age, the cyclist rapidly grows old; his fame and his existence are ephemeral, because he exacts from his muscles and blood a pressure to which the human heart is unequal.

Only for those who use it with caution is cycling an advantageous exercise, and several Alpinists have told me that it helps to train them. This is not due to the exercise of the legs, because the muscles which put the pedals in movement are not all those called into activity when we walk. One may, in fact, be an excellent cyclist, and a very bad walker. The use of cycling, considered as a sport, lies in the vigorous exercise of the heart, because a slight degree of cardiac hypertrophy such as is produced by moderate bicycle exercise, is an advantage to those who undertake ascents.

Life in the mountains is best adapted to re-invigorate the human race. The recorded experience of centuries has taught us this, and modern medical art confirms the statement by means of the climatic cures through which numerous lives have been saved from the deplorable effects of disease. Frequent walks, the sight of nature, the colder and drier air leave in us a pleasing sensation, as though our energy had increased. The apathetic shake off their indolence, the languid are revived by the intenser light. But training, above all, is a factor in these resurrections. In the mountains we see weak persons take lengthy walks and endure exertions such as they would never have borne in town. The varied landscape, the desire to see new things, a certain amount of common emulation increases the resistance. In the Alps all feel a greater need of movement. The wish to strengthen our organism, to reconstruct it by means of the new life amid the awe-inspiring scenes of mountains and glaciers, the craving for exertion are the inexhaustible springs which will keep mountaineering for ever flourishing.

Greeting the arrival of a mountaineering party at the Regina Margherita Hut.

CHAPTER XII

MOUNTAIN-SICKNESS

I.

IN 1760 Saussure published a notice in all the parishes of the Valley of Chamonix, intimating that he would give a considerable reward to any who found a path by which the summit of Mont Blanc might be reached. At the same time he promised to pay the day's work to those whose attempts should prove fruitless.[1]

These promises effected nothing. Only fifteen years later four mountaineers from Chamonix attempted the ascent. Everything seemed to promise success. The weather was splendid and the travellers neither met with crevasses too wide, nor slopes too steep. Only the reflected rays of the sun and the motionless air produced a suffocating heat which made them feel an

[1] Saussure, *Voyages dans les Alpes*. Histoire des tentatives que l'on a faites pour parvenir à la cime du Mont Blanc, tome iv. p. 389.

aversion, disgust even, for food. It was after this essay that Jorasse told Saussure it was useless to carry eatables, an umbrella in one hand and a bottle of smelling salts in the other being all that was needed.

Six years later three others crossed the glacier with the intention of going to pass the night on the mountain La Côte, and had climbed a considerable height when one of them, the most robust, was seized with an invincible inclination to sleep, whereupon they turned back.

Before Saussure's time it was considered dangerous even to climb as high as Montanvert.[1] The aptitude and strength for climbing seem, like the resistance to mountain-sickness, to have developed gradually in Alpinists.

In speaking of mountain-sickness Saussure writes :—

"I have observed rather a curious fact, and that is, that for certain individuals there are clearly defined limits at which the rarity of the air becomes insupportable to them. I have often taken peasants with me, who, although otherwise very robust, experienced suddenly at a given height such a sense of discomfort that they were absolutely unable to mount higher; neither rest, nor cordials, nor the most lively desire to reach the summit of the mountain could make them pass this limit. Some were seized with palpitation, others with vomiting, some fainted, others suffered from a violent attack of fever, and all these phenomena disappeared as soon as they breathed a denser air. I have seen, although in rare cases, that indispositions of these kinds obliged the sufferers to stop at 800 toises above the level of the sea, the limit for others was at 1,200 toises, for several, at 1,500 or 1,600."

After the works of Saussure, we must next consult the work of Meyer-Ahrens[2] in our investigation into the causes of mountain-sickness. It is a book of only 140 pages, written with great erudition, which, so far as the historical part is concerned, seems to have served as model for Bert's[3] great work. All the old theories respecting mountain-sickness are recapitulated and explained with great clearness. For the present study of man in the Alps Paul Bert's book served as authority and encyclopædia. Some years later, Dr. Payot[4] issued a valuable thesis on mountain-sickness, which, however, added little to what was already known.[5]

II.

There is not the least doubt that mountain-sickness is not caused by the diminished atmospheric pressure, although the primary effects of the rarefied air may become the cause of other disturbances. Each of these disturbances has been in turn considered as the sole cause of mountain-sickness.

Fatigue and the difficulty in moving the legs, which, as we shall presently see, is a very complicated fact announcing an incipient disorder in the func-

[1] Ed. Whymper, *Chamonix and the Range of Mont Blanc*. London, 1896, p. 13.
[2] Conrad Meyer-Ahrens, *Die Bergkrankheit*. Leipzig, 1854.
[3] Paul Bert, *La pression barométrique*. Paris, 1878.
[4] Alexander Payot, *Du mal des montagnes*. Thèse. Paris, 1881.
[5] In the *Dictionnaire de Physiologie* of Charles Richet (tome ii., 1896) the ancient and modern bibliography of this subject has been collected by Carvallo. A valuable article was recently published by G. v. Liebig (*Die Bergkrankheit*. Deutsches Vierteljahrschrift für öffentliche Gesundheitspflege. Vol. xxviii.) In a future work I shall consider another writing of G. v. Liebig as well as the publications of Loewy and Aron, who studied the pressure of rarefied air in the alveoli of the lungs. As I am convinced that their explanation of mountain-sickness is not sufficiently borne out by facts and does not satisfactorily explain the phenomena of the indisposition, I postpone the detailed discussion of the work till later. The technical terms of experimental criticism would be tedious to the general reader.

tions of the nerves, were thought by Alexander von Humboldt to be a simple physical effect of the diminished pressure. "The thigh-bone," he says, "tends to slip out of its socket in the pelvis, because the pressure of the air does not suffice to keep it in its place. On this account we must first perform a greater muscular effort, and afterwards can no longer move the legs with ease." This explanation, enunciated at the beginning of the century,[1] was universally accepted, many applying it also to the knee-joint, where we feel a sort of relaxation of the ligaments when we are attacked by mountain-sickness. This hypothesis is now abandoned, because it has been shown that the leg remains in its place in spite of its weight, even when in the pneumatic chamber the atmospheric pressure sinks below that prevailing on the highest mountains.

The two best known, and I might almost say, most popular causes of mountain-sickness are fatigue and indigestion. The sudden increase of fatigue during the last part of an ascent where the mountain is steepest, the lack of strength to proceed, the pain felt at every step, led many to believe that the contraction of the muscles was the cause of mountain-sickness.

In the descriptions of expeditions up the highest mountains of America we sometimes read of persons who did not suffer from the rarefied air while riding, but who on alighting from their mules were immediately seized by mountain-sickness.

Tschudi, in his *Peruanische Reiseskizzen*, relates that he had already been one year in Peru, and had travelled several times over mountains from 4,000 to 4,500 metres high without ever suffering from mountain-sickness. One day, however, without having breakfasted, he rode up to a height of 4,500 metres on a mule, and then lost the road. The mule was tired and Tschudi was obliged to proceed on foot, pulling the mule on behind him by the reins, while he clambered about in search of the path. His fatigue was certainly increased by mental agitation, and he immediately began to feel the influence of the diminished atmospheric pressure.

"An indisposition, such as I had never felt before," he relates, "caused me increased discomfort at every step; I had to stop to draw breath, without being able to find sufficient air to relieve me. I tried to walk on and was seized by an oppression which forced me to halt; my heart beat so violently that I could hear its palpitations. My breathing was short and broken; it seemed as though a great weight were pressing on my chest. My lips chapped, the little blood-vessels of the eyelids burst, and the blood trickled into my eyes. My senses became inert, a mist spread before my sight, I trembled and had to stretch myself on the ground." After half an hour spent in an almost unconscious state he was able to remount the mule and proceed.

It was also Saussure's first idea to attribute great importance to the contraction of the muscles in the production of mountain-sickness.

"If this exhaustion were caused by imperfect respiration, how should a few instants of repose during which the same air is breathed, apparently restore our strength so completely?"[2]

---

[1] "Rather let us examine the probability of the influence of decreased air-pressure on lassitude, when the legs move in regions where the atmosphere is very much rarefied, since, according to the memorable discovery of the two *savants* Weber, the leg, fixed to the body, is only supported in moving by the pressure of the atmospheric air." Humboldt, *op. cit.*, p. 419.

[2] Saussure, *Voyage dans les Alpes*. Tome ii. p 311.

A sufficient proof that mountain-sickness may manifest itself in the absence of muscular fatigue is furnished by the sufferings and the death, in some cases, of aëronauts.

III.

A more complete study of mountain-sickness may be made in a few years' time when the Jungfrau railroad is opened. By means of a tunnel and a lift hundreds of persons may be easily conveyed every day to a height of 4,166 metres. The Virgin, as this mountain has antonomastically been christened from the dazzling purity of its snowy slopes, will have lost part of its charm by the beginning of the next century; its frequent avalanches will be no longer feared, and the most timid of our species will ascend to the summit to hear the rumbling of the glaciers and to revel in the glorious sunsets, a sight which as yet few have enjoyed.

The federal government of Switzerland, before approving the plans for this railway, asked Professor Kronecker of Berne "if the construction and subsequent use of this railway were possible without inflicting injury on human health?"

A great responsibility was laid on physiology by this inquiry. By means of a few observations in the pneumatic chamber and on the mountains, Professor Kronecker had to foresee the whole complicated series of phenomena which may become manifest when an inquisitive crowd of healthy and suffering persons is conveyed to the summit of the Jungfrau.

Professor Kronecker's account is one of the most important works which have been written on mountain-sickness; from it I make the following extracts, which treat of the experiments made on the Breithorn.

"On the 13th September, 1894, I left with my wife and assistants for Zermatt. On the 14th Professor Sahli, director of the medical hospital in Berne, and his wife joined us. Our expedition was composed of seven persons: a boy of ten years of age, an old peasant of seventy, Dr. Archer, of thirty, and us four.

"In Zermatt, on the 14th September, the sphygmographic curve of each member of the party was registered, the pulse-rate, vital capacity, and the quantity of hæmoglobin in the blood being likewise ascertained. On the 15th September, at 3 a.m., we left Zermatt by the light of the moon, which was at its full, and in a slight fog. The caravan consisted of about sixty individuals. The seven persons who were to act as subjects in the experiments rode on mules, each of which was led by one man. The laboratory servant who had to prepare the physiological experiments and a hospital attendant, sent to us by Dr. Seiler, also joined the cavalcade. Two guides preceded us, forty-two porters were told off for the transport of scientific apparatus, rugs, provisions, and carrying-chairs. The ride by night was rather dangerous owing to the fog, but the majority of the seven subjects were not aware of the risk.

"After a warm breakfast in the lower hut of the Théodule, the seven subjects seated themselves in the carrying-chairs, six porters being told off for each one. But soon this number no longer sufficed. One porter turned back as he was suffering from mountain-sickness. Relays of eight were necessary to carry any heavier member of the party, and no less than six for the boy. Dr. Archer had on this account to cross the glacier on foot. The last ascent was performed very slowly, so that we only arrived on the Plateau at 11.30 a.m. I decided to remain there and give up the idea of reaching the summit of the Breithorn, as for this two more hours would have been necessary and we should then no longer have had sufficient time for experiments. A strong wind was blowing on the summit as might be seen by the gathering and dispersion of the mists upon it. Our prudence was well rewarded. We found at this comparatively low halting-place (3,750 metres) all the principal signs of the alterations which the influence of altitude produces in vital functions. We determined the frequency and form of the pulse, the capacity of the lungs and the general state in repose and during the performance of moderate work. The characteristic differences resulting shall shortly be published.

"All felt well when they remained motionless and at their ease; there was no great thirst and wine was distasteful. The pulse was much more rapid, the pulse-curve showed a diminution in the tension of the arteries, except in the case of the old man in whom the arteries had lost their elasticity. The vital capacity was less in all. These symptoms were the same in full-blooded and in rather anæmic persons. Professor Sahli was of opinion that all had a slight degree of cyanosis, the skin being bluish although there was no wind and the air was almost tepid.

"The most important and most appreciable symptom was the pernicious influence of the slightest movements. Twenty steps on the slightly sloping glacier, on which one could easily walk, were sufficient to cause a feverish pulse (from 100 to 160 pulsations per minute). Even in the guides and robust porters, twenty steps caused the pulse to rise from 100 and 108 to 120 and 140 pulsations per minute. Most of us felt a palpitation of the heart and an oppression in breathing when we moved. Stooping caused discomfort as also the lightest work which required attention, as, for instance, the registration of the pulse. Taking photographs and preparing or packing up instruments were still more fatiguing and could only be accomplished with intervals of repose.

"At 7 p.m. all the party had returned to Zermatt in the best condition.

"A co-ordination of all these symptoms convinces me that mountain-sickness originates in circulatory disturbances. Persons seized with it appear as though suffering from heart-disease. The cyanotic (bluish) skin bears out this classification. Deep breathing gives little relief. The diminished pressure produces a dilatation of the blood-vessels in the lung in consequence of a stagnation of the blood in the smaller circulatory canals, and this gives rise to a dilatation of the right ventricle of the heart. Strong irritation of the skin may produce a reflex contraction of the blood-vessels (hence the beneficial influence of the wind when it is not too cold). Muscular exertion excites the heart already abnormally irritated in consequence of congestion. The dilated veins contain so much blood that the pressure diminishes in the arteries and even the brain receives an insufficient quantity of blood (somnolence, fainting); the gorged condition of the *vena porta* causes the failure of appetite, nausea, and vomiting. These phenomena cannot arise from the lack of oxygen, for in that case the breathing would become profound, the indisposition would disappear on the greater intensity of respiration, and would augment in the same proportion as the oxygen diminishes."[1]

[1] H. Kronecker, *Ueber die Bergkrankheit mit Bezug auf die Jungfraubahn*. Bern, 21st Nov., 1894, p. 21.

IV.

Conway recently performed a journey through the Himalayas, of which I have already made mention in the preceding chapters. After his return to London he consigned the material of his physiological observations to the distinguished physiologist, Roy, for examination.

"On the peak we felt much worse on slopes than on the arête," Conway writes,[1] "we had difficulty to restrain ourselves from taking to the cornice." This observation was repeatedly made, and Roy gives it as his opinion that the indisposition was caused by an alteration of the air. I shall here quote a passage from Roy's memoir:—

"Conway's observation that more distress was experienced in hollow places than when walking on an arête confirms what has been noted by others. This may be due to the fact that water takes up more oxygen than nitrogen from the air, so that when on a high peak the sun falls upon the snow, melting a certain part of it, the neighbouring air is robbed of some of its oxygen."[2]

Thus the old opinion of Saussure that the air is altered in the strata touching the snow is presented to us again in a new dress and supported by the authority of an eminent physiologist. But in 1830 Boussingault showed that only the air held within the pores of the snow contains less oxygen, this gas being more easily soluble than nitrogen in water, and rejected the opinion which he had at first accepted from Saussure, namely, that in melting the snow draws the oxygen from the air. These views Boussingault maintained, not only as borne out by his analysis of air, but also because of the correct reflection that if Saussure's explanations were reliable, mountain-sickness ought also to manifest itself in the plain in winter. Later Frankland analysed air taken on the summit of Mont Blanc and found that its composition was the same as that of Chamonix.

The chemical analyses of the air made by my brother, and by Zuntz and Lœwy, on the summit of Monte Rosa, confirmed the fact that, on the top, at a height of 4,560 metres the composition of the air is constant. The movement of the atmospheric ocean is so continuous, the currents, even where heat is most suffered from, are of such extent and velocity that slight alterations such as those produced by the melting of the snow do not sensibly modify the composition of the air. This need not surprise us when we remember that the most minute chemical analyses of the air in forests have not revealed any influence of the vegetation on the air under the trees. So much the less probable does it appear that man should feel the effects of minimum variations since much greater alterations pass unnoticed.

The fact that mountain-sickness is very intense in its effects on bare, rocky mountains also militates against this theory. Zurbriggen told me that he suffered more on bare mountains than on snow or ice.

V.

We must distinguish two forms of mountain-sickness: the acute and the slow form. The acute form breaks out suddenly on the entrance into rarefied air, the slow form manifests itself later, and other debilitating causes,

---

[1] *Climbing and Exploration in the Karakoram-Himalayas*, p. 113. London, 1894.
[2] C. F. Roy, *Mountain-Sickness*. Based on notes by Mr. W. M. Conway of his experiences in the Karakoram-Himalayas, p. 119.

besides the barometric depression, often contribute to produce it. The greater frequency of the pulse, nausea, vomiting, physical prostration, which may even incapacitate one for movement, the livid colour of the skin, the buzzing in the ears, dimmed sight, fainting-fits, are all phenomena characteristic of the acute form.

The slow form is not accompanied by nausea and vomiting, the diminution of appetite and the other disturbances of the digestive system are less serious than in the acute form, the difficulty in breathing, the palpitation of the heart and lassitude cause much less annoyance although they are more persistent.

Whymper[1] who, amongst mountain climbers has devoted more particular attention to mountain-sickness, classified the phenomena which we are now considering as *transitory* and *permanent* phenomena. I should willingly have accepted this classification did it not exclude certain common symptoms of the malady. Often all the symptoms are transitory, as one often notices in the Alps where some Alpinists suffer only on the first day of the expedition, even though they may afterwards ascend to greater heights.

Conway remarks that on the Ispar Pass, 17,650 feet high, not one of his party suffered from mountain-sickness, whereas lower down the malady had made several victims. Those who are well trained and resistant only suffer the slow form of the sickness. Thus, for instance, the brothers Schlagintweit after ascending the Ibi Gamin as high as 22,230 feet suffered fatigue such as they had never felt in their lives before, but nothing else.

Neither did Conway suffer from the acute form. He describes as follows his condition on arriving at the greatest altitudes of the Himalayas which have as yet been reached : "The night at the highest camp *after* the ascent of Pioneer Peak was our worst night; palpitations constantly woke me up. In the descent we felt discomfort (such as was experienced in the ascent between Junction and Footstool Camp) down to a much lower level, as far as Corner Camp (13,000 feet), than we had felt in the ascent. We seemed to become continuously *less* able to hold out against altitude the longer we remained at a higher level. I several times took my temperature, but never hit it at anything but normal."[2]

It must be borne in mind that in this division of mountain-sickness acclimatisation ceases at great heights, because, in consequence of the ever-increasing weakness, we become more sensitive to the action of the rarefied air; thus we see from the foregoing quotation that Conway and his companions felt worse when they descended to lower levels.

The necessity of distinguishing the effects of weakness from those of rarefied air now becomes apparent. During the ascent one is stronger and more resistant, whereas in descending one is attacked by mountain-sickness at lesser heights owing to the state of greater exhaustion brought about by the casualties of the excursion. This is the reverse of what takes place in the acute form, which disappears, as we have seen, when one passes from thinner into denser air.

Even on Monte Rosa at an altitude of 4,560 metres the acute and slow forms of mountain-sickness are easily distinguishable. Several of our party suffered from nausea and vomiting, violent headache, physical prostration

---

[1] Edward Whymper, *Travels amongst the Great Andes of the Equator.* London, 1892, p. 374.
[2] W. M. Conway, *Climbing and Exploration in the Karakoram-Himalayas.* Scientific Results, p. 113.

with loss of appetite and sleep. In myself and others, on the contrary, phenomena of the slow type manifested themselves.

Many will have noticed old people apply their outstretched hands to their sides, while they erect the vertebral column, at the same time drawing a deep breath. During our sojourn at the Regina Margherita Hut these movements became habitual to me. Conway likewise mentions that on the Himalayas he experienced discomfort when his arms hung down by his sides, and relief when he supported them on the hips.

Whymper and Carrel on Chimborazo had no other symptoms than the difficulty in breathing and fatigue. At an altitude of 16,664 feet they could no longer work, whereas Mr. Perring, who was with them, was quite well. At a height of 17,000 feet Conway felt his heart beating, he could not sleep on the left side and experienced discomfort on changing his position. He breathed fifteen times in the minute, suffered when taking topographical observations, and from laboured breathing even when only reading the thermometer and barometer.

There are some Alpinists who affirm that they have never suffered from mountain-sickness, and books which relate the story of the great ascents in the Alps without even mentioning this malady :[1] this arises from inadequate observation. Thus does incipient deafness escape notice so long as we only listen to the usual voices and noises, whereas the defect of hearing becomes immediately apparent when a more delicate test, such as the ticking of a watch, is applied.

VI.

After his ascent of Mount Etna in 1671 the celebrated physiologist Borelli described the phenomena of mountain-sickness and endeavoured to explain them by the theories of the effervescence of the blood and of force. I need not consider these hypotheses at length, because the analysis of physiological phenomena has progressed so greatly in the course of two centuries that Borelli's opinions on this subject have no practical importance, remaining of interest only as part of the history of physiology.

Mountain-sickness is experienced on Mount Etna when the temperature is mild and there is no snow. Some indeed maintain that the average of cases is higher there than on other mountains of the same height.

From amongst the many observations on the occurrence of mountain-sickness on Mount Etna, I select that of Dr. Faralli [2] which will give an idea of the frequency of the malady on that volcano :—

Early on the morning of the 18th September, 1880, we started from Biancavilla in two squads, the first, composed of thirty-two individuals a-foot, the second, of over seventy persons, besides guides and muleteers, all mounted.

The number of cases of mountain-sickness amongst my companions was, I noticed, much greater than is usual on other mountains of the same height as Mount Etna.

Though only attaining a serious degree in a few individuals, sufficiently characteristic although mild phenomena of the sickness soon began to develop in a relatively large number of persons. Even on the short stretch through the Grotta degli Archi one of us, in spite of his having till that moment performed the journey riding, began to suffer from a difficulty in breathing which forced him to halt after a few steps and follow my advice of drawing deep

---

[1] Levasseur, *Les Alpes et les grandes ascensions.* Paris, 1889.
[2] Giovanni Faralli, *Il congresso alpino di Catania e l'ascensione dell' Etna, 16-20 Settembre,* 1880. Annuario Società degli Alpinisti Tridentini.

inspirations so as to recover breath sufficient to enable him to cover the few tens of metres which lay between him and the doubtless longed-for refection.

When we arrived at *Casa Etnea* (alt., 2,942 metres) about thirty individuals showed manifest symptoms of mountain-sickness, lassitude in the members, difficulty in the breathing at the slightest movement, dryness of the throat, nausea, in some cases vomiting, headache, sadness and apathy during the glorious sight, to which all had looked forward, of the setting of the sun and rising of the moon. Of these thirty sufferers only two belonged to the walking party, the others had ridden almost the whole way on their mules. Of the two foot-travellers, the phenomena were in one so insignificant that although he could take but little food, he was yet able to climb the cone of the mountain, whereas the other victims of the evening before had neither the necessary physical force, nor the will to attempt the climb to the summit which had been the object of their ambition at starting.

Dr. Faralli attributes the greater frequency of mountain-sickness observed by him on Mount Etna to the greater rapidity with which the barometer falls.

The greater number of ascents are not performed starting from the sea-level, but from a greater or lesser elevation at which the equilibrium in the gaseous exchange in the lungs has already become re-established.

On Mount Etna, therefore, time is lacking for the establishment of the necessary compensation.

To this must be added the rapid fall of the temperature, which is more precipitate perhaps than on any other ascent. During our excursion the minimum observed at *Casa Etnea* was 0·4°. If we compare this low temperature with that of 40° prevailing at that time in Catania, we can easily form an idea of the nutritive effort necessary to maintain the equilibrium of the animal temperature while that of the air undergoes so rapid a change. This therefore is a factor not indeed capable alone of producing mountain-sickness, but of favouring and hastening the appearance of the phenomena when the necessary tension of oxygen begins to be lacking in the air.

Statistical data which have till now been collected relating to mountain-sickness leave much to be desired in point of accuracy, and yet the investigation is interesting enough to encourage observations of the greatest exactitude. The maximum percentage of cases recorded on an ascent has perhaps been furnished by the expedition up Mount Etna described above: out of a hundred persons thirty suffered from mountain-sickness at an altitude below 3,000 metres, and of these thirty only two had performed the ascent on foot, the others had ridden. We must not think, however, that these hundred persons who climbed Mount Etna on the 18th of September, 1880, were all mountain-climbers. In the South, when there is a festival or a congress, the natural enthusiasm and holiday mood of the outside public lead them to take more part in it than elsewhere. In this case we must remember that the ascent was greatly facilitated, and that the public reception encouraged many to join the expedition who would otherwise perhaps never have undertaken the ascent. Precisely on this account this datum of 30 per cent. is important because it shows how great is the number of cases, furnished by the population of a southern city in which only a few mountain-climbers are to be found.

VII.

Reports of ascents accumulate in the Alpine reviews with such wonderful rapidity that some really important climbing expeditions undertaken before the institution of Alpine Clubs are gradually being forgotten. To these belongs the ascent of Mount Demavend, the *Jasonius Mons* of the ancients, the highest peak of the Elburz Mountains, accomplished in 1862 by Michele

Lessona, professor of zoology at the University of Turin. After the descent from Mount Demavend, which is nearly 5,670 metres high, Lessona wrote a letter to Signora Lessona from Tedgrisch on the 18th of August. It was his intention to write a book about his travels in Persia, but unfortunately this work was never begun. In publishing a few fragments of this letter, given to me by Signora Adele Lessona, it is a pleasure to me to think that thus a document important to the history of mountaineering is saved from oblivion and that I render a tribute of gratitude to the memory of my master. In these pages devoted to observations on mountain-sickness, the artistic nature of the writer and that love of the Alps which kept him young until the very last of his busy life, manifest themselves notwithstanding.

"We started on August 9th, at 2 p.m. from Tedgrisch: Ferrati,[1] De Filippi, Clemencich, Doria, Orio, Centurioni, the Englishman Champain and I. We had thirty mules with us for mounts and baggage-carrying, two European servants, of whom one was Clemente, five Persian servants amongst whom two cooks, provisions of food, rugs, &c. The Englishman took two tents with him such as are used by the Sepoys in India, and an Indian servant of his, who speaks Arabian pretty well. For two hours we skirted the mountain foot in an easterly direction, then we turned to the north and began the ascent, climbing up high mountains and down into valleys and admiring the sure tread of these incomparable Persian mules. At eight o'clock, by a beautifully clear moonlight, we arrived at the village of Afgià where we meant to pass the night. We were lodged in a house now the property of the Shah, which a few years ago belonged to his Prime Minister or Sadraazan, Mirza Aga Khan, a man who was the richest and most powerful in Persia and is now the poorest and most unhappy. His sad story I shall tell you later by word of mouth. The village of Afgià is situated half-way up the slope of a high mountain, it is surrounded by trees and has an abundance of very pure water. On the 10th we breakfasted early, mounted our mules and began to climb the steep. At midday we reached the summit of Mount Valdera in glorious sunshine. Beneath us lay the majestic stretch of the Lar valley, through which winds the river of the same name. These mountains have a peculiar aspect, there is an absolute lack of vegetation, no trees surround the villages, but the valleys are so wide and the heights so immense that compared with them our Alps seem like little hills. Do not think that I mean to speak ill of our Alps or that I disdain them; they are still to me the most beautiful thing I have ever seen, but here what is lacking in grace and beauty is made up for by wild and awful grandeur. We descended to the Lar valley dotted over with the tents of nomadic shepherds. Leopardi's poem 'To the moon,' and his 'Song of the nomadic Asiatic shepherd,' came to my mind. Then we climbed upwards again and down once more, stopping to drink some wonderfully clear water in a little valley full of springs. We then crossed valleys full of herbaceous plants which we had never seen before, finally pitching our tents at 5 p.m. in the lovely little valley of Allar Rhan. A rapid winding stream runs through this narrow dale which closed behind us, while before us, to the east, it opened, disclosing to the left, at no great distance, the lofty and snowy pile of Mount Demavend, the goal of our exertions. We

---

[1] Ferrati was professor of geodesy, De Filippi, of zoology, in the University of Turin, Marchese G. Doria is actual president of the Italian Geographical Society, Clemencich was captain of the staff, Marchese Centurioni was from Genoa, Orio from Milan was a bacologist.

dined with excellent appetite in that rather fresh but very salubrious air, hunted a few rare birds, collected little water animals, and slept marvellously well. On the 11th we walked all day, arriving in the evening at five o'clock at Ask, a village which, were it in Europe, would be celebrated and rich beyond expression on account of its medicinal waters. Just imagine, with us every little thread of ferruginous water is cherished with the greatest care, whereas here, near the entrance of the village, runs a veritable torrent of the kind! In the village at every turn warm sulphur springs bubble forth. Ask is situated on the left bank of the Lar, which whirls and eddies through the deep and narrow valley. A bridge connects the village with the opposite bank, on which is a single little house at which we stopped to pass the night. Here there are no inns of any description, nor are there any in all Persia, but one always finds some one who, for a pecuniary compensation, will clear a room where the traveller may spend the night. The room is bare but the traveller has his mats, mattresses, and rugs with him.

"We left Ask very early on the morning of the 12th and climbed a mountain of very singular geological formation. Near Mount Demavend all the mountains are of volcanic origin and the variety and disposition of the rocks gave us an opportunity for observations and the collection of important specimens. No geologist, no naturalist had visited these spots before us. After three hours' fatiguing ascent on muleback we arrived at Abilaron, a village where there is a thermal spring of such high temperature that it is impossible for a bather to withstand it. The water which spouts out is therefore led in smoking brooklets to a bathing-place situated somewhat lower, where it cools. It is a unique spectacle to see these steaming brooklets running down the mountain. I have made some interesting observations on the temperature of these springs and on the temperature at which certain small plants are first found growing in them. We here made a slight refection, then re-mounted and went on our way, continuing to ascend more and more difficult slopes until in the evening we arrived at the foot of the great mountain which we proposed to attack on the morrow. Before reaching this point we had already passed the glacier-line and were at an altitude of 3,600 metres above the level of the sea. The cold was keen, and Doria began to suffer from the effects of the rarefaction of the air, being troubled with a nausea, which prevented him from eating. I proposed to call this place Thompson after the daring Englishman who first passed the night here (as we were doing, reserving the ascent for the morrow), and my suggestion was unanimously agreed to. The road which leads here is most awkward; the mule that was carrying our tents fell so that we could only expect our tents the next day; on this account we were obliged to sleep in the open air. Well it was for us that we had rugs in plenty, for the cold was severe; Clemente, who has taken quite a motherly care of me on this journey, covered me up from the chin to the toes in such a manner that, at a lesser altitude, I should have perspired like a circus-horse, and this protected me effectually from the cold; nevertheless, after I had fallen asleep, Clemente came back to put a woollen cap on my head, as he thought I was not sufficiently wrapped up at that part. We had all placed our mattresses one beside the other and fell asleep all nestling together, while looking at the stars and at the snowy Demavend which looked down at us from above. On waking a wonderful spectacle met our view, the peaks of the mountains below us peered out like little islands in the midst of a wide sea of dense fog, a sight which we greeted with a unanimous cry of admiration. We rose, and in order to obtain water had to break the crust of ice on the little brook which was fed from the neighbouring glacier.

"We then took two good cups of tea each, and as the ground still permitted of it, we mounted our mules to ride to that point beyond which it would be impossible for the animals to advance.

"This was the morning of the 13th of August, and we started at 5.45 a.m. After three-quarters of an hour the climb became so steep that it was impossible for the mules to go a step further. We dismounted and proceeded on foot, taking ten guides with us to show us the way. The ground during this first part of the climb was formed entirely of large pieces of lava on which we should have run the risk of slipping had we been wearing our usual shoes, but the guides had shod us in a way of their own, putting our feet first into enormous woollen stockings and then into laced shoes of kidskin with the hair on, and in these the feet adapt themselves to that sort of ground. After ascending for half an hour Doria began to suffer so seriously from the rarefaction of the air that he was obliged to turn back; he was troubled with vomiting and oppressed breathing, could gain no relief before returning to our place of encampment, and even there he still suffered, nor did he recover until we returned to Ask on the morrow. His sorrow at being incapacitated for reaching the summit was compensated for by the collection of plants and insects which he was able to make at the mountain foot.

"After we had passed the masses of lava their place was taken by pebbles and sand on the precipitous slope, which rendered the ascent still more arduous.

"After a certain time De Filippi felt his breath fail him, and was obliged to descend with the European servant who had likewise undertaken the ascent with Clemente and with us. Clemente went on undaunted like the hardy mountaineer he is. We climbed for five hours, and then came to a pass called here *Bemsè Bend*, which, literally translated, means the Cat's Pass.

"This is a pass over snow which presents some difficulty, easily overcome, however, with the help of the guides. The Englishman and I, by the bye, were the only ones who needed no assistance from the guides either in ascending or descending. Justice reminds me that I must mention Clemente's name as well. After the Cat's Pass the climb becomes ever steeper and more fatiguing; at every few paces we had to stop to stretch ourselves in order to regain our breath and to put a little snow in our mouths. In erecting myself during one of these halts I caught sight of the outer rim of the crater partly covered with snow and in part glistening with crystals of purest sulphur. With an exclamation I pointed it out to the Englishman who was near me, and it gave fresh courage to both of us.

"We crossed rather a wide stretch of snow, which is the second part of the ascent presenting some difficulty, and found ourselves then with our feet on the sulphur with which the highest part of the mountain is entirely covered. Another half-hour of painful exertion and we were at the summit. The first to arrive was Signor Orio, who waved his silk handkerchief tied to the end of his stick as a species of banner, and made the solitude echo to the sacred cry of 'Long live Italy!' We are the first Italians who have set foot up there. After Orio the Englishman Champain reached the top, then came Clemente, then I, then Clemencich and Ferrati, then the Marchese Centurione from Genoa.

"My guide, to whom I had given my mantle to carry, was suffering so much from the rarefaction of the air that he could not reach the summit: it was cold at the top, but I did not much feel the lack of extra covering; I had my shooting suit of fustian and a sturdy flannel underneath.

"The companions who arrived with me at the crater suffered very little from the rarefaction of the air—I, not at all. The summit of Mount Demavend is a real crater, in part covered with snow, in part with sulphur. Neither fire nor lava ever issue from the crater, but powerful streams of aqueous vapour and an abundance of sulphur, which emanates in a gaseous state, then solidifies, covering the rim of the crater and the highest slopes of the mountain. Then the snow falls on the sulphur layer, and the sulphur again on the stratum of snow, and so on in perpetual alternation. We remained at the top for an hour. Ferrati began to make barometric observations. I at first fell into a reverie, full of emotion, thinking of my country and of all our dear ones alive and dead; but Clemente reminded me presently that we must collect something, and so I began to seek together some beautiful samples of crystallised sulphur. From the summit we ought to have seen the Caspian Sea to the north and the forests of Mazanderan, but we only saw a wide stretch of clouds on every side. We, too, were enveloped in a little cloud up there, and the guides who, only two or three in number, had followed us so far, began to urge an immediate return, saying that the mountain might become covered with clouds and the road rendered difficult."

The ascent of Mount Demavend, a height of 5,670 metres, described by Lessona, is of importance also to the statistics of mountain-sickness. Mount Demavend is in the same latitude as Mount Etna and is almost double the height; the party was composed of eight persons, and two only suffered from mountain-sickness at four-fifths of the ascent. Their resistance had not been acquired by means of previous ascents, but by the simple inurement to exertion given by three months' journeying by land and sea.

Filippo De Filippi, in his account of his journey in Persia with Lessona, writes:—

"The rarefaction of the air occasioned me more distress than the cold; at an altitude of 3,600 metres I suffered from a severe attack of nocturnal asthma.

"The effect of the rarefaction of the air soon made itself felt in some of us. First one of the guides halted, seized with a fit of vomiting, then Doria, and at last, at four-fifths of the ascent, I was obliged enviously to renounce the idea of reaching the summit of the great volcano, the glory of which achievement I had hoped to share with my companions. My symptoms were nausea, dizziness, oppressed breathing, and an invincible desire to sleep as soon as I stopped to rest a little. I had to give in, therefore, and return to the encampment accompanied by one of the guides." [1]

---

[1] F. De Filippi, *Note di un viaggio in Persia*. Milano, 1865, p. 266.

Arrival of an expedition at the Regina Margherita Hut.

CHAPTER XIII

AN EXPEDITION UP MONT BLANC IN 1891

I.

BY chance I came into contact with a part of the expedition of 1891. I was acquainted with Dr. Jacottet, who died of inflammation of the lungs on the summit of Mont Blanc, and went with the guides from Chamonix in search of Herr Rothe and of a guide who had perished under an avalanche in a crevasse of the Petit Plateau.

This expedition had been organised by the engineer Imfeld, who was charged with the construction of the Mont Blanc observatory under the direction of Janssen and Eiffel.

On August 13th Dr. Egli-Sinclair and Dr. Guglielminetti left Chamonix and stayed two nights at the Grands Mulets (alt., 3,050 metres) in order to accustom themselves to the rarefied air. On the 14th the engineer Imfeld joined them with about twenty guides and porters. The next day they started at 3 a.m., reaching the Vallot Hut at Rocher des Bosses (alt., 4,265 metres) at 10 a.m. in good condition. In the hut, however, their state underwent a change; they felt oppressed, sleepy, suffered from headache and a difficulty in breathing which obliged them both to go out in order to breathe the fresh air. Dr. Egli-Sinclair gives the following description of his condition:— [1]

"I sat down before the hut, but felt even worse; I had to breathe deeply and frequently without even then feeling that I had got sufficient air. I felt more and more that the accessory respiratory muscles were in action; they hurt me, a painful tension of the humeral muscles causing great discomfort, and I thought with compassion of patients whom I had often seen struggling for breath. Headache and slight nausea completed my distress. Guglielminetti came and sat down near me; he, too, breathed frequently and deeply —the comical comparisons which he made relieving us not in the least. We remained seated for an hour without noticing any improvement; our optimistic views of mountain-sickness were considerably shaken now that we were observing its first and more peculiar symptom: breathlessness; for a breathlessness which becomes manifest after exertion, which continues and increases, cannot be attributed to fatigue. We had to rise, for our feet threatened to freeze.

"Glad we were to have people at our service who took off our boots and gaiters and put on our sabots, all of which would have cost us some trouble to perform ourselves. In this way we were made ready to take our soup; impossible to say, however, whether it was good or bad, for we had no taste. The red wine tasted like ink, the white like vinegar; only black coffee did not disgust us—I took it after swallowing two grams of phenacetin, the effect of which became presently noticeable, for I began to feel better.

"If sleep forsook me, it was not because of my hard, cold bed, nor of the tempest which howled the whole night through, but always because of the same thirst for air. Three or four times I had to get up in order to breathe deeply, but without obtaining relief; exhausted and discouraged I had to lie down again.

"On the 17th of August—the third day, that is—I still noticed the lack of appetite and the rapidity of the respiration.

"On the fourth day of our sojourn our state began to improve little by little. The respiration was still slightly accelerated, but it did not force itself upon our notice; only when making some effort—in climbing into one's field-bed or getting out, in pulling on one's coat, in lying down—was it necessary to breathe deeply."

The average rate of the breathing was from 20 to 28 per minute. In all the pulse was accelerated. Egli-Sinclair had from 85 to 96 pulsations in the minute; Guglielminetti from 72 to 84; Imfeld from 93 to 103. Between the 13th and 25th of August Egli-Sinclair lost 7 kilograms in weight, Guglielminetti 3·5, and Imfeld 3 kilograms.

The description which Dr. Guglielminetti gives of this expedition is likewise comfortless enough.[2] They suffered a great deal, he says, during the first four or five days; were troubled with vomiting, loss of appetite, oppressed breathing at the slightest movement, and serious indisposition. It is evident that the two days' halt at the Grands Mulets had not sufficed to accustom them to the rarefied air. Guglielminetti says: "My physical energy was almost gone."

The natural predisposition of Dr. Egli-Sinclair and Dr. Guglielminetti to

---

[1] Egli-Sinclair, *Sur le mal de montagne*. Annales de l'Observatoire météorologique du Mont Blanc. Paris, 1893, p. 118.

[2] E. Guglielminetti, *Trois semaines au Mont Blanc*. L'Echo des Alpes, 1894, No. 2, p. 133.

mountain-sickness was, doubtless, augmented by the cold. The circumstance, which they recorded, that there was a broken pane in the hut during the storm, the confession that they could not study the circulation of the blood because "their fingers were numb with cold," show that the expedition was not well organised and that the stove was not in good working order. They refrain from saying so out of politeness towards their host, Imfeld. I consider it a mistake to have abolished the use of wood in the Vallot refuge. If I am able to revisit Mont Blanc, I mean to write this line from Horace on the door of the hut :—

"Dissolve frigus ligna super foco."

Dr. Guglielminetti says clearly what the temperature was in the hut. "On the morrow, the third day, the weather improved, but it was still very cold, the thermometer barely rising above 0°, and outside it was —10°. The ink had frozen during the night, and we woke up with icicles hanging to our moustaches."

Cold predisposes to mountain-sickness and aggravates its phenomena; this has been clearly shown by Conway in his account of his last journey in the Himalayas. Another testimony to the cold suffered in the Vallot Hut during the sojourn of the expedition of 1891 is borne by Schrader,[1] who says that the members were always well clothed, "because even in the rooms the temperature sinks to several degrees below zero. Incessant efforts were made to heat the room, in which the temperature had fallen to —7°, and where we shivered in our superadded garments."

II.

In speaking of the physiological observations which he made on Mont Blanc, Dr. Guglielminetti says : "The porters felt better than we did, because the greater part of them had been employed for some days previously in enlarging the hut. All, however, said that they had suffered during the first three or four days, and had become acclimatised afterwards with the exception of two of their number, who, in spite of everything, and notwithstanding the inhalation of oxygen, were obliged to return to the valley."

"One of the most curious results of mountain-sickness," says Dr. Guglielminetti, "was the annihilation of the will and the complete indifference towards ourselves and others. I had to make a supreme effort in order to determine the bodily temperature, which was normal in all of us (36·8° to 37·5°). Pulse accelerated, between 96 and 103. Respiratory movements, from 23 to 30 per minute."

The quantity of urine decreased by 900 grams per day, but less was drunk than in the plain. The dynamometer did not indicate any change in the muscular energy.

These observations were made the first day, but evidently the effects of mountain-sickness still continued, for Dr. Guglielminetti adds : "The second night was very bad again. Scarcely had we warmed ourselves a little under our rugs than one of our guides came to tell us that a young Parisian was being brought into the hut in a state of total exhaustion. I endeavoured to rise in order to have something prepared for him, but it was absolutely

[1] F. Schrader, *Une tourmente au Mont Blanc*, 1891. Annuaire du club Alpin Français, 1895, p. 28.

impossible. Nothing in the world could have given me the necessary energy."

Dr. Egli-Sinclair made researches on the quantity of hæmoglobin contained in the blood, and in his account he gives a tracing, from which it appears that there was a manifest diminution in all three. He is of opinion that a close connection exists between the amount of colouring substance in the blood and mountain-sickness, but his observations were made under conditions so unfavourable that the results are not reliable. Moreover, Prof. Kronecker has pointed out that the phenomena of mountain-sickness appear and disappear with such rapidity that they cannot certainly depend on the blood, for the hæmoglobin cannot be destroyed and reproduced with such promptitude. Certainly cold brings about a different distribution of the blood-corpuscles and serum in the blood-vessels. A sufficient proof that these experiments are of questionable value is given by Guglielminetti's remark: "Egli-Sinclair counted under the microscope the number of corpuscles contained in a drop of blood extracted once a day from the tips of our frozen fingers."

Later I shall consider all the studies on the blood made during ascents, and shall show that the present methods of investigation are not sufficiently exact. These observations of Egli-Sinclair are also rendered less reliable for other reasons which it is here unnecessary to enumerate. The psychic state of the experimenters was not such as to ensure accuracy in the results of their researches. Egli-Sinclair admits this himself. "In order to count the blood-corpuscles it was necessary, while examining them with attention under the microscope, slightly to hold the breath, which caused me much distress; it is therefore comprehensible and excusable if the reckoning was less exact than might have been desired."

The lack of the necessary calm for investigations prevented Dr. Egli-Sinclair and Dr. Guglielminetti from agreeing as to the value of the observations made. The latter attributed the diminution of hæmoglobin observed by Egli-Sinclair simply to a diminution of red corpuscles, and says:—

"On August 12th, in Chamonix, I had 6,400,000 corpuscles to the square millimetre, and only 4,000,000, on the 17th, in the hut, the number increasing, however, to 5,000,000 on the 21st. In himself the number seemed to me to have fallen to 3,000,000. Although Egli maintains that the correctness of these figures cannot be certified, I must, nevertheless, uphold the fact of the decrease in the number of red corpuscles, as it gives great importance to the diminution of hæmoglobin on Mont Blanc, to the anoxyhæmia that is noted in some drops of blood."

On my expedition up Mont Blanc I learnt one thing, namely, that oxygen is of no use against mountain-sickness. This disappointed me, because Paul Bert's entire physiology is based on the hypothesis that mountain-sickness is due to a lack of oxygen, and that the presence of this gas ensures an immediate recovery. Now we are all convinced that the carrying of supplies of oxygen into the mountains is useless, as also the administering of it to the dying, not one of whom certainly was ever saved by it.

After having performed the ascent of Mont Blanc Dr. Guglielminetti says, in speaking of the descent, when he felt very ill: "I tried to inhale oxygen, but did not obtain the least relief."

While we were in the hut at the Grands Mulets the weather was very bad. I invited M. Frédéric Payot and the guides to drink a glass of wine with me in the inn of the old cook Marie. Afterwards M. Payot asked me to his house, or rather, to the hut which he had had constructed near as a depôt for the Janssen observatory which was to be erected on Mont Blanc. The first thing which struck me was a heap of iron cylinders piled up in one corner of the hut, and which contained compressed oxygen.

I had seen some of these cylinders carried up, but was surprised at the number of them. As we sipped our wine I began an inquiry, on my own behalf, which I continued afterwards in Chamonix, by talking to the workmen who had suffered from mountain-sickness. To my astonishment not one of them spoke of any benefit obtained from inhalations of oxygen. That evening as the guides sat drinking, one of them broke out with the remark that the wine was better than oxygen, and this was repeated by all as a good joke.

III.

A terrible storm burst over Mont Blanc in the night of August 19th, and the thunder continued to roll all through the next day. On the 21st the provisions in the Vallot Hut began to run short. The workmen who were engaged in constructing the tunnel and in seeking the rock under the dome of Mont Blanc were discouraged. Joseph Simond, who had tried to work while the snow was falling on the summit, had come down with a frozen foot and his hands completely insensible. It was decided to send a few men down from the Vallot Hut. Two other travelling parties went down at the same time, Count Favernay's and Herr Rothe's.

These parties left the hut separately; having met on the road they joined, only one rope being used for all. There were five workmen from the Janssen observatory, three guides, and two porters. The weather was bad, and when they arrived at the Petit Plateau an avalanche began to descend from the Dôme du Gouter. It was so dark that although they heard it approach they could not see it. The last five men on the rope were precipitated by this avalanche into a crevasse. The rope broke, and Count Favernay, one guide, and a porter were afterwards extricated. Rothe and the guide, Michel Simond, perished under the avalanche.

When the news came to Chamonix a rescue-expedition was immediately organised. I offered to go as physician to the scene of the disaster, Dr. Jacottet, whose acquaintance I had made, ceding me his post, as he was indisposed. At 3 a.m. we were ready, but the inclemency of the weather prevented our departure. In the meantime I talked to Count Favernay, who had a wound in his forehead.

At about 10 a.m. we left in the rain, our party being fifteen in number. On the road we met a part of the expedition, some of whom were proceeding more slowly, as they had injuries. A porter showed me the broken rope. One guide, whose injuries I attended to on the way, had a wound on the head and another in the hand, which seemed as though caused by some sharp weapon. When the ice moves with velocity, it can cut, with its sharp angles, clean through any rope.

During the night I slept little and badly. The old servant Marie, at the Grands Mulets, after having told me how lively and full of fun Rothe was led me into the room which he had last occupied. She turned down the sheets of the humble bed and wished me good-night. On the little chest of drawers lay a book, which I immediately recognised as a *Baedeker's Guide*. On the yellow cover was written :—

"*H. Rothe, Allemagne,
Braunschweig.*"

It was a sad night. At three in the morning we started again, the weather being still very bad. The scene of the disaster was a deep crevasse, which was half filled by the avalanche. The guides shouted "Michel!" And then all listened, stretching their necks over the abyss. In order to reach the avalanche snow it was necessary to let one's self down perpendicularly to a depth of more than thirty metres. In a moment all was ready; five guides held the rope, by which they slowly let down one of their companions, who was furnished with an axe. Immediately afterwards another guide was lowered in the same way.

The blows of the axe clearing the throat of the crevasse sent up a dreary, mournful sound, and looking down from above the faces of the workers seemed of a livid, corpse-like hue from the bluish reflection of the ice. The wind blew furiously in our faces, and from the dark sky a fine snow fell, which rebounded like grains of sand. Those few inactive hours, spent amid the fog, and smarting under the icy wind, with all one's powers of commiseration roused by the heart-breaking scene, will always remain in my memory as the most terrible hours I have spent in the Alps.

We were convinced that all our efforts would only result in the disinterment of two dead bodies. The leader of the guides, seeing that the weather was growing worse, gave orders to suspend the undertaking; we roped ourselves together and began the descent.

When we arrived at Chamonix it was raining fitfully. At one of the first houses on the left side, near the entrance to the village, a woman came to the threshold with a baby in her arms, and looked at us fixedly, with red eyes, without speaking. It was the wife of Michel Simond. We passed by her with bent heads; not one had the courage to greet her. As I looked at her I felt my own eyes fill with tears.

IV.

The workmen, cast down by this misfortune, refused to go up again, although the weather was splendid. On August 24th all the members of the expedition came down from the Vallot observatory, and on the 28th Imfeld went up again, accompanied by Dr. Jacottet. I had visited the latter, and had jestingly reminded him that the old Piedmontese had shown more justice towards his predecessor, Dr. Paccard, for the Academy of Sciences of Turin had nominated him corresponding member. Now the name of the physician of Chamonix who first ascended Mont Blanc is gradually being forgotten, and no public testimony of honour has been awarded him.[1]

Dr. Jacottet was a robust, broad-shouldered young man. A few days later, when I was returning to Italy, I read in the newspapers, to my great sorrow, that he had died on September 2nd on the summit of Mont Blanc. Thus was another tragic incident to be recorded in the annals of that ill-starred expedition.

[1] Ed. Whymper, *Chamonix and the Range of Mont Blanc*, London, 1896, p. 24.

I give a few brief notes relating to Dr. Jacottet's death, kindly placed at my disposal by Dr. Guglielminetti and Dr. Wizard, who performed the autopsy in Chamonix.

"On the 1st of September, after two days' rest in the hut, during which Jacottet seemed to feel better than he did at first, he climbed to the summit, remained there an hour, and then returned to the hut. During the night he did not sleep and coughed much, and complained at breakfast of headache and lack of appetite. During the morning he wrote a letter to his brother at Vienne, in which he remarked that he had passed so bad a night that he would not wish the like to his worst enemy. His distress increased to such a degree that Imfeld advised him to descend to Chamonix, but he refused. He wrote another letter to one of his friends, telling him that he could not write at greater length because of the sick feeling which was tormenting him, that he was suffering from mountain-sickness like the others, but that he meant to study the influence of atmospheric depression and acclimatise himself. This was, alas! his last letter. He afterwards threw himself on his bed, trembling with cold.

"On the 2nd September, from 3 a.m., violent shivering fits had seized him, and soon he was no longer able to carry his glass to his mouth himself; he seemed as though paralysed, and began to wander. *Oxygen was given to him to breathe, but without result.* The respiration was very superficial (60 to 70 breaths per minute), the pulse irregular (between 100 and 120), the temperature 38·3°. Towards six o'clock in the evening he suddenly ceased to speak, became somnolent, and then the death-agony began. His face grew pale, and towards 2 a.m. he expired in that glacier hut, a victim to his devotion to science, like a soldier on the field of battle."

From Dr. Wizard's post-mortem examination [1] it appeared that Dr. Jacottet had died of capillary bronchitis and lobular pneumonitis. The more immediate cause of death was therefore probably a suffocative catarrh accompanied by acute œdema of the lung.

I have gone into the particulars of this sorrowful incident because a case of inflammation of the lungs occurred also during our expedition, on the summit of Monte Rosa, from which, however, the sufferer fortunately recovered.

[1] Copy of Dr. Wizard's post-mortem report on Dr. Jacottet, Chamonix, September 4, 1891:—

"Vigoureuse constitution, nombreuses lividités, cyanose marquée des lèvres, du visage, des extrémités, cerveau très-bien constitué. Méninges notamment congestionnées. Pas d'adhésions. Vaisseaux de la pie mère augmentés de volume et gorgés de sang. État piqueté de la substance grise, et blanche. Rien de particulier dans les centres, si ce n'est toujours l'état congestif secondaire à un état asphyxique.

"*Thorax.* Pas d'adhérences, pas d'épanchement.

"*Cœur* normal, valvules suffisantes. Les cavités pleines de caillots.

"*Poumon* couleur violet, gonflé, foncé, congestion bilatérale, œdème considérable, muqueuse bronchique injectée fortement. Le liquide de la coupe est écumeux. Congestion égale partout. Foie, rate, reins normaux. Pas d'œdème des jambes."

CHAPTER XIV

OBSERVATIONS ON MOUNTAIN-SICKNESS

I.

MOUNTAIN-SICKNESS as observed at the Gnifetti Hut (alt., 3,620 metres) is generally less serious than at the Grands Mulets on Mont Blanc, although the former is 570 metres higher. The reason of this difference is that on Monte Rosa we reach heights corresponding to those on Mont Blanc with greater ease and less suffering from cold.

At the Col d'Olen, a few metres below the inn, lies a great rock. I once asked why it was called *the devil's stone*. I was told that people felt ill when passing it. Probably by this the first symptoms of mountain-sickness are meant, which begin to manifest themselves at a height of 2,800 metres. It was a guide who gave me the information, to which he added the remark: "You see, however, that that bit is the steepest part of the ascent."

During my sojourn on Monte Rosa I took notes of those places where mountain-sickness makes the most victims. In the visitors' albums in the inns on the slopes of Monte Rosa and in the huts I found remarks written on visiting cards or leaves of paper, and left behind by the travellers as a souvenir. A perusal of these documents showed that there are three points which present the greatest difficulty to those predisposed to mountain-sickness. The first is a steep a little above the Gnifetti Hut; the second a slope leading to Lysjoch; the third Gnifetti Peak, on which is the Regina Margherita Hut. These are all places where the ascent is steeper and the fatigue, in consequence, greater.

A friend of mine had fits of vomiting, although fasting, a little above Gnifetti Hut, but, nothing daunted, he continued the ascent, and arrived at the Regina Margherita Hut in a condition so much improved that he was able to eat there. One Alpinist did not suffer in climbing the Vincent Pyramid, but was attacked by the sickness during the descent, and vomited the whole night in Gnifetti Hut.

Signor B., a lawyer, suffered repeatedly at a height of 2,800 metres from mountain-sickness with somnolence, corpse-like pallor, vomiting. He fell down, and remained for several minutes incapable of moving.

An Alpinist who was crossing the Lys glacier against the wind experienced a sensation of nausea, which disappeared when he halted and turned his back to the wind.

The Deputy, M. de Cristoforis, one of the best known physicians of Milan, left the following writing in Gnifetti Hut:—

"I am sixty-one years of age. This ascent occasioned me not the slightest muscular fatigue. My daughter and a nephew, ten and a half years old, were with me, and, so far as our muscles were concerned, we could have continued the ascent for six hours longer. We felt the lack of oxygen, had a sense of constriction and oppression in the epigastrium, and the thorax was tired from our deep breathing. My pulse had risen from its normal of 60–64 beats per minute to 125–140. This exaggerated circulation lasted all day and all night, notwithstanding that I was in perfect repose. We all felt a disgust for food, the guides as well. I ascended for two hours and a half beyond Gnifetti Hut; the others (my brother-in-law who weighs 105 kilograms, my wife who is slightly built, my daughter twenty-three years old, and a boy ten and a half years of age) went as far as the Regina Margherita Hut. The higher they climbed the more intense became the phenomena of oppression and nausea. They returned with superficial erysipelas and livid in the face."

Some had written on their visiting cards that the first night, on arriving at the Olen Inn, they had suffered from nausea, vomiting, or insomnia; in spite of this, however, several had reached the Gnifetti Hut, and some even the summit of Monte Rosa.

Another traveller had left the following interesting account, which I copy: "We left Gressoney St. Jean and reached Gnifetti Hut, where we found another numerous party. We all slept badly and left again at 3 o'clock by moonlight. Before reaching the Col du Lys the most robust of our party was seized with mountain-sickness. He felt dizzy, complained of fatigue, and often lay down on the snow. We think that we performed the ascent too rapidly, because in an hour and a half we had arrived at the great level whence we saw the sun rise. Having returned to the hut, we passed the night alone. The next day the man who had suffered from mountain-sickness proved the best walker on the tour to Lyskamm."

The celebrated English physiologist, Huxley, suffered from mountain-sickness, and had to stop at the Grands Mulets on his ascent of Mont Blanc in company with Tyndall. Similarly, I have seen other mountain-climbers of advanced age indisposed at Gnifetti Hut. I had thought that the young resisted longer and more vigorously than the old, but various instances convinced me that neither do they enjoy any immunity from the malady. An acquaintance of mine, who now performs the most difficult ascents, had a fainting-fit at Sella Hut when he was fifteen years old. He had been quite well during the ascent from Gressoney, but while the party was at table in the hut he suddenly fainted.

II.

Mountain-sickness (like every other illness) manifests itself in various ways, according to the constitution of the sufferer. The fundamental cause (that is, the rarefaction of the air) has been, however, confused with the predisposing causes. A proof of the imperfection of our knowledge of the malady is that, though its symptoms have been catalogued, its seat has not yet been accurately determined, and even as to its development a satisfactory description is still lacking; we have no diligently prepared collection of the accounts of patients which would enable us definitely to classify its forms. Physicians would do well to direct their attention to this disturbance of the physiological conditions of the organism, whereas as yet the scientific material has been almost exclusively collected by mountain-climbers. I myself was not able during my sojourn on Monte Rosa to study this pathological process as I could have wished; I noticed, however, that its progress includes several periods, and that it manifests itself by fits even during a state of profound repose. I communicate one of these instances in order to show how the functions of the nervous centre are altered during mountain-sickness.

Signor Koeppe arrived at the Regina Margherita Hut in the worst possible condition. This gentleman was forty years of age, had come from Zermatt, and complained that he had not been able to move his legs easily after being seized with mountain-sickness. In the morning the weather had been fine, and he had borne the ascent pretty well, traversing the Grenz glacier and arriving at the Col du Lys, where he began to feel very tired, and was troubled with nausea and vomiting, although he was fasting. At this juncture it began to snow, and he took six hours to reach Col Gnifetti, so frequent were the halts he was obliged to make. When he arrived at Regina Margherita Hut his pulse beat 120 times per minute, his breathing was laboured, and his lips were livid. In half an hour his condition had considerably improved. He had taken a glass of hot wine, and was standing near the stove. The vomiting had disappeared, and all seemed well, only from time to time he said he felt ill. At these moments he was troubled with palpitation, the respiration becoming deeper and more rapid. During one of these attacks he had asked for a little coffee to drink, but remarked to me when it was given to him that he could not swallow as usual. The following numbers suffice to give an idea of the irregularity in the breathing, which I counted every minute for about half an hour: 16, 17, 16, 17, 18, **21, 21,** 17, 16, 17, 19, **20, 24,** 19, 18, 18, 17, 19, **29, 22,** 19, 18, 19, 19, 17, 16, 16, 17.

It is important to notice that the centre of deglutition was also affected. When the respiration becomes laboured, the heart beats more frequently, and the centre of deglutition is likewise influenced. This proves that the seat of the physiological lesion is in the medulla oblongata—that is, in the most important vital centre. We do not know why attacks of the malady

Col du Lys, 4,277 m.

Vincent Pyramid, 4,215 m.

—Gnifetti Hut, 3,620 m.

—Hoheslicht, 3,369 m.

[*V. Sella.*

Naso—

View of the Lys glacier and of the continuation of the Hoheslicht rock, on which Gnifetti Hut stands.

recur periodically during complete repose. This is one of the profoundest secrets in the nutrition of the nervous centres, and one of the obscurest points in medical science.

The great complication of the study of mountain-sickness is due to the concomitant causes which determine its manifestation and aggravate its intensity. In the case of Signor Koeppe it is probable that the storm and the cold had rendered the phenomena of the sickness more violent, because, having gained the shelter of the hut, he vomited no more and passed a fairly good night. The fact that mountain-sickness makes victims during violent storms even amongst the most intrepid Alpinists has been frequently observed ; as an instance I need only mention Zsigmondy who twice suffered at night-time from nausea and general prostration ; once, on the south side of Monte Rosa, and again in the Swiss Hut on the Matterhorn, both times during a furious tempest.

The electric tension observable during storms favours the outbreak of mountain-sickness. We were in Gnifetti Hut on the 7th August when, towards evening, a storm rose. We noticed a party coming up across the glacier, and some of us went out to welcome the new-comers. I went down to the little hut to meet them. As I reached the door I heard a buzzing as of a number of wasps in the hut, but on looking there was nothing to be seen. I listened again and became aware that it was the corners of the hut which emitted a characteristic hissing sound, which I at once understood to be an electric phenomenon. As the weather was threatening and the flashes of lightning very close I took refuge under the arcade of the upper hut. Desiring to write some notes I took a knife to sharpen a lead-pencil and noticed that the chips of wood stuck to the blade and to the finger-tips. The peals of thunder were very near and the sky was so dark that one could not see to a distance of a hundred metres on the glacier.

My companions, who returned shortly afterwards, told me that they had experienced the effects of the electricity in a very remarkable manner. Bizzozero and Corporal Camozzi had repeatedly seen sparks darting round the axe and had felt pricks as from an electric discharge. Corporal Jachini had twice taken off his cap thinking there must be pins in it which were pricking him ; then he felt what seemed to be a heavy hailstorm pattering down on his head ; he passed his hand over his crown and convinced himself that there was nothing. Dr. Abelli and Beno Bizzozero who had often walked to the same distance for pleasure, arrived panting and exhausted, nor could they get over their astonishment at returning in this condition, with laboured breath, uncertain gait, and slight dizziness.

We concluded that bad weather must be avoided on expeditions for this reason, besides others, that it depresses the functions of the organism and produces mountain-sickness.

III.

About the half of the travelling parties performing the ascent of Mont Blanc from Chamonix stop at the Grands Mulets. The number of those who, from the Gressoney and Macugnaga side, succeed in accomplishing the ascent of Monte Rosa is perhaps a little larger. In these statistical data not only the weather, which may change after a party has set out, but also all the other possible mischances of an excursion enter as factors ; but to a certain degree this average serves to indicate the actual frequency of mountain-sickness.

During the sojourn at the Regina Margherita Hut I noticed that there is little or no difference between the travellers arriving from Zermatt and those from the Italian side. Perhaps the parties coming from Zermatt suffered a little more because the ascent is longer and more fatiguing. Out of a party of five persons only one was exempt, and even the two Swiss guides were ill. The restlessness and sufferings of these poor victims accorded ill with the common wish of our party to be left in peace and sleep a little. The wind was blowing so furiously that the hut creaked. One had a complete illusion of being on board ship; the continual retching and moaning lent such a terrible reality to dreams of a shipwreck on a stormy sea, that I shall certainly never forget that night.

The keepers of the Regina Margherita Hut told me that when the snow is deep and soft so that one sinks into it up to the knees, travellers suffer more from mountain-sickness.

The effects of fatigue are cumulative in mountain-sickness. The manifestation of the noxious action of rarefied air is thus often retarded. I convinced myself of this by examining the workmen who constructed the Regina Margherita Hut on Monte Rosa and the Janssen observatory on Mont Blanc. The miners who went on to Monte Rosa to level the rock on which the hut was constructed, did not suffer at all during the first days, but afterwards, when they were fatigued, they experienced such distress that they declined to continue at any price.

This cumulative action produces, so to speak, *posthumous* effects of rarefied air. Thus it frequently happens that the sickness assails us more violently during the descent than the ascent. I experienced this myself on an expedition up Mont Viso. I had slept little the night before, and when I arrived on the summit I worked diligently at the taking of pulse and respiratory tracings. During the descent, when I had reached the spring of Sacripante, I was seized with vomiting and serious indisposition, a condition which lasted about half an hour.

Mountain-sickness tends rather to diminish than to increase, and on this account one must not attribute too much importance to it. This is advisable too, because it is a fact that those who give way to depression involuntarily aggravate the phenomena of the malady and their condition becomes worse.

Zurbriggen and other guides had assured me that bleeding at the nose always affords relief when one is suffering from mountain-sickness. While I was in the Regina Margherita Hut a gentleman had rather a violent hemorrhage from the nose immediately after his arrival. I observed him but did not notice that the bleeding had any effect. The gentleman was a mountain-climber from Milan, strong and robust; he continued to vomit through the night, and in the morning when he began the descent the symptoms still remained the same.

Many will have heard that horses and mules suffer from mountain-sickness as we do. Saussure, in speaking of his expedition to the glacier du Théodule, relates that his mules could not proceed, such difficulty had they in breathing in consequence of the rarefied air, and that one of them emitted a tone of distress in breathing such as he had never heard from these animals in the plain, not even when the exertions performed were much greater.[1]

In Peru when animals are in this condition and are unable to walk, it is the custom to bleed them under the tongue. This can certainly do no good, much less give strength; but thus it is with all popular remedies: if they do not kill outright, they are thought by many to be of benefit.

[1] *Op. cit.*, tome iv. p. 380.

IV.

Mountain-sickness breaks out even during the night's repose. It often happens that one is aroused suddenly from sleep by a sense of discomfort unfelt before, with a weight on the chest and a difficulty in breathing. Any one who has passed a night at a great height will remember that either himself or some friend has risen in order to facilitate the breathing. As this is a phenomenon which demands some discussion, it will be well to quote some competent mountaineers who have mentioned being seized with the sickness during the night, the doubt being thus removed that other causes besides the rarefied air may have come into play. We have already seen that Zumstein experienced this nocturnal effect on Monte Rosa. The brothers Schlagintweit in 1855, and recently Conway in the high regions of Asia, experienced the same phenomenon, waking in the night with an indisposition unfelt during the day. They attributed this, however, to the slight wind which blew during the night.

Mrs. Hervey in the account of her celebrated journey across Central Asia,[1] mentions suffering more through the night from palpitation of the heart and oppression on the chest than at other times, after reaching an altitude of 5,700 metres.

The same phenomenon has been observed in America. I only mention those who suffered from it at inconsiderable heights, as for instance D'Orbigny at La Paz (alt., 3,468 metres). Guilbert mentions being seized with palpitation at night-time in other cities of Peru and Bolivia, Pœppig suffered similarly at Cerro de Pasco (alt., 4,350 metres). "It is the night," the latter writes, "which causes the greatest degree of suffocation; it is a martyrdom, for one cannot remain lying down."[2]

In the Regina Margherita Hut I became convinced that this was not owing to the altered air nor to its temperature. My brother, who suffered more than the rest of us in this way, often sat up in bed through the night on account of shortness of breath. Sometimes he rose and took a few steps in the hut without opening the window or going out (which was often an impossibility), then went back to bed and slept. My brother was subject to this inconvenience during the whole of the sojourn at the height of 4,560 metres, breathing more easily when up than when lying down. We began therefore to discuss this phenomenon which, from one point of view appears, so to speak, paradoxical. When we are lying down we consume less oxygen because the state of repose is greater; as soon as we rise, a great number of muscles enter into activity, the heart beats more rapidly, blood-pressure is augmented: if it were merely a chemical question, a question of oxygen, we should evidently feel better lying down.

My brother often slept so profoundly that he did not notice fairly loud noises near him, then afterwards he would wake spontaneously with an oppression on the chest.

I am of opinion that the origin of mountain-sickness is to be sought in a depression of the nerve-centres, in a slight weakness of the heart, in a momentary diminution of the energy of this organ, and in a subsequent slackening of the circulation which gives rise to the shortness of breath. Fatigue which has weakened the heart, is, doubtless, one of the principal factors in

---

[1] M. Hervey, *The Adventures of a Lady in Tartary, Thibet, China, and Kashmir.* London. 3 vols., 1853, p. 152.
[2] Ed. Pœppig, *Reise in Chile, Peru und auf dem Amazonenstrome.* Leipzig, 1832, 1836.

these attacks which grow more violent during sleep and milder when we stand upright, because the augmented pressure of the blood stimulates and excites the cardiac muscle, terminating the inertia of its innervation.

V.

Alpine life disposes us to the internal observation of ourselves, to judge by the abundant observations with which Alpinists spontaneously furnished me. Perhaps the solitude and the gradual disappearance of every trace of life the higher we ascend fill us with the desire to learn how our own organism works in those deserted regions.

From amongst the important physiological observations kindly placed at my disposal I quote the following on the activity of the pulse communicated to me by the Signori Natale Carini and Achille Bertarelli on their arrival at the Regina Margherita Hut :—

	Olen Inn.	Gnifetti Hut.	Regina Margherita Hut.
Bertarelli	80	85	74
Carini	90	90	86

These two gentlemen had left the Olen Inn on August 13th, had performed the ascent without difficulty after sleeping well at Gnifetti Hut, and arrived at the Regina Margherita Hut just as the sickness was beginning to manifest itself. Their pulse was very weak and slower than the normal, their face and hands were livid. The last part of the ascent had seemed to them very arduous. Sig. Bertarelli was so weak that when he was at a distance of only ten paces from the door of the hut, we saw that he was begging the companions to whom he was roped to make a halt.

It is an unexpected fact that the pulse, in spite of the preceding fatigue and the height of 4,560 metres, should be less frequent at this altitude than at lower stations. In this case, as in other conditions of life, there are causes acting in contrary directions, and thus counteracting each other. Fatigue, high temperature of the blood, rarefaction of the air, and mental agitation tend to accelerate the pulse, but depression, nausea, vomiting, overstrain of the heart tend to slacken its movement.

The rapid changes of the pulse observed during ascents, and more especially during mountain-sickness, are due to the state of the blood-vessels. When these dilate, the resistance opposed to the circulation of the blood is diminished and the heart beats more rapidly. If, however, the phenomena of accompanying failure of strength continue, nausea makes itself felt, the pulse may slacken and sink, from an exceedingly rapid rate, to one even below the normal.

When our skin is much reddened and we are in a state of profuse perspiration we are more easily seized with mountain-sickness. This explains how, in certain gorges and closed valleys the guides foresee that those of the party whose gait is already unsteady, will feel worse. The heart, exhausted by fatigue and from the frequent changes from cold to heat, offers less resistance to these sudden variations of the blood-pressure. We are, as it were, more anæmic when the sun and the heat redden the skin.

VI.

Sometimes mountain-sickness appears as the consequence of a simple emotion. A friend of mine, a good mountain-climber, the lawyer Sig. B——

left Courmayeur in good condition. When he arrived at Lake Combal an old guide who came down from Mont Blanc dissuaded him from attempting the ascent, telling him that the weather was bad, the snow very unfavourable, and that he would certainly fail in the undertaking.

Sig. B—— had in his party a colleague of whose powers of resistance he had some doubt. This anxiety, he says, gave him, immediately, a feeling of fatigue and of uncertainty in the legs. This doubt as to the decision which it behoved him to take, affected him so that at the hut, at a height of 3,200 metres, he could not eat, and slept badly. In the morning the weather had become fine and they set out for the summit of Mont Blanc. Until the height of 4,000 metres was reached he vomited several times; on his arrival at the Vallot Hut he was in fair condition and afterwards recovered his usual excellent health.

That fear may cause the outbreak of mountain-sickness I had once an opportunity of observing in passing in haste across a gully. There were only fifty steps from one wall to the other. From time to time stones rolled down, small indeed, but which might at any moment be followed by bigger ones. Besides this danger, which it was not in our power to avoid, there was the rapid inclination of the gully on which a false step would have imperilled one's life. The guide warned us to be on the alert, and we first fixed upon various points past which the crossing might be more easily accomplished. We were at a height of 3,200 metres. A friend of mine, as soon as he had reached the other side, clutched the rock and had an attack of nausea and vomiting.

There is a certain disagreement in the facts which I have collected relating to the effect of emotions. This, however, was to be foreseen. The observation made by many regarding sea-sickness applies likewise to mountain-sickness. It is an old observation which was published by Darwin's grandfather. A friend of his, Darwin [1] wrote, a good and reliable observer, assured him that he had noticed more than once that, in a vessel in great danger of being wrecked, sea-sickness ceased instantaneously, breaking out afresh as soon as the danger was past.

Forel made some important observations on this subject on Monte Rosa. I prefer to quote them in his own words as follows:— [2]

"The most interesting fact which came under my notice during this expedition is the disappearance at the beginning of the climb up the Botzertolle of the symptoms of mountain-sickness. Before starting I had been careful to obtain information from all those persons who know Monte Rosa as to the point at which one suffers most from mountain-sickness. It is well known that in this respect every mountain has its special locality; it is not, as a rule, on the airy, windy summit, nor on the dangerous or interesting arêtes that the sickness is most keenly felt, but more especially on snowy slopes which are shut in, well protected from the wind and tedious, as, for instance, the Mont Blanc *corridor*. All the reports given me were unanimous: all travellers and often even the guides were most severely put to the proof at the Botzertolle, before reaching the Sattel. On the arête of the summit on the contrary, nobody thinks of being mountain-sick. I prepared, therefore, for a careful study of this Botzertolle. I had the beginning of it pointed out to me by the guides, and from the first I forced myself to ascend it rapidly and without stopping, with the object of exaggerating by fatigue the symptoms

---

[1] Darwin, *Zoonomia, or Laws of Organic Life*, 1793.
[2] Forel, *Opera citata*, p. 110.

from which I had been suffering before attacking it. But, strange to say, I felt these symptoms disappear one after the other; as I directed my attention more especially to one or the other I felt it die away. Fatigue, lassitude, depression, headache, left me one after another, and I covered this tedious passage in perfectly good condition to the stupefaction of my guides, who had seen me seriously affected in parts much less disastrous to other travellers. Attention, scientific interest had therefore had for me in this case the same curative effect as danger; no one suffering from mountain-sickness in dangerous parts.

"This action of the mental faculties, and, of attention in particular, on mountain-sickness should be pointed out, and merits more consideration than has hitherto been given to it in the study of the malady; I restrict myself to the present indication"

When Forel published this observation, however, other mountain-climbers had already affirmed the contrary. As we have here to do with contradictions towards which the reader is always little indulgent I may mention that another physiologist, Le Pileur, said that MM. Bravais and Martins had a sensation of nausea whenever they observed their instruments with great attention [1]

VII

In mountain-sickness one often sees that the lips of the sufferers are livid, the hands and cheeks bluish. In my Alpine travelling-notes, written above the height of 3,500 metres, I often find the word *cyanosis*.[2] This is the medical term indicating a violet colour of the skin. The cyanosis which is observed in the Alps is the mildest, almost physiological form. Weakness of the heart produces cyanosis, on this account it is observed in almost all diseases of the heart, disappearing when the heart, through its own action, or in consequence of remedies, rectifies the circulation of the blood. It is clear that in circulating more slowly through the vessels of the skin the blood must become more venous, and therefore darker containing as it does less oxygen.

If the pressure of the blood is diminished, as after over-exertion—a night spent in dancing, for instance—the veins dilate. Round the eyes where the skin is thin and the veins abundant, a blue circle appears. By whatever excess the nervous system is exhausted, the same effect is produced. Even ascents cause the appearance of a livid circle round the eyes in many climbers. A characteristic dilatation of the veins is that which gives rise to the blue colour of the skin of chilblains. In serious forms of frost-bite the bluish colour of the skin is due to an alteration of the vessels. A pinch also leaves a leaden-coloured mark on the skin, if the mechanical pressure on the blood-vessels has been at all forcible. If we merely dip the hand into hot water and then, when it has become red, into iced water, the fingers assume a violet tinge such as we have all seen produced by the action of the cold in winter or on the Alps. The little arteries contract and in the capillaries and little veins in which contractile muscular fibre is lacking, the blood becomes stagnant or at least sluggish, gradually loses its oxygen and the skin becomes violet. This is the origin of the cyanosis occasioned by cold. The same process occurs in fever when face and hands become bluish during a shivering fit.

[1] *Comptes rendus*, 1845, tome xx. p. 1200.
[2] κύανος in Greek means blue. From this root the word cyanosis has been formed to indicate the livid colour which the skin assumes in certain diseases.

But in the Alps cyanosis remains even after the action of the cold has ceased. Several days after our arrival in the Regina Margherita Hut in which the rooms were well heated, cyanosis had not yet disappeared. In these cases it must be another mechanism to which it owes its origin: it is the weakness of the heart, the diminished pressure of the blood and the languid peripheric circulation to which the persistence of the phenomenon is due. In mountain-sickness, so far as I was able to observe, cyanosis is invariably present.

When H.M. the Queen of Italy arrived at the hut which now bears her name, her cheeks had a slightly bluish colour. The last part of the ascent, which is the most difficult, had necessarily been performed on foot. Her Majesty told me that she had not suffered at all, but had a feeling of constriction at the temples as though there were a band of iron round her head. This was an unaccustomed phenomenon to her Majesty who has never suffered from headache, and gave a sensation as though the veins of the temples must burst.

A corner of the Alpine Laboratory.

CHAPTER XV

CHEMICAL ACTIVITY OF THE RESPIRATION ON THE ALPS

I

SAUSSURE says that the fire did not burn so well on Mont Blanc and that it was necessary to blow continually on the ignited coals, as they otherwise immediately died out. Saussure's party consisted of eighteen persons and they remained about four hours on the summit. They melted snow in order to obtain water to drink. Cold water was the only liquid which they drank with pleasure; wine and liquors were disagreeable to all. On Mont Blanc water boiled at 84·3°. Notwithstanding this, the vessel containing the water took half an hour to come to the boiling-point. The same vessel, with the same quantity of water and alcohol boiled in 12 minutes at the sea level.

Frankland and Tyndall had already found that on Mont Blanc stearine candles are less rapidly consumed than in the plain. They attributed this difference to the cold, but that is not the cause. Dr. A. Benedicenti,[1] assist-

[1] A. Benedicenti, *La combustione nell' aria rarefatta*. Rendiconti Accademia dei Lincei, 17 Maggio, 1896.—This memoir also contains the bibliography of the subject.

ant in my laboratory, undertook at my request to study combustion in rarefied air, and found that the consumption of combustible matter is less at a diminished pressure, even when the temperature of the surrounding air is constant. I refrain from communicating these experiments, as this would entail the description of complicated apparatus and the quotation of a long series of figures.

For the first experiments we made use of candles, afterwards we employed small oil lights with asbestos wick, which burn with much greater regularity than the stearine candles. The intensity of the flame corresponded to that of a night lamp. Now if one of these flames at an ordinary pressure and at a temperature of from 12° to 13° consumed in one hour 2·1930 grams of oil, at the same temperature but with a pressure reduced to 360 mm. (which corresponds to a height of 5,950 metres above the sea-level) it consumed only 1·9119 grams, that is, 0·2811 grams less.

We then sought to ascertain whether the combustion were perfect and obtained an affirmative result. I refer the reader who desires further particulars to Dr. Benedicenti's memoir in which Tyndall's [1] first investigations on the subject are rectified.

II.

These observations of Dr. Benedicenti are intimately connected with the study of the respiration on the Alps, because, since the celebrated experiments of Lavoisier, it is a well-known fact that breathing in many respects resembles combustion.

I may here mention that the flame of a light is much more sensitive than man and animals to the lack of oxygen. A candle goes out where man continues to live and even to breathe. These experiments were performed by Tommaso Laghi [2] towards the middle of the last century in Bologna. He placed under a large bell a bird, rat, or cat, and a lighted candle, and saw that the animals continued to live for hours in that closed-in air after the candle had gone out.

Giovanni Francesco Cigna, professor of anatomy and physiology at the University of Turin, began in 1760 physiological studies on the action of rarefied air. [3] The apparatus constructed by Cigna consisted in a large glass bottle, capable of containing fifty pounds of water, of which the neck, wide enough to admit a sparrow, was closed by a large copper screw-stopper. Two lateral glass tubes branching off from the neck were put into communication, the one with a pneumatic machine, the other with a mercurial manometer which indicated the inner pressure. Cigna stated that under the pneumatic bell also animals live as on the mountains, provided the air be continually renewed.

I communicate one of Cigna's experiments, because his apparatus is the same as that used a century later by Paul Bert.

"In order to learn more exactly what degree of atmospheric rarefaction animals can bear, I made the following experiment. I put a sparrow under the pneumatic bell and let the aspiring pump act until the manometer

---

[1] Tyndall, *Hours of Exercise in the Alps*, p. 56.
[2] Thomae Laghii, *De animalium in aere interclusorum interitu*. De Bononiensi Scientiarum Instituto, Commentarii, Tomus Quartus, 1757, p. 89.
[3] G. F. Cigna, *De causa extinctionis flammae et animalium in aere interclusorum*. Mélanges de philosophie et de mathématique de la Société royale de Turin, 1760-1761, p. 176.

marked 19 inches (513 mm.). The height of the barometer was 27 inches and a half (742 mm.) Then I let air enter until the manometer indicated two inches less (54 mm.) Hereupon I began to pump again until the manometer again indicated the first depression (513 mm.), and in this manner I continued to give and take away air for half an hour together, so that an air-current sufficient for the maintenance of life was kept up. The sparrow vomited at first, then recovered, and when, half an hour later it was taken out, it was hale and hearty; but afterwards dyspnœa reappeared, it was seized with convulsions and died shortly after it had been released."

This sparrow had resisted for half an hour a pressure of only 229 mm. as shown by the barometer, which corresponds to a rarefaction of the air greater than that found on the highest mountain in the world, for on Mount Everest, at a height of 8,840 metres, the pressure is only 248 mm.

III.

The picture on page 195, which is the reproduction of a photograph, shows how the experiments on the chemistry of breathing were made in the Regina Margherita Hut. Beno Bizzozero has the gutta-percha mask on and is breathing through the gas-meter which is seen to the left. The inspired air passes into the gas-meter, then into the first valve before entering the lungs. The expired air passes through the second valve which is rather in the shade, and then, before issuing from the apparatus, into a caoutchouc bladder and into a third valve seen in the middle of the figure. My brother, by means of a syringe in communication with the elastic bladder, takes a certain quantity of the expired air and impels it through six glass tubes, seen in the background of the picture, full of baryta-water which serves to fix the carbonic acid. These experiments were described by my brother in two memoirs laid before the Accademia dei Lincei.[1] I need not therefore dwell on the particulars of the analysis of respired air, but shall restrict myself to the communication of the results.

The first halt was made at Gressoney la Trinità (alt., 1,627 metres) where we arrived on July 18th. The soldiers camped in the open and the experiments were made under a tent which served as laboratory.

EXPERIMENTS MADE AT GRESSONEY LA TRINITÀ (ALT., 1,627 METRES).

	Serial number.	Date.	Time.	Temperature of the air.	Barometric pressure.	Litres of air inspired in half an hour.	Grams of CO_2 eliminated in half an hour.	Grams of CO_2.	
								Contained in a litre of air per	kilog. and per hour.
Jachini	1	21, vii.	9.25 a.m.	17°	65 cm.	261·075	15·423	0·434	0·059
,,	2	21 ,,	2.4 p.m.	18°	,,	285·010	17·036	0·479	0·059
Solferino	3	22 ,,	3.0 ,,	21°	,,	206·223	11·998	0·375	0·053
Sarteur	4	23 ,,	3.0 ,,	25°	,,	207·983	13·003	0·400	0·062
,,	5	24 ,,	1.30 ,,	26°	,,	177·203	9·224	0·284	0·052
Solferino	6	24 ,,	3.55 ,,	24°	,,	289·633	18·380	0·574	0·063

[1] Ugolino Mosso, *Apparecchio portabile per determinare l'acido carbonico nell'aria espirata dall'uomo*. Rendiconti Accademia dei Lincei, 15 Marzo, 1896.—*La respirazione dell'uomo sul Monte Rosa. Eliminazione dell'acido carbonico a grandi altezze*. Archives italiennes de Biologie, tome xxv. Ibidem, 12 Aprile, 1896.

On July 13th the expedition left Gressoney and camped in a locality called Alp Indra (alt., 2,515 metres), situated on a level flanked on three sides by mountains and at the foot of the glacier of the same name. The next day we began the experiments.

EXPERIMENTS MADE ON THE ALP INDRA (ALT., 2,515 METRES).

	Serial number.	Date.	Time.	Temperature of the air.	Barometric pressure.	Litres of air inspired in half an hour.	Grams of CO² eliminated in half an hour.	Grams of CO² Contained in a litre of air per	Grams of CO² kilog. and per hour.
Jachini	7	26, vii.	10.45 a.m.	15º	60 cm.	290·405	17·676	0·497	0·061
Solferino	8	26 ,,	4.30 p.m.	16º	,,	208·561	12·383	0·386	0·059
,, ...	9	29 ,,	9.35 a.m.	10º	,,	240·421	9·528	0·298	0·039
Sarteur	10	29 ,,	10.50 ,,	10º	,,	174·990	9·965	0·306	0·057
Jachini	11	29 ,,	2.16 p.m.	12º	,,	283·126	17·563	0·494	0·062

On the 30th July we continued the ascent and halted at a height of 3,047 metres, at a short distance from Linty Hut, on a level which has served as camping ground to Her Majesty Queen Margaret on her expeditions up Monte Rosa.

EXPERIMENTS MADE NEAR LINTY HUT (ALT., 3,047 METRES).

	Serial number.	Date.	Time.	Temperature of the air.	Barometric pressure.	Litres of air inspired in half an hour.	Grams of CO² eliminated in half an hour.	Grams of CO² Contained in a litre of air per	Grams of CO² kilog. and per hour.
Jachini	12	1, viii.	2.30 p.m.	15º	51 cm.	243·898	13·926	0·388	0·053
Solferino	13	2 ,,	3.39 ,,	13º	,,	303·660	16·483	0·515	0·054
Sarteur	14	3 ,,	3 ,,	12º	,,	220·354	12·601	0·392	0·057

At this height, although the air is rarefied by about a third there is no phenomenon observable in the respiratory functions referable to a lack of oxygen.

On August 5th we reached Gnifetti Hut (alt., 3,620 metres). This hut is surrounded on every side by glaciers, to the north rises a counterfort which protects it from the wind. The experiments were made in the hut.

EXPERIMENTS MADE IN GNIFETTI HUT (ALT., 3,620 METRES).

	Serial number.	Date.	Time.	Temperature of the air.	Barometric pressure.	Litres of air inspired in half an hour.	Grams of CO² eliminated in half an hour.	Grams of CO² Contained in a litre of air per	Grams of CO² kilog. and per hour.
Jachini	15	7, viii.	2 20 p.m.	10º	48 cm.	231·649	14·388	0·405	0·062
Solferino	16	7 ,,	4.20 ,,	5º	,,	231·866	16·597	0·518	0·071
Sarteur	17	8 ,,	5.25 ,,	7º	,,	218·828	11·216	0·345	0·051

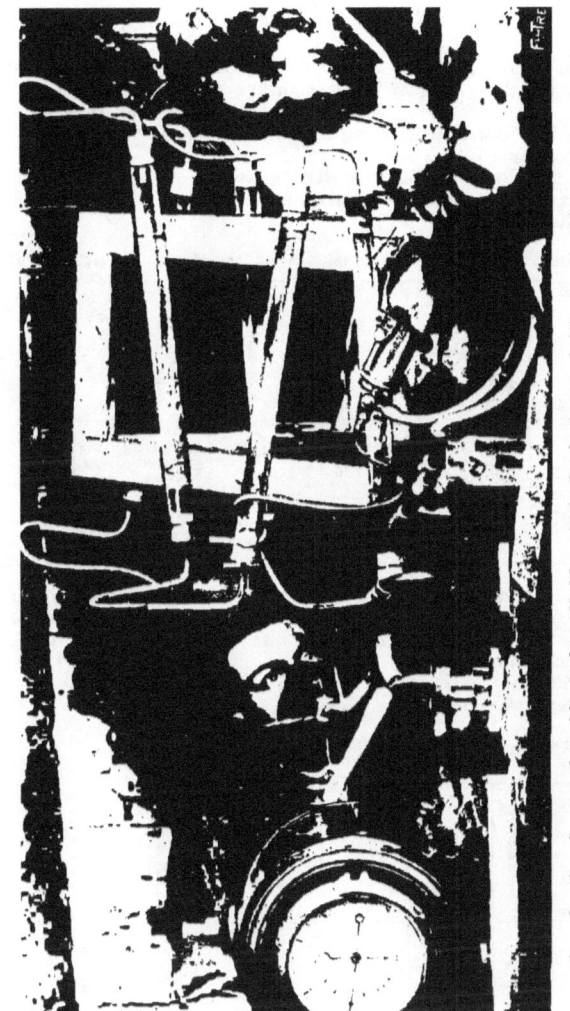

FIG. 48.—Experiment performed by Professor U. Mosso in the Regina Margherita Hut in order to measure the quantity of carbonic acid eliminated in half an hour by Beno Bizzozero.

At this height appeared the first symptoms of an alteration in the respiratory functions, as may be seen in the tracings at the beginning of the book. The breathing, especially during sleep and sometimes also during waking hours, assumed a decidedly periodic form. There was no change observable in the soldiers.

On the 8th the expedition moved on to the Regina Margherita Hut (alt., 4,560 metres). After recovering from the fatigue of the ascent we remained here ten days.

EXPERIMENTS MADE IN THE REGINA MARGHERITA HUT (ALT., 4,560 METRES).

	Serial number.	Date.	Time.	Temperature of the air.	Barometric pressure.	Litres of air inspired in half an hour.	Grams of CO_2 eliminated in half an hour.	Grams of CO_2.	
								Contained in a litre of air per	Kilogr. and per hour.
Jachini	18	12, viii.	4.26 p.m.	7°	43 cm.	276·427	15·282	0·430	0·055
,,	19	13 ,,	5.30 ,,	13°	,,	289·296	16·096	0·454	0·055
Sarteur	20	16 ,,	4.35 ,,	12°	,,	192·065	11·284	0·347	0·058
,,	21	17 ,,	10.25 a.m.	18°	,,	151·830	8·698	0·268	0·057
Solferino	22	18 ,,	10.20 ,,	20°	,,	267·220	14·595	0·456	0·054
,,	23	18 ,,	1.45 p.m.	19°	,,	259·171	12·703	0·396	0·050

The minimum of carbonic acid eliminated during all these experiments was 8·698 grams exhaled by the soldier Sarteur in half an hour in the Regina Margherita Hut. In Corporal Jachini also we found the production of carbonic acid diminished.

After the return to Gressoney la Trinità (alt., 1,627 metres), the last series of experiments were made.

EXPERIMENTS MADE AT GRESSONEY LA TRINITÀ AFTER THE RETURN FROM MONTE ROSA.

	Serial number.	Date.	Time.	Temperature of the air.	Barometric pressure.	Litres of air inspired in half an hour.	Grams of CO_2 eliminated in half an hour.	Grams of CO_2.	
								Contained in a litre of air per	Kilogr. and per hour.
Sarteur	24	23, viii.	10 a.m.	15°	65 cm.	161·229	8·938	0·275	0·055
Jachini	25	,, ,,	11.20 ,,	12°	,,	301·973	18·411	0·518	0·060
Solferino	26	,, ,,	3.40 p.m.	12°	,,	197·861	10·454	0·336	0·053

IV.

Knowing that candles burn less vividly on the Alps,[1] we desired to learn whether the flame of life burns likewise less intensely at great heights than in

[1] Davy, Frankland, and Tyndall have studied this question: other references are to be found in the memoir by Dr. Benedicenti above-mentioned, *Archives italiennes de Biologie*. Tome xxv. p. 473

the lowlands. This was the object of the researches made by my brother on the chemistry of breathing on the summit of Monte Rosa.

To facilitate the survey of the results, I introduce the following table in which is shown the weight (in grams) of carbonic acid, eliminated by the three subjects in half an hour at different heights.

WEIGHT OF CARBONIC ACID ELIMINATED IN HALF AN HOUR AT DIFFERENT ALTITUDES BY THE SOLDIERS JACHINI, SOLFERINO, AND SARTEUR.

	1,627 met.		2,515 met.		3,047 m.	3,620 m.	4,560 met.		1,627 met.
Jachini	15·423	17·036	17·676	17·563	13·926	14·388	15·282	16·096	18·411
Solferino	11·998	18·380	12·383	9·528	16·483	16·597	14·595	12·703	10·454
Sarteur	9·224	13·003	9·965	...	12·601	11·216	11·284	8·698	8·938

It appears evident that the rarefaction of the air rather produces a diminution than an augmentation of the carbonic acid eliminated.

The quantity of air inspired in half an hour did not undergo any noteworthy variation, as may be seen from the following table :—

LITRES OF AIR INSPIRED IN HALF AN HOUR BY JACHINI, SOLFERINO, AND SARTEUR AT DIFFERENT ALTITUDES.

	1,627 met.		2,515 met.		3,047 m.	3,620 m.	4.560 met.		1,627 m.
Jachini	261·075	285·010	290·405	283·126	243·898	231·649	276·427	289·296	301·973
Solferino	206·223	289·633	208·561	240·421	303·660	231·866	267·220	259·171	197·861
Sarteur	207·983	177·203	174·990	...	220·354	218·826	192·065	151·830	161·229

From these data we see that when one remains tranquil and in repose, no great modifications appear at great heights in the elimination of carbonic acid, nor in the volume of inspired air.

Our body is not, therefore, an economical machine which adapts itself to surroundings and to circumstances. When there is a diminished quantity of oxygen in the air we cannot alter our expenditure and burn the substance of our organs less rapidly. The chemistry of the body cannot bear further reductions, and this is a proof that its consumption is lowered to the minimum compatible with the continuance of its activity. This fact, established by Prof. U. Mosso, is important. It shows that it is not possible to moderate the chemical processes of life, and that we cannot adapt ourselves to a diminished ration of oxygen, for even in rarefied air the organism needs its normal amount.

Should the doubt suggest itself that the cold may have produced a greater consumption of material in the organism, and that the consequent augmentation of carbonic acid may have compensated for the slackening of the chemical processes due to the rarefaction of the air,[1] I may answer that the influence of the temperature certainly did not modify the results of our analyses, as we

[1] The investigations of Speck, and the more recent ones of Wolpert, have shown that there is no difference in the elimination of carbonic acid when the surrounding temperature fluctuates between 5° and 25°. *Archiv für Hygiene*, xxvi., pp. 1 to 32.

also took care that the temperature of the Regina Margherita Hut should not sink below 7°, nor rise higher than 20° during these experiments.

Dr. W. Marcet stayed three days at the Col du Géant in 1880, in order to study the carbonic acid eliminated by man at a height of 3,365 metres.[1] He made experiments on himself and on a young friend, collecting the exhaled air into an impermeable caoutchouc bag, and found that he had emitted 12 per cent. and his companion 16 per cent. less than in the plain. Dr. Marcet thinks that such a diminution of the internal combustion was due to the cold, for the temperature that day was only of 6°, but probably there were other complications.

V.

The brothers Lœwy, of Berlin, and the son of Prof. Zuntz[2] performed last year on Monte Rosa an important series of investigations on the chemical activity of the respiration. These researches may be considered as the continuation of those which Schumburg and Zuntz made the year before on the other side of Monte Rosa in the Bétemps Hut, at a height of 2,800 metres, and on the glaciers at the height of about 3,800 metres.[3]

It was a pleasure to me to notice with what ability my colleagues conducted these Alpine investigations, and I regret that lack of space does not allow me to explain the ingenious technique of their experiments, obliging me to restrict myself to a brief mention of the results obtained at the Col d'Olen, and the huts Gnifetti and Regina Margherita. The weather was unfavourable during their sojourn on Monte Rosa.

These investigators found the rate of the pulse and of the respiratory movements increased from the time they left Berlin to the arrival at the Col d'Olen and Gnifetti Hut. They noticed, however, that they gradually accustomed themselves to these heights, because in Gnifetti Hut, which is at an altitude of 3,620 metres, the frequency of the pulse was less than at the Col d'Olen, which is at a height of only 2,865 metres, and during their stay in Gnifetti Hut, the pulse continued to decrease in all three.

The researches into the consumption of oxygen were made while walking in the plain, or in performing the short ascent to the Col d'Olen or on the glacier near Gnifetti Hut. For Dr. J. Lœwy and L. Zuntz the consumption of oxygen during muscular work was greater on Monte Rosa than in Berlin. For Dr. A. Lœwy the augmentation in the consumption of oxygen was less considerable than for his two companions. They are of opinion that an Alpine climate stimulates the material change in our organism. They emphasise the circumstance that in none of their experiments did they meet with any effect which would indicate a lack of oxygen. In spite of this their climbing powers were notably diminished; the work performed every minute during the easy ascent of a sloping plain was less at the Col d'Olen than in Berlin, and less again at Gnifetti Hut. The diminution of the amount of work which may be performed without discomfort at different heights had already been observed the year before by Zuntz and Schumburg on the other side of Monte Rosa, and I, too, had been able to establish the same fact by means of work accomplished with the ergograph at the various halting-places

---

[1] William Marcet, *A Contribution to the History of the Respiration of Man*. London, 1897, p. 11.
[2] Drs. A. Lœwy, J. Lœwy, and L. Zuntz, *Ueber den Einfluss der verdünnten Luft und des Hohenklimas auf den Menschen*. Pflüger's Archiv. Bd. 66, p. 477.
[3] Schumburg and Zuntz, Pflüger's Archiv Bd. 63, p. 461.

of my expedition. It is an important fact because it shows that it is not the lack of oxygen which diminishes our aptitude for work, and lowers, so to speak, the limit of our strength. I think it well to introduce here a table taken from the work of the above-mentioned authors, as we have here a new species of study before us which will certainly be fruitful in results and shed new light on the physiology of man in the Alps.

AVERAGE WORK (IN KILOGRAMMETRES) PERFORMED PER MINUTE IN WALKING ON A SLOPING PLAIN IN BERLIN AND ON MONTE ROSA.

	A. Lœwy.	J. Lœwy.	L. Zuntz.
Berlin : gradient 37 in 100	570 kgm.	580 kgm.	809 kgm.
Col d'Olen : gradient 30 in 100	440 ,,	504 ,,	574 ,,
Gnifetti Hut : gradient 35 in 100	475 ,,	559 ,,	580 ,,

Hoar-frost on the Regina Margherita Hut after the storm of August 13, 1894.

CHAPTER XVI

ANALYSIS OF ASPHYXIA AND OF MOUNTAIN-SICKNESS

I.

PAUL BERT was the successor of Claude Bernard in the chair of physiology at the Sorbonne. His name is known in politics, in literature and in science. It was Paul Bert with his mechanical talent, his apparatus and his analyses of the blood who laid the foundations of a physiology of man on the Alps. His voluminous work on barometric pressure was published while he was fighting a memorable battle, rich in results, in the field of politics, when, as he wrote in the preface, he "was often torn from the laboratory by the severe call of civil duties." His premature death in Tonquin, where he fell a victim to the climate and a sacrifice to his country, who had sent him to govern that colony at a critical moment, endears still more his memory.

The vastness of the scientific work began by Paul Bert exceeded his strength, nor need our wonder be excited if others after him have rectified the results of some of his investigations. In studying the modification of the gases in the blood in an animal placed in rarefied air, Paul Bert found that a fall of only 20 centimetres in the height of the barometer (observable for instance at the Hospice of the Gt. St. Bernard) is sufficient to diminish the quantity of oxygen contained in the blood.

Paul Bert seemed thus to have confirmed by his experiments Jourdanet's opinion and to have discovered the cause of mountain-sickness. Jourdanet was a French physician, who had spent many years on the plateaus of Mexico, where he conceived the idea that at a certain height on the mountains there must be a lack of oxygen in the blood, as there is no longer a sufficient quantity of oxygen in the air to saturate the hæmoglobin. It was this physician, author of two volumes on the influence of atmospheric pressure on human life,[1] who gave to Paul Bert the means of constructing the splendid apparatus of the Sorbonne. Bert recognised the worth of this benefactor of science; he concludes the work dedicated to Jourdanet as follows : "The diminution of barometric pressure acts on living beings only by diminishing the tension of the oxygen in the air which they breathe, and in the blood which animates their tissues (*anoxyhæmia* according to M. Jourdanet), and by exposing them thus to the dangers of asphyxia."[2]

Fraenkel and Geppert of Berlin began the criticism of Paul Bert's theory. They showed that the method adopted by him for the analysis of the blood, was not sufficiently exact, and that down to a barometric pressure of 41 centimetres (corresponding to a height a little above that of Mont Blanc) the blood still contains the same amount of oxygen as at the sea-level.[3]

Bert's work contains two fundamental conclusions: (1) That at the height of the Gt. St. Bernard the arterial blood contains less oxygen than normally; (2) That a little higher than Mont Blanc the arterial blood is already so poor in oxygen that it contains less than venous blood at the sea-level. The simplicity of this theory favoured its acceptation, and it remained unattacked till 1883.

The fact demonstrated by Fraenkel and Geppert that the amount of oxygen in the blood of a dog is not appreciably altered at a height of 4,915 metres has not much elucidated the physiology of mountain-sickness, because we know that many persons suffer somewhat seriously from the rarefaction of the air below this limit. In order to explain the appearance of mountain-sickness below a height of 4,900 metres, Fraenkel and Geppert recur to the theory of Dufour, who maintained the dependence of the indisposition on the excessive work of the muscles. We know, however, that not all recover from mountain-sickness with repose. I knew many persons in the Regiña Margherita Hut who vomited all night, and who even continued to feel unwell the day after their arrival. Others, I noticed, slept through the night and vomited the next day. These cases are not explained either by the Dufour hypothesis or by the analyses of the blood of Fraenkel and Geppert.

II.

The nostrils and the mouth cannot be kept closed at the same time longer than a minute. There are exceptional cases in which the time is longer, but the majority of persons are obliged to breathe even after the lapse of only half a minute.

This irresistible necessity is due to the fact that mouth and nose are like

[1] Jourdanet, *Influence de la pression de l'air sur la vie de l'homme.* Paris, 1875.
[2] P. Bert, *Pression barométrique*, p. 1153.
[3] A. Fraenkel und J. Geppert, *Ueber die Wirkungen der verdünnten Luft auf den Organismus*, Berlin, 1883, p. 112.

the chimney over the fire; if they are closed, the smoke suffocates us. We know that the blood circulates through the lungs and yields in its passage its carbonic acid to the air from which it draws its supply of oxygen. If the lungs remain closed, a moment soon comes in which the blood lacks a sufficient amount of oxygen, containing instead too large a quantity of carbonic acid. From this moment the blood which circulates in the arteries begins to have a certain resemblance to the blood in the veins. This similarity goes on increasing. The nervous centre imperfectly fed with oxygen remains excited. The whole organism feels the effect of this change in the blood and the will becomes incapable of holding in the breath any longer.

If mountain-sickness were, as Paul Bert said, a sort of asphyxia, one ought to be still less able to keep the nose closed on high mountains. The above simple experiment gives us an idea of the rapidity with which internal chemical processes are accomplished, and of the supplies of oxygen which we have stored up in the blood and in the tissues.

I communicate one of these experiments made on the soldier Cento, on the 11th July, 1894, at 3 p.m., the respiratory curve of the thorax being taken with Marey's double pneumograph. The top line of Fig. 49 shows the normal tracing. Towards the

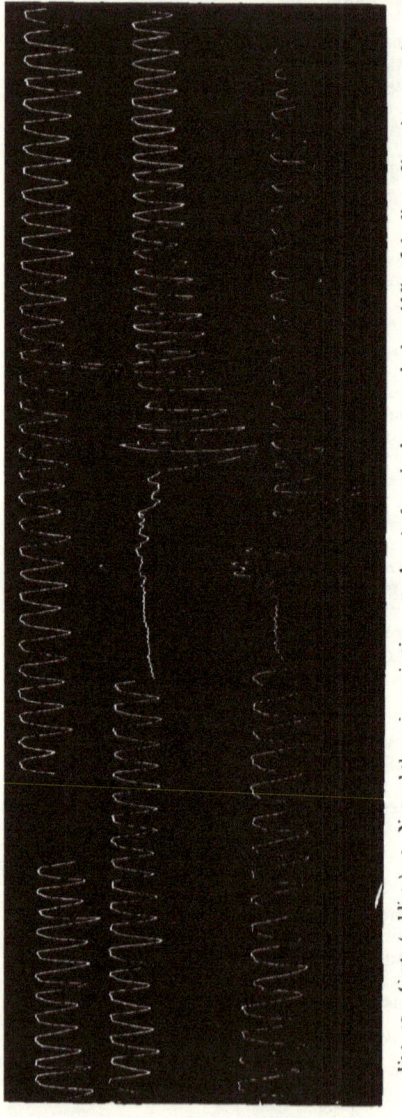

FIG. 49.—Cento (soldier.)—1. Normal thoracic respiration. 2. Arrest of respiration towards the middle of the line. Experiment made in Turin. 3. The same experiment with arrest of breathing made in Gnifetti Hut (alt., 3,620 metres).

middle of the second line I closed his nose, compressing the nostrils with my fingers at the end of an inspiration. The line, which has become horizontal, shows that the thorax is still and the breathing suspended. The slight undulations are caused by the beating of the heart. After 45 seconds, not being able to hold his breath any longer, he opened his mouth. Even before this we see that the thorax has become restless and the line irregular, then a deep breath is drawn, followed by other strong inspirations of gradually decreasing vehemence. Soon the normal breathing returns.

On the 5th of August I repeated the same experiment in Gnifetti Hut. The tracing obtained is shown in line 3. We see that the amplitude of the respiratory movements is somewhat greater than in Turin while their frequency is diminished. As the temperature of the air was 27° when the preceding tracing was taken in Turin, and only 10° in Gnifetti Hut, it may be thought that this difference in the breathing was due to the temperature. Some small influence it may possibly have had, but there is certainly an effect due to the rarefaction of the air.

The most striking fact

is that Cento resisted the suspension of the breath only half the usual time, when he was at a height of 3,620 metres. Nor must this be considered as an accidental circumstance, for I repeated the experiment several times on Cento in Gnifetti Hut and always with the same result. This seemed strange to me, because only in him did this diminished barometric pressure suffice to reduce the duration of the suspension of the breath. A few days later I thought I had found the explanation of this circumstance, in the fact that Cento had suffered from mountain-sickness in ascending Gnifetti Peak, whereas the others had not felt in any way indisposed.

On August 11th Cento started for Regina Margherita Hut with 18 kilograms on his shoulders. When he was half-way up, his load had to be lightened as he was walking very laboriously over the glacier. At the Col du Lys he showed such signs of suffering that Dr. Abelli, who was with him, considered it imprudent to let him proceed to Regina Margherita Hut, and therefore sent him back with the guides.

If we examine the tracing (Fig. 49) more closely, we notice that although Cento showed less resistance in line 3, written at a height of 3,620 metres, the detriment to the organism in consequence of the arrest of breathing was not greater, for in less time than before the respiration has become normal again. This, too, surprised me. I had supposed that in rarefied air a longer time would be necessary to remedy the internal changes produced by an arrest of respiration.

This supposition was, I found, verified in myself in Regina Margherita Hut (Fig. 50).

On the 11th of July, 1894, I made two experiments, one after the other, in Turin, obtaining the same results as is seen in the tracings 1 and 2, which are precisely similar. After two days' rest in the Regina Margherita Hut, I repeated the experiment (line 3), and found that in my case also the resistance to the suspension of breathing was diminished, and that a longer time was necessary for the respiration to regain its former rhythm and form. The barometric depression produced a diminution of the frequency and a greater amplitude of the respiratory movements. I am convinced that this difference is not due to the temperature, as I had had the room heated which served as a laboratory. In the respiratory curves obtained on the summit of Monte Rosa on the other members of the party, it was not possible to discover the slightest difference from those taken in Turin on the same persons.

III.

All mountain-climbers who have been high up on the mountains will have noticed the discomfort caused by the interruption of the breathing, and the disturbance of the circulation when one has to stoop or exert one's self in any way.

I had thought that the arrest of the breath would prove a convenient method for studying the predisposition to mountain-sickness, this supposition seeming reasonable to me, not only because of the resemblance between asphyxia and mountain-sickness, but also because in Zurbriggen I had found a resistance superior to the average. As may be seen from Fig. 51 he is able to remain from 50 to 60 seconds with nose and mouth closed, whereas the majority of persons cannot even resist asphyxia for half a minute without opening the mouth. I must, however, confess that the matter is much more complicated than it seems. As this question had not been previously studied with sufficient accuracy I found myself so beset with difficulties in the few experiments performed on Monte Rosa, that after my return to Turin I had to begin all over again. I begged the students of my medical course to let me examine them, with a view to establishing, first, the relation between the capacity of the lungs and the duration of the resistance to suspended breathing. The height and weight of the subjects were of course duly ascertained. In the following table the various measurements resulting from the examination of fifteen students are given. In Fig. 52 these values obtained are graphically represented for the sake of greater clearness.

INDIVIDUAL DIFFERENCES IN THE RESISTANCE TO ASPHYXIA IN RELATION TO VITAL CAPACITY, WEIGHT OF THE BODY, AND STATURE.—MEASUREMENTS TAKEN ON STUDENTS OF THE THIRD YEAR.

Serial number.	Name.	Respiratory suspension in seconds.	Vital capacity.	Weight in kilograms.	Stature in metres.
1	Francesco Devecchi	72	3,250	56·900	1·68
2	Giuseppe Cambiano	40	2,750	61·100	1·71
3	Carlo Succi	38	2,400	71·500	1·71
4	Alfredo Golzio	35	3,200	62·200	1·63
5	Adolfo Casazzo	34	4,600	73·100	1·95
6	Piero Giordano	25	5,000	79·500	1·90
7	Gerolamo Cesare	31	4,500	74·500	1·72
8	Luigi Gedda	29	2,500	55·200	1·67
9	Silvio Demonte	22	3,500	66·	1·80
10	Pompeo Rivalta	28	4,468	72·300	1·76
11	Davide Bazzi	24	3,640	61·	1·62
12	Antonio Mosso	22	3,300	76·500	1·70
13	Cesare Provera	18	2,834	66·500	1·67
14	Vittorio Flick	17	3,950	64·200	1·75
15	Giacomo Cardini	19	3,250	64·	1·71

The dotted line indicates the vital capacity, the thicker, continuous line, the duration in seconds of the respiratory suspension.

The subject No. 1 for instance, as we see by the indication to the higher left-hand corner was able to hold out 72 seconds. This was the maximum observed in this series of observations. The vital capacity of this student was small, amounting only to 3,250. Subject No. 6 had the maximum vital capacity and resisted only 25 seconds.

If we follow the course of the two lines in Fig. 52 we see at once that a strict relation between vital capacity and the duration of the respiratory suspension is lacking. Neither are we able to say that it is the weight of the body or mass of breathing substance which enters as a preponderating factor. Subject No. 8 for instance is lighter than all, has a lung-capacity superior to that of No. 3, and yet resists asphyxia less than the latter and many others. We may conclude from this that the quantity of air which we have in the lungs is not that which gives us the means of resisting an arrest of breathing for a greater or lesser length of time. It is not this supply of oxygen, nor the weight of the body which determines the long or short duration of the respiratory suspension, but the nervous system which dominates these phenomena with its greater or lesser resistance to asphyxia.

Even the outward aspect by which we judge whether a person is rich in blood or anæmic, is deceptive, for one student, Sig. Gambarotta, who held out longer than all the rest, remaining 1 min. 33 sec. without breathing, is pale and rather anæmic. Others with a vital capacity below the average also resisted for a long time.

I had hoped to find a greater resistance to asphyxia in Alpinists who do not suffer from mountain-sickness, but I met with many exceptions. Francioli and Quaretta, the two keepers of the Regina Margherita Hut, have only an average resistance to respiratory suspension although they are accustomed to live in rarefied air. Dr. Benedicenti showed by the analysis of air that the duration of the respiratory arrest is, within certain limits, independent of the quantity of oxygen consumed.[1]

Having recognised by means of the experiments contained in this section that the nervous system exercises a preponderating influence on the resistance to asphyxia, it is now easier to understand that the phenomena of mountain-sickness depend also on the greater or lesser resistance which the nervous system opposes to the deficiency of oxygen, to the hunger for this element which is one of the most indispensable to life.

IV.

When we see a duck dive in search of food, we are surprised that it can remain so long without breathing. I have often measured this length of time, and, in order to render the experiment more exact, while one held the duck over a large glass vessel, another kept the head under water. The duck holds out for six or seven minutes and has not even convulsions. A dog or a man submersed in this way would die in half that time.

P. Bert's explanation of this prolonged resistance was that ducks must

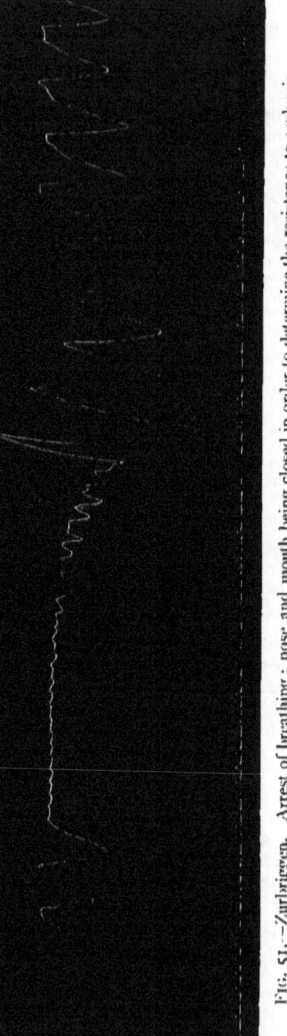

FIG. 51.—Zurbriggen. Arrest of breathing: nose and mouth being closed in order to determine the resistance to asphyxia. The lower line marks the seconds.

---

[1] A. Benedicenti, *Sull' arresto del respiro nell' uomo e le cause che ne modificano la durata.* R. Accademia medica di Torino, 1897.

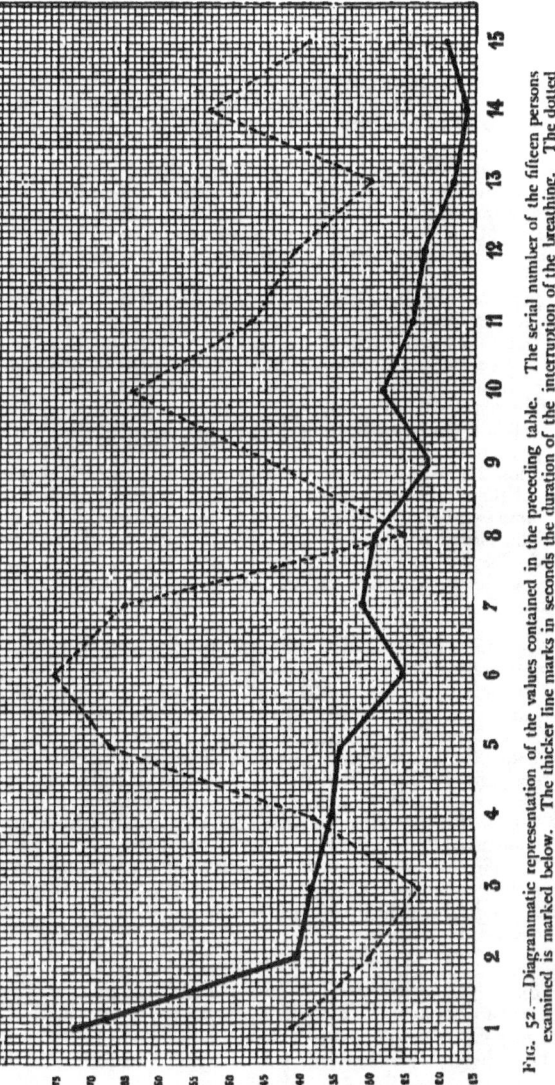

FIG. 52.—Diagrammatic representation of the values contained in the preceding table. The serial number of the fifteen persons examined is marked below. The thicker line marks in seconds the duration of the interruption of the breathing. The dotted line represents the vital capacity of each of the fifteen subjects.

have a greater amount of blood. Richet[1] proved that this is not the case. Neither have divers necessarily a greater quantity of blood or a greater development of the lungs. In the preceding section it has been shown that these differences arise from the greater or lesser resistance of the nervous system to asphyxia.

The fact that the duck opposes more prolonged resistance to asphyxia than other animals would lead us to believe that it must also resist longer the action of rarefied air. On the contrary it resists rarefied air for a much shorter space of time than respiratory suspension; and less than animals more easily and seriously subject to mountain-sickness, as the dog and the monkey.

If we put a duck under a large pneumatic bell and reduce the pressure to 14 or 16 centimetres of mercury, the animal falls after the lapse of one minute. If we then take it out of the rarefied air and put it on the ground, it appears to be dead, shortly afterwards, however, recovering and regaining its legs. The phenomena presented by the duck during the minute in rarefied air cannot be obtained in any way by asphyxia. A respiratory arrest lasting only one-sixth or one-seventh of the time, during which the duck resists asphyxia, produces most serious disturbances. Even five or six minutes after its reanimation the duck still keeps its legs with difficulty. This proves that the action of the rarefied air on the nerve-centres was very rapid and intense. Death in these two cases is brought about in different ways.

I had the pleasure of performing some of these experiments before my friend Prof. Ch. Richet when he came to Turin, the results obtained being published by him in his physiological dictionary.[2] I quote his description which is that of an eye-witness, expressing my thanks to him for its publication.

"In death from asphyxia there are convulsions, violent agitation, dilation of the pupil, great distress, expulsion of fæces and urine, while in death caused by barometric depression, the pupil attains its maximum contraction; instead of frantic agitation, a sort of coma is observed, there is a general numbness, a great weakness of all the muscles, no phase of excessive excitement and convulsions invariably observed in simple asphyxia."

The breathing of ducks becomes more laboured under the pneumatic bell than that of dogs, they do not sleep as the latter often do, and die suddenly after forcibly shaking the head; it being impossible to save them after the manifestation of the phenomena which announce the approach of death. The difference is due to the fact that when the atmospheric pressure diminishes, there is not only a decrease in the weight of oxygen contained in the air, but also in the quantity of carbonic acid in the blood as we shall see in Chapter XXII.

V.

If we draw three or four deep breaths one after the other we notice that afterwards, for a certain length of time, we no longer feel the need of breathing. The respiratory centre having breathed more than is necessary for a few seconds may then rest, remaining for a time in inaction. To this state physiologists have given the name of *apnœa*.

If it were true, as the majority of physicians maintain, that mountain-

---

[1] Malassez et Richet, *Comptes rendus*. Société de Biologie, 17th Nov., 1894. 8th Dec., 1894.
[2] Ch. Richet, *Dictionnaire de Physiologie*, tome ii. p. 36.

FIG. 53. — A. Mosso. Line 1: Involuntary respiratory arrest after three deep inspirations in Turin. Line 2: The same at the Regina Margherita Hut. Line 3: The same in Turin again.
(The rotatory velocity of the cylinder was not the same in these three experiments.)

sickness originates in a state of the blood similar to that in asphyxia, it should be more difficult to effect this respiratory pause on high mountains. For this reason I made some researches also on apnœa during my expedition up Monte Rosa.

I communicate three observations made on myself (Fig. 53). The top line of Fig. 53 shows my respiratory curve in Turin, registered with Marey's double pneumograph applied to the thorax. At the sign A three deep inspirations were executed. The breathing ceases naturally for nineteen seconds, the line meanwhile marking the beating of the heart, after which the respiration recommences spontaneously with somewhat forcible movements. This is the effect of apnœa.

When I was on Monte Rosa I repeated this experiment and obtained the tracing 2 of Fig. 53. We see here, too, that the respiratory frequency at the altitude of 4,560 metres is slightly diminished, and that the inspirations are rather deeper. I again drew three deep breaths, which were followed by an interval of seventeen seconds. There is, therefore, only a minimum difference between this respiratory pause and that of the foregoing experiment. In this case, as in that of respiratory suspension consequent on the closing of nose and mouth, I have found that the results obtained are subject to variations from day to day. The duration of apnœa at the ordinary pressure is sometimes much longer, as may be seen by line 3. If we compare the maximum duration observed in Regina Margherita Hut with the maximum obtained in Turin, it would appear that at a high altitude apnœa is of shorter duration.

Nevertheless, in the soldier Chamois I found that apnœa was more pronounced at a height of 4,560 metres than where the ordinary barometric pressure prevails. This observation, which to many will seem paradoxical, is the most evident proof that on high mountains the conditions are different to those produced by asphyxia. The novelty of the case is clearly shown in Fig. 54. In the first experiment (lines 1 and 2) Chamois executed nine deep inspirations which affected very little the course of the breathing, as is the case in many persons in whom the phenomena of apnœa are less evident. The second line was written without interruption immediately after the first, as I noticed that the respiratory curve had not recovered its normal form, owing probably to a slight emotion and to the transition from profound abstraction to the mental and physical activity which forced breathing necessitates.

When we had arrived at Regina Margherita Hut, I performed another experiment of the same kind, making use of the same cylinder with the same velocity of rotation. We see in the bottom tracing that after nine inspirations there is a complete pause, the like of which I never obtained on this subject in the plain, and the breathing further shows a tendency to stop which it had not before.

It occurred to me that this paradoxical phenomenon might be an effect of fatigue of the respiratory centre which only became apparent at that altitude, because the nervous centre was there weaker. Could we maintain that the nine forcible inspirations executed one after the other had produced an exhaustion of the respiratory centre, the explanation would be simple, but I fear that in reality it is much more complicated. To the psychic state must certainly in part be due so profound a modification of the breathing. In Turin the subject was wide awake, here he was drowsy, but not asleep as was proved by his executing at a given sign the nine deep inspirations. Immediately afterwards, however, he closed his eyes. Whatever the explanation may be, it is strange that the conditions of the respiratory centre should be such at an altitude of 4,560 metres as to produce a respiratory pause never previously observed. This tracing cannot be explained by means of Hert's theory. This is another fact, therefore, which militates against prevailing ideas, and which transports us as it were to the antipodes in the interpretation of the effects which rarefied air produces in the organism. From the above observations it appears evident that the medulla oblongata, under these conditions, no longer acts normally, and in the direction thus suggested we must pursue our investigation.

VI.

Let us first examine what changes take place in the organism when one ascends at the rate of about 1,000 metres per week, and during a sojourn of ten days at an altitude of 4,560 metres. In the following tables are registered the observations which we made on five soldiers in a state of complete repose, the rate of pulse and breathing that is, and the rectal temperature. I have

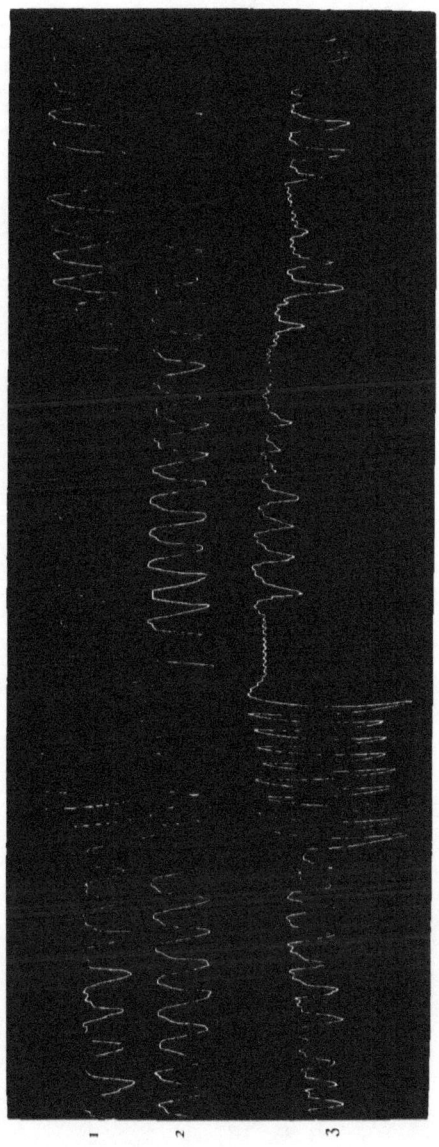

already mentioned on page 32 that for two months in succession Dr. V. Abelli and I made these observations in turn, in the morning before the soldiers were out of bed, and in the evening between three and five o'clock, before they dined. For the sake of brevity I only communicate the statistical results relating to the five soldiers, which are in perfect agreement, however, with those furnished by the observations on the other members of our expedition. The data of those days when the subjects were not well rested I have omitted, as we know that the fatigue of an ascent makes itself felt even on the day following.

The observations made in the morning are the most reliable; in the afternoon we made the subjects remain for ten minutes in a horizontal position before we examined them.

TABLE I.

Rate of Pulse and Breathing, and the Rectal Temperature in the state of repose at various altitudes.

Corporal EUGENIO CAMOZZI (Height, 1·70 m.; weight, 65·600 k.).

Altitude	Month	Date	Time A.M.	Time P.M.	Pulse A.M.	Pulse P.M.	Breathing A.M.	Breathing P.M.	Rectal Temperature A.M.	Rectal Temperature P.M.	Temperature of the Air A.M.	Temperature of the Air P.M.	Remarks
Turin, 276 m.	June	20	5.15		56		20		37°		20°		Pulse slightly irregular
	,,	20		3.45		80		24		37·7°		26°	
	,,	21	6.0		66		19		36·6°		20°		
	,,	21		3.30		78		25		37·3°		26°	
	,,	26	5.0		60		16		36·5°		25°		Pulse slightly irregular
	,,	26		3.0		67		23		37·1°		29°	
	,,	29	5.0		58		17		36·5°		18°		
	,,	29		3.0		70		20		37·2°		24°	
	July	11	8.0		62		16		37°		21°		
	,,	11		3.30		68		20		37°		25°	
	,,	12	8.0		62		16		36·6°		25°		Pulse rather irregular
	,,	12		3.30		74		18		37·6°		27°	
	,,	13	8.0		48		21		36·5°		25°		
	,,	13		3.30						37·5°			
Gressoney, 1,627 m.	,,	20	7.0		62		17						Pulse rather irregular
	,,	20		5.0		82		18		37·5°		13·5°	
	,,	21	5.30		61		16		36·6°		7·8°		
	,,	21		5.0		77		13		37·3°		18°	
	,,	22	5.30		56		13		36·65°		6·9°		
	,,	22		5.0		68		14		37·2°		16·3°	
	,,	23	5.30		56		13		36·4°		8·1°		
	,,	23		5.0		72		15		37·2°		17·7°	
	,,	24	5.30		54		14		36·3°		9·8°		
	,,	24		5.0		72		12		37·2°		22°	
Indra Camp 2,515 m.	,,	26		5.0		76		10		36·8°		11°	* The temperature of the air was measured in the tent where the soldiers slept. This explains why sometimes the morning temperature is higher than that of the afternoon.
	,,	27	5.0		61		12		36·3°		0°		
	,,	27		5.0		74		12		37·1°		8°	
	,,	28	8.0		66		10		37°		13°*		
	,,	28		6.30		80		11		37·6°		10·5°	
	,,	29	5.0		59		10		36·5°		7°		
	,,	29		5.0		90		15		37·6°		14°	
	,,	30	5.0		60		12		36·6°		7°		
Linty Hut Camp, 3,047 m.	August	1	7.0		78		14		36·8°		9°		
	,,	2	5.30		76		15		36·8°		14°		
	,,	3	6.30		68		15		37°		8°		
	,,	4	6.30		70		17		37·1°				
	,,	4		5.0		86		20		37°		8°	
	,,	5	6.30		94		17		37°				
	,,	6	7.30		76		16		37·5°				
Regina Margherita Hut, 4,560 m.	,,	15		5.0		88		12		37°			
	,,	16	7.0		100		10		36·9°				
	,,	16		6.0		98		9		37·2°			
	,,	17	8.0		84		10		37°				Pulse slightly irregular
Gressoney, 1,627 m	,,	23	7.0		65		10		36·9°				

TABLE II.

Rate of Pulse and Breathing, and the Rectal Temperature in the state of repose at various altitudes.

ALBINO SARTEUR (soldier) (Height, 1·73 m.; weight, 64·800 k.).

Altitude.	Month.	Date.	Time.		Pulse.		Breathing		Rectal Temperature.		Temperature of the Air.		Remarks.
			A.M.	P.M.	A.M.	P.M.	A.M.	P.M.	A.M.	P.M.	A.M.	P.M.	
Turin, 276 m.	June	26	5.0		54		13		36·3°		25°		
	,,	26		3.0		68		12		36·9°		29°	
	,,	29	5.0		52		11		35·8°		18°		
	,,	29		3.0		72		13		36·9°		24°	
	July	11	7.0		56		10		36·1°		21°		
	,,	11		3.0		72		18		37·1°		26°	
	,,	12	8.0		55		10		36·2°		22°		
	,,	12		3.0		57		17		36·8°		26°	
	,,	13	8.0		51		8		35·8°		21°		
	,,	13		3.30		62		14		37·1°		26°	
Gressoney, 1,627 m.	,,	20	7.0		50		9		35·9°		36·6°		Pulse slightly irregular.
	,,	20		5.30		62		11					13·5°	
	,,	21	5.30		50		10		36°		7·8°		
	,,	21		5.0		68		17		37·2°		18°	
	,,	22	5.30		56		12		36°		6·9°		
	,,	22		5.0		62		14		36·9°		16·13°	
	,,	23	5.30		67		14		36·5°		8·1°		
	,,	23		5.0		68		13		37·3°		17·7°	
	,,	24	5.30		52		12		36·1°		9·8°		
	,,	24		5.0		58		14		37·3°		22°	
Indra Camp 2,515 m.	,,	26	5.30		59		11		36·5°		11°		* The temperature of the air was taken in the tent where the soldiers slept. This explains why sometimes the morning temperature is higher than that of the afternoon.
	,,	26		5.0		64		13		36·7°		0°	
	,,	27	5.0		56		10		36·3°		8°		
	,,	27		5.0		56		12		36·8°			
	,,	28	8.0		56		10		36·5°		13·0°		
	,,	28		6.30		68		16		37·1°		10·5°	
	,,	29	5.0		60		9		36·2°		7°		
	,,	29		5.0		62		13		36·8°		14°	
Linty Hut Camp, 3,047 m.	August	3	6.30		52		12		36·5°		2·5°		
	,,	3	6.30		54		10		36·5°		8°		
	,,	4		5.0		63		12		36·5°		5·6°	
Gnifetti Hut, 3,620 m.	,,	7	6.15		66		10		37·3°		1°		
	,,	8		6.0		66		11		36·9°		5°	
	,,	9	6.45		70		8		37·4°		13°		
Regina Margherita Hut, 4,560 m.	,,*	11		4.45		74		11		37·1°		11°	* Arrival in the morning from Linty Camp.
	,,	12	6.0		76		10		36·8°		6°		
	,,	15		5.0		80		11		36·8°		7°	
	,,	16	7.0		74		9		36·9°		7°		
	,,	16		6.0		78		8		37·1°		7°	
	,,	17	8.0		67		8		36·8°				
Gressoney, 1,627 m.	,,	23	7.0		63		9		36·6°				

ANALYSIS OF ASPHYXIA AND OF MOUNTAIN-SICKNESS

TABLE III.

Rate of Pulse and Breathing, and the Rectal Temperature in the state of repose at various altitudes.

SANTINO MARTA (soldier) (Height, 1·72 m. ; weight, 71 k.).

Altitude.	Month.	Date.	Time.		Pulse.		Breathing		Rectal Temperature.		Temperature of the Air.		Remarks.
			A.M.	P.M.	A.M.	P.M.	A.M.	P.M.	A.M.	P.M.	A.M.	P.M.	
Turin, 276 m.	June	20	5.15		54		16		37·1°		20°		
	,,	20		3.45		74		18		37·4°		26°	
	,,	26	5.0		54		14		36·8°		26°		
	,,	26		3.30		62		18		37°		29°	
	,,	29	5.0		52		13		36·4°		18°		
	,,	29		3.30		70		20		37·4°		24°	
	July	11	8.0		52		18		36·7°		20°		
	,,	11		3.0		54		18		36·9°		25°	
	,,	12	8.0		47		18		36·8°		25·5°		
	,,	12		3.0		56		20		37·4°		27°	
	,,	13	8.0		58		19		36·7°		25°		
	,,	13		3.15						37·7°		26°	
Gressoney, 1,627 m.	,,	20	7.0		66		19				13·5°		
	,,	20				70		21		37·2°			
	,,	21	5.30	5.0	54		17		36·5°		7·8°	18°	
	,,	21		5.0		69		23		37·3°			
	,,	22	5.30		54		19		36·9°		6·9°	16·3°	
	,,	22		5.0		68		19		37·1°			
	,,	23	5.30		57		16		36·6°		8·1°	17·7°	
	,,	23		5.0		84		25		38·1°			
	,,	24	5.30		50		17		36·6°		9·8°	22°	
	,,	24		5.0		68		18		37·4°			
IndraCamp 2,515 m.	,,	27	5.0		54		15		36·8°			8°	* The temperature of the air in the morning was measured in the tent before the soldiers got up.
	,,	27		5.0		76		22		37·4°	13°*		
	,,	28	6.0		62		20		36·9°			10·5°	
	,,	28		5.0		81		24		37·6°		7°	
	,,	29	5.0		52		14		36·8°			14°	
	,,	29		5.0		62		26		37·4°			
	,,	30	5.0		58		18		36·7°				
Linty Hut Camp, 3,047 m.	Aug.	2	5.30		57		15		36·6°		9°		
	,,	3	6.30		60		17		36·9°		14°		
	,,	4	6.30		63		16		37°		8°		
	,,	4		5.0		70		22		37·5°		20°	
Gnifetti Hut, 3,620 m.	,,	6	7.30		64		18		36·5°				
	,,	7	6.15		68		16		36·7°				
	,,	8		6.0		72		21		37·3°		13°	
	,,	9	6.45		62		20		36·8°		12·2°		
Regina Margherita Hut, 4,560 m.	,,	11	4.45		82		21			37·3°	11·5°		
	,,	12	6.0		64		16		36·8°		6·4°		
	,,	13	6.20		60		18		36·8°		4°		
	,,	15	6.0		76		21		36·8°		7°		
	,,	18	5.30						36·9°				
Gressoney, 1,627 m.	,,	23	7.0		52		15		36·6°				

TABLE IV.

Rate of Pulse and Breathing, and the Rectal Temperature in the state of repose at various altitudes.

Corporal FELICE JACHINI (Height, 1·75 m.; weight 72·100 k.).

Altitude	Month	Date	Time A.M.	Time P.M.	Pulse A.M.	Pulse P.M.	Breathing A.M.	Breathing P.M.	Rectal Temperature A.M.	Rectal Temperature P.M.	Temperature of the Air A.M.	Temperature of the Air P.M.	Remarks
Turin, 276 m.	July	11	8.0		58		16		36·8°		21°		
	,,	11		3.0		62		18		37·1°		26°	
	,,	12	8.0		54		16		36·8°		22°		
	,,	12		3.0		56		19		37°		26·7°	
	,,	13	8.0		52		19		36·8°		21·5°		
	,,	13		3.0		67		18		36·9°		26·3°	
Gressoney, 1,627 m.	,,	20	7.0		60		16						
	,,	20		5.30		59		18		37·1°		13·5°	The temperature of the air was taken in the morning in the tent or in the huts where we slept.
	,,	21	5 30		52		17		36·4°		7·8°		
	,,	21		5.0		64		20		37·5°		18°	
	,,	22	5.30		50		14		36·5°		6·9°		
	,,	22		5.0		57		21		36·7°		16·3°	
	,,	23	5.30		66		14		36·5°		8·1°		
	,,	23		5.0		56		17		37°		17·9°	
	,,	24	5.30		47		16		36·4°		9·8°		
	,,	24		5.0		62		17		37·1°		22°	
IndraCamp 2,515 m.	,,	27	5.0		56		16		36·3°		8°		
	,,	27		5.0		58		17		36·9°		14°	
	,,	29	5.0		63		15		36·6°		7°		
	,,	29		5.0		88		18		37·3°		9°	
	,,	30	5.30		56		15		36·7°				
Linty Hut Camp, 3,047 m.	Aug.	2	5.30		50		14		36·5°		9°		
	,,	3	6.30		56		15		36·7°		14°		
	,,	4	6.30		54		14		36·7°		8°		
	,,	4		5.0		72		17		37·1°			
	,,	6	7.30		60		14		36·7°			5·6°	
Gnifetti Hut, 3,620 m.	,,	8		6.0		86		9		37·4°		13°	
	,,	9	6.45		60		14		36·7°		12·2°		
Regina Margherita Hut, 4,560 m.	,,	13	6.20		70		17		36·6°		4°		
	,,	15	6.0		58		20		36·8°		7°		
	,,	18	5.30		59		17		36·8°		10°		
Gressoney, 1,627 m.	,,	23	7.0		67		16		37°				

ANALYSIS OF ASPHYXIA AND OF MOUNTAIN-SICKNESS

TABLE V.

Rate of Pulse and Breathing, and the Rectal Temperature in the state of repose of various altitudes.

GERMANO SOLFERINO (soldier) (Height, 1·71 m.; weight, 63·900 k.).

Altitude.	Month.	Date	Time.		Pulse.		Breathing		Rectal Temperature.		Temperature of the Air.		Remarks.
			A.M.	P.M.	A.M.	P.M.	A.M.	P.M.	A.M.	P.M.	A.M.	P.M.	
Turin, 276 m.	June	26	5.0		50		15		36·6°		26°		Pulse slightly irregular.
	,,	26		3.0		57		20		37·2°		31°	
	,,	29	5.0		46		15		36·3°		18°		
	,,	29		3.0		58		20		37·1°		24°	
	July	11	8.0		54		17		36·7°		21°		
	,,	11		3.0		66		17		37·2°		26°	
	,,	12	8.0		48		15		36·8°		22°		
	,,	12		3.0		64		20		37·2°		26°	
	,,	13	8.0		48		16		36·6°		21°		
	,,	14	5.0		46		18		36·2°		21°		
	,,	14		5.0		67		23		37·4°		25°	
Gressoney, 1,627 m.	,,	20	7.0		48		15			36·9°		13·5°	The temperature of the air was taken in the morning in the tent or in the huts where the soldiers slept.
	,,	20		5.0		67		24	36·2°		7·8°		
	,,	21	5.30		46		16			37·3°		18°	
	,,	21		5.0		66		23	36·3°		6·9°		
	,,	22	5.30		48		17			37·4°		16·3°	
	,,	22		5.0		60		22	36·4°		8·1°		
	,,	23	5.30		48		17			37·4°		17·9°	
	,,	23		5.0		58		19	36·4°		9·8°		
	,,	24	5.30		50		16			37·5°		22°	
	,,	24		5.0		64		18					
Indra Camp 2,515 m.	,,	26	5.30		51		14		36·2°			11°	
	,,	26		5.0		58		19		36·7°			
	,,	27	5.0		54		17		36·6°		8°		
	,,	28	8.0		49		18		36·5°		13°		Pulse irregular.
	,,	28		6.30		70		22		37·5°		10·5°	
	,,	29	5.0		53		16		36·3°		7°		
	,,	29		5.0		56		21		37·2°		14°	
	,,	30	5.30		52		18		36·6°		7°		
Linty Hut Camp, 3,047 m.	August	2	5.30		52		18		36·2°		9°		
	,,	3	6.30		54		20		36·4°		14°		
	,,	4	6.30		52		16		36·6°		8°		
	,,	4		5.0		76		22		37·1°			
	,,	5		6.30		78		20		37·5°			
	,,	6	7.30		46		16		36·6°				
Regina Margherita Hut, 4,560 m.	,,	11		4.45		76		21		36·9°		11·5°	*Arrival at the hut four hours earlier carrying a load of 20 kilograms. Pulse small; almost imperceptible.
	,,	12	6.0		90		18		36·6°		6·4°		
	,,	17	7.0		90		21		36·9°				
	,,*	18	9.30		100		22				10°		
Gressoney, 1,627 m.	,,	23	7.0		52		17		36·6°				

Two clear facts result from these observations, namely, that in all of us the pulse became more frequent at a greater altitude, and that the temperature of the body was somewhat higher on Monte Rosa than in the plain. In the Regina Margherita Hut the minimum rectal temperature observed in Turin did not reappear. This proves that the organism even in robust individuals is slightly disturbed at that height and that the chemical consumption in repose must be rather greater at the altitude of 4,560 metres.

Jaccoud, Mermod, Armieux, Vacher, Mercier and others have already found that during a sojourn at higher levels the pulsations of the heart increase considerably in rapidity. Vacher, for instance, says that at an altitude of 1,650 metres his pulse beat 78 times in the minute instead of 69 times as usual.

Some even speak of an *altitude-fever*, so considerable was the increased rapidity of the pulse observed at heights not surpassing 2,000 metres. From our observations as a whole it appears that in complete repose the increase in the rate of the pulse is less at the altitude of 4,560 metres than would have been supposed, judging from the results of studies made at lower levels.

The frequency of the respiratory movements on the summit of Monte Rosa is little different from what it is in the plain. As, however, the number of inspirations is not sufficient to give an idea of the respiratory activity, I studied the modification of the average inspiration on the mountains and in the plain by means of the gas-meter and guttapercha mask already mentioned.

The method adopted has been already described on page 38. I have placed the tables of these observations at the end of the volume so as not to interrupt the text by too great an accumulation of figures. From these tables we see that in the waking condition at an altitude of 4,560 metres the volume of air inspired in half an hour is increased in some and diminished in others, but these variations are small considering the height at which the observations were made.

VII.

The first symptoms produced by the rarefaction of the air are not identical with those of asphyxia. In the latter instance the pulse grows slower, in the former, quicker. There are two systems of nerves regulating the action of the heart which may be compared, the one to the reins which check movement, the other to the spurs which incite to greater movement. The two vagus nerves act as the reins which restrain and even arrest the movements of the heart, the accelerator nerves when stimulated increase the frequency of the cardiac pulsations. It was an important question to determine whether, at great heights, the reins of the heart are slackened owing to a paralysis of their nervous centre, or whether, on the contrary, the greater frequency of the pulse is due to the stimulation of the accelerator centres by the rarefied air.

There was no other means of deciding this point than by experiments on animals, for the symptoms of mountain-sickness resemble the phenomena which appear in dogs when the inhibitory nerves of the heart have been severed, that is, vomiting, excessive palpitation of the heart, and diminished respiratory frequency. I therefore put these inhibitory nerves out of action, as in the following experiment.

The heart of a normal dog beats on an average 88 times per minute. When the animal is placed in the pneumatic chamber with the experimenter and the rarefaction of the air is carried to 42 centimetres (a pressure corres-

View from the Regina Margherita Hut.

ponding to an altitude of 4,723 metres) its heart is found to beat 114 times in the minute.

After the section of the vagus nerves the pulse becomes twice as rapid and the rate of breathing sinks from the normal number of 16 to 10 movements per minute. If the animal is now again placed in the pneumatic chamber and the same degree of rarefaction (corresponding to an altitude of 4,723 metres) effected, the rate of the cardiac pulsations is no longer influenced by the diminished barometric pressure. The animal is, however, not so well as before, it is restless and gasps as though for air, although the barometer marks 42 centimetres as before. With the cessation of the rarefaction the dog's condition immediately improves and he breathes quietly.

The facts communicated in the preceding chapters have shown that in mountain-sickness there is a depression of the nerve-centres which have their seat in the medulla oblongata. The increased frequency of the pulse at a height of 4,560 metres is a constant phenomenon which I can only explain as an effect of an incipient paralysis of the vagus nerve. In the soldier, Solferino, for instance, even after a week's repose at Regina Margherita Hut, the heart still performed double the usual number of contractions per minute.

The following is a summary of the facts which tend to prove that neurosis of the vagus must be considered as a factor in mountain-sickness.

We have seen that on Monte Rosa an interval appears between one respiration and the next which was never observed in the plain, and that the respiratory type is altered, the inspiration being longer and the expiration more rapid even in the waking condition. Further, vomiting and difficulty in deglutition were observed. (These are phenomena characteristic of paralysis of the vagus.) The sudden fatigue too, which manifests itself in dogs in which the vagus nerves have been severed, when they try to run, is yet one more point of resemblance with the phenomena observed in mountain-sickness.

VIII.

In Chapter IV. I have already mentioned that the pressure of the blood in Regina Margherita Hut was in us little different from what it was in Turin. As the height of 4,560 metres seemed to me insufficient for my investigations, I performed other experiments in the pneumatic chamber on animals to which a dose of morphia, chloral or chloralose, was administered to prevent their feeling or moving, a manometer then being put into communication with the carotid artery. In all these experiments I found that the pressure of the blood was not altered by a rarefaction of the air corresponding to an altitude of from 6,500 to 7,000 metres. Only the pulse became more rapid and the breathing deeper and accelerated. It is unnecessary therefore to introduce the curves obtained.

Here again is a fundamental difference between asphyxia and mountain-sickness; for in asphyxia the increased pressure of the blood when the respiration becomes inadequate is a constant and characteristic phenomenon. This difference may be explained in two ways; either the changes which take place in the blood when the air is rarefied are different from those produced in asphyxia (on the mountains, indeed, carbonic acid does not accumulate in the blood), or the nervous centre of the blood-vessels becomes less active.

Hüfner's investigations [1] on the blood have shown that we must not seek the cause of mountain-sickness in the physical conditions of the blood,

---

[1] Du Bois-Reymond's *Archiv f. Physiologie*, 1890.

because this fluid only begins to alter at the barometric pressure of 238 millimetres. There is, therefore, no mountain on earth so high as to inspire the fear that should man reach its summit the hæmoglobin of the blood will no longer be able to extract from the air the amount of oxygen which it is capable of absorbing.

That the cause of mountain-sickness is not in the blood is further confirmed by the important fact that after an abundant hemorrhage the effects of barometric depression are not aggravated. This I have repeatedly proved by experiment. If, for instance, we study a dog under the pneumatic bell at a pressure of 32 centimetres (which corresponds to an altitude of 6,888 metres), then take him out and draw off one-third of his blood, we shall find on replacing the animal under the bell, the air then being rarefied to the same degree as before, that there is no difference in the rate and depth of the breathing

That part of the nervous system which manifests the greatest susceptibility to barometric depression is also that which undergoes the most rapid modification in its resistance to deficiency of oxygen. Before his birth man shows an extraordinary resistance to asphyxia as is proved by the fact that the Cæsarean section has often been performed with success after the death of the mother. Paul Bert studied in mice the rapid diminution of their power of resistance to asphyxia after birth. A mouse just born may remain half an hour without breathing and yet survive ; a week later it resists at the most only fifteen minutes, and after two weeks it succumbs after scarcely four minutes.

These changes which certainly take place in the nervous system without there being any sensible change in the composition and quantity of the blood, explain why it is useless to seek in the blood the cause of the rapid acclimatisation to rarefied air or of the individual differences so marked in mountain-sickness. The nervous system is the seat of the evil, for in no other tissue are adaptations so rapid as in the nerve-cells, in no other are there such profound differences between organisms.

The facility with which the organism adapts itself to great altitudes appeared in the successive diminution of the rate of the pulse during our sojourn at Regina Margherita Hut. On the second day my pulse beat at the rate of 93 per minute, whereas during the last days I had a minimum frequency of 54 beats per minute, a rate which I had seldom observed in Turin. The following figures taken from the tables in which is registered the diminution of the pulse on successive days at an altitude of 4,560 metres, clearly show the influence of acclimatisation :—

Marta, 82, 64, 60.   Jachini, 70, 58.
Sarteur, 76, 74, 67.   Camozzi, 88, 84.

IX.

On Monte Rosa, at an altitude of 4,560 metres, the average atmospheric pressure is 423 millimetres. The rarefaction of the air is thus rather less than one-half. If we had not in the lowlands the respiration of luxury, we should be obliged to inhale almost double the usual volume of air at an altitude of 4,560 metres in order to supply the lungs with the same quantity of oxygen. This does not take place, however ; in fact, contrary to all expectation, the soldier Solferino breathed in less air in Regina Margherita

Hut than below at Gressoney. The number of his inspirations increased from ten to fourteen, as may be seen by Table IX. at the end of the volume, but the depth of the respiratory movements decreased; instead of breathing in 6·41 litres per minute, he only drew in 5·54 litres, in spite of the diminished density of the air. In this fact we recognise the functional alteration of the respiratory nervous centre, which, affected by the lack of oxygen, accelerates the movements of the breathing without succeeding, however, in making up for the deficiency, as it is unable to effect deeper inspirations.

In my brother (see Table III.) and in Corporal Camozzi (Table V.), the rate and depth of the inspirations increased. The number of litres of air inhaled by my brother at Gressoney stands to the number inspired at an altitude of 4,560 metres in the proportion of 1 : 1·24 In Corporal Camozzi this proportion was 1 : 1·62. Between Turin and Gressoney I did not find an appreciable difference, although the difference in level is 1,351 metres.

Beno Bizzozero (Table IV.) introduced a greater quantity of air into his lungs on the mountains than in the plain, the rate of the inspirations being increased, their depth diminished, but the litres of air inhaled on the summit of Monte Rosa stood to the amount breathed in at Gressoney, only in the proportion of 1 : 1·05.

In the soldier Sarteur (Table VI.) the rate of breathing remained constant, while the depth was augmented; but the increase in the amount of air inspired was small, the comparison of the number of litres breathed in in one minute at Gressoney, and of the number inhaled at an altitude of 4,560 metres, giving the proportion 1 : 1·03.

The soldiers Chamois and Oberhoffer (Tables VII. and VIII.), who both came straight from Ivrea to Regina Margherita Hut without stopping at the intermediate stations to acclimatise themselves, presented the curious phenomenon of a diminution in the rate of breathing, but of an augmentation of the average inspiration, so that the proportion between the litres of air inspired in Turin, and at an altitude of 4,560 metres, is 1 : 1·15 in Chamois, and 1 : 1·03 in Oberhoffer.

If we take the average of the augmentations observed in the volume of air inspired by six of these persons at the altitude of 4,560 metres, we find that the number of litres of air inspired every minute in the plain stands to the number of litres breathed in on the summit of Monte Rosa in the proportion of 1 : 1·17. We are therefore far from the proportion of 1 : 1·80 which should be found, did the volume of inspired air increase proportionately to the rarefaction of the air.

The modifications manifest in the rate and depth of the breathing at a height of 4,560 metres do not obey a constant law, and all possible combinations were observed by us, namely, augmentation of the rate and depth of the inspirations; diminution of the rate and augmentation of the depth; augmentation of the rate and diminution of the depth; finally as we have seen in the tracings on pp. 33 and 34, there may be a diminution of both rate and depth.

Some figures of these tables do not correspond exactly to the data of the preceding tables; this discrepancy is explained by the circumstances, that in breathing through the meter a slight resistance had to be overcome by the inspiration, and that the wearing of the mask and the subject's consciousness of being observed slightly modified the breathing. To diminish the errors resulting from these circumstances, we used to wait a quarter of an hour after the respiration through the valves was established before beginning the experiment. In spite of the above inconvenience, which can never be quite eliminated, the observations made by my brother (see Table III. at the end of the book) form, together with the observations which have just been discussed, the most reliable material which we as yet possess relative to the study of respiration at great altitudes.

The recent investigations of L. Zuntz[1] (conducted in the Regina Margherita Hut), in which a method somewhat different to mine was followed, suggest the doubt that the subject was still in a fatigued condition, because, if we compare the amount of air inspired per minute at the ordinary atmospheric pressure (4·93 litres) with the amount breathed in per minute in the hut (first 13·74 litres, and in the following experiment 10·55 litres), we find that the volume of air introduced into the lungs was more than doubled. The discrepancy between this result and the results which I obtained experimenting on persons in a state of repose in Regina Margherita Hut, is too great not to indicate the presence of some error.

There are two ways in which the ventilation of the lungs may be rendered more active and the deficiency of oxygen in rarefied air compensated for. The depth of the inspiratory movements may be augmented or the inspirations may follow one upon the other with greater rapidity. Of these two compensatory methods, nature prefers the second, and thus a similar phenomenon is noticeable in the breathing as in the movement of the legs. When we are in a hurry we perform a greater number of steps in the same space of time, that is, we accelerate the rhythm of our steps, the length remaining about the same. The breathing on high mountains follows a similar rule. It is rarely the case that the number of steps (of the respiratory movements, that is) remain the same, while the length is increased as in the soldier Sarteur (Table VI.), or that the steps diminish in number, but become so much longer as to cover a greater space as in the soldiers Chamois (Table VII.) and Oberhoffer (Table VIII.).

In general it may be said that the nervous system prefers to accelerate the rhythm and to repeat a greater number of times the same movement to the extension of which it is accustomed. If this acceleration does not suffice, we execute from time to time a deeper respiratory movement, the distinctive character of breathing on high mountains being that the number of the respiratory movements is increased without any augmentation of the depth (on the contrary the breathing is sometimes more superficial), while from time to time a breath is drawn which is deeper than the preceding ones, and is almost like a sigh. If the need of breathing becomes very urgent we accelerate greatly the rhythm of the movements, as in running, lengthening them at the same time.

Op. cit. Pflüger's Archiv, Bd. 66, p. 517.

The descent of the party from Monte Rosa—The last part of the Garstelet glacier.

CHAPTER XVII

INFLUENCE OF MOUNTAIN AIR ON THE NERVOUS SYSTEM—HEADACHE—THE WIND

I.

THE lower animals also feel the influence of rarefied air. When we put a dog under the pneumatic bell, the fleas jump out from under its hairs, and restlessly seek to escape, a sign that they, too, experience discomfort from the change of pressure.

In order to gain a further proof of this, I experimented on glow-worms in which, owing to their phosphorescent light, the excitement of the nervous system is more easily recognised. The phosphorescence of these insects is due to a chemical process like that which produces the light emanating from phosphorus, although very different as to its actual nature. I thought it would be an interesting experiment to ascertain whether the diminution of oxygen in rarefied air modified this vital phenomenon of light.

I took some glow-worms, therefore, and put them under a large glass bell, in which I slowly effected a rarefaction of the air until the pressure was reduced to thirty centimetres. I was astonished to see that the luminousness of these animals increased in proportion as the oxygen in the air diminished. It is a well-known fact that the light of the glow-worm is intermittent. As soon as the air under the bell began to grow thinner these intermittences ceased, the worms remaining continuously luminous. Even after they had been half an hour or an hour in this air so rarefied that it would have caused the death of a dog or a man, these creatures glowed more vividly than even when they light up our meadows at pairing time. The colour of the light was less yellow, the edge of the segments assuming a deeper, reddish tint.

Any one who picks up a glow-worm on a summer night will notice that only the two segments of the posterior part of the body are luminous. In rarefied air this luminous part lengthens by about three millimetres. The light, as already mentioned, becomes continuous, the former intermittences being replaced by periods of greater and lesser brilliancy.

The opinion hitherto held by physiologists was that the light emanating from these animals was a vital phenomenon standing in close connection with the oxygen of the air. We now see that this view is incorrect. Having ascertained that the luminous cells of the glow-worm are independent of the surrounding air, it will be more easy for us to understand that in ourselves, too, the cells may stand in a less intimate relation to the oxygen of the atmosphere than has till now been thought.

The above experiment renders manifest the fact, without making any further demands on our reasoning or imaginative powers, that the cells of the luminous organs have really in themselves the substances proper to the production of light and need not borrow their energy from the oxygen of the atmosphere. It is the excitement or paralysis of the nervous system which invigorates and stimulates the chemical processes in the cells from which light is evolved, and the luminousness increases in proportion as the oxygen diminishes. This seemingly paradoxical phenomenon is an evident proof of a fact of fundamental importance in physiology.

The fire of life (to use a poetical image, not in its metaphorical, but literal sense) becomes visible in these luminous organs, and the chemical energy of the cells is transformed into the energy of light without the immediate participation of the oxygen of the air in the work.

II.

Has the diminution of the atmospheric pressure any influence on the muscles and nervous system of cold-blooded animals?

I proposed this question to Dr. W. Rosenthal,[1] son of J. Rosenthal, Professor of Physiology at Erlangen, when he came to my institute for the purpose of doing some scientific work. The investigation was one which demanded no little technical ability and ingenuity, but the scope of this work obliges me to refer the reader for all particulars to the original memoir, which also contains a summary of all previous researches on the subject.

Dr. Rosenthal's experiments proved that the diminution of pressure does not exercise any influence on the muscles of the frog. The nervous centres which effect the movement of the heart of the frog are not susceptible to diminished pressure. So far as phenomena of asphyxia are concerned there is no difference between a frog in a vacuum and one in a closed space

---

[1] Werner Rosenthal, *La diminution de la pression atmosphérique a-t-elle un effet sur les muscles et sur le système nerveux de la grenouille?* Archives italiennes de Biologie, tome xxv. p. 418.

deprived of oxygen. The physical and chemical changes which manifest themselves in the muscles and nerves during their activity proceed independently of barometric pressure.

These results, although obtained by experiments on frogs, are of importance to us, because between the functions of the lower beings and man there are only differences of quantity, not of quality. All the properties of the nervous system observed in animals of simple structure are to be met with in the superior animals and in man.

The fact that the most striking phenomena produced in us by the rarefaction of the air on the mountains, are all of a nervous nature, is a sign that the cause of mountain-sickness must be sought in a disturbance of the nutrition of the nerve centres and not in a simple physical effect of diminished pressure. We shall see in the sequel that the greater the development of the nervous system in an animal the more susceptible is it to the action of rarefied air. The nutrition of the nerve-cells is in us more active than in cold-blooded animals and chemical processes are more intense: this is the explanation of the difference.

III.

Generally speaking we may say that headache and tiredness issue the first warning that something abnormal has taken place in the nervous system. Mountain-sickness begins with these symptoms. They are followed by a disturbance in the innervation of the heart and stomach, which produce palpitation, dizziness, nausea, loss of appetite, and vomiting; some time later drowsiness makes itself felt. Many find a resemblance between sea-sickness and mountain-sickness; the phenomena produced by rarefied air seem to me, however, much more complex and varied. The order in which the phenomena manifest themselves depends on the nature of the individual, and on various intricate contingencies.

Only this positive assertion may be made, namely, that the reaction of the organism is the more intense the less the energy of the nervous system. From a number of examples proving this I select the following. As a student I once started from Ceresole with a few friends, and after making the ascent of the Gran Paradiso, we went down to La Thuile by the Rutor. At the Hospice of the Little St. Bernard we were stopped by bad weather, we therefore made the descent to Courmayeur by the Allée Blanche and Lake Combal. We were in good training, but, unfortunately, a friend who had to leave us celebrated his departure by encouraging us to drink more than usual, and we went to bed so late that we only slept a few hours and that badly, being excited by the alcohol consumed.

The next morning we left early for the Col Ferret. When we reached the Lakes de Fenêtre, at an altitude of 2,500 metres, one of our companions began to sit down from time to time, and to lag behind. I waited for him, and he told me that he had a headache and was not feeling very well. He went on walking, but was shortly afterwards attacked by nausea with retching. Even when he sat still his breathing was more rapid, his pulse accelerated and weak. More than all else the palpitation of the heart and the oppression on the chest which took away his breath, as he said, distressed him. We let him lie down on the ground and rest for half an hour, and then, supporting him under the arms, we managed to reach the Col Fenêtre where he had another and more violent attack of sickness. His muscular strength was so diminished that, in spite of our exhortations, he refused to move.

We had already made a sort of tent with our alpenstocks and rugs, and were preparing—two of the party and a guide, that is—to keep our comrade company through the night when others of our companions, who had set out some time before for the Hospice of the Great St. Bernard, returned with lanterns and dogs. The sight of these far-famed dogs, that sprang joyously around us, moved us not a little. The lanterns of the numerous party lighting up the darkness raised the spirits of the inmates of the tent. Our patient picked up courage and managed to descend to the Great St. Bernard Hospice. The next day his condition was perfectly normal.

This was one of the most characteristic cases of mountain-sickness which I have ever observed. The altitude was only 2,500 metres, and the victim was a fairly robust individual in good training without any cardiac defect. The gravity of the symptoms was due to weakness of the nervous system and to lack of sleep. The much greater exertions of the preceding days at greater altitudes had had no similar effect upon him. The sumptuous dinner, the abundance of wine drunk, and the insufficient repose were the causes of the outbreak and aggravated character of the sickness.

A general—to tell an old story which still holds good for modern armies and future mountain-climbers—once said that soldiers must never be led to battle the day after a holiday. We have in the above incident a proof that the remark may be well applied to Alpine excursions.

IV

Amongst the causes which produced such a degree of prostration in our comrade at Col Fenêtre must, I think, be mentioned the sudden darkness caused by fog. During my sojourn on Monte Rosa I often had occasion to observe the depressing influence which fog exercises even on the best climbers. The guides are, indeed, unanimous in maintaining that a dense fog is much more to be feared than a snow-storm.

One day while we were in Regina Margherita Hut two fresh parties arrived, so that we were very much crowded. One of the keepers of the hut and two soldiers, the sturdiest men of our party, offered to go down to Gnifetti Hut, so as to leave us a little more room. They started in high spirits at 4 p.m., with plenty of time before them to reach their destination before night. When they reached the great ice plateau, however, they found themselves enveloped in fog, and it began to snow.

Shortly afterwards they became aware that they had lost their way, but went on walking. They spent an hour wandering about, groping their way, and then discovered to their surprise that they had returned to the point where they had been before the fog had closed in around them. At this their courage failed them. They walked on for a considerable time again, following the holes made by the alpenstocks of another party which had climbed up to the hut; then as the darkness became deeper and the wind and thickly falling snow obliterated all traces, they lost even this clue. Quite out of their reckoning, they began to despair either of finding their way forwards or of retracing their steps. Luckily the sky cleared after a while enabling them to reach Gnifetti Hut after night had closed in.

When they rejoined us on the next day and told me of the fear and agitation which they had suffered, it seemed rather as though they were relating some dream or vision, so different was their talk from what one was accustomed to hear from these sturdy, undaunted fellows. The lack of sight causes moral depression. At night we are less courageous than during the day and fear easily degenerates into panic.

It often happens that a party of mountain-climbers start in the morning with the intention of bivouacking on the summit of some mountain, and then find themselves obliged to make up their minds, before the sun sets, to pass the night on the rock or on a glacier. The state of mind is in this case quite different from that of the Alpinist who finds himself suddenly wrapped round by fog and brought to a standstill on the glacier by darkness. A Mont Blanc guide told me that he once wandered for a long time round Vallot Hut without being able to find it, although he was at the distance of only a few paces, so thick was the fog. Discouragement and psychic depression, like panic fear, stand in no proportion to their causes. The wind carrying away the sound of the voice renders the solitude more oppressive. Fear acts on the organism in such a manner that the phenomena of mountain-sickness appear even in persons who have never suffered from it before. One of the two soldiers above-mentioned told me that he had experienced a sort of dizziness and a feeling of nausea which almost provoked vomiting.

The influence of darkness on psychic phenomena has not as yet been sufficiently studied. Darkness certainly has a depressing influence, as is proved by the greater fatigue which night marches produce. Féré[1] observed that epileptic fits occur in the proportion of two-thirds by night to one-third by day. Our body is constituted by a system of forces in unstable equilibrium, and a passing agitation is sufficient to disquiet the balance in such a manner that it cannot regain its poise, notwithstanding all the efforts of the will. Those who have not known what it is to grope their way through fog on the mountains, in peril of being engulfed in some crevasse, or of slipping down some precipice, cannot understand the Alpinist's dismay and dread when he finds himself in these circumstances. The lack of light may incite to the most desperate acts.

It is mere foolhardiness which leads some climbers to defy the fog; even on the best of days Monte Rosa has its mortal dangers; woe, therefore, to those whom the fog overtakes in the great amphitheatre which lies at the base of its highest peaks.

V.

Were I asked what headache is I should have some difficulty in replying. Perhaps I should venture to say no more than that headache is a warning given us by organic consciousness of a disturbance in the nutrition of the brain. The fundamental parts of our body are insensible. The surgeon's scissors may do their work on stomach, viscera, brain, without the patient's being aware of the operation. And yet, again, sensibility is not utterly lacking. Headache is as the expression of this fundamental and recondite sense, a species of alarm signal issued by the usually dumb organic consciousness. Thus, too, does hunger warn us of approaching detriment from want of food, although it has no special nerves at its disposal. To be well or to be unwell are vague, conventional expressions for a world of indefinable sensations. If any one of the vital functions is altered by fever, fatigue, excessive mental work, vitiated air, or bad digestion, headache, like a warning

[1] Ch. Féré, *Les épilepsies*, 1890, p. 313.

sentinel, arouses our attention. In some parties who came to Regina Margherita Hut while we were there, all the members complained of headache. We had a little medicine-chest with us, because we knew that *nolens volens* we should be called upon to act as physicians. We found that phenacetin was of more benefit than stimulating remedies. Knowing that weakness and exhaustion of the nervous system likewise produce headache, I had hoped that cocaine would have proved useful as a remedy, but I did not observe, even when a dose of one decigram in Marsala wine was administered, that it effected any very speedy relief in case of headache, although it undoubtedly gives strength.

Fatigue, digestive disturbances, insufficient sleep, the dazzling glare of the glaciers, and the action of rarefied air, all contribute to produce the headache which is experienced by all, more or less, on lofty summits.

The headache caused by mountain air has this characteristic, that it increases and diminishes at various hours of the day. The greatest torment which the sense of smell has ever procured me, was experienced during the illness of the soldier Ramella. We had isolated our patient, who was suffering from inflammation of the lungs and pulmonary gangrene, in the last room of the hut, for fear of infection, but owing to our cramped space I was nearly always obliged to work near his bed. The putrid smell of his breath and of the sputum was such, that in less than an hour headache obliged me to pause in my work. I used then to go to the window and on to the balcony, if the weather permitted; in a few minutes I had recovered and was able to return to the sick-room and to my studies.

VI.

In some very sensitive persons more serious nervous disturbances are caused by the action of rarefied air. A colleague of mine at the University of Turin cannot swallow well at a certain height because, as he says, the salivary glands are not in working order.

While we were at Gnifetti Hut a German gentleman, Herr Kolbe, arrived in company with a friend of his, Dr. Weber. When they started for the Col du Lys the weather was uncertain; they walked for an hour over the glacier, but the halts became more frequent and Herr Kolbe kept growing paler. His breathing was so laboured that, in spite of his own courageous insistence, the retreat became imperative. They had both before had an attack of nausea with retching, but this had caused them little anxiety. It was the appearance of a livid colour in their faces which decided them to turn back. The thermometer marked 6°.

On their return to Gnifetti Hut they repeatedly expressed astonishment at the sudden improvement of their condition. Two or three minutes after they had turned and begun to descend, every trace of indisposition had disappeared and they came down almost at a run. After an hour and a half they were sitting at table eating, the only remaining inconvenience being that Herr Kolbe had some difficulty in forming the bites of food in his mouth and in swallowing. We did not ascertain whether this was due to a slight paralysis of the motor nerves, or to a diminution of sensibility; probably the cause was a degree of paralysis of the vagus.

Dr. Weber examined the heart of his companion and found it normal. Some explanation of Kolbe's serious indisposition and rapid recovery is furnished by his age of sixty years. I have seen only two men older than he ascend Monte Rosa : Senator Perazzi, who was the Nestor of Italian Alpinists, and the guide Anthamatten from Saas, who was sixty-seven years old, and the oldest guide, I believe, still on active service.

Parrot,[1] who was the first to ascend Parrot Peak, the most beautiful of the peaks of Monte Rosa (of which I have introduced an illustration taken from a photograph by Vittorio Sella in Chapter VII., p. 111), relates, that during his journey through the Caucasus he once lost his voice. This, too, is a phenomenon arising from paralysis of the vagus. He did not feel ill, was not dizzy, only very weak. He could not see so far, either, nor so distinctly as before. He rested for half an hour and was then able to speak again.

Paul Güssfeldt, in his book on Mont Blanc, says: "The brain has certainly a greater productive efficiency at lower levels than at great altitudes. Probably it, too, would accustom itself to rarefied air like the heart and lungs. At least my experience suggests this. I tried once to continue some work in the mountains which had, however, no connection with my surroundings. I dragged on with it with the greatest difficulty and what I wrote I had afterwards to erase. As soon as I had returned to Germany the thoughts came to me easily, and the work was finished within a very short space of time."

During the ten days which I spent on Monte Rosa, at an altitude of 4,560 metres, I did not notice any difference in the activity of the brain. My brother and I made the experiment of noting the number of seconds which we required to make the addition or multiplication of certain given figures, and found that for the same operations there was no difference in the time taken in Turin and on Monte Rosa.

This holds good for a state of complete repose only, exertion alters the case, arithmetical operations are then no longer accomplished with the same rapidity. Speck affirms that when one is surrounded by an atmosphere containing only 9 per cent. of oxygen one loses one's memory. The same phenomenon is produced by oxide of carbon, and it may, I think, be generally maintained that memory fails as soon as the nutrition of the brain is disturbed.

VII.

Cats are, perhaps, more susceptible to the action of rarefied air than any other animal. In South America cats are never seen in places higher than 3,500 metres.

In his *Peruanische Reiseskizzen* Tschudi relates that the attempt has often been made to carry cats up to the villages on the Cordilleras, where all other domestic animals thrive, but without success. They do not try to escape nor bite, but soon sicken, are dejected, and are then seized by convulsions of an epileptic character and die. Dogs of finer breed are likewise subject to this malady. In South America mountain-sickness is called *soroche*, and those animals that sicken in rarefied air are termed *azarochados*.

In order to show the action of slight barometric depressions I shall communicate an experiment on a full-grown cat which has lived for a long time in the laboratory. The servant, Giorgio Mondo, to whom the animal is much attached, entered the pneumatic chamber with it on his arm.

June 18th. Barometric pressure 743 mm. Temperature 20°. While the cat appeared to be sleeping on Mondo's knees, at 8.20 a.m., I counted the normal rate of its breathing, which ran thus for five consecutive minutes: 32, 30, 30, 31, 30.

---

[1] *Reise in die Krym und den Kaukasus von M. von Engelhardt und F. Parrot*, Berlin, 1815, i. Theil, p. 202.

INFLUENCE OF MOUNTAIN AIR ON NERVOUS SYSTEM

The rarefaction of the air was then begun by setting the pump in motion and slightly diminishing the entrance of air.

8.40. Pressure 533 mm. (= 2,825 m.). Breathing 28, 26, 26, 24, 24.
The normal pressure was then slowly re-established. The animal continued to slumber.
9.22. Pressure 743 mm. Breathing 30, 32, 30, 30.
We then began to rarefy the air again.
9.36. The pressure of 533 mm. is again reached. Breathing 26, 26, 24.
9.48. Normal pressure. Breathing 28, 30, 32, 34.
The animal continued to slumber and did not move. Every time that the air was rarefied we noticed the same phenomenon, namely, that the breathing became slower and more superficial.

It is thus shown that in the cat a barometric depression of only 21 centimetres (= 2,800 metres) reduces the rate of breathing by 10 movements per minute.

VIII.

The first time that I detected an irregularity in the action of my heart (with which I am well acquainted, as I have studied it for many years), was on Monte Rosa, where, from time to time, a more rapid beating was noticeable. In Beno Bizzozero, in my brother, and in others a similar acceleration was observable.

These accelerations, of which I must now speak, are more forcible and more irregular than the periodic variations in the frequency of the pulse shown in some tracings in Chapter IV., p. 58.

As this is one of the more serious symptoms of mountain-sickness, and one to which I should like to direct the attention of mountain-climbers, I here communicate a few observations made on myself.

On August 9th, at 1.15 p.m., I arrived at Regina Margherita Hut, not very tired, as I had been determined to walk very leisurely, and had thus taken five hours to accomplish this ascent for which four would have sufficed. Immediately on my arrival I ascertained the frequency of the pulse, which was 102 per minute, and of the breathing, which was 22 to the minute. The rectal temperature was 37·9°.

After four hours' rest, two of which I spent lying down and the other two in putting my instruments in order, the pulse was 68, the rate of breathing 15 per minute, the temperature 36·9°. The effect of fatigue and of the rarefied air is slight, because, in the plain under normal conditions, the pulse would have been 60, the respiratory frequency 13, the temperature 36·8°.

The next day, August 10th, at the same hour, I did not feel so well; the pulse was from time to time irregular in its frequency and was sometimes strong, sometimes weak. At my request Beno Bizzozero counted the pulse for ten minutes in succession while one of the soldiers wrote the numbers announced, which ran as follows: 73, 76, 75, 76, 93, 80, 84, 80, 76, 75. The rate of breathing was irregular, on an average 22 per minute. Temperature, 37·4°. This disturbance in the physiological condition is important; I had not gone out of the hut, it was not therefore caused either by cold or fatigue, but solely by the barometric depression. The thermometer outside of the window facing towards the north, used for meteorological observations, marked 9°, but within it was warm, because there were two stoves lit all day, one in the observatory and one in the kitchen.

On the fourth day, August 12th, that is, the irregularities in the pulse had disappeared and my heart had resumed its customary slow, regular beating

Dr. Abelli and Beno Bizzozero, astonished at the slowness of my pulse, both counted it repeatedly while I was lying down and found from 54 to 55 pulsations per minute, the rate of breathing being from 16 to 17 and the rectal temperature 36·6°. All the phenomena caused by the depression had therefore disappeared. Only the breathing was quicker than usual; for in Turin, before rising, I only breathe from 11 to 12 times in the minute. One inconvenience which never left me was the sense of discomfort which I experienced in stooping, the venous circulation of the blood being then impeded.

During the first days at Regina Margherita Hut I observed the same augmentations in the rate of the pulse in Beno Bizzozero, and his face changed colour from time to time; sometimes his cheeks were red and sometimes pale, without any other cause than some deep-seated modification in the state of the nerve-centres which regulate the movements of the heart and blood-vessels.

This convinced me that mountain-sickness may appear in all at not very great altitudes, that in Regina Margherita Hut there are conditions favourable to the carrying out of a study of this kind, and that only by minutely describing the first symptoms of the indisposition can a sure foundation be laid for the pathology of mountain-sickness.

IX.

The wind exercises a compressing or else an aspiring action. While we were in Regina Margherita Hut the storms often gave us practical demonstration of the movements of the air such as one is seldom treated to in the plain. When the wind was blowing in a direction at a tangent to the door, one no sooner tried to open the latter than a flame darted out from the stove aperture and the smoke was drawn forcibly towards the door.

This is the principle of the scent-bottle with spray-diffuser which acts when one blows in a direction at a tangent to a tube immersed in the perfumed liquid. The current of air rushing past the tiny opening of the tube drags with it part of the air contained in the tube immersed in the liquid, other particles of air follow and this air in becoming rarefied draws after it the liquid, until the latter, having reached the top of the tube, is dispersed in a very fine cloud. These two forces of the wind, the compressing and the aspiring force, must exercise an influence, too, on respiration: some attempt I have made to prove this, but I do not venture to draw conclusions, as the discomfort caused by exposure to the hurricane was too great to encourage pursuance of the study.

If we breathe with our back turned to the wind, we find that respiration is easier, but I do not think that this is an effect due to aspiration. To front the wind causes much greater discomfort because the current then acts on the uncovered face and on the eyes. More especially is the accompanying sensation of cold distressing.

Prevailing opinions on the effect of the wind on respiration are contradictory. The popular belief is well known. In accordance with it, it is thought, for instance, that any one falling from a tower is suffocated from want of breath before reaching the ground, as though in the rapid passage through the air, it had been impossible to fill the lungs with air.

Tissié, in a recent study,[1] expresses himself on this subject as follows:—

[1] Tissié, *L'entraînement physique.* Revue scientifique, 25 Avril, 1896, p. 516.

"The greater the velocity of progression, the greater is the difficulty of breathing; the strata of air traversed being perpendicular to the axis of buccal expiration act as a gag which is the more resistant the greater the velocity. It is in order to breathe better that one instinctively bends the head down when it is very windy; the two axes of respiration are thus displaced."

In order to study the modification of the breathing in a violent current of air, I set up in my laboratory a ventilator which was made to act by means of a gas-meter. In form this ventilator was similar to those used in foundries and factories for the production of a strong air-current. As the ordinary anemometers did not suffice to measure the very violent current thus generated, I determined its velocity by means of Lind's method,[1] making use of a water-manometer, of which the tube was 28 millimetres in diameter. One of the legs of this U-tube was curved again in such a manner that the air issuing from the ventilator blew straight into it. The water in the manometer rose to from 18 to 20 millimetres at the distance of 10 centimetres from the tube whence the air poured out.

Reckoning according to the tables drawn up for this purpose, I found that the height of 20 mm. corresponds to a velocity of 34·6 m. per second—that is, of 124 kilometres per hour, the velocity of cyclones.

I then first determined the modification in the pressure of the wind when it reaches the lungs by the passage of the nose and larynx. This experiment had of course to be performed on a corpse. I placed the head with the same tube in the trachea in such a manner that the current of air struck the nostrils full in front and found that the pressure was only 15 mm. This proves that part of the pressure of the wind is lost before the air reaches the lungs. When the head of the corpse was bent, as we bend ours when walking against the wind, the manometric pressure sank to 12 mm. These data are easily understood and demand no further explanation.

The influence of the wind on the respiratory form was then studied by means of the graphic method. Tracing 55 shows the result of an experiment performed on myself. The first part to the left is the normal respiratory curve. At the sign a the machine was put in motion and the subject thus exposed to the influence of the strong current of air travelling at the above-mentioned rate. During the first moment the thorax remains somewhat dilated; it then recovers the position which it had before at the end of the expiratory movement. The inspirations are deeper and slower. At the sign ω the action of the wind is stopped and the breathing regains its previous form and rhythm.

In Dr. Perrod the modification of the breathing under the influence of the wind is very marked at the beginning, afterwards disappearing. This may be seen in Fig. 56. The first part to the left shows the normal thoracic respiration while seventeen breaths are being drawn in the minute. At a the current is established, the breathing becomes accelerated and more ample. Twenty breaths are drawn in the minute. The thorax resists the pressure and does not dilate, as in the foregoing experiment. The respirations ascend higher than in the preceding normal tracing. In the second minute the rate has fallen to 18, the amplitude is normal. In this part of the curve we have the proof that a very strong wind (travelling at the rate of 34 metres per second) such as is perhaps never experienced in the Alps, as man would be swept away before it, exercises no visible influence on the breathing.

[1] Gehler's Physikalisches Wörterbuch, x. B., p. 2184.

In other persons I have seen that the wind reinforces the respiratory movements and slackens the rate. As for the form of the single respiratory phases, which were taken by giving a more rapid rotatory movement to the cylinder of the registering apparatus, I have not met in them with any appreciable difference. As, however, so strong a current of air on the face produces an uncomfortable sensation of cold, this alone suffices to give rise to a nervous disturbance which modifies the breathing without the participation of the mechanical action of the lungs.

The draught produced by this ventilator was so strong that only few could face it without experiencing great discomfort. The mechanician of the laboratory became dizzy when he approached the apparatus. This explains why some persons are more liable to mountain-sickness when they walk against a violent wind.

X.

On the glaciers when one is obliged to halt during a snow-storm, it is advisable to make a hole in the snow with the ice-axe and then thrust in the legs up to the calves so as to prevent the feet from freezing.

In Dr. Perrod I took the temperature of the skin of the cheeks with a special thermometer made for measurements of this kind, and found it to be 34° on the surface of the skin. After the subject had been exposed for two minutes to the action of the ventilator the temperature had fallen to 25°. Another time I put an ordinary thermometer into the subject's mouth, so that the bulb touched the inner skin of the cheek. It indicated 35·6°. The experiment with the ventilator was then repeated, Dr. Perrod keeping his mouth shut, and the thermometer still being in the position indicated, while the current struck him in the face. In two minutes and a half the temperature of the mouth was diminished by three degrees. The temperature of the air measured in the current of the ventilator was 12·5°.

We have nerves which are susceptible to heat and others susceptible to cold. The skin of the face is more sensitive to cold than that of the hands. The tips of the fingers feel more pain from cold than the palm. I mention this as an indication of how sensitiveness is distributed over the surface of the body. A typical case is that of the *membrum virile*, which feels heat, but is, towards the apex, insensible to cold.

When exposed to wind or cold the eyes fill with tears. This is a complex phenomenon, not well studied as yet. From observations made on myself, I am inclined to think that there is not an increased secretion of tears. Perhaps a contraction diminishes the orifice of the canal through which the tears run towards the nose, or else there may be some change in the manner in which we wink.

The opinions of Alpinists as to cold are not in agreement. Saussure says: "The only thing which did me good and increased my strength was the cold air of the north wind. If, in ascending, I had my face turned in that direction and could swallow great breaths of the air coming from that quarter I could accomplish twenty-five or twenty-six steps without stopping."

The brothers Schlagintweit, on the contrary, mention that they and their party experienced a sense of suffocation when the wind was blowing, and in the evening the wind made them feel so ill that they lost their appetite and scarcely cooked any dinner, whereas in the morning when the air was calm they felt better.

FIG. 55.—Action of wind on respiration.—A. Mosso. The first part of the curve to the sign *a* represents the normal breathing written with Marey's pneumograph. At *a* the face was turned towards a current of air travelling at the rate of 34 metres per second. At *b* the current is stopped and the last part of the curve represents the normal breathing again.

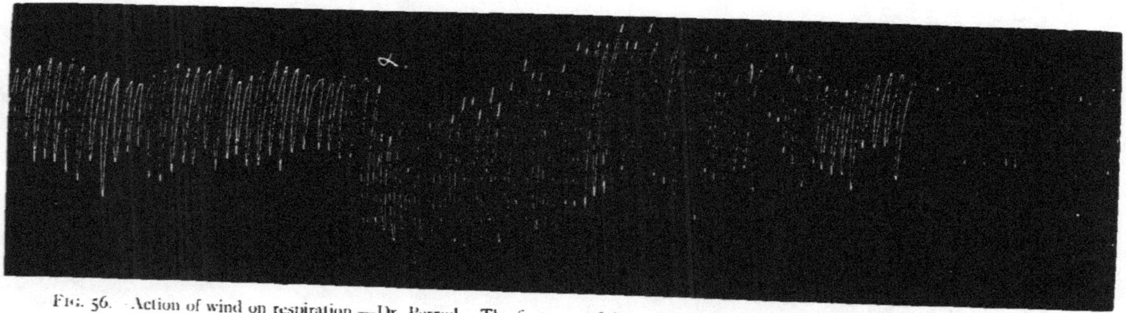

FIG. 56. Action of wind on respiration.—Dr. Perrod. The first part of the tracing to the sign *a* shows the normal respiratory curve. At *a* the action of the wind begins with the above-mentioned velocity.

Conway,[1] when at the same altitude in the Himalayas, complains of the calm air and fine weather. To quote his own words:—

"The connection between heat, still air, and human discomfort at high altitudes is a close one, and calls for explanation. A climber is forced to take account of it. In attempting the ascent of a high peak he should, if possible, approach by a north-south valley, so as to win as much shade as possible, and then he should endeavour to climb by an exposed ridge rather than by gullies or snow-slopes, for thus he will the more probably avoid stagnant air. Finally, he should work in bad weather and by night as much as possible, and should avoid a route which will expose his back to the sun for any considerable length of time."

[1] W. M. Conway, *Climbing in the Karakoram-Himalayas*, p. 509.

Lyskamm.

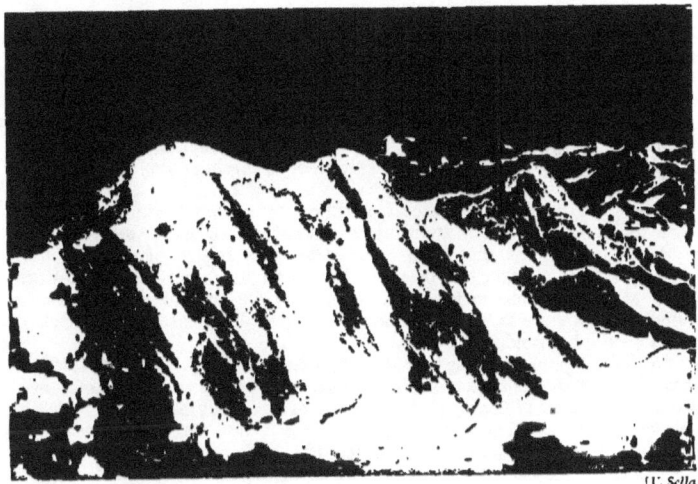

[V. Sella.

Panoramic view taken from the Regina Margherita Hut.

CHAPTER XVIII

CIRCULATION OF THE BLOOD IN THE HUMAN BRAIN

I.

IT was my wish to find some man with a hole in his skull who would have been willing to come with me on the Monte Rosa expedition, but I was not successful in my search. Some other physiologist will, I hope, be luckier. For the present we must content ourselves with the observations which I made in the pneumatic chamber on two persons in whom the brain was uncovered.

Several writers have attributed mountain-sickness to a disturbance in the circulation of blood in the brain. Some, like Tschudi, say that the diminished barometric pressure produces a cerebral congestion; others, and amongst these Lœwy,[1] ascribe mountain-sickness to anæmia of the brain. I should detain the reader too long were I to recall the theories which have been propounded in order to explain the morbid phenomena resulting from an augmentation or diminution of the barometric pressure on the surface of the body. In general it may be said that mechanical theories predominate. P. Bert tried to substitute a chemical for the mechanical theory, but the phenomena are so closely connected that it seems impossible to look upon

[1] Lœwy, *Untersuchungen über die Respiration und Circulation bei Aenderung des Druckes*, Berlin, 1895, p. 15.

either theory as alone sufficient. As a proof of this I may instance Le Pileur, who, at an altitude of 3,046 metres, on Mont Blanc, was seized with dizziness when he merely lifted his head.[1] H. Vivenot maintains that the drowsiness which often troubles the workmen in the caissons full of compressed air, is due to cerebral congestion.[2] He says that the blood is forced towards the inner parts by the compressed air, and that to the diminution of the blood at the periphery must correspond a congestion of the brain and spinal cord which is the cause of somnolency.

These, however, are hypotheses, no direct researches having, so far as I know, been made as yet on the subject. It suffices to show the little value of these suppositions that both anæmia and congestion of the brain have been considered as the cause of somnolency and the other nervous disturbances which are produced by the changes of the barometric pressure, as though, in other words, the influence of over-abundance and of lack of blood on the brain could be identical.

My investigations of 1877 on the physiological action of compressed air showed that the distribution of blood in the organism does not change even when the pressure of the air on the surface of the body becomes double the normal, a weight which would crush us were it not counterbalanced at all parts of the body internally and externally. We shall now see that the mechanical theory of the displacement of the blood is also inadequate to explain the morbid phenomena which become manifest when the air is rarefied.

The method which I adopted for the registering of the cerebral circulation of the blood, is that described in my book,[3] which it is here, therefore, unnecessary to repeat. Fig. 59 shows the application of a tube to the opening in the skull of the youth Favre, in such a manner that the pulsations of the brain are transmitted to a lever, which writes the curve of the circulation of the blood. Let us now consider the construction of the pneumatic chamber and the disposition of the registering apparatus when the brain-pulse was to be traced without disturbing the subject of the experiment.

The large vertical cylinder seen to the right in Fig. 57 is the pneumatic chamber. It is of iron and is made like a steam-boiler, terminating at the upper end in a flattish cupola, while the lower open end is encircled by a thick and perfectly level iron rim. This rim is covered by a large tube of india-rubber which rests on a thick marble slab and closes the cylinder hermetically like a pneumatic bell. A man may stand with ease in this iron chamber as it is 1·85 metres high, and 0·80 metres broad, the capacity being therefore of about one cubic metre. A window of very thick glass admits light to the interior.

The cylinder is easily raised and lowered as it is held in equilibrium by a counterpoise and by two pulleys fixed to the wall. In the figure this part of the iron support is not visible, only in the middle of the cupola the ring is seen to which the suspending rope of the bell is fastened. By means of the handles at the sides the cylinder is raised to the height of a man, this causing no exertion as it is kept in equilibrium by an equal weight at the other end of the rope.

[1] *Comptes rendus*, 1845, vol. xx. p. 1200.
[2] B. v. Vivenot, *Zur Kenntniss der physiologischen Wirkungen der verdichteten Luft.* Erlangen, 1868, p. 494.
[3] *Der Kreislauf des Blutes im menschlichen Gehirn*, Leipzig.

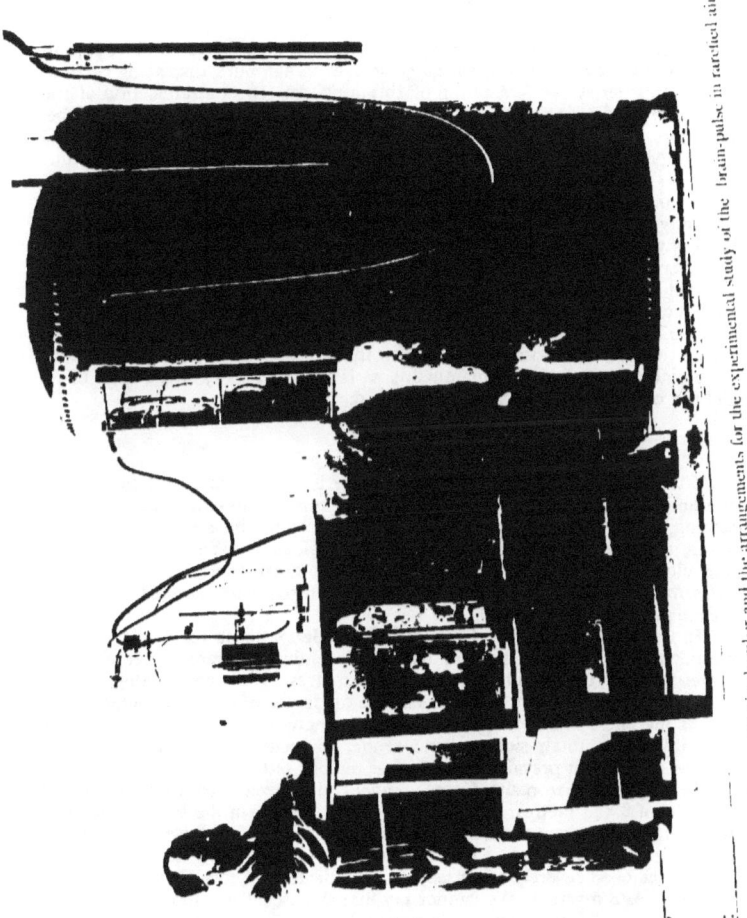

FIG. 57.—Showing pneumatic chamber and the arrangements for the experimental study of the brain-pulse in rarefied air.

Instead of an ordinary air-pump I make use of a gas-motor which keeps in movement a piston which performs 30 strokes in a minute, displacing two and a half litres per stroke. A pump of this kind can effect a rarefaction of the air corresponding to the altitude of the highest mountains on the globe. During rarefaction, the air is continually renewed within the chamber, because in one part, which is not seen in the figure, there is a tap which admits a current of air. The internal depression is effected nevertheless because the pump takes away more air than enters by the tap. The afflux of fresh air is not only continuous, but also more abundant than is necessary for man's breathing. We have repeatedly analysed the air in the pneumatic chamber, and even when it was very much rarefied, and the supply of fresh air therefore reduced to a minimum, we found that after the experiment had continued for an hour, the carbonic acid did not surpass one per cent. of the air. In summer, whenever it was necessary to cool the air, this was effected by letting it pass through a frigorific mixture by means of a serpentine pipe of lead. Two mercurial manometers, the one outside, as is seen in Fig. 57 at the right hand, and the other inside, indicated the pressure.

II.

Till now physiology has profited little by balloon ascents and indeed one can understand that the necessary calm for minute investigations on man is lacking, when one finds one's self floating through the air. The restricted space, too, and the motion of the car are serious and perhaps insuperable difficulties. For a long time, therefore, we must content ourselves with *artificial ascents*, as I call the experiments made with rarefied air in the pneumatic chamber.

In the laboratory of the Sorbonne, Paul Bert [1] constructed a large pneumatic chamber in which he and his friends endured a rarefaction of the air corresponding to an altitude of 8,000 metres. G. von Liebig, Speck, Kronecker, Zuntz, Lœwy and others have made use of similar apparatus.

As the one I have constructed is very economical, I hope it may facilitate the study of mountain-sickness and render unnecessary the exposure to the intense cold which prevails in the higher regions of the air.

In 1875 the aeronauts Croce Spinelli and Sivel died in a balloon at a height of 8,540 metres, as was found on the opening of the barometric tubes which had been given them by Janssen.[2] What was the cause of their death at a relatively low altitude I find it impossible to say. This expedition of the Zenith has been severely criticised,[3] but the death of Croce Spinelli and Sivel still remains a mystery. We cannot say that the ascent was too rapid, because my brother and I have repeatedly been subjected, within a space of time four times less, to a barometric depression in the pneumatic chamber corresponding to an altitude of 7,400 metres, scarcely 1,000 metres less, that is, than the height at which the two aeronauts met their death.

The action of the cold may have been a partial, but certainly cannot have been the only cause of their death, because at an altitude of 7,000 metres the temperature was only —10°. It is my opinion that apprehension rapidly exhausts the nervous system and aggravates in an unexpected manner the effects of the barometric depression. There is a whole unconscious psychology, a whole world of emotions which courageous persons may keep under control

---

[1] P. Bert, *La pression barométrique*, p. 631.   [2] *Op. cit.*, p. 1067.
[3] L. Germe, *Recherches sur les lois de la circulation pulmonaire*. Paris, 1895, p. 354

and hide, but which refuse to be suppressed and exhaust the potential energy of the individual. Perhaps these concealed ravages provoked the sudden outbreak of mountain-sickness in its worst form before the rarefaction of the air was such as to be alone sufficient to cause death.

Even in the pneumatic chamber serious phenomena are sometimes observable which are not proportionate to the rarefaction of the air, and which are probably due to unconscious fear. As a proof of this I communicate an experiment of Paul Bert. On the 24th February, 1874, he entered the pneumatic chamber at 2.37 p.m. with a bag of air very rich in oxygen. After thirty-five minutes the rarefaction of the air corresponded to a height of 4,150 metres, the barometric reading being 450 mm. The pulse rose from 64 to 84 beats per minute, and Bert had a sensation of nausea. Two minutes later, while the pressure was still 450 mm., he began to feel dizzy and to see indistinctly.

After one hour in the pneumatic chamber, Bert felt a convulsive trembling in the calves of his legs and in the muscles of the thighs. His condition at 3.57 p.m., when the pressure was 420 mm. (which corresponds to the height of Mont Blanc), he describes as follows: "I felt unwell; having determined the number of my pulsations in twenty seconds to be 28, I had the greatest difficulty in multiplying this number by three, and I wrote in my notebook *difficult to calculate.*"[1]

An artificial ascent is therefore not so harmless an experiment as it seems at first sight, but luckily not all are so susceptible to the action of rarefied air as Bert was in this case. Important experiments were made in the summer of 1891 by Professor Hugo Kronecker[2] in the pneumatic chamber of Schöneck near Beckenried. He says that after having subjected himself to a pressure of 450 mm., which corresponds to the height of the Breithorn, he suffered for almost two days from feverish sensations accompanied by heaviness of the head. The experiment was repeated several times, and on the fourteenth day he did not feel himself in any way affected. On the first day, after three minutes' exercise in stair-climbing on a special apparatus in the pneumatic chamber (barometric height: 450 mm.), dizziness and difficulty in breathing prevented the continuation of the experiment. On the fourteenth day the same exercise at the same pressure (which corresponds to a height of 4,173 metres) could be continued with the same ease as in ordinary air. We see from these experiments that Professor Kronecker is likewise very sensitive to diminished barometric pressure; nevertheless his organism easily accustomed itself to the depression, a result probably of the rapid adaptation of the nervous system to the rarefied air.

The fact that Paul Bert suffered from mountain-sickness before the pressure was reduced to 41 centimetres, shows that the theory of Fraenkel and Geppert is not quite correct. According to this theory the blood of a dog retains all its oxygen down to a pressure of 41 centimetres. Even were we to grant provisionally that this statement holds good in the case of man also (which has not yet been proved), the fact that mountain-sickness breaks out at altitudes corresponding to a higher pressure than 41 centimetres, without the additional element of fatigue, would oblige us to seek another explanation.

[1] *Op. cit.*, p. 752.
[2] H. Kronecker, *Ueber die Bergkrankheit mit Bezug auf die Jungfraubahn.* Bern, 1894.

III.

In balloon-ascents, as there is no fatigue resulting from movement, the phenomena caused by the rarefaction of the air appear in general much later, and it is said that a height double that of the mountains must be reached before corresponding symptoms of indisposition are felt. This statement is confirmed by the experience of my brother, who, at an altitude of 3,620 metres, in Gnifetti Hut, felt about the same degree of indisposition as at the artificial altitude of 7,400 metres in the pneumatic chamber.

On the 22nd February, 1895, wishing to determine at what pressure artificial mountain-sickness begins, my brother remained in the pneumatic chamber until the rarefaction of the air corresponded to the barometric height of 31 centimetres, which is equal to an altitude of 7,141 metres. He did not suffer from dizziness, but felt his mental faculties blunted, and he had some difficulty in reading the seconds of the watch. Twice he was unable to count his pulse in spite of the concentration of his attention. His handwriting was much altered, and his memory weakened; he forgot what observation he had intended to make, and on coming out of the chamber he had only a partial recollection of his condition at great depressions. At the beginning of the indisposition his eyes became dull and his face more serious and apathetic.

During these experiments at great depressions the psychic phenomena which came under our notice seemed to us the most striking. Every little mischance which occurred during an experiment became to us an insurmountable obstacle. Even the most insignificant circumstance, such as letting fall a lead pencil, proved an effectual hindrance, for either we had no desire to pick it up, or else it did not occur to us that the trifling exertion of stooping to recover it would enable us to continue the experiment.

I have a collection of notes written by various individuals under these conditions which would certainly interest psychologists, but which lack of space prevents my inserting.

Dr. Z. Treves and Dr. Daddi also endured the rarefaction of the air until the first symptoms of indisposition—nausea, palpitation, drowsiness, and trembling—appeared at altitudes between 6,000 and 7,000 metres. These experiments could be interrupted by the subject at will by turning a tap in the interior of the chamber. Notwithstanding this facility it never happened that one of us admitted a current of outside air in order to relieve his condition. Perhaps the depression of the nervous system gradually renders us indifferent. Some, as though rousing themselves from a sleep, complained all at once of indisposition. Thus Dr. Daddi, when the pressure was 340 mm. (corresponding to an altitude of 6,500 metres, the height of Chimborazo), suddenly wrote: "*I feel very ill, I need . . .* " after which came an undecipherable word, which might mean either "air" or "to become."[1] Even before he raised the leaf up to the window for me to read, I had understood, because he had turned pale and his hands trembled as he wrote. I therefore immediately turned the tap so as to admit a strong current of air.

When the pressure was 540 mm., he smilingly informed us that he was feeling better, and that we might increase the pressure more slowly.

Dr. Daddi's normal respiration at 3.25 p.m., after sitting for an hour near the bell, was twenty in the minute. Until the barometric height was 380 mm.

---

[1] Ital. *Vento* = air. *Diventare* = to become.

he had felt well. Suddenly at a pressure of 360 mm. he began to feel his temples compressed as with a band, an oppression in the epigastrium and painful palpitation. Not only did his heart beat more forcibly than usual, but this accelerated pulsation was accompanied by actual pain. Then trembling and dizziness seized him. It was then that he decided to ask for help. The rate of the pulse had risen from 80 to 92 beats per minute when he began to feel ill. The rate of breathing did not change. When the subject came out of the bell the pulse only beat 73 times in the minute. He began to walk up and down in the room, and remarked that the floor seemed less hard to him, and that probably the sensibility of his legs was slightly diminished. Immediately afterwards, however, this phenomenon disappeared.

IV.

Cesare Lasagno, a blacksmith's apprentice fourteen years of age, fell from the second storey while he was leaning on his stomach over the banisters, and sliding down as boys do, and received a wound in the middle of the forehead

FIG. 58.—Cesare Lasagno.—Cerebral pulse.—A. Normal curve. B. Curve of cerebral pulse taken when the rarefaction of the air corresponded to an altitude of 5,111 metres. C. Subsequent normal curve.

with a fracture of the skull. He was carried to the hospital and treated by Professor Carle. When he came to my institute in October, two months had passed since the accident, and the wound had become a pulsating cicatrice. I applied a gutta-percha cap to his head, and took the curve of the cerebral pulse which is shown in A of Fig. 58. In order to register the cerebral pulse in rarefied air, I placed a large glass bell of the capacity of 60 litres on a marble slab as is shown in Fig. 57; the rim of the bell was ground, so that with the application of a little grease, a hermetic closure was effected between it and the slab. Under the bell was a smoked cylinder of which the axis could be made to turn from the outside. In Fig. 57 we see that the axis of the cylinder is furnished at its base with a pulley of wood round which a cord runs; a similar pulley was placed in the axis of a clock-work apparatus, not visible in the figure, which transmitted the rotatory movement to the cylinder. A metal tube with an inner lining of greased tow effects the hermetic closure of the bell in that part where the axis turns. These arrangements enabled me to take the pulse-curve in an apparatus situated outside of the pneumatic chamber which I could manipulate, modifying its velocity, stopping it or putting it in motion, unknown to the subject within the chamber.

While the air was being rarefied in the pneumatic chamber a corresponding rarefaction proceeded under the glass bell, for by means of a tube made of thick india-rubber a communication between the two receptacles was established.

The movements of the brain were transmitted to the registering tympanum within the glass bell by means of another india-rubber tube which passed through the side of the pneumatic chamber and through the neck of the glass bell. Care was of course taken to close hermetically the apertures of passage. A water-valve placed within the chamber as a continuation of the tube which passed from the brain to the cylinder allowed of the expansion of the air in the capsule and above the brain in proportion as the barometric pressure decreased. In this way the pressure remained the same in the glass bell and in the pneumatic chamber. I was thus enabled to follow every movement of the cerebral pulse and circulation without being obliged to enter the chamber, in which case the alteration of the air produced by the breathing of two persons would have rendered the experiment more difficult, perhaps even impossible.

The curve B of Fig. 58 was taken while Lasagno was subjected to a pressure of 400 mm. (corresponding to an altitude of 5,111 metres, the external pressure being 740 mm.). The rate of breathing, which was at first 28 to 30 per minute, had fallen to 22 and 24. The pulse, on the contrary, had increased from 80 to 89 beats per minute.

The atmospheric pressure of 740 mm. being re-established within the chamber, the last curve C (Fig. 58) was taken. In it we see that the cerebral pulse had recovered the rate and height which it had at the beginning of the experiment. The rate of breathing was 20 to 22 in the minute.

If we examine these curves with a magnifying glass the difference between the curve of the brain-pulse in rarefied air and at an ordinary atmospheric pressure becomes evident. Normally the apex of the brain pulsations presents three points, as I have shown in my first work on the circulation of the blood in the brain. In the curve B, written during the action of the rarefied air, the dicrotism appears lower down and the pulse is no longer anacrotic. This change may be due to a relaxation of the walls of the blood-vessels and to a diminution of their tonicity. A very slight increase in the volume of the brain, which gradually disappeared while the pressure within the chamber continued at 400 mm., was in fact observable.

The statement that the cerebral vaso-motor centre is likewise less active in rarefied air would thus seem to receive confirmation. The augmentation in the frequency of the pulse, unfailingly observed in persons in the pneumatic chamber, is also due to a paralysis of the centre whence the nerves which slacken the beating of the heart branch off.

The observations made on Cesare Lasagno enable me to affirm that the diminished barometric pressure produces neither congestion nor cerebral anæmia. The causes of mountain-sickness are therefore not to be sought in a change of the cerebral circulation; they are deeper-seated and are of a chemical nature. It is the vitality of the nerve-cells in the most important vital centres which becomes modified at great altitudes owing to other causes, not to a disturbance of the cerebral circulation.

If the augmentation in the volume of the brain during the action of rarefied air was only slight, this must be ascribed to a weakening of the heart. In no other way can I explain the absence of a greater dilatation of the blood-vessels, while their tonicity diminished. The pulse was smaller and more rapid, I therefore consider it probable that the force of the cardiac contractions diminished at the same time as the activity of the vaso-motor nerves in the brain decreased.

As far as the artificial altitude of 5,111 metres the circulation of the blood in the brain of the lad Lasagno underwent only a very slight modification. I did not wish to subject him to a greater rarefaction of the air, fearing, that as I could not be beside him in the pneumatic chamber, he would be frightened when he began to feel unwell. There was therefore, as remarked, no indication of congestion or anæmia consequent on the diminution of the barometric pressure, the only alteration which appeared being the slight diminution in the tonicity of the blood-vessels of the brain. In order to explain mountain-sickness we must add to the phenomena already considered in the first chapters, namely, incipient paralysis of the respiratory muscles and of the heart, these other phenomena indicating a diminished activity of the nerve-centres, the failure of the memory, the psychic depression observed during artificial ascents and the paralysis of the blood-vessels of the brain, of which a proof was furnished by the experiment on the youth Lasagno.

All these facts, which agree with each other, serve as basis for a theory of mountain-sickness in which the depression of the nerve-centres is recognised as the principal cause of the phenomena observed.

V.

In order to see what changes take place in living organisms when the proportion of oxygen in the air is diminished, while the atmospheric pressure remains the same, I made a series of experiments on man and animals in which *artificial air* was breathed. By *artificial air* I mean air diluted with azote (as wine is diluted with water, if I may be allowed to compare wine to air and water to azote), or air from which a portion of oxygen has been subtracted. In this way we can obtain an artificial air of any given degree of rarefaction. Whatever precautions may be taken in following other methods, it is only by means of artificial air that we can eliminate the mechanical pressure indicated by the barometer, and thus study the chemical effects due to a lack of oxygen apart from all others. It is known that in 100 parts of air, 20·78 are oxygen and 79·22 azote (roughly speaking we say the air contains 21 parts oxygen and 79 parts azote). If we fill a tube of iron (in size and form resembling the barrel of a gun) with copper filings, then heat it until it becomes red and finally send a current of air through it, the oxygen combines with the copper and from the further end of the tube issues pure azote, which is then collected in a gas-meter resembling the one shown in Fig. 59.

Before trying the effect of artificial air on man, I made some experiments on animals. I communicate one of these in order to show the modifications taking place in an organism in extremely rarefied air, when the barometric height is only 16 centimetres.

February, 1895. Barometric reading, 743 mm. Temperature, 16°. A little dog weighing 2,500 grams was put under a large glass bell such as that shown in Fig. 57. As he was accustomed to similar experiments he lay down on the towel we had put inside and curled himself up as though to sleep. After he had been quite still for about ten minutes, I counted the number of respiratory movements every minute in succession for a quarter of an hour. The results ran as follows :—

16, 17, 16, 18, 16, 16, 17, 16, 19, 16, 15, 15, 14, 15, 14.

I then effected a rarefaction of the air until the pressure within the bell was only 334 mm., which corresponds to an altitude of 6,571 metres. The breathing became more rapid and more forcible. The dog got up at first and then lay down again, his nose to his tail, as dogs do when they want to sleep. The respiration had become quicker when the dog moved, it then diminished again in frequency so that the successive counting for every minute of a quarter of an hour gave the following results :—

18, 20, 21, 25, 20, 26, 20, 18, 19, 20, 26, 22, 24, 23, 24.

The animal was now quiet and seemed asleep. I increased the depression in order to produce a state in the dog resembling, as far as possible, mountain-sickness. The barometric reading was now 243 mm. which corresponds to an altitude of 8,500 metres.

A gas-meter placed at the point of entrance of the air indicated that every minute five litres of air were let into the bell, a quantity sufficient to ensure the purity of the inner atmosphere. The dog got up again, showing signs of indisposition and lassitude, and then lay down once more. Respiration: 26, 26, 25, 41, 42. The animal was evidently suffering, he tried to get up but could not. Irregular breathing, first 38 then 25 movements per minute. He contracted the corners of his mouth when breathing inwards.

The rarefaction of the air was continued until the barometer marked 250 mm., the barometric pressure being thus reduced by two-thirds.

Breathing : 21, 22, 23, 24, 32, 37, 41, 39, 44, 40, 40, 38, 36.

The pressure was then further diminished to 162 mm. Breathing, 37 per minute. The dog had an attack of convulsions and expelled urine. Breathing : 106, 69, 70. The animal then again fell into a fit and forcibly extended his limbs. Breathing deep. Expulsion of fæces. The dog then squealed. Two minutes later, as I noticed that the breathing had become weaker and slower, I admitted a supply of air as I feared the animal might succumb. He recovered at once. When placed on the ground he walked with difficulty, his legs evidently being insensible. In three or four minutes he had regained his normal aspect.

Experiment with artificial air.

We prepared 300 litres of artificial air corresponding to the barometric pressure of 162 mm. With the aid of special apparatus made according to Hempel's model, we analysed the air contained in the big gas-meter and found that it only contained 4-5 parts of oxygen in 100, instead of 21.

On the next day at the same time we again put the dog under the glass bell and counted the respiratory movements every minute for several minutes in succession, obtaining the following numbers :—

15, 14, 14, 15, 14, 15, 14, 14, 15.

When we had assured ourselves that all was in order the tap of the gas-meter was opened. In order to prevent the immediate entrance of the artificial air into the bell we caused it to pass through a large bottle of the capacity of six litres, like the one seen in Fig. 59. By means of a meter we ascertained that four litres of air passed through the bell per minute.

When we were convinced that all the air had been renewed, and that the dog was really breathing an air which contained as much oxygen for its volume as possible at a barometric height of 16 cemtimetres, we observed that the animal's breathing was becoming more and more frequent and more ample, as may be seen from the following numbers written for several minutes in succession :—

17, 18, 20, 23, 30, 41.

The breathing was so laboured that the animal moved the corners of the mouth at every inspiration. He lay curled up with closed eyes and sighed from time to time. Then he was seized with convulsions, squealed, staggered to his feet and expelled urine. After the lapse of a minute he seemed better and fell into a doze. Breathing, first 82, then 70, then 69 per minute.

Eight minutes after the first attack of convulsions another occurred.

The animal squealed and stretched his legs in tetanic tension. His tongue, which was paler than usual and slightly cyanotic, hung out of his mouth. He seemed unconscious. Two attacks of convulsions followed with an interval of one minute between ; the dog squealed and expelled fæces. Breathing irregular, about 80 in the minute.

After the dog had breathed this artificial air for half an hour the experiment was suspended.

When the ordinary pressure was re-established the animal did not immediately rise; his condition had, however, already improved. When he was put on the ground, he kept his legs but walked with difficulty, and one could see from the manner in which he pressed his paws on the ground that his legs were insensible.

Artificial air, owing to its rarefaction, produces the same effects as those due to a diminution of barometric pressure. We may therefore conclude that mountain-sickness is not caused by the mechanical action or the diminished weight of the atmosphere, but by its rarefaction, which acts chemically on the metabolism of the nervous system.

VI.

Emanuele Favre is a boy thirteen years of age, who came from Savoie to Turin in order to receive medical treatment from Prof. Carle at the Hospital Mauriziano. While helping his master to chop wood in a forest near Bramant, by laying the branches on the block, he had bent too far forwards and the axe of the master struck him on the head. He fell unconscious to the ground, but recovered his senses shortly afterwards and was able, being supported under the arms, to walk several kilometres to his home.

When I saw this boy he was almost cured, but the great gash in the skull still showed the pulsations of the brain. I applied to his head a gutta-percha cap which, greased round the rim with vaseline, closed hermetically round the edges of the wound. An india-rubber tube, as is seen in the figure, transmitted the movements of the brain through the medium of the air to a registering tympanum. As I obtained excellent curves of the cerebral circulation, I determined to study the modifications which take place in the brain when we breathe air containing only half the usual amount of oxygen.

Into a large gas-meter, such as is seen in Fig. 59, I admitted 300 litres of air, to which were then added 300 litres of azote obtained in the manner already mentioned. In every litre of this artificial air was only half the quantity of oxygen contained in a litre of ordinary air. In breathing this air the same amount of oxygen is supplied to the lungs as would be introduced into them in an atmosphere reduced by one-half, at an altitude, that is, of 5,520 metres. This experiment excited our keenest interest, as we were thus enabled to observe the chemical action of the rarefied air on man apart from its mechanical action. There is, in fact, no other way of avoiding the reduction of the barometric pressure and yet of diminishing by one-half, the amount of oxygen inhaled. In spite, therefore, of the tedious work necessary to fill the large gas-meter with artificial air, we prepared sufficient azote to fill it twice. We were thus able to repeat the interesting experiment on the boy Favre three times.

So as not to let him breathe at once air deprived of half its oxygen, I intercalated two large bottles full of air, one of which may be seen in Fig. 59. A portion of the artificial air contained in the gas-meter was allowed to mix with the ordinary air contained in these bottles. Every fresh supply of artificial air from the gas-meter expelled a further amount of normal air so that that inhaled by the subject became gradually poorer in oxygen.

The weight of the zinc bell was sufficient to keep up the current of artificial air which, by means of a thick forked tube, was led from the large bottle under the gutta-percha mask made expressly to fit the face of the boy Favre. By means of putty the mask was made to close hermetically round the bones of the nose, the cheeks, and the chin. A bandage fastened at the back of the neck kept the mask in its place, as may be seen in Fig. 59. The expired air issued through a thick india-rubber tube several metres in length, which is seen on the table in the figure. In adopting this method I had been able to do without the valves. A constant current of artificial air being kept up in the tube which carried the air from the gas-meter to the mask, and the rapidity with which the air issued from the gas-meter being determined by means of a bottle of lye, I was sure that only artificial air could enter the lungs at every inspiration.

FIG. 59.—Emanuele Favre. Registration of the cerebral pulse during the respiration of artificial air.

This apparatus had the advantage of acting under almost no pressure. Every experiment lasted about half an hour.

The upper curve of Fig. 60 is that of the normal brain-pulse registered on a rotating cylinder. Favre was breathing twelve times in the minute; we had told him to make a sign with the hand when he wished us to leave off, and we should do so at once. The experiment which I here communicate was the third and last. As the boy knew by this time what our purpose was, the emotion of fear was almost entirely excluded. When he began to breathe the artificial air there was a slight augmentation in the volume of the brain, and after a few minutes a diminution. The second curve of Fig. 60 was

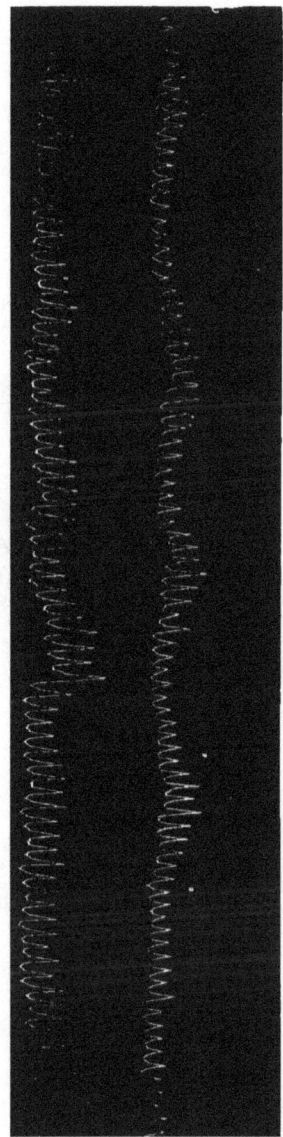

Fig. 60.—Circulation of the blood in the brain of the boy Favre. A. Normal curve. B. Curve registered during the respiration of artificial air when the subject was seized with dizziness.

traced during this period of decrease in the volume of the brain and shortly before the respiration of the artificial air ceased. We took the mask off Favre as soon as this curve was registered: he then told us that he felt as though he were drunk, that he could not hear so well as before because of a singing in his ears, and that he had a headache.

In this experiment with artificial air there was the same augmentation in the rate of the cardiac movements, and the same decrease in the frequency of the respiratory movements as in the experiments with rarefied air in the pneumatic chamber, in which the breathing, consequent on the depression, first becomes quicker and afterwards slower. Favre's normal rate of breathing was 12 to 13 per minute: during the respiration of artificial air the rate sank to 10 and 11 movements in the minute. This seems at first sight a paradox, because, as the amount of oxygen breathed by this subject was reduced by one-half, the frequency of the respiratory movements should have become doubled. This, however, I did not find to be the case, either in this experiment or on Monte Rosa, as I have already mentioned in Chapter III. Neither must we think that the respiratory movements are more forcible; I convinced myself of the contrary by observing the thorax, and the statement is further confirmed by an examination of the curves in Fig. 60 endways. In the upper part the pulsations form, as it were, a festoon which answers to the rhythm of the respiration. This influence, clearly seen in the normal curve A, is lacking in the curve B owing to the superficial character of the breathing. This is an important fact, as it shows us that the air has a depressing effect when it contains less oxygen. The reduction of the oxygen in the air we breathe by one-half has therefore not the effect of increasing the activity of the respiratory centre, on the contrary this centre shows a diminished activity in rarefied air.

The upper curve of Fig. 60 has towards the middle a cerebral pulsation which suddenly sinks while the pulsations following gradually return to the original height. This was caused by a movement of deglutition on the part of the subject, as is provoked in all of us by the saliva, otherwise the pulsations are about equal. During the respiration of the artificial air we see that four times a sort of wave is formed in which the pulsations become greater. The lower profile of the curve B in Fig. 60 sinks and forms a festoon. These variations are apparently due to a change in the tonicity of the blood-vessels. In Fig. 27 we have already seen that the blood-vessels on the summit of Monte Rosa were more unstable than in the plain: in the present case we have a repetition of the same phenomenon in the blood-vessels of the brain. The heart has become weaker and the pulsations of

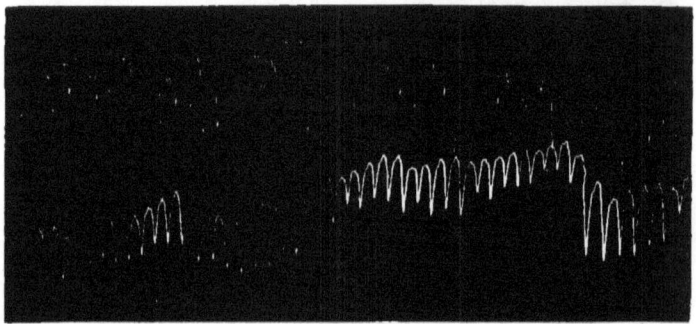

FIG. 61.—Continuation of the experiment on Favre. C. Brain-pulse immediately after the subject ceased to breathe the artificial air. D. Curve registered two minutes later.

the brain are lower during the respiration of the artificial air. The indications of a paralysis of the vessels of the brain such as was observed in Lasagno at a barometric depression little different are, however, lacking.

Fig. 61 shows the cerebral pulse-curve in Favre immediately after the mask had been taken off his face at a sign he had given us to leave off. The respiration has become deep, and in the twelve inspiratory movements executed during the tracing of the upper curve we see that the volume of the brain diminishes at every inspiration, and increases in the expiration following. After about a minute the breathing has become normal again, the influence of respiration on the pulsations of the brain disappears, and this organ, as may be seen in the second curve of Fig. 61, rapidly augments in volume.

The greater height of the cerebral pulsations observable in this curve shows that, during the action of the artificial air, there had been a disturbance in the nutrition of the brain.

The more forcible pulsations, which we feel in a finger, for instance, on which we have received a blow, are due to the more active irrigation which is immediately set up in any part of the body which has been injured. A similar phenomenon is here observable in the brain, in which the hunger for oxygen, the inanition caused by its subjection to the influence of artificial air, calls for compensation.

In both these persons the heart beat more rapidly when they were placed in conditions similar to those which give rise to mountain-sickness. As this increased activity was accompanied by a slackening of the respiratory movements it must probably be attributed to a paralysis of the vagus nerve, because, when we feel well, if the heart begins to beat more rapidly, the breathing undergoes a corresponding acceleration, whereas here the rate abated.

If we examine the curves registered at the moment in which these two persons complained of feeling unwell, none who have had practice in similar studies of the circulation in the brain would venture to affirm that the changes observed in the cerebral pulse are the cause of the indisposition. Our conclusion is, therefore, that the characteristic modifications observed in the sensibility, intelligence and capacity for movement in those who have performed ascents in balloons or up mountains, cannot be explained by the hypothesis of cerebral anæmia or congestion. The blood circulates in a sufficient quantity through the brain and in a manner little differing from the normal as far as an altitude of 5,520 metres.

Matterhorn.   Dent Blanche.

[*V. Sella.*

Panoramic view taken from the Regina Margherita Hut.

CHAPTER XIX

SLEEPINESS DURING ASCENTS—EXPERIMENTS ON MONKEYS AND MARMOTS

I.

"I SLEPT as I walked in spite of the efforts I made to keep myself awake; one of the two guides experienced the same effect."[1] Such was the condition of the physiologist Le Pileur in crossing the plateau to the south of the Breithorn, about 3,600 metres in height. Bravais and Martins were seized by an invincible desire to sleep at an altitude of 3,800 metres on Mont Blanc. Lortet, too, mentions having slept while walking on Mont Blanc. Prof. Forel of Lausanne suffered from sleepiness at an altitude of 3,400 metres on the Col du Géant: when he was within a quarter of an hour's walk from the Col, he had to stop and sleep on the snow in spite of the danger. I might give other instances taken as these are from the writings of physiologists, but the above suffice for our purpose.

Once while descending from Monte Rosa, I met a party coming from Zermatt, at the foot of Dufour Peak. I stopped to talk to the guides and learnt that one gentleman occasioned them great anxiety, owing to his

[1] Le Pileur, *Mémoire sur les phénomènes physiologiques qu'on observe en s'élevant à une certaine hauteur.* Paris, 1845, p. 35.

perpetually sleeping. The case aroused my interest, so I introduced myself to the gentleman, whom I found more annoyed than disheartened. He had a bottle of smelling-salts of which he made frequent use. He told me that during the first few days he always suffered from sleepiness after reaching an altitude of 3,000 metres, but that ammoniac helped to keep him awake. The guides informed me that he walked better near the crevasses and other dangerous places as he then suddenly woke up, but that as soon as the snow was good he began to lag behind, letting himself be pulled on by the rope, to stagger sideways as though drunk, and even to fall without waking up.

Generally speaking, we may say that at great altitudes sleep is less continuous, although it may be just as profound as in the plain. Only rarely did I sleep all through the night without waking, although, of course, it must be borne in mind that in the huts the travellers must sleep together on the benches, and that, in consequence, the movements of one rouse the rest. My brother slept so soundly on Monte Rosa, that even loud noises failed to wake him; once the mattress next to him was changed, while overhead there was, at the same time, a great noise, and yet he did not wake, but shortly afterwards, in spite of the deep sleep he had been in, he suddenly sat up, complaining of shortness of breath. One's sleep is often broken, too, by the snoring of one's companions, which is louder than in the lowlands. Those who lie on their side snore less. When one lies on one's back, the snoring is rougher, as the soft palate and uvula then fall against the posterior part of the pharynx. The relaxation of the muscles produced by sleep, narrows the space by which the air must pass to the nose, thus giving rise to that noisy breathing produced by the vibration of the soft palate, to that prolonged and terrible sound which renders the nights in the Alpine huts lugubrious. Some habitual snorers amongst my companions snored much more loudly in the Regina Margherita Hut than in Gnifetti Hut or in our lower encampments.

Snoring is due to the falling of the tongue, by its own weight, further into the throat. As the arms relax and drop, so also does the tongue, which is a very voluminous muscle, sink into the throat when we fall asleep.

It is usually said that no one notices his own snoring, but this is not the case. I do not snore generally if I lie on my side, but occasionally when resting on my back, and then I often notice the moment when the snoring begins. This happens more especially on summer afternoons when I am overcome by sleep. When tranquilly reclining I gradually lose consciousness, but wake up the moment I hear myself snore, and then become aware that mental pictures have been passing before me which are without the least connection with the former train of thought; that I have, in fact, been sleeping. I have determined the rate of succession of these periods, and have found that scarcely two or three minutes elapse between them. In the plain I have some difficulty in making these observations, whereas in the Alpine huts when I lie down on my back to sleep, I am immediately annoyed by my own snoring. Fatigue certainly helps to produce this diminution of the muscular tone which appears on the cessation of consciousness.

II.

"The god of sleep flees the more rapidly, the more ardently we invoke him. I believe he only touched my lids lightly once or twice."[1]

[1] Re-translated from the Italian.

Thus did Tyndall poetically express himself. Nevertheless, Alpinists are agreed that the night is the most prosaic part of an ascent. In the Alpine refuges, when several parties are lodged together, one sleeps badly. The constant turning and sighing which tell of wakefulness, the snoring, the difficulty of breathing in an atmosphere vitiated by the number of human beings all herded together, leave but a sorry recollection behind.

A bivouac in the open air is preferable, and more poetical. All those who have had to break up the ground with the pick in order to have a softer bed, who have sheltered themselves from the wind in the hollow of a rock and nestled under their warm sheep-skins, or have thrust their heads out of their sleeping-bags to look at the glittering stars or the moon silvering the Alpine peaks, will never forget the emotion which such nights, the happiest of their youth, aroused in them.[1]

Celebrated Alpinists sleep little during ascents. Senator Perazzi told me that he rested well only once on an Alpine expedition, and that was on the Matterhorn, in the old hut now full of ice and snow; in it he had found an india-rubber mattress which had served him as a bed. Tyndall, whose name will ever be connected with the Matterhorn, has given us an account of a night passed in that humble shelter.[2]

"A lover of the mountains and of his kind had contributed an india-rubber mattress, on which I lay down, a light blanket being thrown over me, while the guides and porters were rolled up in sheep-skins. The mattress was a poor defence against the cold of the subjacent rock. I bore this for two hours, unwilling to disturb the guides, but at length it became intolerable. On learning my condition, however, the good fellows were soon alert, and, folding a sheep-skin round me, restored me gradually to a pleasant temperature. I fell asleep, and found the guides preparing breakfast, and the morning well advanced, when I opened my eyes."

Not idle curiosity, but sincerest admiration prompts me to recall these incidents in the expeditions of the pioneers of mountaineering.

Two authors, Durier and Vallot, have already written the story of the Mont Blanc huts. Soon, I hope, some lover of the Alps, inspired by the memories clinging to the huts of Monte Rosa and the Matterhorn, will pen the history of these Alpine shelters now rapidly falling into ruins. A feeling of respect has always filled me on approaching these modest refuges, forsaken amongst the rocks, covered with snow, or full of ice. A poetical, almost religious sentiment, takes possession of one in contemplating these ruins of the first halting-places erected by the conquerors of the Alps. But, unfortunately, there are mountain-climbers of a coarser fibre who look upon these old houses merely as so much combustible material; in these the claims of personal comfort leave no room for Alpine archæology.

It would certainly be a commendable innovation, were it made obligatory by the statute for the enrolment of guides, for every party to carry with them sufficient wood for a bivouac. This precaution is indeed necessary, because in the mountains no one can say how the day may end. When a storm bursts, travellers must remain in the huts, and if the bad weather continues they have no other means of warming themselves than by burning the tables,

---

[1] Some Alpinists have rendered themselves celebrated by their bivouacs. See, for instance, *Bivouacs dans les Alpes françaises.* Paul Guillemin and André Salvator de Quatrefages, Annuaire du Club Alpin Français, 1878. They bivouacked for a month on the Alps on the frontier between Italy and France.

[2] J. Tyndall, *Hours of Exercise in the Alps,* p. 281.

benches, and even the doors. A bundle of wood, with a visiting card to inform the next travellers who was so fortunate as not to need fuel, is the most welcome souvenir which a climber can leave behind for his colleagues. The storing-up of fuel in the huts should be systematically provided for by the sections and by the guides, as one of the most efficacious means for preserving the health and life of mountain-climbers.

III

At the Hôtel Riffelberg, at the altitude of the Col d'Olen, few sleep well the first few nights. My friend Sommier, noted for his anthropological studies and his travels in Lapland, suffered from sleeplessness at a height of only 1,200 metres. When he arrived at Gressoney St. Jean, he was immediately troubled with wakefulness, whereas in Florence he enjoyed very sound sleep.

Zuntz and Lœwy slept badly at the beginning of the ascent of Monte Rosa, and attributed their wakefulness to the barometric depression as, at the Olen Inn, where they stayed, there could be no question of inadequate physical comfort. Other physiologists have met with the same experience.

These observations contrast with those, perhaps still more numerous, of persons who sleep better on the slopes of the Alps than in the lowlands. The notebooks in which for many years I have collected material for an Alpine physiology, are full of remarks transcribed from the visitors' albums, similar to the following, taken from one of the last pages:—

"July, 1895. In Turin I have some difficulty in falling asleep, often lying awake for an hour or two first. At Gressoney la Trinità I fall asleep as soon as I go to bed. The temperature of the room where I sleep is 13° to 15°, in Turin it was between 24° and 27°."

One is at first inclined to think that the cold is conducive to sleep, but then how to explain the fact that in summer almost all of us experience an irresistible desire to sleep in the afternoon? The reply to the query is, I think, that the lighter sleep through the night obliges us to doze more during the day.

A slight degree of warmth or coolness promotes sleep, while extreme heat or cold are alike unfavourable. One of the most distressing nights I have ever spent on the Alps, was on the Roccia Melone. I slept at an altitude of 2,824 metres in the Cà d'Asti, a church situated at a greater height than any other in Europe. Unluckily I had only a light rug and had to lie down on the brick paving. I endeavoured to shield myself from the cold by wrapping newspapers round my body under my clothes, but the coldness of my legs still prevented me from sleeping.

A study of the various methods of protecting one's self from the cold would certainly be valuable, but here I must refrain from entering on the subject. The celebrated mountain-climber, Zsigmondy, private teacher of surgery at the University of Vienna, has left us a description of his bivouacs on Monte Rosa in his book, *Les dangers dans la montagne*.

Once, when he had started from Macugnaga with the object of reaching the summit of Monte Rosa, he was obliged to halt and pass the night at an altitude of 2,900 metres. He took off his shoes and thrust his legs up to the knees into a sealskin bag, which thus served him as a foot-warmer, tied a handkerchief round his hat so as to cover his ears, and felt perfectly comfortable.

Speaking of another bivouac, Zsigmondy writes, "The foot-bag did not seem to me sufficient that evening, so we wrapped the rope round our knees, a very practical innovation. According to our old custom we took off our overcoats so as to make use of them as covers; one is kept warmer in this way than by wearing the coat. The back soon communicates a little heat to the rock, and one is protected on all sides, whereas otherwise the cold immediately strikes one's hands and arms."[1]

IV.

We are more sensitive than dogs and cats to the rarefaction of the air. The greater the development of the nervous system in any animal, the more sensitive is the animal to the action of rarefied air, falling asleep under its influence with greater facility.

Under equal depressions in the pneumatic bell monkeys suffer more than dogs, and dogs more than marmots. Birds suffer less than rabbits, guinea-pigs and mice, while frogs are less sensitive than all. I shall not, however, try the reader's patience with a detailed account of the observations made on all sorts of animals. I merely add that in every species I found individual differences, some members suffering more than others at a relatively slight diminution of pressure.

Why man and monkeys are more liable to fall asleep under diminished barometric pressure I do not know. Perhaps the activity of the brain and the force of attention are greater in them and the conditions of their nervous system more easily altered. Perhaps the equilibrium of nutrition is more unstable in the nerve-cells when the functions of the latter are more complex. Perhaps, when the brain is larger in comparison to the body, the quantity of scoriæ and poisons which are produced and cannot be destroyed or eliminated with sufficent promptitude in rarefied air, is greater. However this may be, we must at present content ourselves with the vague statement that man and the superior animals are more intensely sensitive to barometric depression.

In order to study mountain-sickness during artificial ascents, I bought three monkeys (*Cercopithecus*). I communicate some of the experiments made on these animals so as to establish a clear comparison between the phenomena presented by them and by man in the same conditions. Sometimes we took the monkeys with us into the pneumatic chamber, at other times we placed them under the large glass bell, shown in Fig. 57, and which has a capacity of 60 litres.

MONKEY No. 1.

January 30, 1895.—Barometric pressure from 734 mm. to 320 mm.

A pet monkey which had been bought with the intention of teaching it tricks, and which was so tame that it allowed itself to be carried about on one's arm, was put under the bell at 2.5 p.m. After the lapse of ten minutes the pressure within was only 430 mm. At this degree of rarefaction, which corresponds to the height of Mont Blanc, the monkey was still observant and sometimes played with its tail. It was plain, however, that it was less lively than usual.

When the pressure within was 494 mm. the rate of breathing diminished, the animal only

---

[1] E. Zsigmondy, *Les dangers dans la montagne*, Paris, 1886, p. 101.

drawing 48 breaths per minute, whereas at the ordinary pressure the rate was 60. It now sat motionless, looking absently at the ground.

At the pressure of 420 mm. (corresponding to an altitude of 4,837 metres) the monkey closed its eyes and fell into a doze, breathing 42 times in the minute. From time to time it opened its eyes, but the lids seemed to be heavy. It sat with its hands between its legs and with bent head, in the position natural to it when sleeping. The respiration was rather irregular—sometimes we counted 50, sometimes 40 breaths per minute. By day we had never before seen it sleep. When we tapped on the bell with our knuckles it lifted its head, looked round stupidly and immediately closed its eyes again, while its head began to nod again between its legs.

So as to be sure that the current of air was sufficient for breathing purposes we made use of a gas-meter which measured the quantity of air penetrating into the bell. At the greatest degree of rarefaction 16 litres entered per minute, that is, a ration sufficient not only for a monkey but for a man. We took the same precaution in all subsequent experiments.

At 2.35, seeing that the monkey continued to sleep, while the pressure remained constant at a point corresponding to an altitude of 4,800 metres, we suspended the rarefaction.

I opened a little the tap which gave passage to the air and the pressure began to increase. The manometer had not sunk one centimetre when the monkey awoke, showing signs of restlessness and fright. It turned round with raised arms and then fell down as though seized with convulsions. When it was taken out of the bell, it remained in an agitated but apparently unconscious state; when placed on the ground, it fled, but staggeringly as though drunk.

This same monkey accustomed itself so rapidly to rarefied air that a few days later it only fell asleep at a pressure corresponding to an altitude of 6,470 metres.

V.

The most of those who subject themselves to the rarefaction of the air in pneumatic chambers or to compressed air in caissons, are troubled by violent pain in the ears. This pain is due to the pressure exercised by the external air on the membrane of the tympanum, when there is not a counterpressure at the inner surface, within the middle ear. During storms, such rapid and pronounced changes take place in the barometric pressure that some complain of a noise in the ears. Even during ascents some climbers notice that their hearing is not so good as usual. To overcome this inconvenience one need only close nose and mouth and execute a forcible expiratory movement, or else swallow the saliva, or finally, take a drink.

In monkeys, the air issues easily from the middle ear, when the outer air is rarefied, and for this reason they do not suffer during the artificial ascent. But when the pressure of the air is increased again it would seem that the Eustachian tube is so formed that it does not permit the air to penetrate into the middle ear with equal facility. Hence the pressure on the membrane of the tympanum, which is forced inwards, producing violent pain, dizziness and convulsive attacks.

If the pressure is increased very gradually it will be seen that even in monkeys these serious nervous phenomena do not manifest themselves.

Monkey No. 2.

February 9, 1895.—Barometric pressure from 737 mm. to 337 mm.

9.25 a.m. The monkey is placed under the bell at the usual pressure and performs 62 respiratory movements per minute.

9.35. The rarefaction is begun.

9.38. Pressure, 490 mm. Breathing, 44 per minute.

9.40. Pressure, 337 mm. First 50 rather deeper respirations in the minute, then 46. The monkey keeps its eyes open, it lies curled up and motionless, except for the nodding of its head and frequent yawning.

9.42. It protrudes its muzzle and makes a few efforts to vomit, then vomits.
9.43. The monkey sleeps. The pressure is kept constant at 337 mm. (corresponding to an altitude of 6,476 metres). Breathing 66 per minute. From time to time the animal bends its body so far downwards that it loses its balance, then it erects itself again, as a person does who is dozing.
9.45. It wakes as we knock on the bell with our knuckles, looks up, but without any interest in what it sees. Its face is stupid.
9.47. The monkey no longer lifts its head at the knocking on the glass, nor opens its eyes. Breathing, 68. It has expelled fæces without moving. It lies down, stretching itself on its right side. Only the diaphragm moves, the thorax does not appear to dilate during the breathing. We now turn the tap so as to let in the air and conclude the experiment. At 370 mm. pressure the monkey awakes, at 410 mm. it stands up and has an attack of convulsions, after having twice beaten its head against the wall of the bell in an attempt to escape.
9.58. We offer the animal an apple; it would like to take it, but has not the strength to stand upright.
10.0. The right leg of the animal is paralysed, and drags after it when it moves.
10.4. The monkey has completely recovered and has regained its normal aspect. The breathing is, however, slower than it was before, there being only 36 respirations in the minute.

VI.

The great facility with which monkeys vomit when the pressure of the air is diminished in the pneumatic bell proves that mountain-sickness is not due, as the majority of climbers think, to digestive disorders. I might give a list of maladies in which the sufferer is much troubled with vomiting although the stomach is healthy and empty. All causes which disturb the circulation and the nutrition of the brain may produce vomiting. The cause of nausea and of retching is often to be found in the state of the blood. When, for instance, the kidneys are inflamed and cease to act well, one of the first symptoms which informs the physician that the blood is being poisoned with urea is the vomiting which appears even when the patient is fasting. It is probable that the cause of vomiting in fatigue is also due to a poisoning of the blood, because I have seen vomiting caused by the injection of the blood of a tired dog into a dog in a normal condition.

Vomiting is a characteristic symptom of *angina pectoris*. When, during an attack, the pulse becomes rapid and weak and the patient grows pale and feels an oppression on the chest as in mountain-sickness, vomiting almost invariably follows.

The reason of this similarity of phenomena must be sought close at hand, in the connection between the centres of breathing, of vomiting, of the vaso-motor and cardiac nerves in the medulla oblongata. If we feel the pulse of a person who has taken an emetic we notice that the rate alters from time to time, becoming more rapid whenever vomiting begins. We observed similar variations in the pulse at Regina Margherita Hut, even when vomiting was not the first sign of the action of barometric depression. It is probable, therefore, that these are the causes which give rise to vomiting in mountain-sickness. One of these causes is central: the depression of the nervous centres; the other is peripheric: the incipient paralysis of the nerves of the stomach. Dogs, cats, marmots and especially monkeys vomit whenever they are placed in rarefied air under the pneumatic bell. The cause of vomiting in these cases, as in mountain-sickness, I hold to be the paralysis of the vagus. If this nerve is severed a persistent vomiting is produced.

Monkey No. 3.

January 28, 1895.—Barometric pressure from 733 mm. to 330 mm.

A male monkey, put under the bell at 2.58 p.m., breathes from 56 to 60 times in the minute.

3.4. The rarefaction of the air is begun.

3.15. Pressure 370 mm. (=altitude of 5,732 metres). The monkey is well, licks the grease on the rim of the bell. It breathes 36 times per minute.

3.20. Pressure 330 mm. (=altitude 6,643 metres). The animal does not sleep, and stands less steadily on its legs. It protrudes its muzzle as though about to vomit. The red tint of the lips is not altered, the bluish colour characteristic of mountain-sickness, often observable also in monkeys, has not appeared. The animal breathes 40 times in a minute.

3.25. Retching and vomiting. The monkey immediately eats what it has thrown up. It is unsteady on its legs and falls at a second attack of vomiting.

We did not succeed in sending this monkey to sleep, even though the pressure was diminished as much as possible. It became motionless and apathetic. There are amongst monkeys as amongst men great individual differences, which are rendered apparent by the experiments here communicated.

In monkeys, too, we noticed that the barometric depression caused an acceleration of the pulse and a diminution in the rate of the respiratory movements.

In ascents, when the difficulty of breathing becomes such that one is obliged to keep one's mouth open, the dryness of the throat gives a sense of burning heat and a feeling of discomfort which may provoke nausea and vomiting. For this reason we must endeavour during ascents to keep the mouth moist, when, owing to fatigue, the secretion of saliva begins to decrease. The fear that a morsel of snow or a piece of ice put into the mouth may prove injurious, is exaggerated. We, at least, my companions and I, experienced no ill effects from it, and I consider this remedy preferable to that of drinking alcoholic liquor whenever one feels one's mouth dry.

VII.

Having observed that rarefied air produces sleep, it remained to be ascertained whether narcotics act more intensely when the barometric pressure is diminished. A small dose of morphia, for instance, otherwise insufficient to cause sleep, produces it when the air is rarefied.

This is shown by the following experiment.

Effect of Morphia on a Monkey.

April 2, 1895.—Barometric pressure from 733 mm. to 340 mm.

At 2.0 p.m. the monkey is placed under the bell. It breathes 33 times in the minute.

2.10. Pressure 340 mm. (=5,232 metres altitude). The monkey cowers down, breathing 34 times in the minute. From time to time it protrudes its muzzle as though from a feeling of nausea and then begins to retch.

2.12. The animal still takes an interest in what is going on around it, but it looks cast down and half closes its eyes now and then. It sits huddled together, its head between its knees, breathing 30 times in the minute. The trunk oscillates while it sleeps; from time to time there is a slight movement of the ears.

2.16. The pupil of the eye seems smaller than before. The monkey has not yet moved from its position. From time to time its sleep becomes sounder and its head drops lower between its knees.

April 3, 1895.—*Barometric pressure from* 734 *mm. to* 339 *mm.*

2.15 p.m. The monkey is put under the bell after an injection of 5 milligr. of morphia has been made under the skin of the thigh.

2.25. Inside pressure 339 mm. (=alt., 5,171 metres). The animal begins to protrude the muzzle from nausea, yawns and appears more dejected than on the day before.

2.37. The monkey breathes 36 times in the minute and begins to retch. It half closes its eyes at intervals.

2.45. It sleeps soundly. Breathing, 26. It vomits and has a suffering look. It falls over on to its side. To judge by its face the animal would seem to be dying. It does not open its eyes nor move at any noise we make in knocking on the bell.

2.56. The tap is turned to let in the air but so that the normal pressure is slowly re-established. The serious lethargy ceases. When taken out of the bell and placed on the ground, the monkey walks at first unsteadily, but recovers shortly afterwards.

It is thus proved that a small dose of morphia, otherwise insufficient to produce sleep, becomes the cause of serious phenomena when acting under reduced atmospheric pressure. If the effects of morphia are heightened by rarefied air and *vice versâ*, it is a sign that the action of both is identical.

VIII

Why is mountain-sickness more alarming at night-time? Tschudi, Pöppig, and many others who have travelled in the most elevated regions of the earth, have already noticed this fact, and there are few mountain-climbers, I think, who have not been sometimes roused by a feeling of indisposition when passing the night at great altitudes.

Lœwy[1] says that during sleep the respiratory movements become irregular, and that the ventilation of the lungs being less active, the diminution of the tension of oxygen in the pulmonary alveoli is a sufficient explanation of the indisposition which breaks out at night on the mountains. The observations which I made on Monte Rosa on respiration and the tracings reproduced in the third chapter demonstrated so profound and unusual an alteration of the respiratory movements by night on the mountains that we can no longer recur to the inadequate ventilation of the lungs to explain the sense of oppression and difficulty in breathing, because the change of the breathing is the effect and not the cause of the phenomena which we here wish to study.

There is a similarity between the preceding experiment in which morphia was injected and the phenomena arising from rarefied air thus aggravated, and the origin of sleep. These experiments[2] made it clear to me that the lesser activity of the nerve-centres, caused every day by sleep, acts in the same way as the depression which rarefied air produces in the vitality of the nerve-centres, so that our condition is aggravated by the acting of these two factors in the same direction.

If mountain-sickness were due to the lack of oxygen one ought to feel better when one sleeps soundly, because during sleep the chemical processes slacken and one needs less oxygen. The contradiction between the old theories and the facts here communicated proves that Paul Bert's theory, according to which mountain-sickness was considered as a simple form of asphyxia or a poisoning due to the carbonic acid of the blood, must be abandoned.[3] My opinion is that there is, on the contrary, a smaller quantity

---

[1] A. Lœwy, *Untersuchungen über die Respiration und Circulation*, p. 20.
[2] See the account of experiments by U. Mosso. *Archives italiennes de Biologie*, tome xxv. p. 242. [3] P. Bert. *Op. cit.*, p. 1044.

of carbonic acid in the blood at great altitudes and that the fundamental cause of mountain-sickness is a diminution in the chemical activity of the brain and of the spinal cord.

Sleep is the commonest and most constant symptom amongst those phenomena which reveal a depression in the vitality of the nerve-centres. Excessive cold, too, produces sleep.

Any one who allows himself to be overcome by sleep on the Alps and lies down to rest on the frozen ground, is lost. One must dread sleep at great altitudes. As soon as the first symptoms appear, we must seek to excite the nervous system by all means in our power, so as to fan the languishing flame of life and rouse the body to activity, so that those stores still remaining for the heating of the organs and the blood may be consumed, the circulation reinforced, the vigour of the heart maintained and the abatement of the energy of the nervous system prevented.

The well-known saw of the older physicians that when nature beckons we must follow her, does not hold good on the Alps. We have then to do with a defect, not with a perfection of our organism. Natural sleep tends to re-establish the exhausted strength of brain and muscles. The sleep which befalls us during storms and on the ice is a morbid phenomenon. If we succeed by an effort of the will in overcoming our reluctance to move and in shaking off our mental sluggishness, drowsiness disappears and we feel better, as though the internal heat had melted some obstacle.

In this case cold is the cause of death. Sleep caused by rarefaction of the air may, on the contrary, be considered as beneficial, as we have seen in the case of Tissandier, who, on the descent of the "Zenith," survived because he fell into a lethargy sooner than the others.

Regnault and Reiset, in their celebrated chemical researches on the breathing of animals, observed that a marmot during hibernation lives for a considerable length of time in air deprived of oxygen, whereas, were it awake, this same air would kill it in a few instants.[1]

A not less celebrated experiment is that of Claude Bernard,[2] who, having put a bird under a glass bell, saw that, although it was weakened by the deficiency of oxygen, it was yet able to live in this atmosphere for several hours, whereas the air was already so greatly altered that another bird put into it directly, immediately died of asphyxia.

A similar experiment may easily be performed by putting a dog and a fowl together under a pneumatic bell. If the dog, as often happens, falls asleep, the barometric pressure may be diminished until only one-sixth of an atmosphere remains. Fowls at this pressure of 130 or 120 mm. generally die, whereas the slumbering dog survives. Even ducks, which we should suppose to be the animals opposing the greatest resistance to asphyxia, die before dogs, because they cannot fall asleep in rarefied air. Considerable depressions are reached before they present any serious phenomena, then suddenly they open their bill, shake their head and die, before the experimenter has time to save them by letting in a current of denser air.

Sleep is therefore a means of protection, rendering us more resistant to the action of rarefied air.

[1] Annales de chimie et physique, 1849, p. 515.
[2] Cl. Bernard, *Leçons sur les substances toxiques*, 1857, p. 126.

IX.

In our camp near the Alp Indra we were in the midst of a marmot settlement; and as far as an altitude of 2,800 metres we met with the holes to their burrows. These animals greeted us with shrill whistling sounds from the lonely rocks and from the last grassy levels of the mountains, where no shrubs grow, and to which no goat, no mammal of any kind ventures to climb. The wish immediately took possession of me to study these rodents, whose winter sleep makes them of such importance to Alpine physiology, under a pneumatic bell. I had no difficulty in procuring six living marmots. I shall now briefly relate the experiments made on these animals.

During their deep winter sleep marmots are so insensible that even though a gun is fired close to them, they do not wake, and if they fall to the ground from the height of a metre and a half they do not move nor does the rhythm of their breathing alter. The insensibility of their internal parts is less pronounced, however, and changes of barometric pressure easily rouse them, as Valentin [1] showed in his work on the hibernation of the marmot.

Dubois [2] maintains that the sleep of these animals is caused by an excess of carbonic acid in the blood. He epitomised his theory of the origin of their lethargic sleep in a sentence which well expresses his idea: *autonarcosis due to carbonic acid.*

Were this a correct hypothesis, it ought to be easy to induce sleep and insensibility by causing air mixed with carbonic acid to be breathed. The attempts made in this direction were utterly unsuccessful. For this reason, therefore, I cannot hold Professor Gayet's idea that sleep has a special centre in the brain, to be correct; rather does it seem to me that this idea is contrary to what is as yet known to us respecting the physiology of sleep. It is however inopportune here to open a discussion on a subject which is perhaps the most obscure in the domain of physiology. Some mention of it is necessary as, were the autonarcosis of Dubois an indisputable fact, the origin of the sleep which comes over us on the Alps would be perfectly clear, Bert having observed that arterial blood becomes gradually poorer in oxygen in rarefied air, so that at an altitude of 6,500 metres, it has already lost almost the half of what it contained in the plain, resembling venous blood in its composition more and more the higher one ascends.

Dubois, basing his theory on Valentin's researches, maintained that the waking up of the marmot when placed under the pneumatic bell, is caused by the loss of the excess of carbonic acid in its blood. I repeated these experiments, but took the precaution to effect the depression slowly. I then found that the marmot does not wake even though the barometric depression is very great. When these animals are in their deep winter sleep, they breathe so little that often in a minute they execute only one inspiration, which is so superficial as to be scarcely noticeable. When we put marmots under the pneumatic bell we must take care not to shake them, and to prevent any change taking place in the surrounding temperature. By letting the air-pump act slowly, and allowing of the passage of a faint current of air under the bell so as to ensure a continual renewal of the inside atmosphere, I have succeeded in keeping marmots for two or three hours in air rarefied to the barometric pressure of from 13 to 14 centimetres, that is to one-fifth and one-sixth of the

---

[1] G. Valentin, *Beiträge zur Kenntniss des Winterschlafes der Murmelthiere.* Moleschott's Untersuchungen, i. Bd. p. 211.
[2] B. Dubois, *Physiologie comparée de la Marmotte,* Paris, 1896, p. 253.

ordinary pressure, without their waking. In general, when the atmosphere surrounding them was of 2 or 3 degrees, these animals executed only two respiratory movements in the minute, after having been subjected for two hours to this enormous depression.

The most important fact is, that marmots do not wake so long as they are in rarefied air, but rouse themselves immediately when the rarefaction of the air begins to decrease and the usual barometric pressure is gradually re-established. They then often execute lively movements, and remain restless for a long time. The fact observed in the circulation of the blood in the human brain, namely: that the blood-vessels dilate beyond their normal size when common air is breathed again by a subject who, for a certain time, has been breathing air containing a smaller amount of oxygen, renders apparent a peculiar reaction of the nervous system, and hints at cerebral changes as causing the wakening of marmots when the depressing and paralysing action of the rarefied air ceases.

My experiments convinced me that even when the barometric pressure is reduced to one-fifth it has no effect on the lethargic sleep of marmots. Under a pressure so greatly diminished the venous blood must contain less carbonic acid, as we know that this gas is held in solution by the blood: when the barometric pressure diminishes the blood can only hold a lesser quantity in solution. The theory of autonarcosis cannot therefore serve as an explanation of the lethargy of marmots, nor does it shed any light on the sleepiness felt during ascents.

X.

When awake, marmots are more sensitive than any other animal to the rarefaction of the air. This is one of the most curious observations which I have made, and certainly no one would have suspected that marmots, which in summer live higher up than any other mammals, and which in winter offer such resistance both to cold and asphyxia, feel the effects of barometric depressions so slight that they remain without the least influence on man and on other animals. Let us first consider the facts and then seek to build up a hypothesis.

EXPERIMENT ON A MARMOT.

May, 1896—Pressure, 741 mm. Temperature of the air, 18°.

A tame marmot weighing 3,400 grams, which allows itself to be carried on one's arm, and manifests its delight when we enter its cage by clambering up our legs, is put under the pneumatic bell at 7.40 a.m. It makes a resting-place for itself with towels which we had put under the bell. By means of the pump a weak current of air is kept up by which 6 litres are introduced into the bell per minute. The breathing, which at first was very rapid, begins to slacken. The following numbers, written almost without interruption every minute, show how great was the influence of emotion, and likewise the effect of attention on this animal. As soon as it was put under the bell the marmot had walked round, standing erect on its hind legs, and had then lain down, when we began to count the breathing: 66, 64, 60, 54, 56, 54, 55, 54, 45, 30, 28, 20, 18, 18, 18, 24, 24.

At 8.30 the marmot had already taken up a sleeping position, curling itself up with its head between its legs. Breathing: 22, 20, 20, 18, 18.

The animal wakes, lifts its head, and then returns to its usual sleeping position. Breathing: 21, 15, 18, 20, 18, 16, 15, 16, 16, 15, 17, 17.

It wakes again. Breathing: 20, 17, 17, 16, 15, 15.

At 9.0 we begin to rarefy the air, the barometer in the bell which till then had marked 30 mm. less than the external pressure, which was 741 mm., rises 180 mm. The inside pressure has therefore sunk from 711 to 531 mm. (= to a difference in altitude of 2,324 metres).

This pressure had been reached in two minutes, and was then maintained. The rate of breathing increased slightly: 18, 21, 18, 19, 18, 19, 19, 20, 17, 19, 17, 18, 17.

The animal moves, raises its head, and then falls asleep again. Breathing: 20, 19, 18, 19, 18, 19, 20, 19, 20, 20.

9.44. Seeing that the animal continues to sleep, we re-establish the former pressure of 711 mm. Breathing: 17, 16, 16, 16, 16, 15, 15, 16, 17, 15, 13. The marmot wakes, and then curls itself up again. Breathing: 14, 15, 13, 14, 16, 16, 15, 15, 14, 13.

The slackening of the breathing is evident.

10.15. The air is again rarefied. In two minutes a pressure of 531 mm. is established. Breathing: 18, 18, 17, 17, 17, 17, 17, 18, 17, 17, 17, 18, 17, 18, 19, 17, 16, 17, 17, 17, 18, 18, 19, 20, 19, 18, 18. This time, too, the rarefaction of the air (= altitude 2,324 metres) produced an augmentation in the rate of breathing.

At 10.50 the pressure of 711 mm. is slowly re-established, and the breathing slackens: 17, 17, 16, 15, 16, 15, 15, 14, 14, 14, 14, 13, 12, 13, 14, 13, 12, 13, 14, 13, 12, 12. When the bell was lifted up the marmot remained curled up and motionless, unaware that it was released.

This marmot breathed more rapidly during sleep in a rarefaction of the air corresponding to the altitude of 2,324 metres.

The average number of breaths drawn per minute at 8.30 was ... ... 17·9
At a pressure of 531 mm. the average number of breaths drawn per minute was ... 18·8
The usual pressure being re-established   „   „   „   „   15·9
The pressure of 531 mm.   „   „   „   „   „   16·6
The usual pressure   „   „   „   „   „   14·9

As the marmot slept the breathing continued to become calmer and slower; nevertheless, in this animal as in other marmots the acceleration and reinforcement of the breathing appeared as a constant phenomenon at inconsiderable changes of barometric pressure below the limit of 41 centimetres, established by Fraenkel and Geppert as that at which the alteration of the blood begins.

There is, therefore, something else which modifies the conditions of the breathing besides the hæmoglobin of the blood, or else there are changes in the blood which we have not yet discovered, and which act when the barometric pressure is diminished.

Nothing takes place in nature which has not its *raison d'être*. It is my opinion, therefore, that the greater susceptibility of the marmot to barometric depression must be a consequence of the special functions of its nervous system. The partial suspension of life during the winter months, the diminution of the activity of the nervous system when the external temperature sinks, must be due to the absence in these animals of those regulating forces which we possess, and which serve to reinvigorate the chemical processes of the organism when surrounding conditions are changed. Perhaps this difference may put us on the track of other characteristic differences in their nervous system, of which the functions must be in close connection with the variations which take place in the outside air, as we see in this case. The lethargic sleep of marmots may perhaps find its explanation in the diminished resistance which their nervous system opposes to the surrounding air, and in the lack of a regulating mechanism which, in superior animals, renders the vital phenomena constant.

De Saussure's camp at the Col du Géant (alt., 3,365 metres). Reproduced from a drawing executed by De Saussure's son in 1788.

CHAPTER XX

THE ACTION OF LIGHT—PERSPIRATION—COLD

I.

THE light on the Alps is different from the light in the lowlands, because in travelling to our earth it passes through a smaller stratum of air and loses less of its intensity. That the air, notwithstanding its transparency, absorbs luminous rays, is shown by the splendid colours of dawn and of sunset and by the seemingly deeper blue of the sky.

"Further, we find that the blue light of the sky is *reflected* light; and there must be something in the atmosphere capable of producing this reflection . . . when the solar beams have traversed a great length of air, as in the morning or the evening, they are yellow, or orange, or even blood-red, according to the state of the atmosphere. . . ."[1]

"The 'rose of dawn' is usually ascribed, and with sufficient correctness, to transmitted light, the blue of the sky to reflected light; but in each case there is both transmission and reflection."[2]

[1] J. Tyndall, *Glaciers of the Alps*, London, 1860, p. 258.
[2] Idem, *Hours of Exercise on the Alps*, London, 1871, p. 297.

"What mainly holds the light in our atmosphere after the sun has retired behind the earth is, I imagine, the suspended matter which produces the blue of the sky and the morning and evening red."[1]

Our skin is more susceptible to the action of light towards the end of winter, when one has become unaccustomed to the more vivid rays of the sun. I noticed this when I climbed partly up Monte Rosa in the spring of 1894, in order to select suitable places for our camps. I scarcely reached an altitude of 2,600 metres, and yet my neck and the backs of my hands were so sunburnt as never before, even in summer when I had stayed in Gressoney, from which place I had visited the same localities.

This phenomenon is observable in plants also. Those who have some knowledge of hot-house culture will remember that plants must be gradually accustomed to light. The leaves of begonias, for instance, turn yellow at the edges and then dry up if the full light of the sun is suffered to strike them in the first days of spring. The leaves of amaranths curl up and other plants wither. If, instead of this, they are gradually inured to the light, they may afterwards be set outside and exposed to the scorching rays of the sun without suffering in any way. In these phenomena, not heat, but light plays the most prominent part.

On Monte Rosa, at the Riffelberg, a French physicist, M. Cornu,[2] showed that the violet rays in the sun's light are there more abundant. Investigations on this subject have also been made on the mountains of America. Photographs of the spectrum are visibly different when taken on the Alps from what they are in the plain.

Our eye is not sensitive enough to perceive that the light on the Alps is richer in violet rays, but what the eye does not see, the skin feels and informs us by its inflammation that there has been an intense action of the violet rays on the tissues beneath the epidermis.

Tyndall says that no sunlight on the Alps ever scorched him so intensely as the electric light while he was working at the lighthouse of the North Foreland. Widmark[3] of Stockholm was, however, the first to prove that only the violet rays produce the inflammation of the skin and of the eyes.

Dr Ogneff[4] has recently studied eye and skin diseases, which were already known on the Alps, in a large metallurgic factory in Russia, where iron is melted by means of electric currents. One of Widmark's most striking experiments was that showing that the electric light no longer exercises an inflammatory action on the skin when it passes through glass or a thin stratum of water which holds a little alum in solution.

The aqueous vapour contained in the atmosphere does not alone suffice to withhold the ultra-violet rays. This explains the well-known fact that the skin may become sunburnt even when the sky is cloudy or we are enveloped in mist. This cutaneous affection experienced at first by almost all mountain climbers is called by the Germans *kalte Verbrennung* (cold sunburn) in order to indicate that it is not an inflammation caused by heat. The redness of

---

[1] J. Tyndall, *Hours of Exercise on the Alps*, London, 1871, p. 298.
[2] Cornu, *Observation de la limite ultra-violette du spectre solaire à diverses altitudes*. Comptes rendus. Tome lxxxix. p. 808. *Sur l'absorption par l'atmosphère des radiations ultra-violettes*. Tome lxxxviii. p. 1285. *Sur la substance absorbante dans l'atmosphère les radiations solaires ultra-violettes*. Tome xc. p. 940.
[3] Widmark, *Skandinavisches Archiv für Physiologie*, vol. i. p. 264 ; vol. iv. p. 281.
[4] J. Ogneff, *Einige Bemerkungen über die Wirkung des elektrischen Bogenlichtes auf die Gewebe des Auges*. Archiv f. d. gesam. Physiologie, 1896, vol. lxiii. p. 209.

the skin produced by heat lasts a much shorter time than the inflammation due to light.

Amongst the more recent publications of dermatologists on solar erythema the monographs of Hammer[1] and Bowles[2] must be mentioned. Bowles made some experiments on the effect of the sun's rays on the skin on the Gornergrat, at the foot of Monte Rosa. Having dyed his face brown (he does not say, however, with what substance), he observed that in about 100 persons who were at the Riffelalp he was the only one who did not suffer from the action of the light.

During our expedition up Monte Rosa I made a methodical series of observations in order to determine which colour most effectually protects the skin, and whether vaseline and grease are of any use in this respect. I took with me turmeric, red ochre, blacklead, and soot. So as to ascertain the effects with still greater accuracy, I sometimes dyed one-half of the face of one colour and the other half of another colour, or else the nose with one colour and the cheeks with another. Generally, however, the whole of the face and the backs of the hands were dyed with the same substance. I need not go into the particulars of these experiments, which certainly kept us in a cheerful mood and proved a great source of merriment to the mountaineering parties with whom we came into contact. I found that the blackening of the face with a burnt cork is a sufficient protection against inflammation of the skin, in fact, this thin layer of soot is so efficacious that a single trial will recommend it. Mr. Vallot and other mountaineers in Chamonix have this year tested my method and found it very useful.

It cannot be said that grease is quite useless, since it prevents too rapid an evaporation at the surface of the skin, but it does not shield the skin from the irritating action of the violet rays. Vaseline, lanoline, and cold cream did not prove efficacious.

II.

The light reflected by the snow is the origin of various diseases of the eye which were first studied towards the end of the last century. In 1793 the revolutionary government of France, after sending king and queen to the scaffold, solicited an alliance with Piedmont. In that year the Piedmontese soldiers, who were obliged to cross Mont Cenis and the St. Bernard several times during the winter, suffered greatly from ocular affections. This is the first instance on record of hundreds of persons being attacked in this way at the same time.

Numerous works have been issued on this subject[3] on which I shall therefore not enlarge, only adding a few words on observations personally made.

Once when I was at the Col du Théodule I met a mountain-climber, a veritable Tartarin, who, although he had never before been on a glacier, set off, in the face of the guides' protests, without glasses, to perform the ascent of the Breithorn. This despised precaution, even on so short an excursion, had its not undeserved consequences. In the evening when our mountaineer returned, and we sat down together to supper with the hostess, Signora

---

[1] Hammer, *Einfluss des Lichtes auf die Haut*, Stuttgart, 1891.
[2] B. Bowles, *Ueber den Einfluss der Sonnenstrahlen auf die Haut*. Monatshefte für praktische Dermatologie, N. 1, xviii.
[3] J. W. Hoffman, *Ueber die Schneeblindheit*, Mittheil. deutsch. u. Oester. Alpenvereine, N. 6, 1886, p. 64.

Pesson, no evil effects were as yet noticeable; but in the morning when the gentleman woke, his eyelids were so swollen that he could not open them. This is sufficient proof that the somewhat similar incident related by Dr. Paccard is no exaggeration. On coming down from the summit of Mont Blanc after his first ascent with Balmat, Dr. Paccard's eyes were much fatigued by the glaring light. In the morning he remarked to his companion on waking—

"How strange! The birds are singing before sunrise!"

"No, it is your eyes that are swollen," Balmat informed him.

I had to treat a case of this kind in the Regina Margherita Hut. A workman left Gressoney in order to repair the balcony which runs round the hut. I had seen him in perfect health when he halted at Gnifetti Hut. Three days later I found him lying in Regina Margherita Hut in such a condition that he did not venture to descend, so great was the suffering which even a feeble light caused him. He had crossed the glaciers without glasses, and the day afterwards his eyelids were swollen, and he began to feel sharp pains in his eyes and to see everything as through a mist.

The swelling of the eyelids is certainly very distressing, but much less serious than the alterations which may take place in the retina. Professor Schiess,[1] of Bâle, relates that the Italian workmen who cross Mont St. Gothard on foot when they go to Switzerland at the beginning of the spring, are often attacked by this ophthalmia, especially when the wind is blowing from the north. He had several cases of the kind in his hospital, some of the sufferers being almost blind.

There are other affections of the eyes which grow worse towards evening, but the alteration of the retina, due to fatigue caused by the too vivid light, of which we are speaking, is favourably influenced by twilight. A less intense light renders the sight clearer.

Loeb[2] says that the feeling of fatigue is diminished if one takes off one's glasses on the glaciers. It may be that this acts as a momentary stimulus, like cold air which makes us feel better for a while. I should not, however, advise any one to keep the glasses off, as fatigue is thus certainly increased and much harm done to the eyes.

One of the many mountain-climbers whom I interrogated on the subject of mountain-sickness, told me that he attributed it to the too intense light of the glaciers. He supported this by telling me that as a rule he did not suffer from mountain-sickness, but had been attacked by it once, after he had broken his spectacles. This man was of a nervous temperament, to whom any strong light was so annoying that in the evening, when walking through the city, he endeavoured to avoid passing chemists' shops from the windows of which those vases full of coloured liquid illuminate the street by means of a reflector placed behind them.

Siemens noticed, too, that some of his workmen suffered from nausea and vomiting when working by very vivid electric light.

III.

The lungs and skin are subject to a continual evaporation which prevents the blood from growing too hot. When, in summer, we have water sprinkled

---

[1] Schiess, *Archiv für Ophtalmologie*, vol. xxv.
[2] Quincke, *Ueber den Einfluss des Lichtes auf den Thierkörper.* Pflüger's Archiv. Tome lvii. p. 100.

over the floors of our rooms to cool the air, few think that there is a similar arrangement for the cooling of our body. The chemical function of perspiration may be left almost disregarded, because the substances eliminated are in minimum quantities only. The water perspired has the office of providing for the cooling of the body by evaporation. When dogs bask in the sun or are hot they immediately begin to breathe with greater rapidity; we do the

FIG. 62.—Roman balance made use of on the Monte Rosa expedition.

same, although in a lesser degree, when the temperature of our body rises, because the evaporation thus set up in the lungs helps to cool us.

The panting which seizes us during ascents, when muscular work has increased the temperature of the body, is therefore a means of defence, one of the many automatic mechanisms which we have in our body, which act unknown to us and sometimes even against our will, in order to maintain an equilibrium within the organism.

On my expedition up Monte Rosa I had taken with me a Roman balance with a weighing capacity of 100 kilograms, and which instead of the scale had a seat of wood on which a man might conveniently place himself. This balance was susceptible of a difference in weight of four grams.

At half an atmosphere, all other conditions being the same, a double quantity of water should evaporate, because, according to Dalton's law, the quantity of liquid evaporating from a given surface in a unity of time stands in inverse proportion to the atmospheric pressure. Besides the diminution of the pressure the air on the mountains is drier, and for this reason, too, the quantity of water evaporating in a unity of time ought also to be greater on highlands than in lowlands.

The free end of the graduated beam of the balance bore an index in front of which there was a scale marked on a piece of paper. When a subject had seated himself on the wooden board we waited till the beam of the scale had become horizontal (its index then corresponding to the sign A), then noted the time at which this equilibrium was established. As the weight of our body diminishes on the average by 60 grams every hour, a weight of 10 grams had, after a certain time, to be placed on the subject's shoulders so as to bring the index back to A. We may say that on the average ten minutes elapsed before the additional weight was rendered necessary, that is to say that the weight of the body in a person of medium height and weight decreased, in Turin, by about one gram per minute. Another method which we adopted was to weigh accurately some person and then, the time having been noted, to repeat the weighing with the same exactness one or two hours later, in order to ascertain what loss of weight had been sustained during this time through perspiration.

I need not communicate all the results obtained in these weighing experiments; it is sufficient to say that in general there is a less active perspiration on the Alps. Many explanations may be given of this unexpected fact, but unfortunately my experiments were not sufficiently numerous to justify positive statements. It is probable that the blood-vessels of the skin are less dilated and that the cutaneous circulation and secretion of perspiration are therefore less active. The diminished vigour of the circulation and respiration cause a diminution of pulmonary and cutaneous perspiration. All these circumstances together form perhaps a sufficient explanation of the fact that, in some cases, we found the loss of weight within a given time diminished by half on the Alps, at an altitude of 4,560 metres, whereas one would have expected to find it doubled.

The difference in the temperature of the air was small and could not, in my opinion, give rise to the phenomenon. The cause of the difference lies possibly in a flagging of the chemical processes. Man gives off on an average one gram of carbonic acid every two minutes. If the organic combustion diminishes, this loss (which is measured by means of the Roman balance together with the evaporated water) ought to become manifest. The observations of my brother, which show that there is little variation in the quantity of carbonic acid eliminated every half-hour in Turin and in Regina Margherita Hut, make against this hypothesis.

One advantage resulting from the above observations was that they made me acquainted with the influence which the Alpine climate exercised on the weight of the various members of our party. In the following table I give the average weights as determined in Turin before the start and in Gressoney before we separated after the descent from the summit. Competent authorities will know how great are the differences between one day and another in weighings of this kind, in spite of all the precautions taken, so that a long series of observations, longer than I was able to perform, is necessary to ensure absolute accuracy. Nevertheless, we see clearly that some members of our party lost weight during the sojourn on Monte Rosa, these being Ramella, who had had an inflammation of the lungs, Oberhoffer, Marta, Sarteur, Solferino and myself, whereas others grew heavier, Beno Bizzozero gained 4 kilograms, Corporal Camozzi 1,200 grams, Corporal Jachini 1,170 grams.

WEIGHT OF SOME OF THE MEMBERS OF THE MONTE ROSA EXPEDITION.

	Before.	After.
Camozzi	65,600 gr.	66,800 gr.
Oberhoffer	58,300 ,,	57,100 ,,
Marta	71,200 ,,	71,100 ,,
Sarteur	64,820 ,,	63,800 ,,
Solferino	64,100 ,,	63,800 ,,
Jachini	73,560 ,,	74,730 ,,
Chamois	62,680 ,,	62,600 ,,
Cento	69,120 ,,	69,600 ,,
Beno Bizzozero	56,340 ,,	60,500 ,,
Ramella	62,920 ,,	60,800 ,,
A. Mosso	74,500 ,,	73,400 ,,

IV.

A cyclist examined by Tissié in the Velodrome at Bordeaux covered 620 kilometres in twenty-four hours. Taking duly into account the liquids imbibed (amongst which were two litres and a half of milk) and the losses of liquid incurred, it appeared that his body had lost 7·710 kilograms in weight. As his weight had first been 70 kilograms his body was lighter after the race by one-tenth.

These figures will give the reader an idea of the considerable losses which we are continually incurring, and which in medical phraseology are said to be due to *insensible perspiration*. Certainly such a diminution of weight as that in the cyclist studied by Tissié and which, in lesser degrees, may be found in all of us when we perform an ascent, is in part due to the elimination of carbonic acid through the breathing. I regret not having been able to make experiments on the loss of weight during ascents. It was my intention to do so, but the bad weather forced me to give up the project.

Some may say that the balance is unnecessary for investigations of this kind, as we have a special and very delicate sense, *thirst*, which warns us when the water in the organism is diminishing. It would thus apparently suffice to observe carefully whether we are much tormented by thirst on the Alps in order to resolve the question. The matter is, however, much more complicated than it appears. When performing an ascent we sometimes breathe with our mouths open, and this alone provokes great thirst, as we have all experienced, when, in consequence of a cold in the head, we have had to breathe through the mouth. The dryness of the throat excites a sensation identical with that of thirst, even when the body contains sufficient water. During fatigue and owing to the influence of the rarefied air the secretion of saliva diminishes. This is another serious complication which would mislead us were we to place exclusive reliance on so indefinite a sensation as thirst in pursuing a study of this kind.

Professor Oertel, in comparing the various methods adopted in medicine to effect a diminution of the weight of the body, showed that mountain-climbing causes the more rapid loss of a greater quantity of water.[1]

In conclusion I may say that at altitudes above 3,000 metres on Monte Rosa I did not notice that thirst was more intense owing to a more rapid evaporation of water. The regimen followed by myself and my companions, whom I had begged to assist me in this matter by attentive observation, enables me, even in the absence of more exact data, to pronounce an opinion with sufficient confidence. The amount of wine and coffee distributed, the quantity of snow which we had to melt every day at Gnifetti and Regina Margherita Huts always remained the same, and no one ever complained of thirst.

V.

Saussure says that we feel the heat of the sun much more on the Alps than in the lowlands, and adds that it was the heat, not the cold, which made the first mountaineers who attempted the ascent of Mont Blanc turn back. I incline to the belief that there is some exaggeration in this statement. Let us, however, consider the facts as the celebrated Genevan physicist has himself related them. Saussure, M. Bourrit, and the son of the latter were at the foot of Mont Blanc at an altitude of about 3,700 metres. Saussure had one parasol and M. Bourrit another, and neither could stand in the sunlight without this protection on account of the great heat.[2]

"I tried to do without it while adjusting the barometer, but could not; I was forced to take it up again and M. Bourrit was obliged to keep close to his father in order to benefit by the shade of his. And yet these rays which our bodies could not bear, only exercised an effect on the bulb of the thermometer equal to $2\frac{1}{5}$ degrees, this instrument marking $2·5°$ in the shade and $4·7°$ in the sun."

It is a certain fact that the rays of the sun are more powerful on high mountains and that the thermic radiation is there more intense. But the higher we go the colder does it become and the air does not conduct the heat so well.

On our expedition I took a large parasol with me to shield us from the light when we had to work in the open air. We made use of it several times in the midst of snow, at altitudes corresponding to those at which Saussure made his observations, but we were never so distressed by the solar light as one would have expected, judging from Saussure's remarks. Not even my brother, who worked with the ergograph in the sun at the foot of the arches supporting Gnifetti Hut, ever complained of not being able to bear the heat; in fact none of our party suffered from heat while the temperature was so low. We must, therefore, conclude that Saussure and his companions were more sensitive than we were, or that their skin was already inflamed, or else, finally, that in those localities where their observations were made there were special conditions which were absent in our own case.

Saussure says that the thermometer marked in the shade $2·5°$, and that in the sun, where the suffocating heat was unbearable, it marked only $4·7°$. To

---

[1] *Op. cit.*, p. 103. [2] Saussure, *Voyages dans les Alpes*, tome iv. p. 437.

this observation I must make the objection that the thermometer used was not blackened, and that for this reason it absorbed only a small part of the solar radiation so painful in its effects on the skin. It is a known fact that a bright mercurial bulb reflects a great part of the heat which comes from the sun and by no means marks the whole quantity received.[1]

During our sojourn at Regina Margherita Hut we often observed an iridescence of the clouds. One evening while we were standing with our backs to the setting sun, we saw two great halos in the sky which formed two perfect concentric circles coloured like the rainbow. The sky before us was slightly cloudy. Another time when the sky was clear we saw the shadow of Monte Rosa plainly projected upon it. It was on August 14th, at the hour of sunset. A dark triangle began slowly to rise in the heavens. The basis of this dusky shadow stretched beyond the extremity of Lago Maggiore towards Sesto Calende at the right and the Lago di Varese to the left. It looked like the representation of a solitary and conical mountain such as Japanese drawings have made us familiar with. From the vertex of the cone two dark streaks branched off in a direction to the right, similar to the rays of the sun when it sets behind clouds. The triangular shadow of Monte Rosa rose slowly and reached its maximum intensity shortly before the sun sank below the horizon. The illusion was such that for a few instants it appeared to be not a shadow, but a reality. It vanished as the sun dropped out of sight.

VI.

When we are cold our vessels contract, the quantity of blood in the skin and superficial parts of our body being thus diminished. The nervous apparatus regulating the circulation closes, so to say, the flood-gates in the direction of the surface of the body, to prevent the too rapid cooling of the blood which is thus accumulated in the organs in the deeper parts of the body. This is an advantage, but one which has a drawback nevertheless. If the cold continue, the surface of the body may be injured by this diminution of the circulatory movement.

Resistance to cold varies in different individuals. This fact forces itself on our notice when we shake hands with a number of persons who have been for several hours together under the same conditions. The temperature of the hands we touch varies greatly. In general our hands are colder than usual in the morning and only begin to grow warm in the afternoon.

Assisted by Dr. Colombo I made a series of researches on the manner in which the blood circulates in the hands and feet. The differences which we found between individuals were very striking. In some, cold caused such a contraction of the blood-vessels as to impede the circulation. We may easily notice this if we observe the colour of the hands in a number of persons subjected to the same degree of cold. In some the skin assumes a livid hue.

---

[1] For the measurement of the atmospheric temperature I used a thermometer, not blackened, but kept in the shade and well shielded from all irradiation. For the meteorological observations made on Monte Rosa I made use of a box of wood fastened on a pole fixed into the ground. This box, which was open at top and bottom, had holes in the side turned towards the north. I made other observations by putting the thermometer within a paper cylinder open at both ends, or by swinging it rapidly round in the manner of a sling by means of a string 10 or 20 centimetres long, fastened through the eye of the thermometer at one end and held in the hand by the other.

This change of colour is due to the less rapid circulation of the blood in the little vessels, in consequence of which it turns to the colour of blood deprived of oxygen.

It would be useful to pursue a study of this kind in a large number of mountain-climbers. I am convinced that physiology will one day succeed in establishing with certainty what are the capabilities of the individual climber, what amount of resistance he is able to oppose to inclement weather and to the excessive exertion of ascents, thus saving those less fitted from a rash exposure of themselves to dangers which menace their existence. The anæmia of hands and feet produced by a contraction of the vessels under the influence of cold, is one of the conditions preceding frostbite. The excess of defence becomes injurious. The withdrawal of the blood from the surface of the body to save the centres of life, gives the peripheral parts over to death.

Certainly, those who have vessels less sensitive to the cold can, by means of slight muscular contractions (since the circulation of blood still proceeds in their extremities), maintain a degree of temperature in the fingers which protects the latter against the action of frost. These differences were brought under my notice at Regina Margherita Hut during a violent storm, when some persons arrived with feet and hands frostbitten, although perfectly well equipped as to shoes and gloves.

When we are called upon to lend aid to a person whose hands or feet are frostbitten, we must first of all remember to take great care not to injure his body in any way. All know that the process of warming must be very slow and gradual.[1]

An experiment of Dr. Catiano shows this necessity very clearly. By allowing ether to evaporate on the head of a pigeon, the brain may be very suddenly cooled. If the normal temperature is then slowly and gradually re-established, five to eight hours being devoted to the process, the animal shows no sign of any injury inflicted and wakes up little by little. On the contrary, if, after cooling the brain, tepid water is poured on the pigeon's head, the bird shows symptoms of considerable nervous disturbances.

The old remedy of guides and shepherds of rubbing the frozen parts with snow is so bad, that it is certainly better to do nothing rather than this. Dr. Catiano made experiments on animals, in which he froze their legs with cold and then rubbed them in parts with snow. He found that on these parts ulcers subsequently broke out. There are crystals in the snow which graze the skin, and these wounds are liable to become the seat of ulcers or other sores.

When circulation is restored, the skin is so tender, and so liable to become inflamed and canker, that we must be very careful in touching it; even the pressure we exercise on it when applying massage must not be too forcible. For this reason, when any one came to Regina Margherita Hut with feet and hands frostbitten, we used to apply a gentle massage with vaseline, exercising the compression from the tips of the fingers in the direction of the trunk, but very lightly and cautiously, until at last the skin became red and warm again.

Dr. Gurgo had recently a personal experience on an expedition up Monte Rosa of the necessity for caution in applying friction to frostbitten members. "He was able to affirm that the hand on which the friction had been

---

[1] A. Mosso, *Il freddo*. Bollettino, Club Alpino, 1894, vol. xxvii.

less violent, improved and got well more rapidly than the other which had been subjected to more energetic rubbing."[1]

On the re-establishment of circulation the vessels cease to be contracted and become paralysed, and the skin, reacting after the fatigue undergone by the vessels, grows tumid and red. The burning and redness of our hands when we have made snowballs give us an idea of the over-abundant flow of blood to the surface of the body when some frostbitten part is restored. The redness then develops into inflammation of the skin, while the tingling and slight tumefaction of the hands are only a milder form of œdema and blisters, which may give rise to ulceration and the destruction of the skin and muscles by gangrene. The feet of one traveller who arrived at Regina Margherita Hut during a storm swelled so that for three days he was unable to put on his boots, and even when he went on his way he still limped. The ears are more easily restored than the prominences of the cheeks, which I have once seen frostbitten. The nose is kept warm by the expired air.

In some instances frostbite deprives of feeling in the part affected for months. The action of the cold alone, without frostbite, provoked a tingling sensation in the fingers of the Signora Baccelli (who with her husband, the Hon. Alfredo Baccelli, visited Regina Margherita Hut while we were there), which continued even for two days after her return to Gressoney.

Alessandro Sella told me that once while cutting steps in a glacier his hands became frostbitten. The thermometer indicated $-16°$ and there was such a violent storm raging that he and his companions had to throw themselves down on the ground when they reached the summit, so as not to be carried away by the wind. At a certain point his father, Quintino Sella, asked him for help, but he was unable to open his hands, which were clenched round the handle of the pick. The effects of this frostbite lasted for three months, sensibility but not the power of movement being lost. His father had one thumb frostbitten, of which the nail fell off.

VII.

The action of cold on the blood-vessels was one of the first subjects which I studied at the beginning of my scientific career, but the experiments of that time are now so old that no further mention need be made of them.

I am convinced, however, that the study of cold is still of importance to the physiology of man on the Alps. Hermann has recently shown that one suffers more intensely from cold when one passes from slightly heated premises into the open air, than when in winter one goes out of a well-heated room into the cold outside. In accordance with the physiological law of contrasts one would have expected the contrary. The reason of the phenomenon is this: when the temperature of our body has fallen in consequence of our having been for some time in a cold place, a further diminution of temperature, even though slight, is sufficient to cause trembling.[2]

Our greatest source of discomfort on our expedition was the cold, from which we suffered more intensely when we were encamped at altitudes between 2,500 and 3,000 metres, as we could not there warm ourselves by means of a stove. I tried to console myself by thinking of Saussure's encampment on the Col du Géant, where he made a halt of sixteen days at

---
[1] G. Rey, *Una escursione scolastica al Monte Rosa.* Torino, 1897, p. 20.
[2] L. Hermann, *Kleine physiologische Bemerkungen und Anregungen.* Pflüger's Archiv, 1897, p. 599.

an altitude of 3,365 metres, in the last century. He had started from Chamonix at the beginning of July and, after crossing the Tacul glacier, had pitched his tents at the foot of the mountain Tacul. After having explored the crevasses and steep slopes of the glacier of the Aiguille Noire he reached the col which descends towards Courmayeur. Before they reached the summit and when all danger seemed to be past, a cry arose: "Ropes!" One of the porters who had been walking on ahead, carrying Saussure's mattress, had disappeared into a crevasse. Fortunately he fell on to a firm stratum of snow about twenty metres below the mouth of the crevasse, and was saved.

In the account he wrote Saussure complains of nothing but the cold, and neither furs, nor cloaks, he says, gave him satisfactory protection. In the evening, even when the weather was fine, he used to write his notes while he warmed his feet on a heated stone. It was impossible to light a fire in either of the two little tents, which were of canvas, and the hut was in such wretched condition, so full of holes that there was no means of heating it; the coal burned badly, and when the party had succeeded in warming their feet all the rest of the body was frozen by the wind which blew through the walls made of loosely piled-up stones.

The illustration on page 109 shows our camp near Linty Hut. The tent which served as laboratory and in which Dr. Abelli slept, situated somewhat further off, and the tents for our domestic staff are not visible.

The tents of the soldiers were lower than ours and six soldiers were quartered in each. They had lined the canvas with blankets, and as the floor was covered with their mattresses the temperature within was kept high. One morning the thermometer which was hung up in one of the tents marked 14°; without the temperature was, as usual, below zero. As a rule there were from 8° to 9° in the soldiers' tents.

In the evening I used to light two candles in my tent by which to read or write. The temperature, if there were no wind, then rose from 0° to 7° or 8°. This suggested the lighting of the mountaineer's lamp in our tent for an hour or two before going to bed. As regards warmth we were not so well off as the soldiers, but the air in our tents was better. The tents with which officers of our army are provided are too permeable for mountain service, because when the wind blows, it is not possible to create inside a temperature any less cold than that without.

When Alessandro Sella and I made our winter ascent of Monte Rosa we had planned, in case we were surprised by bad weather, to dig a long, deep trench in the snow, and by way of practice we built a snow-house of which the entrance was closed by a great block of ice, during the day we halted at the Col d'Olen. We had fixed a pole in the middle on which to hang up our thermometer, and two other pieces of wood served as a support for the lantern which was to do duty as a stove and warm the air somewhat. We had prepared a soft bed of snow covered with oilskin. How we cherished the project of sleeping in that ice house! When we returned from the Vincent Pyramid, however, we were too tired quite to relish the idea of taking quarters there, so we renounced the plan, consoling ourselves with the recollection that the experiment was, after all, needless, similar attempts having been made by the crew of the *Jeannette*.[1] The Esquimaux, too, construct new ice-huts every year. We know that Saussure also entertained the notion of building an ice-hut on the summit of Mont Blanc, a plan which, however, like us he did not carry out.

[1] *L'expédition de la "Jeannette" au pole Nord*, tome i. p. 177.

The Alp-hut Lavez in the Valley of Gressoney (alt., 2,445 metres).

CHAPTER XXI

CHANGES IN THE BLOOD ON THE ALPS

I.

"THAT climate on high mountains is the best which most effectually restores health and by which a maximum activity in the production of new blood is set up, with a minimum of discomfort in the process of acclimatisation."[1] These words, pronounced in the Congress of Swiss physicians by the celebrated physiologist, Professor Miescher, of Bâle, in 1893, briefly express the opinion generally held by physicians respecting the so-called treatment by altitude.

More than thirty years ago Jourdanet[2] maintained the contrary and affirmed that in America people who live at an altitude beyond 2,150 metres are generally anæmic. This conclusion was the result of a long series of observations which he had made during a number of years spent on the

[1] F. Miescher, *Ueber die Beziehungen zwischen Meereshöhe und Beschaffenheit des Blutes.* Correspondenzblatt für Schweizer Ärzte, October, 1893.
[2] Jourdanet, *De l'anémie des altitudes, et de l'anémie en général dans ses rapports avec la pression de l'atmosphère.—Influence de la pression de l'air sur la vie.* Tome premier, p. 176, Paris, 1895.

plateaus of America. According to Jourdanet there is an intellectual and physical inferiority in the populations living on the slopes of the Himalayas and the Andes, which is due to the lack of oxygen, that is to the chronic anoxyhæmia of the blood.

Paul Bert and Jolyet had the blood of domestic animals, living at an altitude of 3,700 metres, sent to them from America, and found on analysing it that it had an absorptive capacity for oxygen much greater than the blood of animals living at the level of the sea.

Müntz made similar investigations, but with greater exactness. He carried some rabbits up the Pic du Midi (altitude, 2,877 metres) and seven years after examined the blood of their descendants, comparing it with that of rabbits that had always lived in the plain. In the former the blood contained 70 per cent. iron, in the latter 40 per cent.; the density of the blood in the rabbits from the Pic was 1,060, in those from the plain 1,046; the fixed bodies in the first case amounted to 21 per cent., in the latter to 15 per cent.; the oxygen absorbed by 100 cubic centimetres of the blood amounted to 17 cubic centimetres in the Pic rabbits, to 9 cubic centimetres in the others. Similar changes were observed also by Müntz in the blood of sheep after they had been for a few weeks on the mountain at a height of 2,877 metres.[1]

In 1889 F. Viault, professor of histology at Bordeaux, undertook a journey in Peru and Bolivia in order to study the influence which the climate of elevated regions exercises on the blood. The observations made on the Cordilleras, which were laid by Viault before the Academy of Sciences in Paris, tended to show that at the height of 4,392 metres the number of red corpuscles in the blood is much greater than normally. This increase is produced, according to Viault, also by moderate elevations, as in Arosa at an altitude of 1,800 metres.

Regnard obtained precisely similar results in experimenting in the laboratory of the Sorbonne on two guinea-pigs which were kept under a pneumatic bell.[2]

If the reader finds that I am going too much into detail on this subject I must solicit his patience, as the question is one of great importance. Were it true that new blood is produced in us merely by going on to the Alps, and that the altitude treatment is one of the most effectual means for combating many diseases, mountaineering might be considered as resting on the surest of foundations.

In order to comprehend the difficulty of these researches the reader must remember that the composition of the blood is very liable to alter in the different parts of the body, especially under the action of cold and heat. Rovighi and Winternitz first noticed this fact. The subject was followed up by Murri,[3] who showed that a simple cold bath, if the individual remains in it for some length of time, causes an augmentation in the number of the red corpuscles of the blood, this increase after the lapse of a few hours giving place to a diminution of the average number, which decrease, in a chlorotic person, may continue for four or five days.[4]

The amount of blood-corpuscles in these persons remains constant; it

---

[1] Comptes rendus, vol. cxii. p. 208.
[2] P. Regnard, *La cure d'altitude*. Paris, 1897, p. 132.
[3] A. Murri, *Policlinico*, 1894, fascicolo v.
[4] The same results were obtained by Dr. E. Mangianti, in Professor Bozzolo's hospital. *Variazioni locali dei corpuscoli sanguigni per influenze termiche*. Giornale Medico dell' Esercito, 1895.

is only the distribution which varies in the ramifications of the circulatory system. When the cold acts on the blood-vessels their calibre diminishes and the blood at the surface of the body becomes less dense. *Vice versâ*, when the body is heated and the vessels of the skin dilate the quantity of serous liquid contained in the peripheral blood-vessels is greater.

II.

Dr. Kuthy of Buda-Pesth conducted an investigation on this subject in my laboratory. From his article, "On the modifications which the blood undergoes in elevated regions owing to the diminished barometric pressure,"[1] I make the following extracts in order to show in what manner our researches on the blood were carried out.

Grawitz[2] held that this (*i.e.*, the increase of red corpuscles) was due to an inspissation of the blood arising from the loss of water which the more rapid evaporation, consequen- on the rarefaction of the air, effects. Schumburg and Zuntz justly observed that the loss of water which the body would have to sustain before an inspissation of the blood was brought about would be too great. Several litres of water would have to be lost before the number of red corpuscles rose from five to six millions per cubic millimetre. If this were correct, it would have been easily ascertained by a diminution of the weight of the body, in which respect it has not been borne out.

The most probable hypothesis is that it is due to a different distribution of the red corpuscles and of plasma in the organism. A phenomenon of this kind had already been observed by Lesser[3] in the blood of animals after the severing of the spinal cord, and more recently Cohnstein and Zuntz[4] have effected changes in the composition of the blood even greater than those observed in man on the mountains by means of the contraction and relaxation of the blood-vessels.

I have occupied myself with this problem simply from a critical point of view, in order to test the accuracy of other methods hitherto adopted by other investigators and the reliability of the results thus obtained. My experiments may be divided into two parts: in the first I investigated the composition of the blood of rabbits kept under a barometric pressure artificially maintained below the normal, in the second I examined my own blood, that of another person called Giacinto, and of several animals during a sojourn from the 9th to the 14th of May at Gressoney la Trinità, which is at an altitude of 1,627 metres.

These researches are similar to those conducted by Regnard and Jaruntowski. I made exclusive use of rabbits, weighing from 1,500 to 2,000 grams. These animals were placed, one at a time, under a large glass bell of the capacity of 18 litres. Here the rabbits lived quite well for weeks together at a barometric pressure nearly corresponding to the height of Monte Rosa, that is, to 4,560 metres. Every day I had the animals taken out for about half an hour in order to feed them, and, at the same time, to have the bell cleaned.

I counted the red corpuscles according to the Malassez method, and determined the amount of hæmoglobin with the Fleischl apparatus, the density of the blood being ascertained in accordance with Hammerschlag's method. The results of three series of observations on three rabbits are given in a table.

My observations led me to conclude, firstly (and this seems to me of importance), that the methods followed in these researches are inexact, as appears from the disagreement between the results obtained in the three different ways mentioned; secondly, that the composition of the blood in the vessels of the skin of rabbits subjected to the action of rarefied air probably undergoes a change.

OBSERVATIONS ON THE COMPOSITION OF THE BLOOD IN MAN AND ANIMALS MADE AT GRESSONEY LA TRINITÀ (ALT., 1,627 METRES).

I chose Gressoney la Trinità for these investigations because it is one of the highest-situated villages on the slopes of the Alps, and also because I was sure of finding all that was necessary to enable me to keep to the same manner of living at the Thedy inn.

---

[1] Dott. Desiderio Kuthy, Rendiconti Accademia dei Lincei, 6 Settembre, 1896.
[2] E. Grawitz, *Ueber die Einwirkung des Höhenklimas auf die Zusammensetzung des Blutes.* Berl. Klin. Wochenschrift, 1895, n. 33.
[3] Archiv für Anatomie und Physiol., 1878, p. 41.
[4] Schumburg and Zuntz, *op. cit.*, p. 491.

A week before I started I began to examine my blood every day as well as that of the person who was to accompany me to Gressoney. I made a series of preliminary researches on a dog weighing 10,300 grams, and on two rabbits, of which one weighed 1,630 grams and the other 1,550 grams. I arranged matters so that our diet should vary as little as possible during this time and endeavoured always to perform my analyses at the same hour every day in the case of all the subjects. The observations on man were made before lunch, that is, between 10 and 1 o'clock, after which, at 1.30, lunch was taken.

RESULTS OF THE EXAMINATION OF THE BLOOD IN MAN AND ANIMALS IN TURIN AND AT GRESSONEY LA TRINITÀ (ALT., 1,627 METRES).

	Average of the observations made in Turin (alt., 4,560 m.).	Gressoney la Trinità.			
		1st day.	2nd day.	3rd day.	4th day.
RABBIT (weight, 1,630 grams).					
Number of red corpuscles	6,000,000	6,240,000	6,880,000	6,720,000	6,080,000
Hæmoglobin	75–80%	75–80%	80–85%	75–80%	75–80%
Specific gravity of the blood	1·056	1·056	1·058	1·053	1·052
RABBIT (weight, 1550 grams).					
Number of red corpuscles	6,800,000	7,040,000	7,200,000	6,580,000	6,620,000
Hæmoglobin	75–80%	75–80%	80–85%	75–80%	75–80%
Specific gravity of the blood	1·056	1·058	1·061	1·057	1·058
DOG (weight, 10,300 grams).					
Number of red corpuscles	5,160,000	5,960,000	5,040,000	5,240,000	5,120,000
Hæmoglobin	80–85%	80–85%	80–85%	80–85%	80–85%
Specific gravity of the blood	1·057	1·058	1·057	1·056	1·057
GIACINTO (weight, 58 kilograms).					
Number of red corpuscles	4,320,000	4,600,000	4,720,000	5,560,000	4,800,000
Hæmoglobin	95–100%	95–100%	95–100%	100%	85–90%
Specific gravity of the blood	1·058	1·060	1·060	1·061	1·056
DR. KUTHY (weight, 65·5 kilograms).					
Number of red corpuscles	4,300,000	4,040,000	4,880,000	5,600,000	4,960,000
Hæmoglobin	85–90%	80–85%	90–95%	90–95%	80–90%
Specific gravity of the blood	1·058	1·060	1·060	1·060	1·058

The results obtained would seem to show that in the rabbits there was an augmentation in the density of the blood during the two first days after they had been taken to Gressoney, while the amount of hæmoglobin remained the same. On the third and fourth day the blood of the rabbits showed a tendency to regain the composition which it had had before in Turin.

The changes observed in my blood and in that of Giacinto agree with the observations of Viault, Müntz, Egger, and Miescher. In these two cases the increase of red corpuscles was progressive and constant during the first three days at Gressoney la Trinità, and even the determinations of hæmoglobin and of the density of the blood agree better than in the other previous observations, showing that there is an inspissation of the blood in the vessels of the skin.

All the observations which I made at Gressoney would seem, therefore, to indicate that there was an increase in the number of red corpuscles and in the density of the blood.

These observations are, however, not sufficient to establish as a fact that there was a general change in the composition of the blood owing to the barometric depression. These investigations should be repeated with more accurate methods for the examination of the blood. Above all, it is necessary to keep account of the losses of water which our organism undergoes through lungs, skin, and kidneys.

It is probable that the more intense action of the light on the blood-vessels in elevated regions and the colder air produce a change in the circulation, in consequence of which the number of red corpuscles becomes more abundant in the vessels of the skin. In this case the blood-plasma would accumulate in the deeper parts of the body. The least probable of all hypotheses is that which has hitherto been most generally supported, namely, that there is an actual augmentation of red corpuscles.

III.

Another scientific expedition in the same year as mine was made up Monte Rosa by Professor Piero Giacosa. At the beginning of this chapter there is an illustration of the Alp-hut Lavez in the Valley of Gressoney at an altitude of 2,450 metres, where he stayed for a certain time in the years 1894, 95 and 96. The hut is composed of a large stable on the ground-floor and of two rooms upstairs, of which one served as laboratory and kitchen, the other as sleeping-room and laboratory for more delicate work. The situation could not be better for investigations on the mountains. Professor Giacosa has already published a series of articles on the chemical and bacteriological properties of the water and air in that region.

The variations taking place in the hæmoglobin of the blood [1] consequent on the action of rarefied air were studied according to a new method. Professor Giacosa's observations were made in Turin, at the Alp-hut Lavez (alt., 2,445 metres) and in Regina Margherita Hut (alt., 4,560 metres), whither he took an analytical balance of Sartorius.

In examining the blood of Dr. Scofone on an ascent of Monte Rosa, a slight increase in the amount of hæmoglobin was found.

Professor Giacosa had a big dog weighing 25 kilograms, and another, a fox-dog, weighing 12 kilograms, carried up to Regina Margherita Hut, the diet they were accustomed to being strictly adhered to. In the blood of these two dogs the amount of hæmoglobin was found to be the same as in the plain. Giacosa therefore concludes that barometric depression has certainly not the effect of augmenting the quantity of hæmoglobin contained in the blood. In two rabbits also kept for five days in Regina Margherita Hut, no sufficiently important variation was found in this respect to justify the supposition that an altitude of 4,560 metres has an influence on the composition of the blood.

Zuntz and the brothers Lœwy recently studied the influence of rarefied air on the composition of the blood, and made a comparison between the results obtained in Berlin, at Gressoney, on the Col d'Olen and at Regina Margherita Hut. They came to the conclusion that the number of red corpuscles presented a diminution during the first week of their sojourn on Monte Rosa and a slight augmentation during the second week, the results obtained, however, not being higher than those noted in Berlin.[2]

[1] P. Giacosa, *Il contenuto in emoglobina del sangue a grandi altezze*. Rendiconti dell' Istituto Lombardo, vol. xxx. p. 410.
[2] A. Lœwy, I. Lœwy and Leo Zuntz, *op. cit.*, Pflüger's Archiv, 1897, p. 537.

The observations on Monte Rosa would therefore seem to make against the prevailing ideas on the regeneration of the blood in rarefied air. It would, however, be unjust to pass on without saying a few words on the experiments of those physiologists who maintain an affirmative opinion on the subject.

The influence of the climate of elevated regions on the composition of the blood was studied with great zeal in the laboratory of Bâle under the direction of Professor Miescher. It is with a feeling of sorrowful pleasure that I pay a tribute of respect to the memory of this esteemed colleague in recalling the admirable work which was performed by him and under his guidance, and which was, alas! cut short by his lamented death.

IV.

Professor Miescher's conviction that the methods adopted by physiologists to determine variations of the hæmoglobin in the blood were not sufficiently exact, led him to his critical consideration of the instruments used in these investigations. Veillon's work on the hæmometer of Fleischl and Miescher, which serves to measure the colouring matter in the blood, was thus originated.

Dr. Egger[1] during a sojourn at Arosa (alt., 1890 metres necessitated by the state of his health, pursued investigations on the blood for two years, in which time he examined twenty-seven persons. The increase observed by Egger in the number of red corpuscles in these individuals is not perhaps a fact of much importance, as his subjects were, for the most part, invalids; but in six rabbits that he had taken with him from the laboratory in Bâle, he noticed, too, a remarkable augmentation of these blood-corpuscles. On examining the blood of twelve persons with the improved hæmometer of Fleischl and Miescher he found that all but one of these individuals had redder blood.

When the subjects return to the lowlands the blood gradually regains its normal state. That the amelioration of the blood due to treatment by altitude is of brief duration, is a point on which all physicians are agreed.

Having ascertained that a difference of level of 1,626 metres, as between Bâle (alt., 266 metres) and Arosa (1,892 metres)—about the height of Gressoney la Trinità above sea-level—effects an alteration in the blood, Professor Miescher determined to find out the smallest difference of level which would produce an augmentation in the number of the red corpuscles. To this end he made investigations at Champéry (alt., 1,052 metres), at Sernens (986 metres) and at Laugenbruck (700 metres).[2]

The fact that Suter found an increase in the number of red corpuscles per difference of level of 434 metres (between Bâle and Laugenbruck) raises the doubt whether the cause of these changes observed in the composition of the blood really is the diminished barometric pressure. As yet we know no sufficiently plausible reason why the number of blood-corpuscles should be increased by such inconsiderable degrees of rarefaction of the air.

[1] F. Egger, *Beobachtungen an Menschen und Kaninchen über den Einfluss des Klimas von Arosa auf das Blut*. Die histochemischen und physiologischen Arbeiten v. F. Miescher, Leipzig, 1897, p. 464.
[2] J. Kurcher, E. Veillon, and F. Suter, *Ueber die Veränderungen des Blutes beim Uebergang von Basel nach Champéry, Sernens und Laugenbruck*. Op. cit. p. 479.

Until proofs to the contrary are given, we must rather maintain that the cause of the variations observed lies in the climatic conditions, in the more active influence of the sun's rays, in the greater dryness of the air and in the altered manner of living.

V.

The conviction that the number of red corpuscles and the quantity of hæmoglobin in the blood do not increase in rarefied air was borne in upon me on considering the data published by Suter as showing the influence of a difference of level of 434 metres. Suter found an increase of 6·4 per cent. in the number of red corpuscles in six individuals. As we know as yet of no fact which opposes the supposition that the augmentation in the number of red corpuscles is proportionate to the degree of rarefaction of the air, we ought to have found during our sojourn on the summit of Monte Rosa an increase of 64 per cent. because the altitude at which we halted is ten times greater than the difference in level between Bâle and Laugenbruck.

This is incredible; the phenomena observed by us on Monte Rosa and the results of the investigations of Scofone and Zuntz make equally against it.

The problem may be thus formulated. Is there an actual increase in the number of red corpuscles? Does the amount of colouring substance of the blood, of hæmoglobin, that is, increase in consequence of the barometric depression? Or is there merely an altered distribution of the solid and liquid parts of the blood? In spite of the undoubted authority of Miescher, I am of opinion that there is no new generation of red corpuscles either at the moderate elevations above-mentioned, or at greater heights. Suter and Jaquet[1] recently endeavoured to solve the problem definitely, and instead of examining one drop of blood extracted from a wound they bled an animal to death. As such an *experimentum crucis* cannot be repeated on the same animal, the comparison of the results with those obtained on similar animals kept, some at Bâle and some at Davos, immediately complicated the question. The fact that external conditions can produce other changes than those due merely to barometric depression alone suffices to render the experiment less convincing.

Suter and Jaquet came to the conclusion that the rabbits that had lived for four weeks at Davos had a greater quantity of hæmoglobin in their blood. The difference is, however, so small that it would be rash to attribute much importance to it. Such variations may arise from other causes, the rabbit being the animal least adapted for these investigations. Its timidity is proverbial. In my book *Fear*,[2] I have shown that in no other animal are the contractions of the blood-vessels more forcible and more apparent. The rabbit blushes and grows pale more easily than all other animals. For this reason the composition of its blood has a continual tendency to alter. If one bears in mind the condition of its digestive system, which is never empty but in continual activity, the statement that any other animal is better adapted for these researches than the rabbit is justified. The investigations of Suter and Jaquet have therefore not put an end to the controversy but merely indicated the surest way to come to a decision.

The reader will understand the extreme difficulty of these studies, in

[1] F. Suter and A. Jaquet, *Höhenklima und Blutbildung, op. cit.* p. 529.
[2] *Fear.* Introduction IV. London, 1896. Translated by E. Lough and F. Kiesow.

which the object of research is a minimum variation in the composition of the blood. The methods which we adopt are not very accurate, and perhaps the error which the use of them involves is greater than the very variations in the blood which we wish to compute.

The blood is contained in a system of tubes subject to a continual variation of diameter. Under the influence of heat and cold especially, and owing also to other causes independent of barometric changes, they dilate or contract at the surface of the body, or internally in the organs. When they contract the blood is less rich in solid parts, when they dilate there is a more abundant mixture of red corpuscles with the serum of the blood.

The most serious difficulty is that, as physiologists have not as yet any positive knowledge as to the origin of the blood corpuscles, it is impossible for them to try to find out either in animals or in man whether there is a greater activity at their point of origin, in the organs, that is, charged with their formation.

The physicians of the climatic health-resorts, enthusiastic at the success of their treatment, have endeavoured to ascertain the real cause of the improvement of many invalids in elevated regions. The persons they study are those whose condition, owing to their previous suffering, shows a rapid amelioration in mountain-air. Into these researches suggestion is liable to enter as a factor which must not be neglected in our estimation of the results, and which justifies the wish that similar observations should be repeated with more accurate methods on healthy persons.

An expedition similar to mine would perhaps solve the problem. Other physiologists will, I hope, carry out the idea, the physicians of the climatic stations will then be able to apply practically the knowledge resulting from observations on healthy man.

The normal quantity of blood in the body is greater than is necessary, for healthy man keeps at the disposal of the organism a certain amount of blood which may be called into requisition to meet emergencies. In women this surplus compensates for periodical losses sustained; in both men and women it is as a reserve-store in case of accidental losses. This extra supply of blood is so considerable that we cannot admit an immediate production of new corpuscles on slight changes in the atmospheric pressure. Nature is too ingenious, too economical in her methods not to find other means of compensation, without having recourse to an increased activity of the organs which generate the blood. The latter mechanism only acts in extreme cases, when danger is imminent, not at every little, scarcely observable variation in the pressure of the atmosphere.

VI.

Cold rather than barometric depression exercises, as I believe, an intense influence on the composition of the blood on the Alps. It would be useful to make experiments on this subject, similar to those which Albertoni and Novi performed on dogs and Murri on chlorotic women. The amount of iron eliminated with the bile and urine became three times greater in a dog kept in a cold bath for four hours. In winter, weak persons are more liable to suffer from chlorosis than in warmer seasons. Murri has shown that this impoverishment of the blood is due to the deleterious action of the cold on the red corpuscles.

I mention these facts merely as an indication of the serious complications which render the study of the blood on the Alps a matter of so much difficulty. The enumeration shows, too, what problems still demand investigation. The first question to solve is whether there is really a modification of the blood, appearing as a constant phenomenon whenever one goes into the mountains, even when only to altitudes below one thousand metres, as was maintained by Miescher, and after him by all the specialists of climatic health-resorts. Once it is established as a fact that there is a greater number of red corpuscles in the surface vessels of the body, it remains to be ascertained whether in those deeper-situated the blood has become more dense. Our researches are useless until we find out whether there is really a new production of red corpuscles, or whether the change observed is due to an altered distribution of the solid and liquid parts of the blood.

The latter explanation seems to me the more probable of the two, although the last work published on the subject by Schauman and Rosenquist,[1] of the University of Helsingfors, speaks for an increase of the red corpuscles in animals subjected to diminished barometric pressure.

There is, it seems to me, a source of error in all these researches inspired by Bert's[2] theory of mountain-sickness. Paul Bert's conclusion that "tout s'explique par la diminution de l'oxygène du sang," being accepted, in order to explain the fact that after the subsidence of the first sufferings one accustoms one's self to living in elevated regions, it was further maintained that the modification in the composition of the blood is accompanied by an augmented respiratory capacity of that fluid. Professor Miescher and others gave it as their opinion that the marrow of the bones regulates the amount of red corpuscles when the supply of oxygen becomes insufficient. Regnard maintains that the microcytes are transformed into red corpuscles, while others hold that the respiratory compensation is effected merely by an increase of hæmoglobin in the corpuscles of the blood.

As yet it has not been proved that there is a lack of oxygen in the blood at moderate elevations such as those taken into consideration by Professor Miescher whose work, as well as that of others performed later but in the same direction, lacks not only an experimental but also a teleological basis.

Modern medical art attributes greater importance to treatment by climate than to the influence of other remedies in certain diseases. This is a sensible tendency and we physiologists will certainly not combat it. Mountain air may be useful for many reasons, but not because the deficiency of oxygen produces an augmentation of the blood. In his recent work on the treatment by altitude, Regnard has endeavoured to show that the increase of the respiratory elements of the blood is the basis of a method of treatment, and that anæmic persons, the convalescent, those suffering from disturbances of digestion, chronic bronchitis, nervous affections, the neurasthenic and the melancholy, should be sent into the mountains.

I do not think that a sojourn in rarefied air effects an immediate alteration of the blood, "une véritable explosion de microcytes," to make use of Regnard's own words. Neither can I think that the amount of hæmoglobin in the red corpuscles augments, nor that the blood of an animal that has lived in rarefied air always absorbs a greater quantity of oxygen. This victorious struggle of the organism in rarefied air against conditions unfavour-

---

[1] O. Schauman und E. Rosenquist, *Ist die Blutkörperchenvermehrung im Höhenklima eine wirkliche oder eine scheinbare?* Archiv für gesam. Physiologie 68° Band, p. 55.
[2] P. Bert, *Pression barométrique*, p. 1102.

able to life, this radical change in the blood on the mountains is not to my mind so evident as to justify its unconditional acceptance as a truth.

The study of acclimatisation at great heights gave rise to the recent discussions on the treatment by altitude. Paul Bert enunciated the idea at first merely as a hypothesis, facts for its support were sought afterwards. The opposite mode of procedure is, however, generally the surest in science, first facts, that is, and then theories. The red corpuscles have been compared to barks which carry the oxygen of the lungs into all parts of the body. When the weight of the oxygen which each bark can carry has become less on account of the rarefaction of the air, nature, it has been said, wisely increases the number of barks; that is, constructs immediately a large number of red corpuscles. This theory is beautiful, but observed facts militate against it. We have a proof of this in the fact noticed by Conway and other travellers that the natives of Asia and America born at great altitudes suffer more from mountain-sickness than Europeans. Conway says, in fact, that the natives of the Himalayan slopes, born and bred at an altitude of 10,000 feet, suffered as much as he and his party.[1]

We are thus led by another way to conclude that the seat and origin of this malady is in the nervous system, and that acclimatisation is a growing power of resistance and adaptation to the barometric depression acquired by the nerve-centres.

An evident proof that the blood does not become more abundant at great altitudes is easily obtainable by all mountain-climbers who will examine the colouring of the skin and mucous membranes in those individuals who live on the high Alpine pastures. One often meets with poor creatures who spend several months of the year in some lonely valley, herding their sheep and goats at heights above 2,500 metres. I have never found one of these individuals who had the flourishing look of the shepherds and peasants of the plain. Their skin is of an earthen colour, their outer aspect almost inclines one to think that Jourdanet was right in his theory of anæmia caused by altitude.

Many physicians send their patients into the mountains in the hope that they will recover more speedily owing to an immediate generation of a large number of red corpuscles due to the rarefaction of the air. I, too, believe that an Alpine climate may exercise a favourable influence in the case of invalids, if they do not go beyond an altitude of 2,000 metres, but this is not because the deficiency of oxygen gives rise to a reaction within the organism and to an increase of blood corpuscles. The treatment by altitude resembles the hydropathic treatment in its processes and in its effects, only that instead of shower-baths and plunge-baths, we have the sharp air, the wind and the sun which act on the body. Other factors in the treatment by altitude are light and motion which modify the circulation of the blood and lymph, the Alpine surroundings, the obligatory following of the rules of treatment, the more hygienic and natural mode of life.

[1] *Op. cit.* p. 112.

Gressoney la Trinità (alt., 1,627 metres).

CHAPTER XXII

EXPLANATION OF MOUNTAIN-SICKNESS—ACAPNIA

I.

MOUNTAIN-SICKNESS has been thought a simple asphyxia due to lack of oxygen, whereas, in reality, it is a very complex phenomenon, as the arterial blood loses a considerable part of its carbonic acid when the barometric pressure diminishes, and even before the effects due to the lack of oxygen in the air appear the phenomena produced by the diminution of carbonic acid in the blood have already manifested themselves.

From the time when I stayed in the Regina Margherita Hut, and noticed that the respiration there became slower and weaker, I became convinced that in air rarefied to less than half an atmosphere the preponderating cause of mountain-sickness could not be lack of oxygen. In Regina Margherita Hut I had with me Paul Bert's book on "Barometric Pressure," and on looking at the diagram showing the diminution of oxygen and carbonic acid in arterial blood when the barometric pressure decreases, I saw at once that on high mountains there must be a greater lack of carbonic acid than oxygen in the blood. Bert writes, indeed, that "les variations de l'acide carbonique sont considérablement plus étendues que celles de l'oxygène."[1]

[1] *Op. cit.* p. 644.

Frænkel and Geppert, as I have already said in Chapter XVI., found on analysing the blood of dogs in rarefied air that up to a pressure of 410 millimetres the amount of oxygen contained in the body does not alter. We know, however, that on Monte Rosa, and even at an altitude of only 3,300 metres, mountain-sickness may appear in a very violent form, although the barometric reading is only 500 millimetres.

Hüfner, certainly one of the greatest authorities on the physiology of the blood, showed, as I have already mentioned, that solutions of hæmoglobin similar to the blood begin to dissociate only when the barometer marks 238 millimetres. By means of artificial blood, if I may so express myself, Hüfner convinced himself that not even on the highest summit of the Himalayas would the hæmoglobin lose the property of absorbing the normal quantity of oxygen, and that the cause of mountain-sickness, up to an altitude of 9,000 metres, must not be sought in any physical or chemical change in the hæmoglobin of the blood.[1]

The experiments of Frænkel and Geppert, and those of Hüfner, which showed that the saturation of the blood with oxygen does not change at heights much beyond those at which mountain-sickness breaks out, oblige us to attribute this indisposition to some other cause than the diminution of oxygen. This other cause is, I believe, the *diminution of carbonic acid in the blood*.

Mountain-sickness is, indeed, more serious at night and in repose when the consumption of oxygen is lessened, but it is then, too, that the production of carbonic acid is diminished. If not by the lack of carbonic acid in the organism, there is no means of explaining the relief experienced on rising in the night when we are seized with oppression on the chest, palpitation of the heart, and difficulty in breathing. It is not necessary in order to improve our condition to breathe the pure, cold air outside, a little movement, walking a few steps suffices. Muscular contraction in producing carbonic acid, partly re-establishes the equilibrium of this gas in the blood.

Dr. A. Lœwy [2] was the first to notice that in the pneumatic chamber one feels better if one moves about a little. A subject studied by him was unable to withstand a barometric depression corresponding to an altitude below 4,500 metres, if he did not in some way contract his muscles, and merely by working with the ergostat this individual warded off a fainting-fit which menaced him in repose.

The cause of these phenomena appears evident when we study the analyses of the blood made by Frænkel and Geppert. From the table in which their experiments are summed up we see that the dogs from which blood was drawn, for the purpose of analysis, at the usual pressure and in rarefied air, were not always quiet. When animals are restless and breathe with greater intensity, it sometimes happens that in rarefied air there is a greater quantity of oxygen in their blood than at the usual pressure. This must, of course, be considered as an error in the experiment. Similarly at other times a greater quantity of carbonic acid may be found in the blood in rarefied air.

Out of twenty experiments, of which the results are given by Frænkel and Geppert, only seven are in this way disqualified. If we take the average of the remaining thirteen experiments, we find that the arterial blood contains less carbonic acid in rarefied air than at the normal pressure. From

[1] Hüfner, *Ueber die Gesetze der Dissociation des Oxyhämoglobins*, Archiv f. Physiologie, 1890.   [2] *Op. cit.* p. 16.

the analyses of these two investigators we see that the arterial blood of the dog under pressures varying from 460 to 198 millimetres loses 1·63 carbonic acid to 1 of oxygen.

I have found that on the average one-sixth of the usual amount of carbonic acid is lacking in the arterial blood of a dog breathing rarefied air such as is found on the summit of Monte Rosa. We cannot say that this is an insignificant variation, as carbonic acid is a very important substance to which the nervous centre has been accustomed from the very beginning of life. We shall see later on that we are much more susceptible to a given diminution of carbonic acid in the blood than to a corresponding increase of the same.

It was necessary to give some name to this new state of the blood, opposed to asphyxia and which had not as yet been studied by physiologists. I thought to designate the lack of carbonic acid by a Greek word, and as the ancients were not acquainted with carbonic acid and had therefore no name for it I chose the word *smoke* as most resembling it in a physiological sense, and so coined the word *acapnia* from ἄκαπνος, which means *without smoke*.

On mountains of the height of Mont Blanc, therefore, we would seem to be subjected not to asphyxia but to *acapnia*.

II.

There is a simple method of ascertaining whether really the diminution of oxygen alone produces the phenomena of mountain-sickness, or whether the deficiency of carbonic acid plays some part in the matter, and this is to augment the proportion of oxygen contained in the air we breathe, while at the same time the barometric pressure is diminished. If, while the same quantity, in weight, of oxygen is breathed, we see that under great barometric depressions the indisposition of the subject is less serious when carbonic acid is breathed in as well as oxygen, we must conclude that *acapnia* really exists, and that to it mountain-sickness is in part due.

I communicate an experiment of this kind made in the pneumatic chamber, the subject being made to breathe air containing a quantity of oxygen surpassing the normal. For this purpose I made use of compressed oxygen, as furnished by Brin's Oxygen Company, London. This oxygen is contained in large iron tubes which hold 2,800 litres of the gas compressed to 120 atmospheres. Analysis convinced me that this oxygen is almost perfectly pure. By means of a valve which regulates the pressure I caused the oxygen to pass into an ordinary gasometer with a capacity of 500 litres. A tube of thick india-rubber formed the communication between the gasometer and the pneumatic chamber. A tap in the interior of the chamber enabled the subject to supply himself at will with oxygen.

April 6th. Pressure, 744 mm.; Temperature, 15°.

Giorgio Mondo, servant in the laboratory, counts his pulse after remaining seated for ten minutes. Six times in succession the rate is 55 to the minute. Breathing, 11 per minute. At 8.57 a.m. he enters the pneumatic chamber.

Time.	Pulse.	Pressure in millimetres.
8.59	55	664
9.1	55	604
9.5	63	544
9.7	65	514
9.10	64	484

Time.	Pulse.	Pressure in millimetres.
9.13	65	... 464
9.16	67	... 454
9.18	69	... 444
9.20	72	... 434
9.21	74	... 434
9.22	76	... 364
9.23	80	... 344
9.25	81	... 343

Up to this point Mondo, with whom I was able to speak through the window panes in the chamber, had told me that he felt quite well. The colour of lips and cheeks was normal, and he was not sleepy. But now he let me know by touching his head with his hand that he was not feeling quite so well. During the three minutes following his condition rapidly grew worse. He was pale and his face had a suffering expression. The pressure was now 336, breathing 11.

9.28. Pulse, 86. Pressure, 336 mm. Dizziness. Heavy breathing. Nausea. The rarefaction of the air corresponded to an altitude of 6,500 metres. This height had been reached in half an hour.

I make a sign to him to fill a bottle with air¹ for the purpose of analysis: immediately afterwards, at 9.30, he opens the oxygen-tap. At this moment we close the other tap by which the air enters the bell. The pump continues to act. About 100 litres of oxygen pour in.

9.32. Pulse, 73. Pressure, 334 mm. The subject writes that he feels better.

9.34. Pulse, 64. Pressure, 314 mm. By a movement of the hand to the head he makes me understand that the phenomena of indisposition have disappeared. He writes on the sheet of paper which lies before him: "When I took the oxygen I felt my hands and legs tremble."

9.36. Pulse, 63. Pressure, 294 mm.

9.38. Pulse, 63. Pressure, 290 mm. Mondo lets me know that he is feeling well and that all symptoms have disappeared. He draws 19 breaths in the minute.

9.41. Pulse, 66. Pressure, 283 mm. The subject writes: "I feel well, but the pulse is stronger."

9.47. Pulse, 80. Breathing, 13. After replying to certain questions which I put to him, he writes on the sheet of paper, which he then shows to me through the window, "When I speak I do not feel so well." Pressure, 256 mm.

9.57. Pulse, 92. Breathing, 12. Pressure, 250 mm. Mondo writes: "I feel rather dizzy. Breathing difficult."

9.59. Pulse, 102. Pressure, 246 mm. He fills a bottle with air for the purpose of analysis, and immediately afterwards opens the oxygen-tap so that the normal pressure is gradually restored. Fifteen minutes later the subject issues from the pneumatic chamber.

In summarising, we see that Mondo was subjected within thirty-three minutes to a rarefaction of the air corresponding to an altitude of 6,500 metres, the barometer within the chamber marking 336 mm. At that moment, when he was no longer able to withstand it, being attacked by nausea and dizziness, he filled a bottle with air which analysis showed to contain 19·9 per cent. of oxygen and 0·9 per cent. of carbonic acid. The pulse, which at first had beat 55 times per minute, was beating 86 times in the minute at this depression. The rate of breathing which at the normal pressure was 11 was now 12.

When 100 litres of oxygen had penetrated into the pneumatic chamber, the indisposition rapidly disappeared, the pulse fell from 86 to 63, although the internal pressure was not diminished. On the contrary, the rate of breathing rose from 12 to 19, subsequently slackening again in proportion as the carbonic acid, produced by the breathing, accumulated, the access of fresh air being prevented.

After twenty-nine minutes the barometric depression was 246 mm., which

¹ For a description of these bottles see page 302.

corresponds to the highest summit of the Himalayas, that is, to an altitude of 8,800 metres. Mondo became unwell again as at first. The pulse beat 102 times in the minute, and the subject drew twelve breaths per minute. He filled another bottle with air which subsequent analysis showed to contain the following volumes :—

17 per cent. oxygen.
2·2 per cent. carbonic acid.

He took a little oxygen to revive himself and then immediately began the descent.

In fifteen minutes, from a barometric pressure equal to an altitude of 8,800 metres, the subject had reached the usual atmospheric pressure. When he came out he said he felt well and told us that when he filled the second bottle with air he felt a sudden warmth about his head, a trembling of the hands, and a slight dizziness.

The most important part of this experiment lies in the comparison of the composition of the air: the first time, the subject showed symptoms of mountain-sickness at an altitude of 6,500 metres, and the air contained 19·9 per cent. oxygen; the second time, the phenomena appeared at an altitude of 8,800 metres, and the air contained 17 per cent. He was able to ascend higher, if I may so express myself, when the air contained less oxygen. For the sake of greater clearness we must reduce the values of these analyses performed at the ordinary pressure and expressed in volumes, to the value in weight of the proportion of oxygen at the pressure of 336 mm. and of 246 mm. In the footnote [1] these questions are worked out. The result shows

[1] The air contained according to volume—

19·9 per cent.   ...   ... oxygen.

and in weight—

22 per cent.   ...   .   oxygen.

With these data it is easy to find out what was the weight of oxygen in every 100 parts of air at the inner pressure of 336 mm. when the indisposition was severe.

$$760 : 22 :: 336 : x \qquad x = \frac{22 \times 336}{760} = 9\cdot 7$$

Before the introduction of the oxygen, therefore, the air in the bell contained in 100 parts in weight only 9·7 of oxygen. After the introduction of oxygen the analysis of the air showed that the latter contained in volume 17 per cent. oxygen. If we now reduce the volume to weight we have—

$$19\cdot 9 : 22 :: 17 : x \qquad x = \frac{22 \times 17}{19\cdot 9} = 18\cdot 79$$

That is, at the ordinary pressure 17 volumes per cent. correspond to 18·79 in weight per cent. In order to find out what weight of air there was when the pressure in the pneumatic chamber was only 246 mm., that is, when the subject felt ill the second time, we must work out the following proportion :—

$$760 : 18\cdot 79 :: 246 : x \qquad x = \frac{18\cdot 79 \times 246}{760} = 6\cdot 0$$

that at a pressure of 336 mm. the subject breathed 9·7 per cent. in weight of oxygen, and that at a pressure of 246 mm. he only breathed 6 per cent. This fact seems at first sight a paradox as the subject would appear to have withstood the depression better when the amount of oxygen was smaller, in the proportion of 6 to 9·7 ; but if we take the carbonic acid into account the contradiction is explained, because the first time the air contained 0·9 per cent. carbonic acid, whereas the second time there was 2·2 per cent. carbonic acid.

We conclude that, by adding carbonic acid to the air, one is able to withstand a rarefaction of the air corresponding to an altitude of 8,800 metres with a lesser quantity of oxygen than is requisite at an altitude of 6,500 metres.

III.

When the attempt is made to penetrate the more elevated regions of the atmosphere by means of balloons, the aeronauts must not merely take oxygen with them as Paul Bert advised. The foregoing remarks on *acapnia* have shown that a sufficient quantity of carbonic acid must be added to the oxygen in order to re-establish the equilibrium of these gases in the blood. Large stores of compressed oxygen and carbonic acid must therefore be taken. One of the saddest incidents in the history of these researches is that furnished by the disastrous ascent of the *Zenith*. A picture in Paul Bert's book shows the car of the balloon at the solemn moment of departure on the 15th April, 1875. Two hours later Sivel and Croce-Spinelli lay dead within it. The bladders full of oxygen attached to the car were so small that they would not have held out even for half an hour ; the aeronauts died without having consumed this stored-up gas ; perhaps they left off using it when they found that it did no good, perhaps while they were inhaling it acapnia caused the tube to fall from their hands.

If it be allowable to compare the experiments made with rarefied air in the pneumatic chamber to balloon ascents I might say that up till the present day I have reached a greater atmospheric height than any one else, so far as I can judge from the publications which I have read on the subject.

Croce-Spinelli and Sivel died when the balloon had reached a height where the pressure was 262 mm.

Glaisher on his highest balloon ascent,[1] on which he was accompanied by Coxwell, reached the height of 8,100 metres before he and his companion lost consciousness. Probably they did not ascend beyond 10,000 metres. Paul Bert attained in the pneumatic chamber a minimum pressure of 248 mm., but withstood this depression only for two minutes, during which time he continually breathed oxygen.

By inhaling oxygen I was once able to withstand a barometric depression of 220 mm., and at another time of 192 mm. It made a strange impression on me when I found I could cover the whole of the barometric column with the palm of my hand.

ANGELO MOSSO.

April 8th. Pressure, 750 mm. Temperature, 17°.

At 8.50 a.m., after remaining seated for ten minutes, I count my pulse. For five minutes in succession it beats as follows : 59, 59, 58, 59, 58.

At 9.7 I enter the chamber and the pump which rarefies the inner air is put in action.

---

[1] See Paul Bert's critique. Pression barométrique, p. 199.

EXPLANATION OF MOUNTAIN-SICKNESS—ACAPNIA

The large gas-meter was full of oxygen and in communication with the pneumatic chamber, so that I could at any moment effect the passage of oxygen into the latter.

Time.	Pulse.	Pressure in mm.
9.12	63	600
9.16	66	530
9.19	68	510
9.22	69	490
9.25	69	480
9.28	69	470
9.32	69	440
9.34	70	430
9.35	71	410
9.37	71	400
9.44	76	380
9.45	77	370

At this depression of 370 mm., which corresponds to an altitude of 5,700 metres (the limit, according to Fraenkel and Geppert, up to which the blood contains its normal quantity of oxygen), I breathe 14 times per minute. I write that I feel well, unable to find that anything is the matter with me. My condition is normal.

9.50. Pulse, 80. Pressure, 360 mm. I sigh from time to time, my pulse seems to me weaker, there is a slight buzzing in my ears. When I whistle I notice that in running up the scale some of the notes are not so clear as in normal air.

9.54. Pulse, 84. Pressure, 350 mm.

9.55. Pulse, 83. Pressure, 340 mm. The pulse is weaker, but the impulse of the heart is more extended and stronger, as I notice on laying my hand on my chest.

9.56. Pulse, 88. Pressure, 330 mm. I move hands and legs, stretch myself, and feel better after performing muscular contractions.

10.1. Pulse, 92. Pressure, 330 mm. Sudden sensation of warmth about the head. I breathe 15 times per minute, the depth of the respiration being the same as usual.

10.7. Pulse, 92. Pressure, 320 mm.

10.10. Pulse, 92. Pressure, 320 mm. I drink some water, stooping down to lift the bottle from the ground without experiencing any discomfort.

10.15. Pulse, 107. Pressure, 320 mm. In the last five minutes my condition has rapidly grown worse. I feel a slight dizziness. I see near and distant objects through the window quite well, but am no longer capable of the continued attention necessary to count the pulse. I twice make a mistake and break off. I lose two minutes and grow confused, but do not feel sick nor tremble. I am calm but absent-minded and cannot count the pulse. I try to execute a few deep inspiratory movements in order to promote a more active renewal of the air within the lungs, but this seems rather to hurt me than to do me good, because I feel afterwards a slight dizziness due to cerebral anæmia, as I sometimes experience also in ordinary air. The only difference is that now the dizziness comes over me immediately after three or four deep breaths. The rarefaction of the air corresponds to an altitude of 7,141 metres.

At 10.18 I take some oxygen. When the tap is opened the current issuing from the gas-meter strikes me on the chest.

10.20. Pulse, 76. 150 litres of pure oxygen have poured in. The radial pulse has become so weak that I can no longer count it. I am obliged to feel the carotid artery. The inner pressure is reduced to 410 mm.

10.22. The radial pulse is imperceptible. I feel the carotid artery and count 62,76. I feel well, breathe 18 times in one minute, and then 19 times. The impulse of the heart in the thorax has disappeared. I let some air in.

10.28. Pulse, 62. Pressure, 330 mm.
10.32. Pulse, 66. Pressure, 290 mm.
10.35. Pulse, 66. Pressure, 270 mm. I write that I feel well.
10.37. Pulse, 78. Pressure, 240 mm.
10.38. Pulse, 84. Pressure, 230 mm.
10.40. Pulse, 86. Pressure, 220 mm. I write that indisposition is rapidly increasing, I am slightly dizzy, have some difficulty in counting the pulse, and am troubled with nausea. I fill a bottle with air which subsequent analysis showed to contain :—

27·1 per cent oxygen, 1·9 per cent. carbonic acid.

I notice that nervous phenomena are more marked than before although the pulse is less rapid.

I take some oxygen, soon recover, and then effect a speedy re-establishment of the normal pressure. I feel perfectly well on coming out of the pneumatic chamber.

From the calculations in the footnote [1] we see that at 220 mm., since the air contained, according to volume, 27·1 per cent. of oxygen, I breathed only 8·66 parts of oxygen in weight, whereas at the pressure of 320 mm. I breathed 9·26 parts in every 100 parts of air. The analysis showed that if there were less oxygen there was, however, a greater amount (1·9 per cent.) of carbonic acid when the barometer marked 220 mm.

The pulse did not, however, return to the normal rate in spite of the abundance of oxygen, and remained at 62 instead of falling to 58 or 59.

During this experiment I was struck by the rapid aggravation of my condition. After having let in about 150 litres of pure oxygen I diluted the air a little so as to render it less rich in oxygen. While the pressure was slowly decreasing, the composition of the air remaining in all probability constant, I noticed a sudden increase of indisposition. Nausea, which had not troubled me before, suddenly appeared; although the pulse now beat only 86 times in the minute instead of 107 times as before, the nervous phenomena were much more serious—so much so, in fact, that I began to feel some anxiety, and had to break off the experiment by taking some oxygen. This sudden indisposition I have observed at other times; as an explanation of it I suggest that in the organism there may be stores of oxygen which are rapidly exhausted in rarefied air.

Another fact is rendered evident by this experiment, namely, that we must make a distinction, in studying mountain-sickness, between circulatory and nervous disturbances.

The first time, at 10.15, the pulse beat 107 times per minute and the nervous phenomena were bearable.

The second time, at 10.40, the pulse only beat 86 times in the minute and the nervous phenomena were more serious. Probably the oxygen acted with more efficacy on the heart than on the nervous system.

When I began to feel unwell I drew a series of deep breaths in order to renew the air in the lungs, but I felt no resultant benefit.

The beneficial effect of oxygen is therefore evident when we breathe it at barometric depressions corresponding to altitudes above 7,000 metres. As soon as I breathed in oxygen the pulse fell from 107 to 62. I did not breathe pure oxygen because my head was at some distance from the tube. One circumstance which I am at a loss to explain is the great weakness of the heart-beats when I breathe oxygenised air. The radial pulse became so weak that I could no longer count it: when I put my hand on the region of the heart, the impulse of this organ was likewise lacking and I had to lay my fingers on the arteries of the neck in order to determine the rate of the pulse.

[1]
$$760 : 22 :: 320 : x \qquad x = \frac{320 \times 22}{760} = 9\cdot26$$

$$19\cdot9 : 22 :: 27\cdot1 : x \qquad x = \frac{27\cdot1 \times 22}{19\cdot9} = 29\cdot95$$

$$760 : 29\cdot95 :: 220 : x \qquad x = \frac{29\cdot95 \times 220}{760} = 8\cdot66$$

IV.

In the following experiment I directed my attention more particularly to those nervous disturbances from which I suffer when I subject myself to the greatest degrees of rarefaction of the air which I can withstand.

ANGELO MOSSO.

April 25th.—Pressure, 742 mm. Temperature, 16·5°.

At 3.40 p.m. I sit down to rest, and wait in this position until the pulse becomes steady.
4.10. Pulse, 70, 69, 69, 70. Breathing, 19 per minute.
4.20. Pulse, 70.
4.30. Pulse, 70.
4.35. Pulse, 70.
4.41. I enter the pneumatic chamber and the rarefaction of the air is begun.
4.50. Pulse, 74. Pressure, 502 mm. Breathing, 16.
5.6. Pulse, 88. Pressure, 340 mm.
I begin to feel a slight heaviness of the head. I must therefore be subjected within 25 minutes to a rarefaction of the air corresponding to an altitude of 6,400 metres before the manifestation of the first symptom of indisposition. I breathe 11 times per minute. I try to whistle, and succeed while the pressure is 330 mm. I execute muscular contractions with arms and legs and feel better.
5.10. Pulse, 88. My thoughts are liable to wander when I count the pulse. I often have to begin over again, and in order to lighten the task I am obliged to count it only for 30 seconds. Thus, I find the numbers 44, 41, 42.
5.17. Pulse, 44. Pressure, 322 mm.
5.23. Pulse, 83, counted during a whole minute. My indisposition has disappeared; I write in my note-book that I am feeling better. I am again able to count the pulse for one minute together without breaking off or letting my thoughts wander. Pulse, 80, 86. Breathing, 14. Pressure, 292 mm.
5.28. I still feel well. Pulse, 84. Pressure still 292 mm.
5.30. My head begins to feel heavy again. Pulse, 86, 88. Breathing, 14 per minute. Stomachic and intestinal gases escape. I feel neither sick nor sleepy. I see near and distant objects quite clearly through the window.
5.35. I write that I do not feel well. I feel indifferent, apathetic.
5.39. I fill a bottle full of air for subsequent analysis, and then open the oxygen-tap after remaining for about a quarter of an hour at the pressure of 292 mm. (= 7,617 metres).
I feel better as soon as I breathe oxygen. I close the tap letting in the outer air. About 100 litres of oxygen had poured in, the pressure increasing by scarcely one centimetre and diminishing again immediately when I close the tap. During this time I make no observation, as I feel tired.
5.47. Pulse, 64. Pressure, 302 mm.
5.50. Pulse, 65. Pressure, 290 mm.
When I lay my hand on the cardiac area I no longer feel the beating of the heart, the pulse is filiform and I have difficulty in counting it. The rate of the pulse has therefore fallen below the normal, although the pressure is as before. The rate of breathing has, on the contrary, increased, owing to the oxygen, being now 19 per minute.
5.58. Pulse, 66. Breathing, 18. Pressure, 252 mm.
6.0. Pulse, 69. Pressure, 232 mm.
6.4. Pulse, 73. Pressure, 222. I begin to feel my head heavy.
6.7. Pulse, 80. Breathing, 18. Pressure, 202 mm.
6.9. Pulse, 84. Breathing, 18. Pressure, 192 mm.
My handwriting is little altered. I do not tremble, nor feel sick nor sleepy, but overcome with apathy. My lead-pencil, which I lay on the table, rolls off and falls into a pail of water in which are the tubes of the bottles which serve to collect air for subsequent analysis. Seeing that I have no means of continuing to write, unless I stoop to pick up the pencil, which is too much trouble, I break off the experiment although my condition is less distressing than the first time. I fill a bottle full of air and then open the oxygen-tap. In 15 minutes the usual pressure is re-established. On coming out I feel well. Half an hour later I was at dinner at a friend's house. I had, however, less appetite than usual.

In this experiment I withstood the rarefied air longer than the time before, having resisted until the pressure sank to 292 mm., whereas the first time I only held out until it fell to 325 mm. We often find this, namely, that the resistance to rarefied air varies from one day to another. It must, however, be remarked that it is difficult to say when the phenomena of indisposition reach the same degree of intensity. Giorgio Mondo who, in the experiment communicated in this chapter, only withstood the rarefied air until the pressure of 336 mm. was reached, had held out until the pressure sank to 324 mm. two days previously. The indisposition does not augment uninterruptedly, but breaks out periodically, returning with more or less violence as long as the rarefaction of the air continues.

Our observations during these experiments on myself and the one preceding on Giorgio Mondo led us to conclude with certainty that the augmentation in the rate of the cardiac pulsations in rarefied air is not due to mechanical conditions to which the diminished pressure at the surface of the body gives rise, because the pulse fell, owing to the effects of the oxygen, from 88 to 64 (that is, 4 pulsations below the normal rate), while the pressure remained constant at 290 mm. The cause of the modification of the activity of the heart, which here manifests itself with surprising intensity, is therefore chemical in its nature. Not less important is the increase which takes place in the rate of breathing under the influence of oxygen, the number of respiratory movements per minute rising from 14 to 19, although everything would have led one to expect the contrary phenomenon.

From the calculations in the footnote [1] we see that the first time I left off at a pressure of 292 mm., when I was breathing 8·45 parts of oxygen in weight in every 100 parts. The second time I held out till a pressure of 192 mm. was reached, when the air contained 8·14 of oxygen in weight in every 100 parts. Here, too, we find again what I have observed in all similar experiments, namely, that the second time one withstands a greater diminution of pressure although the quantity of oxygen at the disposal of the organism is less. In this second case, however, the quantity of carbonic acid was greater, being in the proportion of 2·1 per cent., whereas in the ordinary air, taken at a pressure of 292 mm. and analysed in the same way, we found only 0·8 per cent. of carbonic acid.

It is important to remember that I might have borne a still greater barometric depression than **192** mm. (=alt., **11,650** m.) and that I concluded the experiment, not because I felt ill as the first time at a pressure of 292 mm., but because of an accident which prevented my continuing to write. If, with less oxygen, I bore a further depression of 100 mm. of mercury, this must be due to the presence of the 2·1 per cent. of carbonic acid in the respired air.

[1] The analysis of the air showed it to contain, in volumes, at a pressure of 292 mm. :
20·1 per cent. oxygen, 0·8 per cent. carbonic acid ;
and at a pressure of 192 mm. :
29·18 per cent. oxygen, 2·1 per cent. carbonic acid.

$$760 : 22 :: 292 : x \quad x = \frac{292 \times 22}{760} = 8\cdot45$$

$$19\cdot9 : 22 :: 29\cdot18 : x \quad x = \frac{29\cdot18 \times 22}{19\cdot9} = 32\cdot25$$

$$760 : 32\cdot25 :: 192 : x \quad x = \frac{192 \times 32\cdot25}{760} = 8\cdot14$$

Dr. Georg von Liebig,[1] who has done much excellent work on the subject of respiration, recently published an article on the causes which render it impossible to whistle in rarefied air. Bert, while experimenting in the pneumatic chamber, found that he could not whistle at a pressure of 500 mm., which corresponds to a height of only 3,334 metres.[2] Dr. Schyrmunski of Berlin found likewise that he could not whistle in the pneumatic chamber in a rarefaction of the air corresponding to the height of Monte Rosa.

When I read these observations I immediately concluded that these two physiologists must be more keenly susceptible to the action of rarefied air than myself, and I remembered that in Regina Margherita Hut the soldiers often whistled, and in the evening they often accompanied the song of some comrade in this way in quite a masterly manner. I have repeatedly tested this observation, as in this last experiment, and have found that at a pressure corresponding to an altitude of 6,600 metres I can whistle quite well, but at a higher degree of rarefaction I experience a certain difficulty in producing the higher notes. Those who suffer probably cannot execute an expiration sufficiently rapid and forcible to produce the whistling sounds. We have already said that even merely speaking, when the air is much rarefied, occasions distress and fatigues one more. Humboldt remarked that on arriving at Quito (alt., 3,000 metres) it became a greater effort to speak.

V.

In 1895 I laid the tracings of breathing and pulse which I had taken on Monte Rosa[3] before the International Congress of Physiologists held in Berne, and gave it as my opinion that they could only be explained by *acapnia*.

Amongst the facts on which I based my hypothesis, the weightiest was that of the respiratory arrest observed in all my companions during sleep, a complete arrest which, in the case of my brother, lasted regularly for 12 seconds. If the amount of oxygen in arterial blood does not vary until there is a pressure of 410 mm., the constant fact of periodic respiration, observed at a pressure of 423 mm. on Monte Rosa, must be due to *acapnia*. It is the deficiency of carbonic acid which occasions long intervals of repose in the respiratory centre, although the ration of oxygen in the air is diminished. I made another communication on the same subject to the Société de Biologie in Paris.[4] Dr. Regnard made the objection to my theory of *acapnia* that the diminution of carbonic acid on the mountains must be very insignificant,[5] but it seems to me that the data given in this chapter prove the contrary.

The stimulus which makes us breathe is a certain degree of accumulation of carbonic acid in the blood. When the carbonic acid in the blood diminishes, the need of breathing ceases. Hering and A. Ewald[6] found that when they made a dog breathe very forcibly by means of a bellows, the blood lost about the half of the carbonic acid which it contained.

It is to this diminution of carbonic acid that, in spite of the contrary opinion of most able physiologists, we must attribute that arrest of breathing

---

[1] G. v. Liebig, *Warum man unter einem stark verminderten Luftdruck nicht mehr pfeifen kann.* Münchener Medic. Wochenschrift, n. 10, 1897.
[2] *Op. cit.*, p. 752.   [3] *Op. cit.*, p. 752.
[4] Société de Biologie, 5 Mars, 1897.
[5] Paul Regnard, *La cure d'altitude.* Paris, 1897, p. 97.
[6] A. Ewald, *Zur Kenntniss der Apnoë.* Pflüger's Archiv, vol. vii. p. 575, 1783.

which is known under the name of apnœa and of which I have given tracings obtained on man in Figs. 52 and 53. This was the opinion of Miescher.[1] This hypothesis, which considers apnœa as arising from the diminution of carbonic acid in the blood, seems to me to cover all the changes which I observed in the breathing on Monte Rosa and of which I therefore hold *acapnia* to be the sole explanation.

As yet physiology has not examined this particular state of the organism in which the blood contains less than the normal amount of carbonic acid.

Lahousse found, indeed, that when peptone, that is, digested albumen, is injected into the veins a diminution of carbonic acid in the arterial blood is produced. Immediately after the injection vomiting appears, the respiratory movements are slackened, and sometimes the thorax tends to stop its movement, while the animal shows signs of breathing with difficulty. Muscular strength diminishes, the animal seems tired and walks unsteadily. The blood-vessels are dilated and the blood-pressure feeble. The rate of the cardiac pulsations reaches a maximum. The animal is sleepy and dejected.[2]

We meet with no other material modification of the organism which may give rise to these phenomena resembling those of mountain-sickness, excepting the defective condition of the blood, which contains less carbonic acid and becomes incapable of coagulating.

The quantity of carbonic acid diminishes almost by one-half. The quantity of oxygen increases by almost 5 per cent. This condition lasts only for a short time and after half an hour or an hour the animal has completely recovered.

The symptoms exhibited by an animal poisoned by an injection of peptone resemble those of mountain-sickness so greatly that I felt it necessary to study the subject. The cause of the indisposition is widely different. The injection of an albuminous body into the blood is so different from barometric depression that one is inclined to think there cannot possibly be any relation between the two. There is, however, one point of resemblance—*acapnia*. The following is an experiment on the subject:—

At 3 o'clock in the afternoon we inject into the jugular vein of a dog, weighing 6,500 grams, breathing 18 to 20 times in the minute, and with a pulse-rate of from 80 to 90 per minute, 30 c.c. of a 10 per cent. solution of peptone. The breathing immediately slackens and falls to 11 per minute, the pulse rising to 156. The animal is dejected. He still fondles us at first, then retires to a corner and appears disinclined to move; when he lifts his legs to surmount an obstacle he seems tired.

After 15 minutes other 46 c.c. of peptone are injected into him. The breathing falls to 8 in the minute and becomes very superficial. There is no doubt but that the peptone acts on the breathing, rendering it less active; the pulse is so rapid and weak that it can scarcely be counted.

In order to find out whether these two characteristic phenomena are due to *acapnia*, I make the animal breathe artificial air rich in carbonic acid.

I had let 500 litres of air into a large gas-meter and added to these 50 litres of carbonic acid, the analysis of the resultant composition showing that this air contained 16·7 per cent. carbonic acid. A muzzle of india-rubber made in the form of a truncated cone is put into communication with the gas-meter by means of a tube, I then open a tap which lets out a strong current of artificial air which the dog is made to breathe.

Pulse (in one minute).		Breathing (in one minute).
194	..	12
182	...	12

The dog breathes air containing 16·7 per cent. carbonic acid.

---

[1] Miescher, *Die histochemischen und physiologischen Arbeiten.* Leipzig, 1897, p. 272.
[2] Lahousse, *Die Gase des Peptonblutes.* Archiv. f. Anat. u. Phys., 1889, p. 77.

Pulse (in one minute).		Breathing (in one minute).
128	...	36
124	...	44
112	...	40
114	...	40
The dog breathes ordinary air.		
160	...	14
168	...	14
168	...	14
The animal again breathes carbonic acid.		
110	...	36
106	...	40
120	...	40
116	...	40
The dog again breathes ordinary air.		
162	...	22
156	...	14
170	...	14

The pulse of the peptonised animal accelerates as in us during apnœa when we draw a series of deep breaths and the breathing slackens as in apnœa, because the reflex excitability of the spinal cord is diminished in these pathological conditions owing to the lack of carbonic acid.

Having thus confirmed several times in succession that carbonic acid always slackens the pulse, we must conclude that this gas is beneficial in *acapnia*.

This is the first time that we see carbonic acid used as a remedy, rendered necessary by a deficiency of this gas in the blood.

A proof of the efficacy of carbonic acid seems to me to be given by the experiences of the two scholastic excursions which met in Regina Margherita Hut.[1] There were forty-five persons altogether, and these had barely one cubic metre of air each; nominally there were 1·29 cubic metres per head, but we must deduct the volume of each person's body, that of the furniture in the hut, of the provisions, and especially of the fuel. The hut being plated over with copper sheets, of which the joints are hermetically closed so as to prevent the entrance of the snow between the planks, the cubic measurement of air for each person may be considered as accurate. There was no other opening for ventilation except the windows, which remained off the latch, and the two stove pipes which kept up the necessary draught. If, under such unfavourable conditions (and they could scarcely have been worse), forty-five persons crowded together within a space with a capacity of scarcely 58 cubic metres, did not suffer, this circumstance must, I think, be attributed to the amount of carbonic acid in the air they breathed.

It seems strange, but we have seen that no other explanation can be found for the exemption of these persons from mountain-sickness in an air which was certainly very poor in oxygen.

VI.

It is a known fact that carbonic acid is of the utmost importance to life, producing, as it does, the respiratory movements, acting on the heart and

---

[1] The dimensions of the Regina Margherita Hut are as follows: length 9.20 metres, breadth 3 metres, height 2.10 metres. The cubical contents divided amongst forty-five persons give 1·29 cubic metres for each.

$$9\cdot 20 \times 3 = 27\cdot 60 \times 2\cdot 10 = \frac{57\cdot 960}{45} = 1\cdot 29$$

effecting the contraction of the blood-vessels. It is likewise known that the accumulation of carbonic acid in the blood is a stronger specific stimulus to the respiratory centre than the lack of oxygen. These studies of mine on *acapnia* show that the diminution of carbonic acid in the blood exercises a profound influence on vital phenomena. Carbonic acid combines doubtless with various substances of the blood, whereas oxygen combines solely with the substance of the red corpuscles, but our ignorance respecting the origin of the former gas and its conduct in the organism is much greater than with regard to oxygen and its properties. It is probable that the barometric depression dissociates certain bicarbonates which are found in the blood, as it does bicarbonate of potash.

There is a very simple experiment often performed in the lecture-room in order to show that certain chemical combinations are so unstable that they disunite when the barometric pressure is diminished. A concentrated solution of bi-carbonate of potash is prepared in a cylinder, at the bottom of which a few crystals are left, and then put under a pneumatic bell. Under barometric depressions corresponding to the heights of Mont Blanc and Monte Rosa we notice a development of carbonic acid, bubbles of this gas detaching themselves in abundance from the crystals, the effervescence continuing so long as the barometric depression is prolonged.

Lœwy[1] had already observed that when carbonic acid is breathed in the pneumatic chamber it is of as much benefit as oxygen alone. Only the mechanism of their action is different, according to Lœwy, the carbonic acid, which causes a greater intensity of respiration, effecting a more active ventilation in the lungs. We have, however, already seen in the foregoing experiment that it is of no use to draw deep breaths and promote a more active renewal of the air in the lungs when the indisposition due to the rarefaction of the air manifests itself. The theory of *acapnia* gives us the key to Lœwy's experiment with carbonic acid.

If we examine more closely these apparently paradoxical facts we see that carbonic acid is useful because it acts on the heart. In the footnote[2] I

---

[1] *Op. cit.*, p. 21.
[2] *Giorgio Mondo.* March 11, 1898. Pressure, 741 mm. Temperature, 18°. The subject enters the chamber while air at the usual pressure is circulating within it.

Time	Pulse	Temperature
9.0 a.m.	60	17°
9.5 ,,	60	...
9.12 ,,	60	...

The rarefaction of the air is begun.

Time	Pulse	Pressure in mm.
9.15 ,,	60	601
9.23 ,,	64	571
9.45 ,,	66	461
9.50 ,,	69	391
9.52 ,,	72	391
9.54 ,,	73	390

We let about 50 litres of carbonic acid into the chamber. I close the air-tap so as to prevent too great a diminution of the inner pressure.

9.57 a.m.	70	411
	66	
10.0 ,,	62	411
	62	
10.2 ,,	60	411

The subject fills a bottle full of air for subsequent analysis. It is found to contain 5·3 per cent. of carbonic acid.

communicate the results obtained when we gave carbonic acid to a person when the distressing effects of rarefied air were beginning to be felt.

We see that as soon as carbonic acid was let into the pneumatic chamber the rate of the pulse immediately diminished. In spite of the barometric pressure of 400 mm., the pulse falls from 73 to 60 beats per minute.

On coming out of the chamber the subject tells us that at a pressure of 390 mm. he breathed with difficulty and had a headache, and that he felt better as soon as he inhaled carbonic acid.

I repeated this experiment on myself, and found that the pulse returned to the normal rate as soon as I inhaled carbonic acid, and that the breathing then became deeper.

The pulse was 71 at the pressure of 422 mm. (which about corresponds to the height of Monte Rosa). As soon as I began to breathe air very rich in carbonic acid the pulse fell to 63 and 62 (the normal rate being 61), although the pressure remained the same. The amount of carbonic acid was 4·7 per cent.

In other persons, as for instance in Dr. Treves, the influence on the pulse was less evident, but the improvement of the condition was confirmed by all. On March 10th Dr. Treves endured a depression of 340 mm. ($=$ 6,405 metres). When he inhaled carbonic acid he afterwards told us the feeling of dizziness disappeared, although the pressure did not alter, decreasing even to 330 mm.

We must now see whether carbonic acid alone is capable of producing a slackening of the cardiac pulsations. To this end I performed a series of experiments in the pneumatic chamber.

The same person, Giorgio Mondo, who had been the subject of the preceding experiment, entered the pneumatic chamber the next day, and counted his pulse while in a sitting position, the pump meanwhile producing a sufficient current of air. Pressure, 734 mm. Temperature, 18°.

Pulse in one minute : 53, 53, 53, 53, 54, 54, 54, 54, 55, 55, 54, 54, 54.
Breathing ,, : 13, 13, 12, 12, 13.
I let into the pneumatic chamber 50 litres of carbonic acid.
Pulse : 53, 52, 53, 54, 55, 55.
Breathing : 18, 15, 15, 16, 17.
On analysis the air was found to contain 4·7 per cent. carbonic acid.

We see that the effect was very small, almost inappreciable, for the pulse did not alter when the subject breathed in 4·7 per cent. carbonic acid. More manifest was the influence on the breathing, which rose from the rate of 13 to 18.

The quantity of carbonic acid administered was, in this case, too great to admit of a comparison with the experiment preceding. We must remember that in rarefied air the weight of carbonic acid diminishes in proportion to the pressure. In the preceding experiment, for instance, we find on working out the necessary formulæ for the transformation of volume into weight, that at the pressure of 411 mm. Mondo breathed only about the half of carbonic acid. In order to establish a comparison I should therefore have to give him only 2·8 per cent. carbonic acid at the usual pressure, so that in a unit of time he would breathe in the same quantity.

I then made an experiment on Mondo, in which I gave him 2·5 per cent., and found that the rate of the pulse did not change, only the breathing rose to 15 from 13.

It is therefore proved that, when one breathes in carbonic acid at the usual pressure in the proportion of 2 to 3 per cent., it has no effect on the rate of the cardiac pulsations, whereas in rarefied air it slackens the movements of the heart.

The cause of this difference is that, at the usual pressure, the augmentation of the tension of carbonic acid beyond a certain narrow limit is of no use, whereas, when we are in rarefied air, as there is a deficiency of carbonic acid in the blood (the cause of the increased rapidity of the heart-beats) the addition of a small quantity of this gas to the air inhaled, slackens the pulse, re-establishing, as it does, the normal conditions of carbonic acid in the blood.

VII.

The reader understands, doubtless, how difficult it is to determine the moment at which a man who is ascending into higher atmospheric regions ceases to be in a normal physiological condition and becomes ill. In the study of mountain-sickness, as in that of all other maladies, physiology and pathology can scarcely be separated, because, from the province of the one, we pass insensibly into that of the other.

The experiments showing the restorative effect of carbonic acid confirm, as it seems to me, the theory of acapnia. I now communicate a few other facts which likewise lend support to that hypothesis. These new observations will make the phenomena which manifest themselves in the blood as we climb higher on the mountains, clearer to us.

Carbonic acid separates itself with difficulty from the blood, and when it passes through the lungs there is not time for it to free itself altogether from that fluid.

If we take a bottle of effervescing water and pour it into a wide dish, in which it forms only a thin layer, and then back again into the bottle in which we shake it, then into the dish again, and so on several times in succession, we shall still find, on putting it in a glass under the pneumatic bell, that carbonic acid is given off in much greater abundance than from the same amount of ordinary water.

However vigorous the ventilation of the lungs, there always remains about one-fourth of the normal amount of carbonic acid in the blood, as has been shown by the analysis of arterial blood performed during apnœa by Ewald.

I shall here say a few words on a series of analyses which I made of expired air collected at different barometric pressures. The method adopted was the usual one of Hempel. Of the numerous experiments made in various ways on different persons, I select one which I give in detail, as the scope of this work, which is rather of a synthetic character, compels me to be brief. I assure the reader, however, that all these experiments showed that the rarefaction of the air draws a considerable quantity of carbonic acid, which is held in solution by the blood, out of that fluid.

A first series of analyses was made of the air which issues from the lungs at different degrees of rarefaction in the pneumatic chamber.

A medical student, Sig. Polledro, breathed into a bottle full of saturated salt solution until it contained about 800 cubic centimetres of air. This bottle was closed at the top by an ebony tap, and was furnished, at the bottom, with a large tube of india-rubber, by means of which the water might issue when the subject blew into it.

I first ascertained what error might be incurred by withdrawing in this way part of the air contained in the lungs at the end of an ordinary inspiration. Five experiments performed, one after the other, at intervals of about five minutes, showed that expired air contains the following proportions of carbonic acid per cent. :—

3·1 per cent. — 3·0 per cent. — 3·5 per cent. — 3·3 per cent. — 3·5 per cent.

The difference of 0·5 per cent. seemed to me too insignificant to disqualify the experiment, which was carried out as follows :—

Oreste Polledro, student, 24 years of age, enters the pneumatic chamber, in which, on a table, are five glass bottles like the one just described, all full of salt solution, closed at the top with a tap and furnished at the bottom with a tube likewise full of salt solution which hung down into a pail full of water. After resting for a time, and while the pump was effecting an active ventilation within the pneumatic chamber to prevent an accumulation of carbonic acid, the subject fills one bottle with air expired at the usual pressure, then a second at a pressure of 580 mm., a third at 420 mm., a fourth at a pressure of 580 mm. again, and the fifth and last at the usual pressure.

In the following table the results of this analysis of the air are given. The experiments were made in the month of January on four different days. From 20 to 30 minutes were allowed to elapse between the filling of one bottle and the next with expired air, so as to ensure an establishment of the equilibrium of the pressure, and of its action as at the corresponding altitudes of 2,150 and 4,600 metres.

QUANTITY OF CARBONIC ACID FOUND IN EXPIRED AIR COLLECTED SUCCESSIVELY AT DIFFERENT BAROMETRIC PRESSURES.

Serial number of experiment.	Pressure 740 mm.	Pressure 580 mm.	Pressure 420 mm.	Pressure 580 mm.	Pressure 740 mm.
I.	6·1	7·8	5·9	4·7	5·5
II.	5·7	7·2	5·4	4·7	4·2
III.	4·1	6·2	4·3	5·0	3·8
IV.	3·5	5·1	4·6	4·3	3·1

It is evident, therefore, that the amount of carbonic acid eliminated with the expired air does not so much depend on the extent of the barometric depression as on the point of time : that is, that a small diminution of pressure extracts at *first* a greater amount of carbonic acid from the body than a diminution twice as great to which the individual is *subsequently* subjected.

Experiments similar to these were made by A. Lœwy.[1] The results of the analyses of air collected by this investigator in the pneumatic chamber showed "that during repose there is an increase in the elimination of carbonic acid in proportion as the pressure diminishes." The above experiment, which was repeated on the same subject, shows that the phenomenon is more complex than has hitherto been thought. The greatest amount of carbonic acid was eliminated in the first half-hour ; afterwards less carbonic acid is extracted from the blood, even though the depression is doubled, passing from 580 mm. to 420 mm.

Here we have a factor which has till now been neglected : the point of time. I have made the experiment of keeping subjects for two hours in the

[1] *Op. cit.*, p. 26.

pneumatic chamber at a pressure corresponding to that in Regina Margherita Hut, and have found that the difference at the end of this time was very small in comparison to the normal, whereas, in the first half-hour, at a pressure of 580 mm., results like those indicated in the preceding table were obtained.

When the normal pressure is re-established, less carbonic acid is eliminated than at first, as this gas begins then to accumulate again in the blood.

Barometric depression acts in a mechanical and physical manner, drawing the carbonic acid out of the blood, without the intensity of the chemical processes of the organism being modified by small differences of pressure (580 mm. and 420 mm.).

In studying the respiratory quotient, we must therefore take the barometric pressure into consideration.

VIII.

It had long been known that on the Alps wine less easily causes inebriation ; but no one had sought to explain this fact. Preliminary studies on *acapnia* suggested to me the idea of finding out, by means of experiment, whether alcohol, which has entered into the blood, issues from the lungs more easily in rarefied air.

The effects of alcohol are, unfortunately, only too well known, but as yet we know little about the transformation which it undergoes in the organism. The old opinion pronounced by Liebig, that alcohol burns and produces carbonic acid and water, thus saving the combustion of other substances of our body, has been abandoned. It is a known fact, however, that part of the alcohol drunk (from 5 to 10 per cent.), issues unaltered from the lungs with the expired air after it has passed into the blood. One part issues unaltered with the secretion of the kidneys and passes into the urine ; the rest is burnt in the organism.

I requested my assistant, Dr. Benedicenti, to investigate this subject. His researches, begun in my laboratory and continued in that of Prof. Rosenthal at the University of Erlangen, confirmed my previous views. In rarefied air alcohol issues more easily from the blood and the phenomena of inebriation are less lasting and also less intense, although the quantity of alcohol taken remains the same.

Dr. Benedicenti drank, for instance, 50 cubic centimetres of absolute alcohol diluted with 200 cubic centimetres of water, and analysed the air he breathed out after half an hour at the usual pressure, and at a pressure corresponding to an altitude of 2,000 metres. He found that even this slight degree of rarefaction of the air had occasioned a more copious elimination of alcohol in the expired air.[1]

The experiments made on animals are more exact. We found, for instance, that whereas, during one hour at the usual pressure 0·0118 grs. of alcohol were eliminated, 0·0156 grs. were eliminated during the same length of time at a pressure of 570 mm. (= 2,300 metres altitude). Subbotin's method, which was followed in these investigations, enables the investigator to recognise even the smallest trace of alcohol in the air expired. The difference of 4·6 milligrams in one hour is not so small a matter as it seems, as

[1] The method adopted was that of Strassmann. For further particulars I must refer the reader to the original article by Dr. Benedicenti, *Ueber die Alkoholausscheidung durch die Lungen.* Arch. f. Anat. u. Physiol., 1896.

the animal did not weigh one kilogram (0·970 kgs.) and the time was comparatively short.

Other substances found in the blood in the form of gas or loosely combined with the corpuscles of the blood, or dissolved in the serum, may likewise be drawn from the blood by means of barometric depression. Dr. Benedicenti found that the action of chloroform is also less intense when the animals dosed with it are placed under the pneumatic bell. The phenomena of poisoning disappear more rapidly in rarefied air, and analysis of the air expired shows that a greater quantity of chloroform is eliminated when the barometric pressure diminishes.

Pohl[1] had already shown that the vapours of chloroform which produce poisoning and anæsthesia, remain dissolved in the blood, but that by means of a current of air kept up through the blood for a considerable length of time, all the chloroform which was administered may be recovered. Carbonic acid forms, probably, like chloroform and alcohol, a very unstable combination with the blood, or else it is held in the blood simply by physical and mechanical influences; in the one case as in the other a barometric depression suffices to set free carbonic acid, alcohol, and chloroform.

IX.

Rarefied air causes an alteration of the lungs similar to that observable after the vagus nerves have been severed at the neck. I consider this change as an important factor in mountain-sickness. We have, therefore, two new ideas which concur to explain the symptoms: a central phenomenon, *acapnia*; and a peripheric phenomenon, the *paralysis of the vagus nerve*.

On page 220 I have already enumerated the phenomena observed on Monte Rosa which are due to the paralysis of the vagus nerve; here I shall give the proofs which show that paralysis of this nerve in rarefied air is an indubitable fact. Whenever dogs or rabbits are subjected in the pneumatic chamber to a rarefaction of the air corresponding to 290 or 260 mm., their lungs become hyperæmic and congested. This change always takes place even when the action of the rarefied air is only kept up for half an hour or an hour. Now that we have found a material change in the lungs of animals subjected to a barometric depression corresponding to an altitude of 7,500 or of 8,400 metres, we may interpret those serious disturbances which appear in man at great heights with the certainty that our explanation rests on a sure basis.

The best way to perform the experiment is as follows: Four young dogs of one litter, and which are three or four months old, are selected. Of these two are put under the pneumatic bell, the air then being rarefied till the pressure within amounts to 29 or 30 centimetres. This pressure is maintained, while at the same time an abundant current of air is kept up within the bell. In another of these dogs both vagus nerves must be severed, the fourth animal being left for the present uninjured in order that the heart and lungs in the other dogs may afterwards be compared with corresponding organs in a normal state. After the lapse of half an hour or an hour, the examination of lungs and heart in the dogs which have been kept in rarefied air shows that in aspect these organs precisely resemble those of the dog

---

[1] Pohl, *Ueber Aufnahme und Vertheilung des Chloroforms im thierischen Organismus.* Arch. f. exp. Path. u. Pharm. xxviii., 1891.

in which the vagus nerves have been severed, and in which consequently there was complete paralysis of these nerves.

The lungs of animals subjected to the action of rarefied air are slightly œdematous. Their colour is not so pale as usual, it has a reddish grey tint with dark, bluish spots. In those parts where the colour has remained normal there are spots of lighter hue irregularly distributed. At the surface, and especially at the edge of the pulmonary lobes, there are circumscribed hæmorrhages, ecchymoses, and extravasations of blood of a dark violet colour.

As the lungs are harder and firmer, they shrink less when the thorax is opened than in an animal in normal physiological conditions. When an incision is made in one of the darker parts of the lung a somewhat frothy liquid exudes.

In full-grown dogs it sometimes happens that we find no hyperæmia and congestion of the lungs after they have been subjected for half an hour to a diminution of barometric pressure as great as that which exists on the highest summits of the Himalayas. This did not surprise me, as it is a known fact that the phenomena observable also after the severing of the vagus nerves vary very much even in animals of the same species.

The congestion of the lungs and dilatation of the heart sufficiently explain the constant and remarkable diminution found in the vital capacity of all those persons who accompanied me on the Monte Rosa expedition (see Table X. at the end of the book).

The disease of the lungs in the case of the soldier Ramella, the report of which is given in the First Appendix, may probably be attributed to the same causes. The paralysis of the vagus perhaps explains the rapid and fatal progress of the malady to which Dr. Jacottet succumbed on Mont Blanc, and the œdema of the lungs found in the autopsy. The death of the brothers Zoja on the Gridone was probably also due in part to the paralysis of the vagus.

Just as the severing of the vagus nerves produces varying phenomena in different animals, so the effect of rarefied air is not in all of us equally intense. The more rapid disappearance in some persons of the less serious effects of paralysis of the vagus is doubtless due to the fact that the disturbances of cardiac innervation, of the nervous system and of the lungs may subside after a short sojourn on the Alps.

This discovery of important alterations in the lungs will perhaps frighten some, but the mountain climber must have confidence in his own powers of resistance, which he may test by preliminary experiments and increase by training. I myself, while studying the effects of paralysis of the vagus consequent on rarefaction of the air, did not hesitate to subject myself to the greatest depressions which man has as yet resisted.

I refrain from entering on the researches which I have made relating to remedies against mountain-sickness and fatigue, in which special attention was given to the properties of cocaine. The results of these investigations will be published later. In a work of a more analytical character shortly to be issued I shall publish an experimental critique on the recent investigations of E. Aron and G. von Liebig, as well as the results of a series of experiments showing the effect of rarefied air on the circulation of the blood in the lungs. It was my purpose to explain simply and clearly certain series of facts in human physiology in the hope of thus rendering a service to mountain-climbers desirous of knowing the scientific reason for the hygienic rules to be followed in mountaineering. If this book should be found to meet the needs of those who, intending likewise to make observations on the phenomena which human life presents on the Alps, wish to become acquainted with the prevailing views on Alpine physiology I shall be fully satisfied.

I am convinced that this work will prove of use to a greater number of readers the less the bulk of the volume and the less abstruse the matter. I therefore now draw it to a conclusion. I have made so many digressions that I almost feel it my duty to ask the reader to pardon me. The interruption of the account of our expedition was, however, unavoidable, in order to elucidate the phenomena observed. The discovery of new facts is of little use unless we succeed in explaining them; the search for causes, which is the noblest task set by science, is full of fascination for the student of nature.

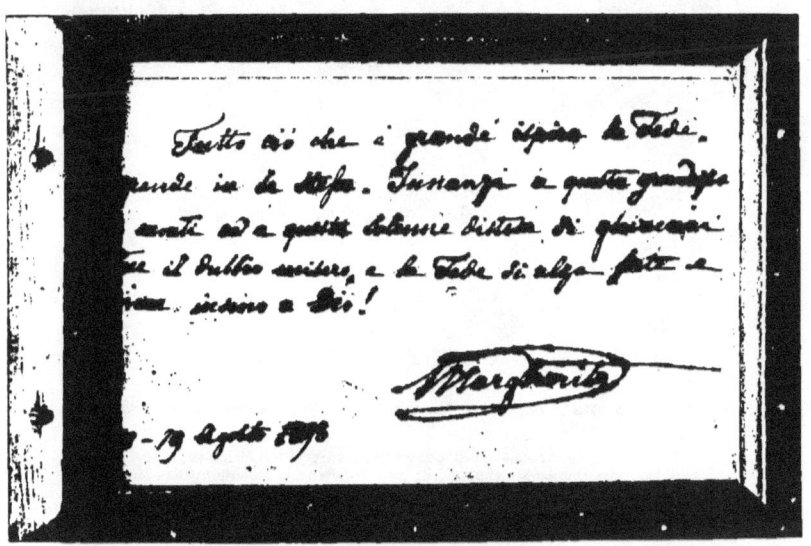

Inscription burnt into a tablet of wood by H.M. the Queen of Italy, in Regina Margherita Hut.

"*All that is grand inspires Faith, which is grand in itself. These mountains in their grandeur, these majestic glaciers silence pitiable doubt, and Faith rises, strong and vigorous, to God!*"
"*August* 18–19, 1893. "*Margherita.*"

The new Regina Margherita Observatory to be constructed in 1898 on the summit of Monte Rosa (alt., 4,560 metres). (Drawing by Sig. Girola, engineer.)

CHAPTER XXIII

THE NEW OBSERVATORY AND ALPINE STATION ON MONTE ROSA

"Of the four great nations whose boundaries march with Switzerland, perhaps none has more thoroughly explored its own frontiers and mountains than Italy."[1]

I.

ON Gnifetti Peak, at an altitude of 4,560 metres, a new observatory is to be constructed this year (1898) in order to facilitate the study of the Alps, the heavens, the physical phenomena of the earth, and life above the snow-line.

The idea of this undertaking originated with H.M. Queen Margaret of Italy. Perhaps the difficulties which we encountered on our expedition up Monte Rosa had some part in suggesting the project to her Majesty, who followed with interest the investigations carried on by Professor Piero Giacosa as well as those laid before the reader in this book. The proposal to construct an edifice on Gnifetti Peak, for the sole purpose of facilitating scientific research, was made spontaneously by H.M. Queen Margaret—it was

---

[1] C. D. Cunningham and Captain Abney, *The Pioneers of the Alps*, p. 128.

not the outcome of any previous suggestion from others. This declaration I feel it my duty to make in homage to the truth. Senator Perazzi communicated this decision of her Majesty to me in 1895, at the same time consigning 4,000 lire to me, with the request that I should form a committee in order to carry out the plan for the building of the new Monte Rosa Observatory.

The Minister of Agriculture and Commerce, acceding to the proposal made by Professor Tacchini, director of the meteorological department and of the observatory of the *Collegio romano*, contributed 10,000 lire in a series of instalments, further assigning a yearly endowment for the expenses of service and the keeping-up of the observatory. H.R.H. Louis, Duke of the Abruzzi,[1] contributed 5,000 lire, and the Italian Alpine Club 4,000 lire.

In a short time the sum necessary for the construction of the observatory by enlarging the Regina Margherita Hut was thus collected. The Commission[2] which was

[1] H.R.H. Louis of Savoy, Duke of the Abruzzi and nephew of King Humbert of Italy, made the ascent of Mount St. Elias in Alaska in 1897.
[2] Those belonging to the Commission are: Professor Tacchini above-mentioned, Senator Blaserna, Professor of Physics at the University of Rome, Dr. Alfonso Sella, assistant in the Physical Insti-

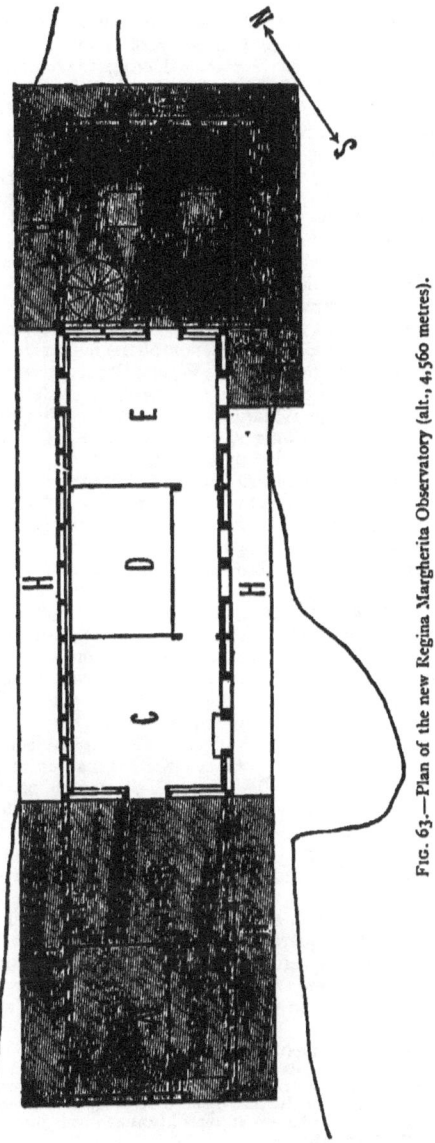

Fig. 63.—Plan of the new Regina Margherita Observatory (alt., 4,560 metres).

appointed came to the decision that the Monte Rosa Observatory should be annexed to the University of Turin and the directorship assigned to Professor Andrea Naccari. During the summers of 1896 and 1897 the weather was so bad on the Alps that the foundations of the building could not be laid, but from the attempts made in 1896 when the ice was cleared away, it appeared that it would not be possible to construct the observatory apart from the hut on account of the absence of rock. In 1897, although the weather was little favourable, the rock was levelled and preparations made for the laying of the foundations, so that towards the middle of July, 1898, we may hope that this part of the work will be completed and the new construction begun.

Fig. 63 shows the plan of the new Observatory. The middle part left white is the old Regina Margherita Hut, composed of three rooms, C, D, E, as already shown in the plan on page 129. The dark part at the two sides represents the new rooms and the observatory now in course of construction at Alagna, under the direction of the engineers Signori Girola and Gaudenzio Sella and of the advocate Signor Grober, president of the Alpine Club, and which will be put together this year on Gnifetti Peak.

The Regina Margherita Hut will be lengthened towards the north by the two-storied wing F, which will jut out beyond the breadth of the present hut and be encircled by a balcony H, H.

The two rooms, situated one above the other, have a side of 4 metres and a height proportioned to the instruments which will be placed within them. The part facing the south where the door of the hut is at present will be lengthened and two new rooms, A and B, constructed in it. That portion of the building destined for the observatory will contain four rooms: D, E, and two above these in the upper storey; for the use of mountain-climbers three rooms will remain, A, B, C. The new entry will be in the middle of the building facing towards the south. Two little pillars, indicated in the last room to the right of the plan, made of stone and fixed into the rock, are to serve as supports for instruments measuring gravity, galvanometers, and other instruments of precision. An inside flight of stairs puts this part of the observatory in communication with the upper floor. Hence by means of an outside flight the upper terrace is reached. This terrace is made in such a manner that it may when necessary be covered over, so as to protect instruments from the rays of the sun. The old hut, completely plated over with copper, is, as it were, enclosed within a lightning-conductor, for, by means of points, and wires which are led down the rock into the ice, electrical discharges are provided against. As this means of protecting the hut against lightning has proved to be effectual, the new part of the observatory will also be coppered over.

At the south side of the observatory a level will be made on a projecting rock, a few square metres in area, for investigations in the open air. In the drawing the irregular line which bulges out before the door indicates the form of the uncovered rock on which the Regina Margherita Observatory is to stand; this line runs on to the right and then along the back part of the building.

tute of Rome, Professor Andrea Naccari, Professor of Physics at the University of Turin, Professor Piero Giacosa, Professor of Pharmacology at the University of Turin, Professor Francesco Porro, Director of the Astronomical Observatory of Turin, Signor Grober, President of the Italian Alpine Club, Signor Gaudenzio Sella, engineer, Signor Cav. Giacomo Rey, who was appointed treasurer, and Angelo Mosso, who was elected president of the Committee.

II.

Many mountain-climbers have seen the Vallot Observatory on Mont Blanc and the more recently erected observatory of Janssen, of which there is a description in the memoirs of the Académie des Sciences of Paris. Whymper, in his book, "A Guide to Chamonix and the Range of Mont Blanc," gives figures of both the inside and outside of the Janssen Observatory, and remarks that the building will gradually sink into the snow. This is perfectly correct, because every year an amount of snow falls on Mont Blanc and the layers below sink downwards. On August 26, 1881, the Vice-President of the Italian Alpine Club, Signor Gonella, crossed Mont Blanc, starting from the Aiguille Grise Hut on the Italian side. When he arrived at the summit of Mont Blanc, which has the form of an arc, he found that it was divided in a perpendicular direction by a large crevasse. He was obliged to skirt this crevasse, climbing down a certain distance on the Italian slope in order to reach the other side. When he had reached the top again, a gust of wind carried away his hat, which was lost in the crevasse, the owner being obliged to descend to Chamonix with a woollen cap. The guide, Alphonse Payot, declares that more than ten years ago he met with a crevasse which was about 100 metres in depth on the summit of Mont Blanc. The engineer Imfeld is of opinion that the present cap of ice which covers the top of Mont Blanc is not far distant from the subjacent rock.

When a tunnel was made in the Mont Blanc calotte in order to find out where the rock lay, a plum-stone was found in the snow at a depth of 12 metres. Janssen's observatory will be buried in the same way little by little by the snow. The calotte of Mont Blanc remains at the same altitude only because every year new layers of snow are added to it, the upper layers taking the place of those that glide down the rock towards the base. Everything tends to confirm the fear that the Janssen Observatory will be swallowed up by the snow before the funds devoted to its erection have been repaid by the hoped for scientific results.

Richard's meteorograph has remained till now inactive, because the cold and the inclination of the observatory, which is slowly sinking at one side, cause the stoppage of all instruments of registration shortly after they are put in movement. The kind of registering apparatus chosen by Janssen is not, as I think, adapted to the purpose. Instead of one single motor it would perhaps have been better for each writing-apparatus to have its own special motor.

The Regina Margherita Observatory on Monte Rosa will have the great advantage of a solid foundation on the rock which will ensure accuracy in the meteorological registering instruments and in those for other geophysical investigations. The importance of an observatory at an altitude of 4,560 metres need scarcely be mentioned; the first results proceeding from the Etna Observatory, at a height of 3,000 metres, give a guarantee that those which will be obtained on Monte Rosa will furnish a valuable addition to the comparative study of data obtained at various altitudes in different latitudes. The new observatory will offer a wide field for the study of geophysics, magnetism, telluric currents, atmospheric electricity, and seismic movements. Physical astronomy will form an important part of the work of the observatory, and for microscopic researches in chemistry and physiology all possible conveniences of arrangement will be made.

On account of the cold the construction of the self-registering instruments, which must act alone for six months in the year, is a problem difficult of solution.

As a sojourn, too, the Janssen Observatory is not practical, as one cannot live, without serious sufferings, in an iron chamber buried in the ice. Fuel, carried to that height, costs 32 lire the myriagramm—four times more than it costs when taken up to Regina Margherita Hut. Living on the summit of Monte Rosa, as was proved by our expedition, is much more comfortable. Soon we hope to be able to offer to the students of the Alps those means which are indispensable to the carrying out of exact researches and with which till now it was impossible to provide one's self at such high altitudes.

To lovers of the Alps the illustration on page 313, from a photograph by Vittorio Sella, will, I am sure, be of interest. It was taken at the moment when H.M. Queen Margaret was about to ascend Gnifetti Peak. The 18th of August, 1893, is a memorable date, because on that day a new epoch in the story of Monte Rosa was ushered in with the inauguration of the Regina Margherita Hut by the august lady whose name it bears, and whose love for science prompted the consecration of this mountain to the service of Nature.

III.

The erection of the Monte Rosa Observatory being now a certainty, it is incumbent on us to plan a system on which it may be satisfactorily worked. This could be effected by the construction of a building at an altitude of 3,000 metres near the inn at the Col d'Olen, which would serve as a centre for the votaries of Alpine studies and those undertaking excursions over the glaciers.

At the sitting of the 7th of November, 1897, I laid this plan of an Alpine station at an altitude of 3,000 metres near the Col d'Olen before the Accademia dei Lincei in the name of the members of the committee. The object of the same is to furnish naturalists with the means necessary for investigation on the mountains, by founding special laboratories provided, so far as the locality permits, with the most indispensable apparatus and instruments of which the carriage presents much difficulty. The new building will probably contain twenty rooms which will serve as laboratory for geophysical, meteorological, biological, botanical, and physiological studies, another larger room will be given up to astronomy and will be furnished with a cupola which will serve as a refractor. The remaining part of the Alpine station will consist of library, collection-rooms, and living-rooms. As an assistant and servant will live here permanently, it is to be hoped that thus a satisfactory impulse will be given to the study of the Alpine world.

Besides the mutual assistance which the various experimenters will be able to lend each other in the station, a greater intimacy and friendlier feeling between the naturalists of different nationalities will thus be promoted, not without advantage to the advancement of scientific work.

Monte Rosa, as may be seen in the illustration on page 183, has a projecting part, the Hoheslicht, which juts out in the direction of the Vincent Pyramid. On a prominence of this ridge Gnifetti Hut was built. This hut is at present the largest which may be easily reached amongst all the Alpine huts at an altitude of 3,620 metres. The position in the midst of the glaciers is wonderful and has not its equal in all the Alps.

During their first attempts to reach the summit of Monte Rosa Zumstein

Dufour Peak, 4,635 m.   Zumstein Peak, 4,563 m.   Gnifetti Peak, 4,560 m.

H.M. Queen Margaret of Italy about to make the ascent of Gnifetti Peak, August 18, 1893.

and his predecessors made this peak their base of operations. The brothers Adolph and Hermann Schlagintweit stayed for two weeks in the Hoheslicht Hut and thence pursued their Alpine studies as a prelude to their explorations in Central Asia.

The highest stations which we have as yet in Europe, besides the station on Mount Etna, are the Sonnblick in the Hohe Tauern, at an altitude of 3,103 metres, and the station of the Pic du Midi in the Pyrenees at a height of 2,870 metres. The proposed station on Monte Rosa would be superior to the others on account of the easy means of communication which the mule-path would afford, of the enormous mass of glaciers which it would overlook, the neighbourhood of the Olen inn, of the large Gnifetti Hut, and the good communication with the Monte Rosa peaks and the Regina Margherita Observatory.

By means of the telegraphic and telephonic communication between the projected station and the summit of Monte Rosa, a field of study will be opened up to meteorology and geophysics unrivalled in its possibilities. Until now the study of the Alpine flora has been made, so to say, *en passant ;* in future the development of the plants, of snows and glaciers may be continuously observed and our knowledge of the modifications which the Alpine climate and the diminished pressure of the air produce on vegetable life will be vastly increased. At a short distance from the site of this station there is an island situated amongst the glaciers where a polar flora flourishes (the so-called Naso). This island may be seen in the illustration on page 183. Bacteriology and pathology will find new paths of investigation opening up before them.

IV.

For four centuries mankind has sought with ever-increasing ardour to reach the pole. The story of Arctic exploration is one of the grandest in the annals of the human race. No legend ever imagined dramas more terrible, in no struggle with the elements has man shown more undaunted heroism. The recollection of the numerous victims, of the sufferings and disasters of those who have perished amid the polar ice, thus paying for their boldness with their lives, does not deter others, fore-doomed, from following in their footsteps, from challenging with fresh hardihood the stormy seas, the icebergs, the winter darkness which lasts four months, the cold, often 45° below freezing point, the terror of ever-imminent catastrophes, and the dread of that most miserable of deaths—death from hunger.

Governments, parliaments, private individuals, offer immense sums as soon as some man who inspires confidence declares himself ready to start on a voyage of exploration to the polar regions ; and scarcely does the fear that some expedition is lost become outspoken, but new expeditions are organised to go in search of the missing explorers with a grand and touching generosity inspired by the love of science and sympathy with its daring followers.

It was once thought that the pole was a cap of ice which covered *terra firma*, possibly an island where man might set his foot ; now we are sure that about the pole there is a deep sea on which lie great fields of ice driven thither by the winds and the ocean-currents. Astronomers had already shown that the pole is not an eternally fixed point, but that its position on the surface of the earth gradually changes. Man will therefore never leave any trace of his passage in these desolate, icy regions. The discovery of the pole will be of little use to science and none at all to commerce. As Nansen [1] says, the desire to reach the pole is at bottom a suggestion of the demon of vanity. And yet, not vanity alone is the motor power but that mystery which exercises such an attraction on hardy spirits. It is the hope of reaching a point hitherto deemed inaccessible which fascinates daring characters, renowned no less for their intelligence than for their courage.

The genius of the pole, whether bad or good, is the same spirit to whom the mountain-climber pays homage. Why, many will have wondered, are those so few in number who have attempted the ascent of the highest peaks on the face of the earth? Gaurisankar, which rises 4,000 metres higher than Mont Blanc, with its untrodden snows, challenges our generation, which, perchance, will pass away, leaving it unconquered. Mount Everest, as this mountain is currently called, after the English colonel who measured its height, must be re-christened when the conqueror whom it is awaiting has reached its snowy summit and taken away the reproach from the mountaineering record that the highest peak of the earth has not yet been climbed, nor man looked down from thence on the plateaux whence the Aryan race moved onwards to subdue the world.

V.

Are the dangers attending an expedition to the pole greater than those of the ascent of the highest summits of the earth? I think not. So far as Mount Gaurisankar is concerned, there is the additional difficulty that it is situated in the independent state of Nepal and surrounded by a warlike population. As, however, the English government has a representative in the capital of this kingdom, it ought not to be too difficult for Europeans to organise a scientific expedition, the more so as Gaurisankar is scarcely 100 kilometres distant in a direct line from the confines of the English possessions in the valley of the Ganges. The travellers who first reached the base of the Himalayas certainly exaggerated the danger arising from the insalubrity of the valleys situated in front of the principal chain. The worst to be expected is that it may be a malarial region. We do not know whether malaria prevails beyond an altitude of 4,000 metres, but, at any rate, with the preventive means which we now possess, this need not be a difficulty to deter an expedition. What causes the evaporation of all enthusiasm is the conviction, till now general, that man cannot withstand the rarefied air of those altitudes. Heroism shrinks from such prolonged suffering as that due to lack of breath. The romantic descriptions of the Himalayas, the poetical enthusiasm of authors carried away by the supreme beauty of these mountains are inadequate to inspire courage to face the danger of a slow malady. I am, however, convinced that man may reach the summit of Gaurisankar without serious sufferings. The experiments and observations collected in this book give us the assurance that man is able slowly to accustom himself to the diminished barometric pressure of the Himalayas. If birds fly to a height of 8,000 metres man ought to be able to reach the same altitude at a slow rate of progress.

Let us make a brief comparison between the dangers attendant on the two enterprises. A polar expedition presents greater facilities in the matter of victualling, as there is always the probability of fresh supplies being

[1] Fridtjof Nansen, *Vers le pôle*, Paris, p. 98.

furnished by fishing and the chase; it is possible also for provision-boats to advance along the lanes which open in the ice-fields. The dogs that draw the sledges afford an excellent means of transport, because when stores run out they may be eaten one after the other. Nature is less desolate in the polar regions than on the Himalayan slopes, and the dangers are less great. Nansen and Johansen were able to travel over a great part of the polar regions on two sledges until at last they reached Franz Josef Land. Two men, whatever their strength and daring, who would attempt to travel alone over the last, unexplored part of the Himalayas would meet with certain death. The eastern part of the chain is much more precipitous than our Alps, owing to the monsoon which there prevails, and the abundance of rain which falls.

A longer preparation and an organisation on a wider basis are therefore necessary. If, as an undertaking, a Himalayan expedition may seem humbler than one to the polar seas, we must not on that account deceive ourselves as to the probable expense which will certainly not fall below that of the latter. As for its scientific and historical importance, it would in this respect surpass even the most celebrated Arctic expeditions. The conquest of the virgin summits of the Himalayas will be the crowning achievement of mountaineering.

VI.

The ascent of the loftiest peaks of Asia, the dream and the ambition of mountain-climbers, has been made the subject of numerous works. Amongst these I should like to mention those of Clinton Dent.[1] In 1854-56 the brothers Schlagintweit climbed to a height of 22,259 feet. Conway reached an altitude of 22,600 feet in the Karakorams. Zurbriggen with FitzGerald climbed this year to a height of 24,000 feet, it is thought, but the figure is not yet quite certain. The data collected by Graham in 1883 admit of discussion. According to the opinion of the natives and of the official surveyors in India, it seems probable that not Mount Kabru but a lower mountain was ascended.

A serious impediment in the way of reaching the summit of Gaurisankar is the difficulty of finding trained individuals who would acclimatise themselves during a slow rate of progress, and reach the top in conditions of health and strength such as to enable them to overcome, if necessary, other unforeseen difficulties. It is probable that when an altitude of 7,000 metres is reached the expedition would have to descend and then climb again up a more distant peak. The victualling arrangements would have to be generously but prudently made, so as to ensure the surmounting of all obstacles, more especially as the last stages would necessarily be performed very slowly. Knowing that a man consumes a little more than one kilogram of food per day, and that beyond an altitude of 5,000 metres it is not prudent to carry per man more than 10 kilograms or to ascend more than 200 metres per day, we may compute the probable number of encampments necessitated and of the individuals who would have to be employed to carry the provisions to each successive camp. The number of porters, if we take into account the additional weight of tents, instruments, and other travelling necessaries, may be represented by a pyramid with its base at the beginning of the ascent, and which keeps growing narrower as it passes from one camp to the next. The

[1] Clinton Dent, *Above the Snow-Line.* London, 1885, p. 300. The Future Mountaineering.

amount of provisions forwarded in this way through a ladder-like system of camps gradually diminishes likewise. For the higher stages European porters and guides would have to be made use of, as these withstand mountain-sickness better than the natives.

Mountaineering expeditions have hitherto adopted too rapid a rate of ascent. This haste has serious consequences: the nervous system has not time to accustom itself to the action of the rarefied air, nor the organism to the cold; the fatigue of the ascent rapidly consumes our strength and leaves us no time to regain it. Under such conditions mountain-sickness renders the strongest men helpless.

If I may compare small things with great, I should say that my colleagues on Mont Blanc (see Chapter XIII.), on an expedition to a lower altitude than that of Gnifetti Peak, suffered much more than we, because they did not accustom themselves to the cold as we did, by ascending slowly at the rate of 1,000 metres a week, and because they did not succeed in keeping up such a comfortable temperature as we did in the Regina Margherita Hut.

Inurement to cold is a subject which is yet to be thoroughly studied. We can accustom ourselves to live for months at a temperature of $-40°$ as Nansen did; the organism must not, then, be suddenly taxed but gradually inured by being subjected to a continually increasing cold. The organiser of an expedition up Gaurisankar ought first of all to ascertain what amount of resistance the various members are able to oppose to the influence of cold. A good preliminary training would be to camp on the vast ice plateau which extends below the Monte Rosa peaks, where, in case of danger from storms, there would be the sure refuge of the Regina Margherita Hut.

For an expedition of this kind it is indispensable to find a certain number of guides and porters as well adapted to mountain-life as Jachini, Marta, and Sarteur of our party, men, that is, in whom mechanical muscular work causes only a minimum consumption of organic material, in whom that nervous excitement, which is the more immediate cause of fatigue, is almost entirely lacking, in whom the internal temperature of the body does not rise even during the greatest exertions. The populations living on the slopes of the Himalayas, though they may be fed at much less expense, would not be of much use as porters on a mountaineering expedition of this kind, because their religious conviction that the summits of the Himalayas are inaccessible to man would rob them of that moral force which long-continued exertion demands. The moderate alimentary needs of these natives is not in itself a recommendation; in enterprises such as the one proposed it is better to choose men with sturdier appetites.

These are new mountaineering problems which call for some study, but it is my opinion that in the end those resist fatigue better who eat heartily, or those who have in their blood such stores of assimilable elements that the other more precious supplies in the tissues may be left untouched. Everything which consumes the organism renders our condition less favourable for resistance to barometric depression. In those individuals who, during prolonged exertion, are able to draw the requisite energy from the blood and not from the stores accumulated in the tissues, the phenomena of fatigue during ascents are less lasting and less serious.

In the new observatory I hope to have constructed an apparatus, such as is shown in Fig. 56, by means of which the resistance of persons may be tested who think to attempt the ascent of the Himalayas. The pneumatic chambers which are made use of in the lowlands are not satisfactory as a means of training for great altitudes. We oppose less resistance, because we have no time to accustom ourselves to the greater depressions. I have been in air rarefied to correspond to the altitudes of 7,600 and 11,600 metres, but I should certainly have suffered less had I been able to accustom myself gradually. Another disadvantageous circumstance attending experiments in the pneumatic chamber in the lowlands is the high temperature of the air. Even in winter the return to the usual pressure after every experiment is a serious inconvenience. On Monte Rosa the inurement to rarefied air is more effectual, as beginning at an altitude of 4,560 metres the pressure may be reduced till it corresponds to altitudes of 8,000 or 9,000 metres, and the investigator may accustom himself slowly, as I hope, to these great depressions. There are apparatus which may be placed in the pneumatic chamber by means of which a person may perform muscular work as during an ascent although remaining all the time in the same place.

Instead of a chamber of iron made all in one piece as that shown in Fig. 56, it will be more convenient, on account of carriage, to construct an aluminium chamber divided into two equal parts, two cylinders, that is, each closed at one end and with the top in the form of a cupola, so that it may the better resist the reduced pressure. Before the door of the observatory a site has been prepared on the rock where a benzine motor may be erected. This motor will work a pump which, by means of the necessary tubes, will effect the reduction of the barometric pressure.

After a course of training at an altitude of 4,560 metres it will be possible to hold out for a greater length of time against depressions which we find insupportable now when we pass rapidly from the normal pressure to that of a height of 8,000 metres.

It is a hope I cherish to be able to complete these studies which were the object and, as it were, the dream of my last expedition to the Alps. Should my desires remain unrealised I may perhaps have the satisfaction of applauding younger, more competent colleagues who will continue the investigations begun by me on Monte Rosa.

Ramella (soldier).

Corporal Camozzi.   Army-Surgeon Capt. V. Abelli.   Marta (soldier).   Corporal Jachini.

FIRST APPENDIX

AN ATTACK OF INFLAMMATION OF THE LUNGS WHICH DEVELOPED ON THE SUMMIT OF MONTE ROSA

I.

THE above photograph was the last which Beno Bizzozero took of our expedition, at Gressoney, to commemorate the safe arrival of our rearguard, composed of the soldier Ramella, who was recovering from an attack of inflammation of the lungs, of Dr. V. Abelli, the two corporals, Camozzi and Jachini, and the soldier Marta.

While we were at Regina Margherita Hut, at a height of 4,560 metres, Ramella was seized by the above-mentioned malady. In publishing an account of this rare case of a malady which developed and was cured at such a height, I may express the hope that if this clinical study is not so complete as one might desire, its deficiencies may be pardoned as due to the cramped space and to the numerous difficulties which beset us during those days of anxiety.

Pietro Ramella, an inhabitant of Oropa,[1] is a mountaineer of 22 years of age; he weighs

[1] This account was written by Dr. V. Abelli, and presented to the Accademia dei Lincei, *Rendiconti seduta*, 5 Luglio, 1896. In the original memoir there are three curves which, for the sake of brevity, are here omitted.

62 kilograms, and is 1·62 metres in height. He is regularly built and his constitution is robust, although he is usually somewhat pale. Vital capacity, measured July 13th, 3,872 cubic centimetres. As a boy he suffered from earache, but does not remember any other circumstances worthy of notice.

In order to give a proof of Ramella's strength, I here instance one of the marches which he accomplished during the period of training, while we were exercising ourselves by trial-marches in the plain and Lower Alps. On July 5, 1894, he left Ivrea at 5 p.m. with some companions, and arrived at Gressoney St. Jean at 7 a.m. the next day. I had gone with Prof. A. Mosso to await the party, at a point an hour's walk below Gressoney St. Jean. Here we found that Ramella had a rectal temperature of 37·4°, a pulse-rate of 98, breathing-rate of 25 in the minute; he was therefore in excellent condition, and started shortly afterwards for Gressoney la Trinità, where he arrived at 10 a.m. This was a march of about 12 hours, leaving the halts out of account, over ground rising to 1,400 metres, and with a weight of about 15 kilograms in a knapsack on his back. By other marches of equal length in the plain between Montanaro and Turin, we reassured ourselves as to Ramella's strength and power of resistance to fatigue.

After we had been for some weeks on the glaciers of Monte Rosa, we sent word to Ramella, who was at Ivrea, to follow us. On August 10, 1894, Ramella left Ivrea with the train at 7 a.m. Having arrived at Pont St. Martin at 8 a m., he went on on foot, arriving at 5 p.m. at Gressoney St. Jean. Here he slept, started again at 6 a.m. the next day with some companions and a guide, and at 5.30 p.m. reached Gnifetti Hut (alt., 3,620 metres), where he slept well. The next day (August 12th) he left Gnifetti Hut at 5.30 a.m., carrying, as he had done the day before, a sack of bread on his shoulders, weighing about 20 kilograms. During the whole of the journey over the glacier, he exhibited no signs of abnormal fatigue, even when the ascent was most arduous. Even at the last part of the ascent, which is the steepest and most difficult, although three of our party had gone to meet the newcomers, as was our custom, in order to offer assistance or refresh them with a little warm wine, Ramella refused help, and carried the sack of bread up to Regina Margherita Hut. The new arrivals, four in number, reached the hut at 9.12 a.m. The weather was fine, the wind high. The temperature of the air in the shade was —9°.

As soon as the four men entered the hut, each of us (we were four physicians) took one and subjected him to an examination in order to find out the phenomena of fatigue and to study the modifications which the organism presents as soon as the altitude indicated is reached. Ramella was assigned to Prof. Ugolino Mosso. From the journal of observations I copy that part which refers to the first hours after his arrival at Regina Margherita Hut.

Pietro Ramella arrived at 9.12 a.m. He felt well, had no headache, but was very tired. His face was somewhat leaden-coloured and the hands were very cold. The shoes and stockings being taken off, the feet were found in a normal condition. I wrapped them in a blanket and Ramella then lay down on a mattress.

	Pulse.	Breathing.	Rectal Temperature.
9.18 a.m.	110	25	37·6°
9.27 „	102	20	37·5°
9.45 „	110	20	37°
3.0 p.m.	123	25	37·8°
5.50 „	120–124	26	39°

He complained of headache, and of a tendency to vomit; as he was much depressed we administered 10 centigrams of hydrochloride of cocaine in half a glassful of Marsala wine. The livid colour of the face had increased and he began to shiver.

In the night the fever increased and the next day, after examining the lungs, I began to suspect a case of inflammation. In the table at the end I have entered the observations made during the illness.

During the two first days the pulse fluctuated between 118 and 100 beats per minute. We could not obtain a curve with Marey's sphygmograph, the pulse being too weak and filiform. I might have tried to register the pulse with Prof. A. Mosso's hydrosphygmograph, which we had with us in Regina Margherita Hut, but it seemed to me needless to trouble the patient, as, with the exception of the great rapidity and weakness of the pulse, the action of the heart and blood-vessels was normal.

The irregularity in the frequency and amplitude of the respiratory movements was evident. Repeated observations convinced me that in Ramella the breathing was more superficial than in all the rest of us. On the third day of the illness the rate of respiration was only 23 to the minute. This arises from the counter-action of antagonist factors, as—fever, the altitude, repose, the lesion of the lungs itself, and the depression of the nerve-centres. With regard to the theory of mountain-sickness, it is interesting to note that in this case the amplitude of the inspiration was less, in spite of the barometric pressure of only 425 millimetres, and notwithstanding that, owing to the inflammation of the lungs, the respiratory area was more limited than the normal.

Another fact worthy of mention is that during the malady the respiration remained periodic. This phenomenon, which was common to all of us during sleep, was manifest in Ramella also in a waking condition, with this difference, that in him the periods were constituted of 10 or 12 superficial breaths, separated by one or two profound inspirations.

The rate of respiration reached its maximum on the second day of the illness, 32 inspirations being executed per minute; it then gradually and continually diminished, falling at last to 18 breaths in the minute. In the plain the average respiratory frequency was in Ramella only 14 breaths per minute. The frequency of the pulse began also to decrease after the second day, falling from 118 (August 13th) to 64, without, however, recovering the minimum observed in the plain after sleep, that is, 50 pulsations in the minute. During the whole of the sojourn at the Regina Margherita Hut the pulse was small and weak.

The progress of the disease was marked by the characteristic course of the temperature, which, even, at the beginning, barely reached 40° (39·9°), fluctuating on the days following between 38·8° and 38°. On the seventh day the condition of the patient improved and the course of the fever during that day may almost be considered as a long lysis.

Lysis, sufficiently rare in acute pneumonitis, denotes an anomalous course of which we must consider the causes. The hypothesis that this inflammation was produced by a chill does not seem very probable to me, for in that case inflammation of the lungs should be of much more frequent occurrence amongst mountain climbers than it actually is. Indeed, the experience which I have had of the Alps leads me to believe that this disease is less frequent in the highlands than in the lowlands.

Although we were unable to examine the sputum under the microscope, the disease in question was in all probability acute fibrinous inflammation. The exceedingly slight cough, the physical qualities of the sputum which had the typical appearance, being rusty-coloured, mixed with blood, firm and glutinous, the lack of other symptoms characteristic of bronchial catarrh encourage the statement that this was a case of infection with the Fraenkel pneumococcus.

As soon as the disease had been diagnosed, the first question which we put to ourselves was whether the state of the patient would be aggravated by remaining at that height, or whether, or the contrary, the atmospheric depression would be favourable to the course of the fever and inflammation. During the two first days we were alarmed at the increase of the livid colour and at the lack of strength. A terrible storm burst at this time over the Alps rendering it impossible to leave the hut, much less to transport our patient to a lower level.

OBSERVATIONS MADE DURING THE ILLNESS OF THE SOLDIER RAMELLA AT AN ALTITUDE OF 4,560 METRES.

Date.	Time.	Pulse.	Breathing.	Rectal temperature.	Observations.
Aug. 12th	9 p.m.			39·5°	Violent headache. Respiration periodic; that is, a certain number of superficial respirations alternated with one or two deep inspirations.
13th	6.20 a.m.	118	32	39·9°	Vesicular breathing in the whole lung except at the right posterior base of the thorax, where it is undetermined. The beat of the heart apex is not noticeable, the area of cardiac dulness is augmented, the sounds not altered but very weak, pulse small, not perceptible at the radial artery. At the right posterior base of the thorax, a crepitating râle is heard, hyper-resonant response to percussion, slight increase of vocal sound. Complete absence of cough; breathing periodic; intense frontal headache; very marked and diffused cyanosis, lethargy; tongue slightly furred.
	9.45 a.m.	102	30	39·5°	
	12 a.m.			38·9°	
	4.30 p.m.			38·6°	
	5 p.m.	104	24	38·5°	
	7 p.m.			38·2°	

Date.	Time.	Pulse.	Breathing.	Rectal temperature.	Observations.
Aug. 14th	7 a.m.			38·7°	Whistling bronchial breathing at the right posterior base; epistaxis; continued headache. Cough absent. Urine scanty, thick, dark.
	10.30 a.m.	98	29	38·6°	
	5.30 p.m.			38·7°	Continued headache; cough still absent; bronchophony, crepitating rále, augmentation of cardiac dulness on the surface corresponding to seat of inflammation.
	9 p.m.	96	24	38·1°	Very manifest periodic respiration.
15th	6 a.m.	94	25	38·8°	Rare, feeble, and subdued attacks of coughing eliminate a characteristic pneumonic sputum, from which a strong putrid odour emanates, insupportable to the patient himself. Headache still more violent. Half a gram of phenacetin is administered and a cup of strong coffee.
	11 a.m.			38·1°	Headache much less violent; the patient drinks the yolk of an egg in Marsala wine, and after two hours some egg broth.
	4.30 p.m.	96	23	38°	
	9 p m.			38·7°	Slight headache; the patient is dozing; has taken some warm wine and some Marsala.
16th	6 a.m.	92	24	38·4°	Headache continued during the night, but was gone this morning; the patient has taken a cup of coffee, has an annoying sensation in the ears, as though there were water in the outer auditory canals, which are, however, normal. Sputum sanguineous; it is got rid of easily, as always, at the first effort to cough.
	5 p.m.			38·5°	Labial herpes noticeable; headache gone; the patient has taken some egg-broth, red wine, and Marsala. He sat up for two hours.
	9 p.m.	95	22	38·3°	Headache returned for three hours; the patient has taken some broth and red wine.
17th	8 a.m.	90	21	37·7°	The patient slept well during the night; has no headache.
	2 p.m.			38°	Patient quiet; has taken some soup. Expectoration diminished; sputum of a lighter colour.
	5 p.m.	86	23	38·1°	Local symptoms almost completely gone; reappearance of vesicular respiration; the crepitating rále has ceased; expectoration almost; pulse filiform, felt with difficulty on the radial artery; cyanosis diminished.
	9 p.m.			37·9°	Patient says he feels better; is sleeping quietly.
18th	6.30 a.m.	90	22	37·8°	Has rested all night. Very little muco-purulent sputum.
	4.30 p.m.	80	19	37·4°	Patient has been up four hours; has eaten; slight cyanosis with pallor, pulse filiform, respiration periodic.
19th	7 a.m.	64	18	36·8°	During the whole of the illness there was no pricking pain in the thorax.

The rapid decrease of the disease made us think afterwards that the rarefaction of the air had exercised a beneficial influence on the progress of the inflammation. Certainly the pneumococcus showed a lesser virulence than it usually does in the plain. The circumstance that the patient was with us for a week, in the confined space of a badly-ventilated hut, without the disease communicating itself to any of us, proves that the bacilli were not very virulent. It is, of course, true that few patients are tended with equal care; we four physicians were with him the whole day, busying ourselves with him, and intent on keeping up his courage. Though isolation was not possible, as we were obliged to live and sleep near the patient, yet all practicable precautions were taken, especially with regard to the sputum, for which receptacles containing a solution of corrosive sublimate were set apart. Everything which he touched in eating or drinking was carefully washed afterwards in corrosive sublimate. For all other sick-room refuse we had a means of absolute disinfection, such as no hospital has at its disposal. When the south-window of the hut is opened, there lies below, at a depth of 1,500 metres, the Vigne glacier. Anything thrown out of this window, towards the valley of the Sesia, falls down vertically to a dizzy depth.

I have inserted the account of this case of inflammation of the lungs exactly as it was written by Dr. Abelli immediately after our descent from Monte Rosa. Subsequent experiments completely altered my opinions as to the nature and cause of the disease, which must, I think, be considered as a typical case of *inflammation of the lungs arising from paralysis of the vagus nerve*. The alteration of the lung due merely to barometric depression which I found in dogs and rabbits in less than an hour sufficiently bears out this diagnosis.

The anomalous course of the malady and the phenomena observed support the view that the etiology of the inflammation can only be sought in the diminution of the barometric pressure.

Ramella had slept well the night before, and arrived at the foot of Gnifetti Peak in such good condition that he would not give up the load of 20 kilograms which he had on his back to those who had come to meet him in order to help him in climbing the last part of the glacier, which is the steepest and most difficult. When he reached Regina Margherita Hut at 9.12 a.m. he told me gaily that he was quite well. In less than six hours his condition became alarming. He began to vomit, his pulse became very rapid and almost imperceptible, so that it could only with difficulty be counted at the radial artery.

One circumstance surprises us in the story of this illness—the high rate of the pulse (123 per minute), which does not correspond to the slight rise of the rectal temperature (37·8°). The serious general depression, cyanosis, vomiting, the increased area of cardiac dulness, the extreme weakness of the impulse of the heart against the ribs, the irregularity in the rate and amplitude of the respiratory movements after the lapse of five hours, the pulmonary gangrene due probably to incomplete deglutition, are all characteristic phenomena which can only be explained as arising from paralysis of the vagus nerve.

Ramella's condition improved, happily, in two days' time. If the paralysis had lasted longer, or had assumed a more serious form, we should perhaps have had to witness the death of our comrade, and to the summit of Monte Rosa would cling to-day the sorrowful recollection of a fatal case of paralysis of the nerves of heart and lungs similar to that which caused the death of Dr. Jacottet on Mont Blanc (see p. 179).

Dr. Burdon Sanderson tells me that on a visit to Zermatt many years ago, a well-known German professor who had attempted a high ascent was brought down by his guide in a state of intense and alarming dyspnœa. His case was recognised as one of pneumonia, and treated accordingly. In a couple of days he was convalescent. Dr. S. thinks it probable that this case was of the same kind as that of the soldier Ramella.

In all such cases we should advise climbers to bring down their friends to a lower level as promptly as practicable.

Orsia above Gressoney la Trinità. Houses at the foot of Monte Rosa, the highest inhabited in winter (alt., 1,800 metres).

SECOND APPENDIX

METEOROLOGICAL OBSERVATIONS MADE IN REGINA MARGHERITA HUT [1]

THE direct observation of meteorological conditions at great heights above the level of the sea is important to our general knowledge of the atmosphere. Every mountain-climber provided with good instruments should collect accurate data and compare them with the data obtained from the registering instruments which were used on Mont Blanc in the Vallot Observatory [2] for about a month in the year 1887.

I here communicate the results of the observations made by us during our sojourn in Regina Margherita Hut, and those obtained by Alfonso Sella from the 22nd to the 26th of August.

The period of observations extends from the 11th to the 26th August, with a break from the 19th to the 21st, during which we came down from the hut and Dr. Alfonso Sella went up. The observations were made, as a rule, every three hours from 6 a.m. to 9 p.m. We used the Goldschmidt aneroid barometer to determine the atmospheric pressure, and a thermometer exposed to the north and protected from the direct radiations of temperature.

I.

ATMOSPHERIC PRESSURE

The aneroid had been carefully verified before use, its constants being directly determined for pressures not widely differing from the normal. The doubt remained, however, that for pressures so low as that on Monte Rosa, these constants might alter, thus causing an instrumental error. A further determination was therefore made under conditions similar to those of the high Alps. The observer entered the pneumatic chamber shown in Fig. 56 with the aneroid barometer and a mercurial barometer. We then began to diminish the pressure, continuing until the aneroid marked the average pressure on Monte Rosa, the indications of the mercurial barometer being observed at the same time. It is easy to understand how, from the comparison of the two, the gradual correction necessary in the values marked by the Goldschmidt aneroid is determined.

In Italy, to obtain the average value of the atmospheric pressure of one day, we take the average of the registrations at 9 a.m., 3 p.m. and 9 p.m., and it may be shown that in so doing average values are obtained which differ only in an inappreciable degree from those which would result were the average taken of the registrations of every hour in the day.

But from our observations it appears evident that the daily period of atmospheric pressure on Monte Rosa, or rather the law according to which the pressure varies in one day at that height, is different from that which regulates these variations near the level of the sea, and, therefore, that the daily pressure can be better determined by taking the average of the pressures observed at 6 a.m., 12 a.m. and 9 p.m. The values corresponding to these hours and the averages drawn from them, are collected in the following table :—

[1] Dr. G. B. Rizzo, assistant at the Astronomical Observatory of the University of Turin put in order the meteorological observations which we had collected and wrote this appendix, for which service I express grateful acknowledgment.
[2] J. Vallot. Annales de l'Observatoire Météorologique du Mont Blanc, 1893.

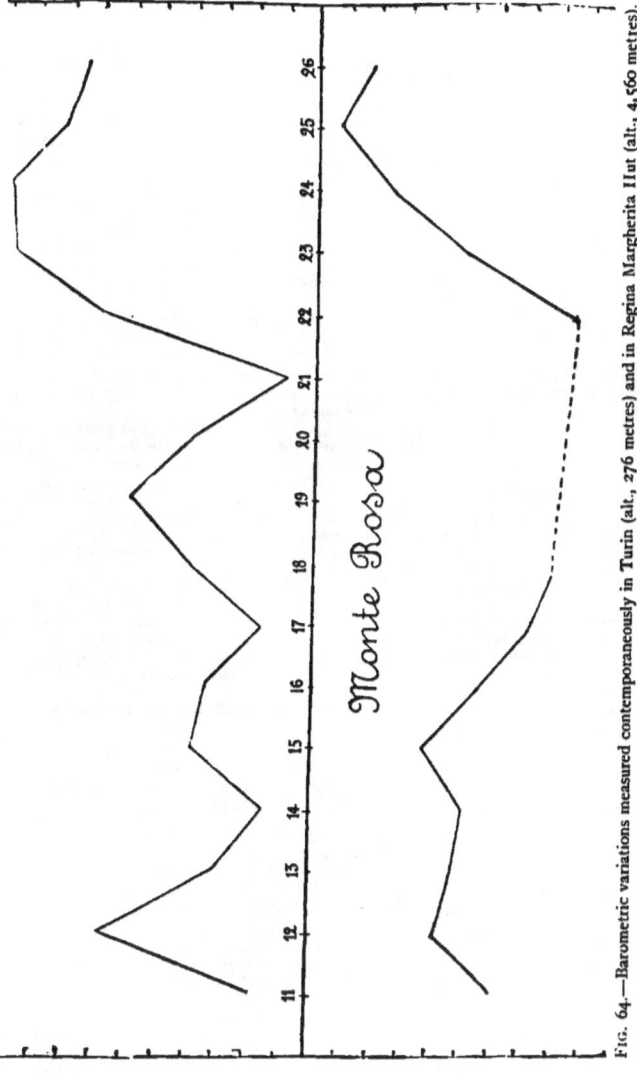

FIG. 64.—Barometric variations measured contemporaneously in Turin (alt., 276 metres) and in Regina Margherita Hut (alt., 4,560 metres).

August, 1894. Date.	Atmospheric pressure in millimetres on the summit of Monte Rosa (4,560 m.).			
	6 a.m.	12 a.m.	9 p.m.	Average.
11	426·2	426·8	427·5	426·83
12	427·2	429·0	430·5	428·90
13	429·0	428·5	427·5	428·33
14	426·2	427·8	430·0	428·00
15	429·0	429·7	429·5	429·40
16	428·0	427·0	427·6	427·53
17	426·0	425·0	427·0	426·00
18	425·5	425·0	425·0	425·17
22	422·0	425·0	426·5	424·50
23	427·3	428·0	429·1	428·13
24	429·2	430·5	431·8	430·50
25	431·9	431·5	430·5	431·30
26	430·8	430·6	429·6	430·33

Only in very rare cases, when some serious occupation prevented the taking of observations at the hour established, the omission was made good by an average drawn from the registrations at the time immediately before and after.

In ordinary conditions, that is, at common altitudes, the atmospheric pressure reaches its maximum between sunrise and midday, because the aqueous evaporation during the morning hours carries into the atmosphere a certain quantity of vapour the tension of which is added to the pressure of the air. Then the augmentation of the temperature at the surface of the earth gives rise to currents which ascend into the air and cause a diminution of the pressure at the level of the sea, a minimum being reached between 2 p.m. and 5 p.m. The pressure then again begins to increase, until, after midnight, owing to the condensation of vapours which collect in the form of dew, it diminishes once more until the rising of the sun, when the increase begins again and the same round is gone through.

These facts are well known to all interested in meteorology, and it is likewise known that at great heights above the level of the sea the laws of variation of atmospheric pressure must be different. There the effect of the tension of aqueous vapour added to the pressure of the air makes itself noticeable later, when the ascending currents which, at the level of the sea, determine the barometric minimum of the afternoon, carry masses of vapour up to the higher regions. The augmentation also continues later when the nocturnal cold is added to the great humidity.

This is fully confirmed by our observations, the average barometric pressure being:—

At 6 a.m. ... ... 427·56 mm.
,, 3 p.m. ... ... 428·03 ,,
,, 9 p.m. ... ... 428·62 ,,

A comparison of the atmospheric pressures on Monte Rosa with the values obtained during the same days in Turin is given in the following table:—

COMPARISON BETWEEN THE ATMOSPHERIC PRESSURE IN TURIN (ALT., 276 METRES) AND ON MONTE ROSA (ALT., 4,560 METRES).

August, 1894. Date.	Atmospheric Pressure.		
	Turin.	Monte Rosa.	Difference.
11	734·69	426·83	307·86
12	739·07	428·90	310·17
13	735·99	428·33	307·66
14	734·52	428·00	306·52
15	736·86	429·40	307·46
16	736·45	427·53	308·92
17	734·60	426·00	308·60
18	736·72	425·17	311·55
22	739·82	424·50	315·32
23	742·74	428·13	314·61
24	742·88	430·50	312·38
25	741·02	431·30	309·72
26	740·47	430·33	310·14

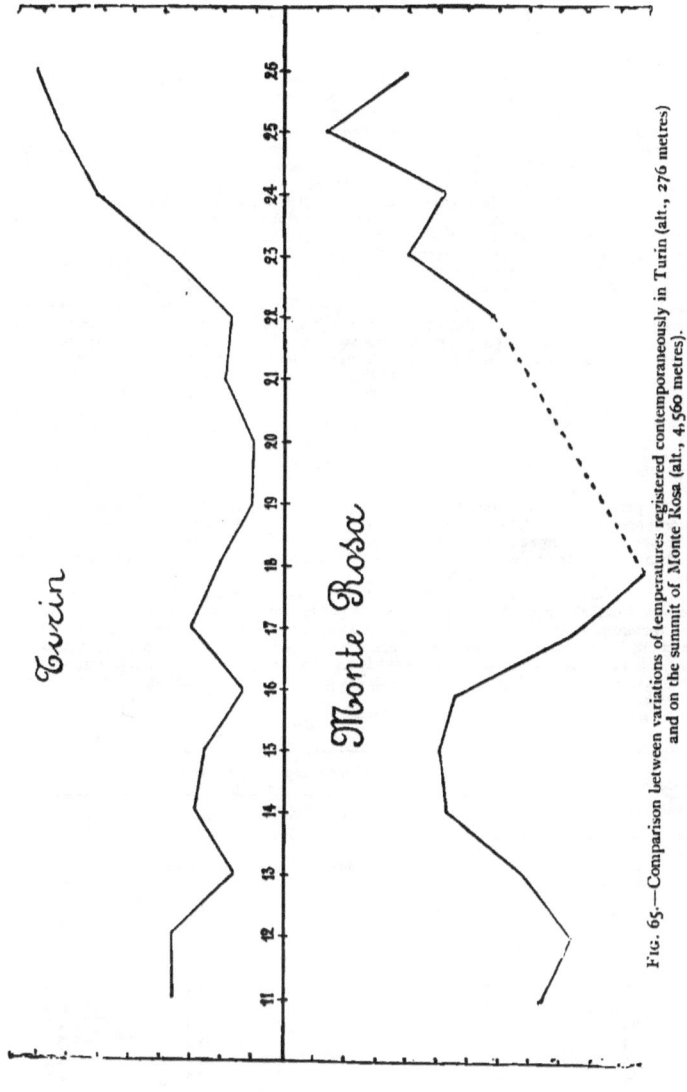

FIG. 65.—Comparison between variations of (temperatures registered contemporaneously in Turin (alt., 276 metres) and on the summit of Monte Rosa (alt., 4,560 metres).

The diagram in Fig. 64 shows the nature of these variations more clearly.

It is seen at once that the great fluctuations proceed along almost parallel lines in the two places, although their amplitude is less on Monte Rosa, and this is natural, because in Turin, the absolute value of the atmospheric pressure being almost the double of that on Monte Rosa, there must be the same proportion also between the variations.

One last remark respecting the atmospheric pressure. The determination of the atmospheric pressure in different places is a practical method to ascertain the difference of their levels. Now, in Turin, the average barometric pressure during the period under consideration was 738·41 mm., on Monte Rosa 428·07. Turin is 276 metres above the level of the sea, Monte Rosa, 4,559 metres. The difference of pressure is therefore equal to 310·34 mm. for a difference in level amounting to 4,283 metres, this giving an average diminution of 1 mm. of pressure for every 13·8 metres of altitude. Between two places nearer to the level of the sea the diminution of pressure with increasing height is more rapid, the rate of decrease being at ordinary altitudes 1 mm. for about every 10 metres. Nor need this cause surprise, because the lower strata of the atmosphere are denser and hence the variations of pressure must be more rapid, the measurement of heights, based on barometric registrations, being carried out by applying certain formulæ in which account is taken of the exact law which unites the variations of pressure to the variations of height above the level of the sea.

II.

TEMPERATURE

At great heights the warmth of the sun's rays is greater, but the pure and transparent atmosphere of those higher regions is not adapted to absorb their energy, the air therefore becomes little warmed, while during the night the soil cools with great rapidity. This explains why, even in the height of summer the temperature there is very low, a fact which our observations clearly confirmed.

The moderating action of aqueous vapour being almost entirely lacking, the temperature on high mountains has a diurnal progress different to that of places near the level of the sea, and therefore the daily average of the temperature cannot be calculated in the same manner as in our Observatories, but from an examination of all the observations made, it seems to me that, as average temperature on Monte Rosa, the average value of the observations made at 6 a.m., 12 a.m. and 9 p.m. may be taken as for the determination of the barometric pressure.

The following are the results obtained :—

August, 1894. Date.	Temperature on the summit of Monte Rosa.			
	6 a.m.	12 a.m.	9 p.m.	Average.
11	—14·0	—2·0	— 9·0	— 8·3
12	— 9·0	—9·0	—10·0	— 9·3
13	—10·0	—4·0	-- 9·0	— 7·7
14	— 5·0	—4·0	— 7·0	— 5·3
15	— 6·0	—2·0	— 7·0	— 5·0
16	— 7·0	—2·5	— 7·0	— 5·5
17	— 8·0	—8·5	—11·5	— 9·3
18	—13·0	—8·0	—14·5	—11·8
22	— 8·8	—5·0	— 7·0	— 6·9
23	— 5·2	—3·5	— 4·0	— 4·2
24	— 6·0	—3·8	— 6·0	— 5·3
25	— 3·5	+2·2	— 3·0	— 1·4
26	— 3·0	—4·0	— 5·0	— 4·0

A comparison of these values with those obtained during the same time in Turin is given in the subjoined table.

SECOND APPENDIX

COMPARISON OF THE TEMPERATURE IN TURIN (ALT., 276 METRES) AND ON THE SUMMIT OF MONTE ROSA (ALT., 4,560 METRES).

August, 1894. Date.	Temperature.		
	Turin.	Monte Rosa.	Difference.
11	21·6°	− 8·2°	29·9°
12	21·6°	− 9·3°	30·9°
13	19·5°	− 7·7°	27·2°
14	20·8°	− 5·3°	26·1°
15	20·6°	− 5·0°	25·6°
16	19·4°	− 5·5°	24·9°
17	21·0°	− 9·3°	30·3°
18	20·1°	−11·8°	31·9°
22	19·7°	− 6·9°	26·6°
23	21·9°	− 4·2°	26·1°
24	24·1°	− 5·3°	29·4°
25	25·1°	− 1·4°	26·6°
26	26·1°	− 4·0°	30·1°

These variations are shown in the diagram, Fig. 65.

The temperature of the air, especially in the mountains, depends on a great number of circumstances: on solar radiation, the state of the sky, on the degree of humidity, the direction of the wind, &c. On this account it is clear that even if the progress of the temperature on Monte Rosa is not, roughly speaking, much different from that in Turin, there may yet be considerable divergencies and mutations in details. But if we consider the temperatures of all the days of the above-mentioned period, taking them all together and again striking an average, we obtain results not wholly without importance.

The average temperature of the period under examination was—

in Turin + 21·6°
on Monte Rosa − 6·5°

the difference being, therefore, 28·1°.

If we now compare this difference of temperature between the two places with the corresponding difference of height above the level of the sea, we find that the diminution of temperature is of about half a degree, or more accurately 0·65° for every 100 metres rise.

The result is in perfect agreement with that found elsewhere by other observers.

Hirsch and Hann, reckoning from a great number of observations taken at different heights above the level of the sea in Switzerland and in the mountains of Germany, found that in the month of April, for every 100 metres of altitude the average temperature decreases—

0·67° in Southern Switzerland,
0·64° in Northern Switzerland,
0·66° in the Harz Mountains.

Carlo Bruno, working on an ample series of observations taken at Mondovì and La Balma in the Maritime Alps, found a diminution of 0·68° in the average summer temperature for every 100 metres.

III.

THE STORM OF THE 13TH–14TH AUGUST, 1894

Before concluding these brief notes on the meteorological conditions observed on Monte Rosa, mention must be made of the violent storm which we experienced in the night of the 13th–14th August.

The barometer had not sunk at all considerably, it was oscillating, in fact, about the average, when in the night of the 13th the wind began to blow furiously from the north, continuing without a break till the following midday. The violence of the hurricane was such as we had never before experienced. The keeper, Francioli, who had gone out of the hut, was thrown to the ground by the wind and bruised his knee. When the storm was over we found that the wind had incrusted the whole hut and balcony with a thick layer of hoarfrost. The icicles were from 12 to 14 centimetres in length. We had never seen anything similar in the Alps. A picture of the frost-covered hut is given on p. 200 with the writer in the foreground according to the wish of the young photographer of the party.

We endeavoured to discover to what conditions the storm owed its origin. The synoptic weather-charts published by the central meteorological offices show that in Europe from the 13th to the 14th the atmospheric pressure was distributed as indicated in the subjoined sketch, Fig. 66.

A strong depression extended over England and Sweden, whereas in the Bay of Biscay and Iberian peninsula the pressure was very high. According to the fundamental principles of atmospheric movement, we know that for our hemisphere the air exhibits in a depression, or, as it is called, *cyclone*, a vertical movement in a contrary sense to that of the hands of a watch, whereas in an atmosphere of high pressure, or *anticyclone*, it moves in the same sense as the clock hands. On Monte Rosa, in the night of the 13th-14th August, 1894, the united action of the British cyclone and Iberian anticyclone gave to the air the movement from north to south and produced the very violent wind.

The day afterwards the cyclone was still in almost the same place, whereas the area of high pressure had removed considerably towards the east, the atmosphere afterwards becoming tranquil again.

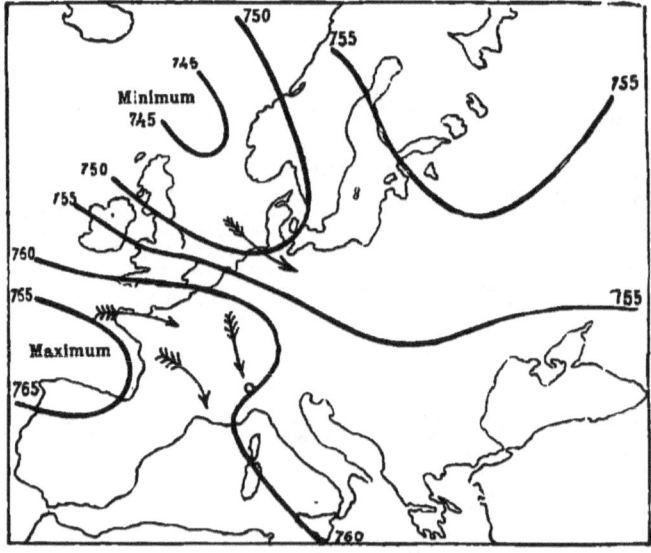

FIG. 66.—Chart of barometric pressure in Europe during the storm of the 14th August, 1894.

TABLES
OF PHYSIOLOGICAL OBSERVATIONS MADE DURING THE MONTE ROSA EXPEDITION.

The most important anthropometrical data furnished by the subjects of my experiments have already been given. Before placing them here again before the reader in tabular form I may mention that only two of my subjects (Corporal Jachini and the soldier Sarteur) had already been on the glaciers at an altitude of about 3,500 metres in their native valley of Aosta. The other soldiers, although they were mountain-soldiers, had never ascended beyond the height of 2,500 metres, and could not therefore be looked upon as accustomed to live at an unusual altitude. In the year in which they accompanied me up Monte Rosa not one of all these mountain-soldiers had been on the mountains. The year before my brother had made an ascent as far as Gnifetti Hut. Beno Bizzozero was a good mountain-climber. In the previous year he had crossed Monte Rosa to Zermatt by the Col du Lys, making the ascent of Zumstein Peak (4,563 m.) on the way. Dr. V. Abelli was an experienced mountain-climber.

In the following table the three last names are those of the soldiers who ascended directly from Ivrea to Regina Margherita Hut. The other members of the expedition, ten in number, without counting guides and porters, mounted slowly at the rate of about 1,000 metres per week.

NAME.	WEIGHT IN GRAMS.	HEIGHT IN METRES.	AGE.
Eugenio Camozzi	65,600	1·70	22
Santino Marta	71,200	1·72	22
Albino Sarteur	64,820	1·73	22
Germano Solferino	64,100	1·71	22
Felice Jachini	73,560	1·75	22
Carlo Cento	69,120	1·71	22
Beno Bizzozero	56,340	1·78	21
Angelo Mosso	74,500	1·70	49
Vittorio Abelli	60,000	1·67	35
Ugolino Mosso	59,500	1·64	41
Guiseppe Oberhoffer	58,300	1·61	22
Pietro Chamois	62,680	1·62	22
Pietro Ramella	62,920	1·62	22

TABLE I.

(See p. 8.)

Comparison between the changes in the rate of pulse and breathing in Turin (276 m.) and in Regina Margherita Hut (4,560 m.) after the exertion of raising two dumb-bells weighing 5 kilograms each above the head at 4-second intervals.

NAME.	ALTITUDE.	DATE.	Number of lifts.	PULSE.		BREATHING.	
				Before.	After.	Before.	After.
Corporal Eugenio Camozzi	276 m. " 4,560 m.	July 12th 13th August 16th	44 48 150	74 89 100	100 112 136	19 22 20	20 18 28
Santino Marta (soldier)	276 m. " 4,560 m.	July 12th 13th August 14th	62 94 185	70 74 92	88 94 134	20 22 24	24 22 24
Albino Sarteur (soldier)	276 m. " 4,560 m.	July 12th 13th August 16th	80 110 143	64 68 96	78 100 132	20 19 16	17 14 22
Corporal Felice Jachini	276 m. " 4,560 m. "	July 12th 13th August 14th 15th	51 56 76 131	66 70 68 80	78 72 104 106	18 18 18 20	22 22 24 28
Pietro Chamois (soldier)	276 m. " 4,560 m.	July 12th 13th August 13th	82 121 119	60 62 96	74 68 128	21 20 22	24 18 28
Giuseppe Oberhoffer (soldier)	276 m. " 4,560 m.	July 12th 13th August 14th	95 124 130	74 70 82	82 86 118	24 23 24	24 22 28

TABLE II.

(See p. 193.)

Volume of air inspired in half an hour at various altitudes.
Experiments made by Prof. Ugolino Mosso during the Monte Rosa Expedition.[1]

Serial Number	NAME	DATE	TIME	Litres of air inspired in 1 minute	Temperature of the air	Barometric pressure	Litres of air inspired in half an hour
		I. Gressoney la Trinità (alt., 1,627 metres).					
1	Jachini	21 VII	9.25 a.m.	8·702	17°	65 cm.	261·075
2	„	21 „	2.4 p.m.	9·50	18°	„	285·010
3	Solferino	22 „	3 „	6·867	21°	„	206·223
4	Sarteur	23 „	3 „	6·93	25°	„	207·983
5	„	24 „	1.30 „	5·77	26°	„	177·203
6	Solferino	24 „	3.55 „	9·65	24°	„	289·633
		II. Indra Camp (alt., 2,515 metres).					
7	Jachini	26 VII	10.45 a.m.	9·68	15°	62 cm.	290·405
8	Solferino	26 „	4.30 p.m.	6·952	16°	„	208·561
9	„	29 „	9.35 a.m.	8·014	10°	„	240·421
10	Sarteur	29 „	10.50 „	5·833	10°	„	174·990
11	Jachini	29 „	2.16 p.m.	9·437	12°	„	283·126
		III. Linty Hut Camp (alt., 3,047 metres).					
12	Jachini	1 VIII	2.30 p.m.	8·129	15°	51 cm.	243·898
13	Solferino	2 „	3.39 „	10·122	13°	„	303·660
14	Sarteur	3 „	3 „	7·345	12°	„	220·354
		IV. Gnifetti Hut (alt., 3,620 metres).					
15	Jachini	7 VIII	2.20 p.m.	7·721	10°	48 cm.	231·649
16	Solferino	7 „	4.20 „	7·732	5°	„	231·866
17	Sarteur	8 „	5.25 „	7·294	7°	„	218·828
		V. Regina Margherita Hut (alt., 4,560 metres).					
18	Jachini	12 VIII	4.28 p.m.	9·214	7°	43 cm.	276·427
19	„	13 „	5.30 „	9·643	13°	„	289·296
20	Sarteur	16 „	4.35 „	6·402	12°	„	192·065
21	„	17 „	10.25 a.m.	5·061	8°	„	151·830
22	Solferino	18 „	10.20 „	8·907	20°	„	267·220
23	„	18 „	1.45 p.m.	8·639	19°	„	259·171
		VI. Experiments made on the return to Gressoney la Trinità (alt., 1,627 metres).					
24	Sarteur	23 VIII	10 a.m.	5·374	15°	65 cm.	161·229
25	Jachini	23 „	11.20 „	10·65	12°	„	301·973
26	Solferino	23 „	3.40 p.m.	6·595	12°	„	197·861

[1] The air was measured by means of the same gas-meter, valves and gutta-percha masks which I made use of. These experiments served to determine the amount of carbonic acid eliminated in half an hour at various altitudes.

TABLE III.

(See p. 222.)

Comparison between the volume of air inspired at Gressoney
and on the summit of Monte Rosa.

Prof. UGOLINO MOSSO.

PLACE.	DATE.	TIME.	Temperature of the air.	Litres of air inspired in 30 minutes.	Litres of air inspired in 1 minute.	Average rate of breathing.	Amount of average inspiration.
Gressoney Trinità, 1,627 m.	24 VII	10.10 a.m.	24°	208·29	6·94	12	0·758
Reg. Margh. Hut, 4,560 m.	12 VIII	7.40 ,,	8·6°	257·87	8·59	13	0·660

Rate of breathing for every minute.	Volume of air in c.c. introduced into the lungs at every inspiration.

GRESSONEY TRINITÀ.

11	602	482	602	602	506	554	554	554	530	506	530			
13	602	482	554	626	530	482	602	554	530	457	530	554	578	
13	530	578	578	602	578	602	723	433	578	578	482	578	530	
14	506	554	385	506	482	457	409	576	530	433	433	361	554	482
13	482	795	578	506	554	457	554	554	457	433	578	409	457	
11	771	650	626	554	650	554	530	482	626	578	530			
12	578	433	578	530	771	530	650	626	650	843	482	506		

REGINA MARGHERITA HUT.

13	964	795	530	554	650	795	650	482	626	698	578	385	626	
13	698	602	433	674	939	698	409	819	602	578	698	602	554	
12	554	1325	602	723	867	698	578	867	482	626	1180	843		
12	698	674	723	891	361	385	723	771	506	674	771	747		
12	747	650	891	578	867	578	723	915	626	626	723	843		
12	554	771	578	674	578	1036	1012	433	1012	1036	698	1012		
13	626	650	626	771	578	747	939	1060	771	602	819	626	626	
13	578	723	867	602	625	891	771	1036	747	626	771	613	602	
13	915	698	939	1132	843	578	1012	843	698	795	650	939	674	
14	674	723	939	578	723	1060	723	530	433	1132	1084	723	771	530

TABLE IV.

(See p. 222.)

Comparison between the volume of air inspired at Gressoney and on the summit of Monte Rosa.

BENO BIZZOZERO.

PLACE.	DATE.	TIME.	Temperature of the air.	Litres of air inspired in 30 minutes.	Litres of air inspired in 1 minute.	Average rate of breathing.	Amount of average inspiration.
Gressoney Trinità, 1,627 m.	24 VII	9.0 a.m.	20°	262·69	8·75	11	0·808
Reg. Margh. Hut, 4,560 m.	12 VIII	8.15 ,,	5·3°	274·74	9·15	15	0·611

Rate of breathing for every minute.	Volume of air in c.c. introduced into the lungs at every inspiration.

GRESSONEY TRINITÀ.

10	723	602	891	747	964	771	1060	1084	723	1180		
10	867	650	843	891	747	843	674	915	939	723		
10	891	795	650	578	819	530	674	626	819	723		
10	723	723	723	723	482	650	578	602	698	747		
11	723	674	771	819	723	843	723	723	771	626		
12	771	723	723	626	650	819	506	771	771	843	626	819
11	482	843	554	602	361	602	723	433	409	409	361	
12	795	843	698	843	723	771	795	795	771	819	939	795
13	915	915	988	771	771	867	578	578	650	361	457	554	482
11	578	747	843	843	915	771	843	843	795	843	674	
9	939	602	723	723	795	819	289	626	578			
10	747	795	891	723	964	891	964	915	674	723		
10	1084	771	843	795	795	674	795	457	698	723		

REGINA MARGHERITA HUT.
12th August, 1894, 8.15 a.m. Temp. 5·3°.

14	771	650	602	674	602	554	650	747	506	578	506	843	723
15	385	482	650	530	530	530	578	602	578	578	674	626	506	578
	602												
16	626	650	457	578	578	723	795	554	530	457	578	650	747	506
	506	602											
15	650	674	771	602	530	578	482	602	457	723	771	578	723	554
	482												
16	578	506	650	506	578	554	530	554	554	530	482	530	602	554
	554	554											
16	626	602	530	554	650	602	602	506	602	698	602	554	554	554
	578	506											
15	650	626	650	747	385	506	482	698	795	698	385	602	506	626
	554												

TABLE V.

(See p. 222.)

Comparison between the volume of air inspired at Gressoney
and on the summit of Monte Rosa.

Corporal CAMOZZI.

PLACE.	DATE.	TIME.	Temperature of the air.	Litres of air inspired in 30 minutes.	Litres of air inspired in 1 minute.	Average rate of breathing.	Amount of average inspiration.
Gressoney Trinità, 1,627 m.	23 VII	9.50 a.m.	18°	140·960	4·90	8	0·587
Reg. Margh. Hut, 4,560 m.	17 VIII	11.40 „	8°	238·59	7·95	9	0·883

Rate of breathing for every minute.	Volume of air in c.c. introduced into the lungs at every inspiration.

GRESSONEY TRINITÀ.

8	602	939	915	939	964	843	915 723
6	1132	1156	843	939	964	988	
7	964	1612	915	843	843	1084	867
6	1156	819	698	1084	1036	1084	
7	964	723	964	964	723	723	337
7	674	530	843	843	723	1200	602
7	602	650	915	723	723	843	578
7	723	964	843	723	650	723	643
8	1325	409	482	626	602	698	602 602

REGINA MARGHERITA HUT.

10	674	747	819	723	819	771	747	795	867 867
10	891	747	771	988	771	939	939	1036	915 1036
11	891	843	867	795	409	433	530	891	723 964 939
9	578	1036	819	915	1060	482	939	1084	747
8	1060	667	915	843	674	578	602	433	
7	795	1084	1205	1397	867	1277	1025		
7	1132	1229	1180	915	1277	891	1180		
7	1229	1277	915	1132	1277	1108	1205		
7	1253	1132	1180	1108	1188	1277	1084		

TABLE VI.

(See p. 222.)

Comparison between the volume of air inspired at Gressoney
and on the summit of Monte Rosa.

ALBINO SARTEUR (soldier).

PLACE.	DATE.	TIME.	Temperature of the air.	Litres of air inspired in 30 minutes.	Litres of air inspired in 1 minute.	Average rate of breathing.	Amount of average inspiration.
Gressoney Trinità, 1,627 m.	24 VII	8.50 a.m.	18°	168·70	5·620	10	0·562
Reg. Margh. Hut, 4,560 m.	14 VIII	8.56 ,,	8°	174·84	5·824	10	0·582

Rate of breathing for every minute.	Volume of air in c.c. introduced into the lungs at every inspiration.
	GRESSONEY TRINITÀ.
8	1205 723 1012 915 891 915 843 1180
8	1229 1180 1108 891 964 1084 1036 843
7	1446 1325 1084 843 964 964 843
8	843 964 843 1084 843 964 964 964
8	843 843 650 795 723 1446 1017 1036
8	1132 1036 1205 747 819 723 626 698
9	650 843 554 650 650 698 771 843 650
9	674 771 795 843 723 602 602 602 650
	REGINA MARGHERITA HUT.
11	482 482 554 482 554 602 650 626 578 530
10	698 482 602 626 602 674 578 626 602 602
11	602 602 602 674 530 723 698 602 554 602 1397
11	795 457 457 385 457 578 506 482 457 530
12	554 457 506 530 482 506 409 409 554 482 409 530
11	554 482 433 626 626 530 482 482 482 433
10	409 433 409 482 626 361 433 385 482 433
11	409 361 361 409 385 385 361 385 361 409 433

TABLE VII.

(See p. 222.)

Comparison between the volume of air inspired in Turin and on the summit of Monte Rosa.

PIETRO CHAMOIS (soldier).

PLACE.	DATE.	TIME.	Temperature of the air.	Litres of air inspired in 30 minutes.	Litres of air inspired in 1 minute.	Average rate of breathing.	Amount of average inspiration.
Turin 276 m.	15 VII	10.0 a.m.	20°	231·567	7·719	18 to 19	0.428
Regina Margherita Hut,	15 VIII	8.50 ,,	9·4°	265·461	8·848	16	0.553
4,560 m.	16 VIII	4.0 p.m.	9°	277·752	9·115	15	0·617

Rate of breathing for every minute.	Volume of air in c.c. introduced into the lungs at every Inspiration.
	TURIN.
18	433 457 408 384 480 480 384 432 504 360 432 409 457 457 409 480 384 480
19	457 433 409 433 409 457 384 432 384 482 457 409 433 457 457 409 480 433 457
19	433 385 409 433 506 385 482 482 409 384 409 457 433 530 385 385 385 457 482
18	457 409 482 506 433 457 409 387 385 409 409 530 409 385 385 433 409 385
18	409 433 409 433 457 457 433 482 482 385 385 409 433 409 433 457 433 482
	REGINA MARGHERITA HUT.
	Chamois arrived at the hut on the 12th. On the 15th I made the observations on the breathing.
16	650 650 650 650 674 723 650 674 482 723 723 698 771 674 747 723
16	674 674 626 723 674 674 723 698 698 747 723 771 698 698 723 698
16	694 723 698 723 723 771 674 723 723 674 650 698 674 650 674 650
16	675 674 650 698 530 698 723 650 626 698 698 626 674 723 674 650
16	771 674 650 698 674 674 554 626 650 650 578 626 650 554 698 626
16	771 674 650 698 674 674 554 626 650 650 578 626 650 554 698 626
17	650 530 602 602 602 578 530 674 578 626 626 650 723 698 626 650 602
	REGINA MARGHERITA HUT.
	Observations made after four days' rest after the subject's arrival at the altitude of 4,560 metres.
15	433 443 530 530 626 554 602 602 650 554 578 626 698 650 650
15	723 430 602 626 650 795 578 723 626 674 674 771 723 578 795
15	723 674 674 723 626 723 819 891 313 771 747 747 819 698 650
14	625 650 626 626 602 650 650 674 602 674 626 626 650 626

TABLE VIII.

(See p. 222.)

Comparison between the volume of air inspired in Turin and on the summit of Monte Rosa.

GIUSEPPE OBERHOFFER (soldier).

PLACE.	DATE.	TIME.	Temperature of the air.	Litres of air inspired in 30 minutes.	Litres of air inspired in 1 minute.	Average rate of breathing.	Amount of average inspiration.
Turin, 276 m.	13 VII	8 a.m.	21°	267·076	8·90	20	0·445
Reg. Margh. Hut, 4,560 m.	15 VIII	8 ,,	7°	275·824	9·19	19	0·483

Rate of breathing for every minute.	Volume of air in c.c. introduced into the lungs at every inspiration.
	TURIN.
20	456 432 480 432 456 408 432 408 456 552 408 384 408 552 408 456 432 408 456 408
20	384 408 408 456 442 456 552 576 384 408 384 384 552 408 408 504 408 456 432 456
21	504 504 384 384 504 408 456 432 504 408 408 384 360 552 552 408 432 432 408 432 552
20	432 456 480 384 384 384 504 408 408 504 456 432 408 504 528 504 408 408 432 432
20	480 456 408 408 504 456 408 456 456 552 552 384 384 552 384 456 456 456 480 480
	REGINA MARGHERITA HUT.
	Observations made after three days' rest.
17	432 456 552 480 576 480 504 744 504 1056 456 408 456 576 360 480 432
19	480 528 504 576 504 480 480 552 480 456 528 480 552 384 312 432 504 576 576
19	552 552 432 480 480 600 600 480 408 456 384 504 528 408 360 552 288 456 432
19	336 360 600 480 456 456 528 480 456 456 456 480 552 600 480 360 432 408 624
20	456 456 456 528 552 504 408 384 384 480 624 456 480 576 528 456 480 600 528 552
17	720 648 792 576 552 648 672 552 672 648 600 576 624 600 504 504 360
17	480 576 504 600 504 480 480 552 504 528 528 504 624 576 504 576 504
15	576 576 528 672 576 672 552 576 576 648 528 552 480 648 648
17	552 480 552 624 528 432 456 528 576 480 576 432 360 552 576 576 504
15	600 576 600 552 864 648 696 744 792 672 648 648 600 360 576

TABLE IX.

(See p. 221.)

Comparison between the volume of air inspired at Gressoney and on the summit of Monte Rosa.

GERMANO SOLFERINO (Soldier).

PLACE.	DATE.	TIME.	Temperature of the air.	Litres of air Inspired in 30 minutes.	Litres of air Inspired in 1 minute.	Average rate of breathing.	Amount of average inspiration.
Gressoney Trinità, 1,627m.	23 VII	8.5 a.m.	10°	192·58	6·41	10	0·641
Reg. Margh. Hut, 4,560 m.	12 VIII	9.45 „	11·6°	166·29	5·54	14	0·390

Rate of breathing for every minute.	Volume of air in c.c. introduced into the lungs at every inspiration.

GRESSONEY TRINITÀ.

Rate											
10	723	530	674	723	602	723	650	650	602	433	
10	530	554	698	554	843	698	747	530	385	650	
10	747	650	650	554	554	578	530	554	482	723	
8	602	694	723	819	723	530	819	771			
9	1036	723	1205	964	843	723	843	1012	723		
9	843	723	723	723	964	843	723	771	578		
10	1084	723	723	795	650	650	819	915	747	964	
9	723	723	723	674	723	867	578	771	723		
9	723	723	602	409	626	602	747	554	795		
9	771	771	626	867	891	819	795	795	723		
10	530	433	482	554	530	602	530	506	530	482	

REGINA MARGHERITA HUT.

Rate												
12	482	409	433	433	337	385	409	433	361	409	385	361
12	457	385	409	385	385	385	482	433	578	433	409	554
12	457	457	385	313	265	289	409	409	457	361	313	313
13	337	337	289	289	361	337	337	361	385	265	409	313	313
14	361	361	241	313	313	241	241	361	361	265	265	265	337	313
13	241	241	241	433	433	361	337	265	241	241	241	241	216
14	192	433	433	409	433	409	385	385	313	289	289	313	289	241

TABLE X.

(See p. 152.)

VITAL CAPACITY

of some of the members of the Monte Rosa expedition, the measurements being taken in Turin (276 m.) and in Regina Margherita Hut (4,560 m.).

(The values given in cubic centimetres were found by taking the average of three successive observations. From four to five minutes were allowed to elapse between one measurement and the next in each individual, so that the lungs might return to their normal state.)

	TURIN.	REGINA MARGHERITA HUT.	
A. Mosso	3,888 c.c.	3,108 c.c.	780 c.c.
B. Bizzozero	4,200 ,,	3,653 ,,	547 ,,
Solferino	4,556 ,,	4,434 ,,	122 ,,
Marta	5,206 ,,	4,651 ,,	555 ,,
Sarteur	5,205 ,,	4,723 ,,	482 ,,
Jachini	4,795 ,,	4,508 ,,	287 ,,

The soldiers Chamois and Oberhoffer ascended Monte Rosa directly from Ivrea without acclimatising themselves.

Chamois	3,678 c.c.	3,276 c.c.	402 c.c.
Oberhoffer	3,179 ,,	2,734 ,,	445 ,,

www.ingramcontent.com/pod-product-compliance
Lightning Source LLC
Chambersburg PA
CBHW032353230426
43672CB00007B/690